Economic Integration and Public Policy in the European Union

Economic Integration and Public Policy in the European Union

Edited by

Christos C. Paraskevopoulos

York University and the Athenian Policy Forum, Canada

Ricardo Grinspun

York University, Canada

Theodore Georgakopoulos

Athens University of Economics and Business, Greece

Edward Elgar

Cheltenham, UK • Brookfield, US

Published by
Edward Elgar Publishing Limited
8 Lansdown Place
Cheltenham
Glos GL50 2HU
UK

Edward Elgar Publishing Company
Old Post Road
Brookfield
Vermont 05036
US

British Library Cataloguing in Publication Data
Economic integration and public policy in the European
Union
1. European Union 2. Political planning – Europe 3. Europe – Economic integration
I.Paraskevopoulos, Christos C. II.Grinspun, Ricardo
III.Georgakopoulos, Theodore
337.1'42

Library of Congress Cataloguing in Publication Data
Economic integration and public policy in the European Union / edited by Christos C. Paraskevopoulos, Ricardo Grinspun, Theodore Georgakopoulos.
p. cm.
Includes index.
1. European Union countries—Economic integration. 2. European Union countries—Economic policy. 3. European Union countries—Social policy. 4. Greece—Foreign economic relations—European Union countries. 5. European Union countries—Foreign economic relations—Greece. I. Paraskevopoulos, Christos C. II. Grinspun, Ricardo. III. Georgakopoulos, Theodore A.
HC241.2.E29258 1996
337.1'4—dc20 95-49721
CIP

ISBN 1 85898 314 2

Typeset by Manton Typesetters, 5–7 Eastfield Road, Louth, Lincolnshire LN11 7AJ, UK.
Printed and bound in Great Britain by Hartnolls Ltd, Bodmin, Cornwall

ERRATA

Page 137 should read as follows

Per capita income will rise if the rate of growth of GNP outpaces that of population. In the last 25 years, however, the growth in real income has dramatically declined. This suggests that the growth in GNP did not keep pace with population increases. To assess how to reverse that trend or avert an erosion in the standards of living we decompose the determinants of per capita income into the components (factors) indicated in the following:

$$(GNP/P) = (GNP/GDP)\ (L/E)\ (E/P)\ (GDP/L)\ldots \qquad (1)$$

where:

GNP = real gross national product
P = population
GDP = real gross domestic product
L = person hours worked
E = employment

Hence equation (1), in an interactive[4] manner, identifies the sources of improvement in the standards of living. Therefore, from equation (1) changes in real per capita income (GNP/P) depend – other things being equal – on changes in the foreign indebtedness and international competitiveness (GNP/GDP); average hours worked per employee (L/E); the employment participation rate (E/P); and labour productivity (GDP/L – output per hour).

Per capita improvements, however, in the standards of living can be attained in at least four ways:

Contents

Figures

Tables

Contributors

Panos Afxentiou, University of Calgary, Canada

Andreas A. Andrikopoulos, Athens University of Economics and Business, Greece

Nicholas C. Baltas, Athens University of Economics and Business, Greece

Bala Batavia, DePaul University, US

Dimitris Bourantonis, Athens University of Economics and Business, Greece

Patrick M. Crowley, Saint Mary's University, Canada

George Demopoulos, Athens University of Economics and Business, Greece

Elias Dinopoulos, University of Florida, US

Richard S. Eckaus, Massachusetts Institute of Technology, US

Miren Etxezarreta, Universitat Autonoma de Barcelona, Spain

Theodore Georgakopoulos, Athens University of Economics and Business, Greece

Dimitris Georgoutsos, Athens University of Economics and Business, Greece

Ricardo Grinspun, York University, Canada

Theodore Hitiris, University of York, UK

Arvind Jaggi, Franklin & Marshall College, US

Richard Jankowski, State University of New York College at Fredonia, US

Nicolaos Karamouzis, Athens University of Economics and Business, Greece

Bernd Kempa, University of Essen, Germany

George M. Korres, University of London, UK

A.G. Malliaris, Loyola University of Chicago, US

Leo Michelis, University of Western Ontario, Canada

Christos C. Paraskevopoulos, York University and the Athenian Policy Forum, Canada

Yannis G. Paraskevopoulos, University of London, UK

John Paschakis, York University, Canada

George C. Petrakos, University of Thessaly, Greece

Mike Pournarakis, Athens University of Economics and Business, Greece

Kyprianos Prodromidis, Athens University of Economics and Business, Greece

Robin Rowley, McGill University, Canada

Apostolos Serletis, University of Calgary, Canada

Constantinos Syropoulos, Pennsylvannia State University, US

Panos Tsakloglou, Athens University of Economics and Business, Greece

Constantine Tsoutsoplides, Athens University of Economics and Business, Greece

Steven Vansteenkiste, Tilburg University, The Netherlands

Nikos C. Varsakelis, Aristotle's University of Thessaloniki, Greece

George Zestos, Christopher Newport University, US

Spyros E. Zikos, University of Macedonia, Greece

Foreword

Richard S. Eckaus

Economic integration is the most noteworthy development in international economic policy of the end of this century. The enthusiasm for the European Union (EU) has been infectious. That and the establishment of the North American Free Trade Agreement (NAFTA) and Southern Cone Common Market (MERCOSUR) in the Western Hemisphere have led to discussions of the possible creation of economic or customs unions in other parts of the world. Yet there are many aspects of the EU and its consequences that still remain obscure and which warrant further careful scrutiny. The essays in this book are an important contribution to this investigation. In addition to analysing some of the familiar issues, they also take up problems that, though usually treated as peripheral, may turn out to be crucial for the success of the EU.

The discussion of the integration of international trade has, overwhelmingly, and understandably, focused mainly on its effects on the levels and composition of interregional and extraregional trade and their consequences for national development. There are several significant contributions to this discussion in the essays in this book.

The essays in Part II continue the investigation of the implications of monetary union and of associated exchange rate policies. These are important because the debates over European integration have been oriented closely to policy. In spite of early enthusiasm, both the feasibility and desirability of a monetary union have been increasingly questioned, as the problems of convergence of domestic inflation rates appear more intractable and the sacrifice of domestic monetary policy receives more sceptical scrutiny.

There are, however, a number of other issues, often mentioned, but seldom studied, that are important aspects of economic integration and are, perhaps, even crucial for its success. These include the politics of union, national fiscal policies and associated social and labour policies. It is now clear that political support for the EU is not uncontested. The issues are featured prominently in popular journalism, but are most often discussed in terms of clichés about drawing people closer together and common citizenship. Thus the analysis here of the politics of regional interests and the practical politics of formulating and implementing policies is particularly noteworthy.

Questions as to the potential harmonization of fiscal and social policies within the EU, although they have been a persistent source of popular debate, have also been relatively neglected in scholarly research. Several of the papers in this book make a contribution in this direction.

Some of the most difficult problems of integration, however, are sectoral. Perhaps the tangled interests of agricultural policy are the most prominent among these, but foreign investment and technological guidelines contain thorns that prick the hands of decision-makers. The special case of Greece, which is the focus of a number of the papers, supplies a context in which many of the general issues of industrial adjustment, investment and politics become quite concrete.

The scope and perspectives of the papers in this volume are unusual and worthy of a broad audience.

Acknowledgements

Most of the contributions to this volume were originally presented at an international conference held in Toronto, Canada, in May of 1994. It was organized by York University and the Athens University of Economics and Business in co-sponsorship with the newly established 'Athenian Policy Forum'. The Toronto meeting was the second major joint activity of the two universities, under an exchange agreement signed in April 1991. We would like to thank the two organizing universities, the Athenian Policy Forum and all participants for their contributions to its success. York University, as host, should be cited for outstanding organization and publicity.

In addition to the editors, who also served as conference chair (C. Paraskevopoulos) and co-chairs (R. Grinspun and T. Georgakopoulos), a number of other colleagues served on the organizing committee or helped in other ways. The editors would like to thank N. Baltas, N. Christodoulakis, G. Eaton, O. Hamouda, A. Kintis, F. Lazar, V. MacKinnon, K. Prodromidis, P. Shum and B. Spotton. Special thanks are due to A. Andrikopoulos for coordinating the Athens' arrangements and J. Smithin for editorial advice.

We appreciate the support (financial or otherwise) provided within the university by: the office of the Vice-President (Academic Affairs); the office of the Associate Vice-President (Research); the Department of Economics (Arts); Faculty of Arts (Office of the Dean); the Economics (FAS); York International; York Ad Hoc Research Fund; Centre for Research on Latin America and the Caribbean (CERLAC). Within the faculty of Atkinson College by: the Department of Economics; the Office of Master; the Atkinson College Student Association; and above all, Dean Skip Bassford for his very significant contribution. And within the government of Ontario by: the ministries of Education, Economic Development and Trade, and Community and Social Services.

We further appreciate the financial support provided by the following non-academic sponsors: The Hellenic Canadian Board of Trade and the significant financial contribution of its members; The Ionian and Popular Bank of Greece SA; the Hellenic Industrial Development Bank SA; and the National Bank of Greece SA. We also thank the following contributors: Ellas Restaurant and Banquet Halls; Astoria Shish Kebob House; Brazilian Canadian Coffee Co. Ltd; Cronos Travel Inc.; Eastside Chevrolet Oldsmobile Ltd;

National Bank of Greece (Canada); Mr. Greek Shish Kebob Restaurants Inc.; and Patris Restaurant.

We would like to thank and acknowledge the special contribution of the following individuals: Agnes Fraser (Conference Secretary), Dawn Freeman (Corresponding Secretary), Elsie Ramkhelawan, Diane Stadnicki, Robin Smith, Laura Eustace of York University; Eleftheria Apostolidou of the Athens University of Economics and Business; Yiannis Stamatakos (Conference Fundraiser), Betty Skoutakis of the Hellenic Canadian Board of Trade; and Eitan Grinspun and Robert Kreklewich.

We would like to thank the anonymous reviewer (referee) of the volume, and above all, the publisher, Edward Elgar for his support and encouragement of this project.

Finally, thanks are due to Dymphna Evans, Jo Perkins and other members of the staff of Edward Elgar Publishing Limited, both at Aldershot and Cheltenham, for their customary high quality work on this volume.

Abbreviations

ABG	Agricultural Bank of Greece
CAP	Common Agricultural Policy
CCAPM	Consumption-based capital asset pricing model
CEC	Commission of the European Communities
CM	Common market
CSFs	Community's structural funds
CU	Customs union
EAGGF	European Agricultural Guidance and Guarantee Fund
EC	European Community
ECB	European Central Bank
ECU	European currency unit
EIB	European Investment Bank
EMCF	European Monetary Cooperation Fund
EMI	European Monetary Institute
EMS	European monetary system
EMU	Economic and monetary union
ERDF	European Regional Development Fund
ERM	Exchange rate mechanism
ESCB	European System of Central Banks
ESF	European Social Fund
FDI	Foreign direct investment
FEOGA	See EAGGF
GATT	General Agreement on Tariffs and Trade
IMP	Integrated Mediterranean Programmes
MCA	Monetary compensatory amount
MNE	Multinational enterprise
NAFTA	North American Free Trade Agreement
RACE	Research and Development in Advanced Communications for Europe
ROW	Rest of the world
SEA	Single European Act
SEM	Single European market
SMEs	Small and medium enterprises
UA	Unit of account

Introduction

Christos C. Paraskevopoulos, Ricardo Grinspun and Theodore Georgakopoulos

Most of the contributions in this volume were originally presented at an international conference held in Toronto, Canada, in May 1994, organized by York University and the Athens University of Economics and Business in co-sponsorship with the newly established Athenian Policy Forum.

The Toronto conference, on the theme 'Economic Integration and Public Policy: NAFTA, the European Union and Beyond', was the second of a series on economic integration – the largest ever conference on the subject – and was a follow-up to the first such conference held in Athens, Greece, in August 1992. Then the theme was 'Economic Integration between Unequal Partners'. The Athens conference in 1992 was an important first step in broadening and deepening the discussion of the implications of economic integration among nations where unequal partners are involved. The Toronto conference in 1994 was a further significant step as it regularized the discussion through the establishment of the Athenian Policy Forum, a research institution dedicated to the support of free and open discussion of the critical issues of economic policy.

The aim of the conference – with specialists in attendance from several different countries and two continents – was to gain a better understanding of the impact of economic integration on public policy at both the national and supranational level. The present volume includes a selection of papers that focus on the European experience. A companion volume, *Economic Integration in the Americas*, also forthcoming from Edward Elgar, and a special issue of the *North American Journal of Economics and Finance*, both focus on integration in the Western Hemisphere.

The chapters in this volume provide a state-of-the-art analysis of key issues facing the European Union (EU). The range of topics, methodologies and perspectives tackled make for an unusually broad presentation that will engage the economic theorist, the empirical social scientist, the policy-maker, and also the informed general reader who wants to understand the challenges and dilemmas facing the EU. The significant number of Greek economists participating in both the conference and in this volume provides a unique perspective. Greek accession to the EU is an important case study dealt with in several of the chapters.

The volume is divided into six parts. Part I presents some general aspects of European integration. In Chapter 1 Chris Paraskevopoulos and John Paschakis discuss the main features of the European monetary system (EMS) and provide a brief history of exchange rate mechanism (ERM) realignments. They also address some of the factors which may have caused exchange rate changes in the ERM. Patrick Crowley and Robin Rowley argue in Chapter 2 that a strong imperative for European economic integration persists despite recent challenges. They address dynamic and practical aspects of economic and monetary union, including the politics of, and alternative paths to, EMU, as well as the currency issues, fiscal strains and the new institutions which are part of this unifying process. Arvind Jaggi argues in Chapter 3 that market dynamics tend to accentuate inequality under integration and that elements of a North–South divide give us an appropriate framework to analyse the integration of disparate regions within the EU. A case is made for a reformed regional and structural policy that fosters a sustained and broad-based development. Chapter 4 by Constantinos Syropoulos and Elias Dinopoulos is theoretical. They develop a stylized model of two trading blocs, 'home' and 'foreign', to analyse the effects of deepening integration within a bloc (i.e. the formation of a common market) on protection and welfare. Their model indicates that if the creation of a common market raises the volume of inter-bloc trade, then tariffs increase and the welfare of both blocs increases. Andreas Andrikopoulos and Kyprianos Prodromidis set Chapter 5 within the 'political business cycles' literature, where governments' electoral interests create cyclical patterns in key policy variables. Their empirical study of 12 member countries of the EU provides significant support for the existence of electoral cycle patterns. They cannot, however, find strong support for the existence of partisan cycles (i.e. patterns characteristic of 'socialist' versus 'conservative' governments).

Part II presents empirical and theoretical analyses of the monetary union. Apostolos Serletis and Panos Afxentiou, in Chapter 6, focus on the importance of convergence between 'laggards' and 'leaders' as a precondition for successful integration. Because convergence in nominal macroeconomic variables is a necessary condition for the success of EMU, they test for the degree of convergence of nominal exchange rates, assuming that these rates reflect the monetary policy pursued by the sampled countries. In Chapter 7 Richard Jankowski addresses possible reasons for government intervention in exchange rate markets. He performs an empirical test of the determinants of such interventions using data from 12 OECD countries, and finds that governments use exchange rate intervention as a countercyclical employment stabilization policy. Dimitris Georgoutsos and Nicolaos Karamouzis present an empirical investigation of the sterling–deutschmark exchange rate in Chapter 8 with reference to the September 1992 crisis in the ERM that led to the suspension of the UK pound and the Italian lira from the system. They test exchange rate band credibility before the crisis; the degree of predictability of changes in these exchange rates; and, finally, the statistical relationship between the two currencies in the two sub-periods before and after September 1992. Leo Michelis develops in Chapter 9 a simple general equilibrium consumption-based capital asset pricing model to explain the *ex-ante* real interest differential among countries in a fully integrated economic union. His theoretical analysis concludes that the real rate differential is expressible as a function of the differences in the riskiness of capital among states in the economic union. Bernd Kempa's empirical study in Chapter 10 sheds light on the question of whether the EU is ready for monetary unification. He investigates the sources of real exchange variability within the EU, and predicts that the current, large degree of variability will not be significantly reduced after monetary unification. He concludes that the implementation of the EMU at present cannot be endorsed either for the EU as a whole or for any group of core countries.

Part III of the volume deals with social policy reform and the structuring of a social union. In Chapter 11 Chris Paraskevopoulos argues that the persistence of high unemployment rates and slow productivity growth, coupled with mounting deficits, have placed an inordinate strain on the maintenance of social programmes and the defence of declining living standards for vast segments of the world's population. Countries are now groping to find ways to protect the living standards of, and provide adequate social protection for, their citizens. He observes that urgent calls for social policy reform dominate the socioeconomic and political agenda. He cautions that policy reform often leads to 'cost-shifting' and, if there is no excess capacity, to a 'hidden tax'. The topic of Chapter 12 by Steven Vansteenkiste is the relationship between economic integration and social security. A survey of social policy in several federal states (but not in the EU) shows that the federal authority plays a major role in the shaping of social security legislation. Given that the EU does not yet have extensive competences in the field of social security, this is a key area of future development. In Chapter 13 Panos Tsakloglou deals with the related issue of social protection for the elderly. In his empirical work he finds that in all EU countries the non-elderly population is better off than the elderly. Moreover, in most EU countries the elderly are not a homogeneous group (i.e. elderly males are better off than females). He warns that the current emphasis on eliminating social security budget deficits will increase inequality and poverty both nationally and within disadvantaged groups such as the elderly.

Public finance and fiscal policy are the subjects of Part IV. In Chapter 14 George Demopoulos and Kyprianos Prodromidis ask how EMU will work without a strong federal institution to help conduct fiscal policy. They analyse fiscal policies from the perspective of the theory of optimum currency areas, the sustainability of the national public debt of each member state, and the related question of defining 'fiscal discipline'. They propose the creation of a federal-type fiscal authority empowered to alleviate chronic fiscal difficulties of member states. Chapter 15 by Theodore Georgakopoulos and Theodore Hitiris focuses on the taxation of intra-union trade following the abolition of fiscal controls. The basic question is whether the 'destination principle' should continue to apply, or whether a shift to the 'origin principle' is warranted. They analyse the allocative and inter-country redistributional effects of a hybrid destination–origin principle for a general value-added tax.

Part V presents analyses of key EU policies, such as agriculture, foreign investment and technology, as well as a case study of accession. In Chapter 16 Bala Batavia and A.G. Malliaris provide a comparative analysis of the Common Agricultural Policy of the EU as it has evolved since 1957, and the agricultural policies of developing countries in recent decades. In contrast to the consistent support for agriculture in the EU, import-substitution industrialization and macroeconomic policies that have been applied in the latter group have produced a strong bias against agriculture. Foreign direct investment (FDI) is the topic of Chapter 17. Mike Pournarakis and Nikos Varsakelis examine the integrating effects of inward-oriented FDI in the EU. Given current FDI policy, which does not adequately accommodate existing regional disparities, the danger looms that transnational activity could become a source of economic rivalry with a mix of integrating and disintegrating effects on the union. In Chapter 18 George Korres and Yannis Paraskevopoulos focus on European technological policies. Such policies aim to reinforce competitiveness, to reduce economic disparities and to achieve convergence among member states. The authors analyse the evolution of 'framework research programmes' and the role of financial and technological flows encouraged through structural funds. Chapter 19 by Miren Etxezarreta presents a sceptical analysis of the Spanish accession to the EU. This accession was not only an economic issue but an important democratic and political achievement. Since 1992 conditions have deteriorated, in part as a result of EMU-oriented restrictive macroeconomic policies. She concludes that Spain has suffered a deterioration of its industrial structure since entry into the EU.

Finally, Part VI analyses the Greek country case. George Petrakos and Spyros Zikos deal in Chapter 20 with the structure of Greek industry and its role in leading Greece toward economic convergence within the EU. The authors examine the changes that have taken place in the industrial structure of Greece, assess the impact of existing industrial policies, and evaluate the prospects for the economy within the integrated European space together with the policies necessary for the period of adjustment. Nicholas Baltas, in

Chapter 21, reports on an empirical study of the determinants of agricultural investment in Greece. He finds that the ready availability of credit on easy terms was instrumental in stimulating such investment until the 1970s. After that period there was a marked slow-down in investment activity, as a result of increasingly tight credit caused by the liberalization of the banking system following Greece's entry into the EU. In Chapter 22 George Zestos asks how the accession of Greece to the EU has affected the Greek economy. He empirically estimates the elasticity of substitution in production between capital and labour in four major sectors of the Greek economy and compares them with the corresponding sectors of the French and German economies. He finds that elasticities of substitution of the manufacturing and industrial sectors of the three countries converged following accession. In Chapter 23 Dimitris Bourantonis and Constantine Tsoutsoplides model a market in which 'political influence' is exchanged for real resources. The fact that Greece is a net recipient of resources from the EU plays a key role in shaping the Greek attitude toward membership (i.e. these resources are 'purchasing loyalty' to the EU). Since the urgency for income improvements will not decrease in the medium term, Greece should be expected to remain in the EU's sphere of influence.

The set of studies presented in this volume on issues and problems concerning economic integration and public policy in the European Union, and laying particular emphasis on the contentious issues which arise in a process of integrating *unequal partners*, will obviously not settle the debates about either the desirability or the viability of these trends. However, it is hoped that the reader will feel that, collectively, they do represent a valuable further step in the ongoing study of these complex phenomena.

PART I

European Integration: General Issues and Problems

1. Systemic and fundamental pressures in the EMS: strong- versus weak-currency countries

Christos C. Paraskevopoulos and John Paschakis

INTRODUCTION

The European monetary system (EMS) was started in March 1979 as part of the process of integrating the economies of the European Economic Community (EEC) countries. It replaced the European common margins arrangement (the 'snake') which had been established shortly after the dollar was floated in 1972. Its creation reflected the dissatisfaction of the Europeans with the experience of floating exchange rates and their conviction that floating rates were harmful to European integration and detrimental to employment and growth in Europe.[1] From the beginning, the Europeans saw the EMS as an important step towards a currency union and closer political cooperation. There are 12 currencies that participate in the arrangement: the Belgian franc (BFr), the Danish krone (DKr), the French franc (FFr), the Greek drachma (Dr), the German Mark (DM), the Irish pound (I£), the Italian lira (L), the Luxembourg franc (LFr), the Dutch guilder (Fl), the Portuguese escudo (Es), the Spanish peseta (Pta), and the pound sterling (£). The Luxembourg franc is equivalent to the Belgian franc by a long-standing agreement between the central banks of those two countries. Therefore, their bilateral central rates are equal.

This chapter has three objectives. First, it discusses the main features of the EMS. Second, it provides a brief history of the EMS realignments. Third, it discusses some of the factors which may have caused exchange rate changes in the exchange rate mechanism (ERM) of the EMS.

THE MAIN FEATURES OF THE EMS

The two major features of the European monetary system (EMS) are the exchange rate mechanism (ERM) and the European currency unit (ECU).

The European Currency Unit (ECU)

The ECU is an artificial currency containing a fixed amount of each of the EMS currencies. The amounts of each currency are negotiated among the member countries and approximate the weights of the respective national economies in the EEC. The value of the ECU in terms of any national currency j is equal to the sum of the currency j values of each member currency i times the amount of currency i in the ECU. That is,

$$S_t^* = \sum_{i=1}^{12} \theta_i S_{it}, \tag{1}$$

where S_t^* is the currency-j value of the ECU in the spot market at time t, S_{it} the currency-j value of currency i in the spot market at time t, and θ_i the amount of currency i in the ECU. The ECU exchange rate S_t^* is therefore a weighted average of its component currencies.

The weights of the member currencies in the ECU are calculated as follows:

$$\sum_{i=1}^{12} \theta_i S_{it} / S_t^* = \sum_{i=1}^{12} \omega_i = 1, \tag{2}$$

where ω_i is the weight of currency i in the ECU and the sum of the weights of the component currencies is 1. Since the number of units of each currency in the ECU is fixed, the weights of the various currencies change over time, as intra-European exchange rates fluctuate. Exchange rate fluctuations thus could move the composition of the ECU far away from the initial set of weights which were based on the economic size of the various countries. To correct this, the units of each currency that make up the ECU are reviewed every five years, or when the weight of any currency has changed by more than 25 per cent. The need for revision can also arise because of changes in the membership of the EEC. The fixed amounts of currency in the ECU were first set in 1979. Since then, they have been adjusted twice. The first adjustment took place in September 1984, when the Greek drachma was added to the basket. The second adjustment occurred in September 1989 with the inclusion of the Spanish peseta and Portuguese escudo.

The ECU has two forms – official and private. The official ECU, which is governed by the rules of the EMS, was to be used as the numeraire for the exchange rate mechanism (to establish bilateral central rates), as the basis for detecting divergencies between Community currencies, as the unit of account for the operations of intervention and credit mechanisms, and as a means of settlement between monetary authorities of the European Community. Official ECUs are created by the European Monetary Cooperation Fund (EMCF) in exchange for three-month swaps by the EMS central banks of 20 per cent of their gold and dollar reserves. All the 12 EEC member countries have signed the EMS Agreement and deposited 20 per cent of their gold and gross dollar reserves in exchange for ECUs.

The private ECU is basically a Eurocurrency. Banks create it by crediting sums to an ECU account. The private ECU markets include all assets and liabilities denominated in ECUs, ranging from current or demand accounts at banks to long-term bonds, as well as various kinds of forward commitments. Neither ECU is coined. The link between the two is that the value of both is fixed to the same basket of European Community currencies. This stability is one of the ECU's greatest attractions (see Pozo 1987). The composition of the ECU as announced on 21 September 1989 is shown in Table 1.1.

The Exchange Rate Mechanism (ERM)

The EMS is based on fixed but adjustable exchange rates among member countries. It is also combined with a policy of flexible exchange rates against the other major currencies. That is, even though each country's exchange rate is fixed *vis-à-vis* the European currency unit, the ECU itself floats against the dollar, the yen and other major currencies. The main objective of this mechanism has been to stabilize bilateral nominal rates among participating currencies with the hope that the discipline of such a mechanism would lead to converging inflation rates and thus more stable exchange rates as well (Ungerer et al. 1986, p. 18).

Each participating currency has a central rate relative to the ECU (ECU parity). The ECU central rates are expressed as a certain quantity of currency per ECU, for example BFr/ECU. Central rates are reference points only and may not be equal to the market rates. The ECU central rates are used to establish a grid of bilateral central rates around which maximum fluctuation margins can be established.[2] The initial fluctuation margins were 6 per cent (plus or minus) for the Italian lira and 2.25 per cent for the other EMS countries. At these margins, the central banks of a pair of member countries are expected to intervene in the foreign exchange market to keep market exchange rates within the range allowed by the upper and lower grid values. Other policy measures include modification of domestic fiscal and monetary policy, changes in central rates and changes in interest rates.

Table 1.1 Composition of the ECU announced on 21 September 1989

EMS currency	Currency amount	Percentage weights
Deutschmark (DM)	0.624	30.10
French franc (FFr)	1.33	19.00
Pound sterling (£)	0.0878	13.00
Italian lira (L)	152.0	10.15
Dutch guilder (Fl)	0.220	9.40
Belgian franc (BFr)	3.30	7.60
Luxembourg franc (LFr)	0.13	0.30
Danish krone (DKr)	0.198	2.45
Irish pound (I£)	0.00855	1.10
Greek drachma (Dr)	1.44	0.80
Spanish peseta (Pta)	6.89	5.30
Portuguese escudo (Es)	1.39	0.80

Source: European Community documents.

The Spanish peseta entered the ERM in June 1989, the British pound in October 1990 and the Portuguese escudo in April 1992. All three currencies were allowed to fluctuate within a band of plus or minus 6 per cent of their central rates. Although the Greek drachma has been included in the definition of the ECU, Greece does not participate in the exchange rate mechanism. But the currency of Greece has been assigned a notional central rate. In the realignment of September 1990, the lira range was reduced to 2.25 per cent. After September 1992, the permissible fluctuation margins for most of the EMS currencies have been changed to 15 per cent of agreed central rates against the other members of the ERM.

The EMS exchange rate mechanism provides for a 'divergence indicator' which is used to single out the currency diverging from its central ECU rate, and to impose upon it the burden of adjustment. The maximum spread of divergence is the maximum permissable movement of a currency's market ECU rate, which is based on actual exchange rates and is therefore variable, against its ECU central rate, which is fixed. It is calculated using the following formulas:

$$M(i) = +/- 0.0225(1 - \omega_i), \quad (3)$$

$$M(i) = +/- 0.0600(1 - \omega_i), \quad (4)$$

where ω_i is the weight of currency i in the ECU basket (calculated using ECU central rates). A maximum divergence of 6 per cent is possible for escudo or peseta or pound, or 2.25 per cent for the other ERM currencies. When a currency reaches 75 per cent of this maximum, it crosses the 'threshold of divergence' and the authorities in the country concerned are expected to correct this. No policy action is compulsory, however, in contrast to the obligation to intervene arising when a currency reaches a *bilateral* margin.

In reality, the indicator of divergence has played almost no role in the ERM because the EMS ended up functioning exclusively around the bilateral parity grid rather than the ECU parities. The Bundesbank did not want to participate in a system characterized by intervention rules that would be able to single out the divergent currency — as opposed to a pair of divergent currencies. It feared that the Deutschmark would diverge upwards and that an ECU-based system would push Germany more often to the front line of intervention.

HISTORY OF THE EMS REALIGNMENTS

This section provides a short history of the EMS realignments and together with later sections discusses some of the factors which may have led to these exchange rate changes.[3] When a realignment occurs, a new set of ECU central rates is chosen. The new ECU central rates give rise to a new set of bilateral central rates in the parity grid and may also affect the position of the fluctuation bands. There have been 13 realignments in the ERM between March 1979 and December 1994.

The EMS experienced its first realignment on 24 September 1979, when the Deutschmark was revalued by 5 per cent against the Danish krone and 2 per cent against other EMS currencies. The second realignment occurred on 30 November 1979, and involved a 5 per cent devaluation of the Danish krone against all other EMS currencies. Both realignments coincided with a weak dollar and strong inflationary pressures in Denmark as a result of the oil price increases in 1979–80. The third realignment, on 23 March 1981, resulted from an acceleration of inflation and current account difficulties in Italy. These pressures led ultimately to the 6 per cent devaluation of the lira relative to the other EMS currencies. On 5 October 1981, the central rates of the Deutschmark and the Dutch guilder were revalued by 5.5 per cent, and those of the Italian lira and the French franc devalued by 3 per cent against the other EMS currencies. This realignment coincided with a number of events such as renewed confidence in the Deutschmark as the German current account performance had improved and inflation moderated, doubts about the stability of the French franc and uncertainties about the policy stance of the new French administration (Mitterrand's victory in French), and worsening inflation combined with a widening trade deficit in Italy. The fifth EMS realignment, effective as of 22 February 1982, consisted of a 8.5 per cent devaluation of the Belgian franc and Luxembourg franc and a 3 per cent devaluation of the Danish krone. The Belgian economy suffered from high unemployment (at 13.1 per cent of the workforce), rising budget deficits and a current account deficit running at an annual rate of US$5 billion and growing external indebtedness. On 14 June 1982, a sixth realignment took place. The French franc and the Italian lira were devalued by 5.75 per cent and 2.75 per cent respectively, while the Deutschmark and the Dutch guilder were upvalued by 4.25 per cent each against the remaining EMS currencies. The main causes were widening trade deficits and continuing high inflation in both France and Italy. The seventh realignment was agreed upon on 21 March 1983, when seven currencies changed their parities simultaneously. The Deutschmark was upvalued by 5.5 per cent, the Dutch guilder by 3.5 per cent, the Danish krone by 2.5 per cent, and the Belgian and Luxembourg francs by 1.5 per cent, while the French franc and the Italian lira were devalued by 2.5 per cent and the Irish pound by 3.5 per cent. The main reasons were high inflation, and big current account and public-sector deficits in France. At the same time, Germany had low inflation and a current account surplus, which put her out of line with the rest of Europe.

The EMS had its eighth currency realignment on 22 July 1985, when Italy devalued its lira by 8 per cent. The lira's devaluation was caused by a public-sector deficit of more than 13 per cent of its gross domestic product, a worsening of the current account and an erosion of external competitiveness. The ninth realignment, announced on 6 April 1986, devalued the French franc by 3 per cent. The Deutschmark and the Dutch guilder were revalued by 3 per cent, and the Belgian/Luxembourg franc and the Danish krone were revalued by 1 per cent. The devaluation of the franc was part of a package of measures designed to liberalize the French economy and restore its competitiveness. The tenth realignment became effective as of 4 August 1986, when the Irish pound was devalued by 8 per cent against the other EMS currencies. It purported to correct the decline in external competitiveness arising from the sizeable appreciation of the Irish pound against the British pound and the US dollar.

The eleventh realignment of the European monetary system came on 12 January 1987. The Deutschmark and the Dutch guilder were revalued by 3 per cent, and the Belgian and Luxembourg francs by 2 per cent against the French franc and the other EMS currencies. The realignment was justified on grounds of a weakening dollar, which sent more money flowing into the Deutschmark than into other EMS currencies.[4] It was also triggered by political events, such as strikes and student demonstrations in France. The twelfth realignment, effective on 8 January 1990, involved a 3.7 per cent devaluation of the lira against the Deutschmark. It reflected a move on the part of the Italian authorities to narrow the lira's band from 6 per cent to 2.25 per cent.

The EMS had the most severe crisis on 16 September 1992, when the British pound and the Italian lira temporarily abandoned Europe's exchange rate mechanism. Both currencies were devalued and allowed to float outside the ERM. Spain devalued the peseta by 5 per cent and Portugal devalued by 6 per cent on 22 November. The Irish pound was devalued by 10 per cent on 30 January 1993, and Spain and Portugal devalued again in May 1993. The ERM had come under strain for several reasons. First, there was the weakness of the dollar as a result of the enormous interest rate gap between Germany and the US. The German government had financed unification by swelling its budget deficit, thereby provoking the interest rate hikes.[5] As investors switched from dollars into Deutschmarks, first sterling and then the lira were dragged down within the exchange rate mechanism. These strains had been exacerbated by uncertainty about the outcome of the French referendum on the Maastricht Treaty on 20 September 1992, and political troubles in Italy. Also, the UK, Italy, Spain and Portugal had high inflation, big budget deficits or large current account deficits. The devaluation of the Irish pound reflected a move on the part of the Irish monetary authorities to restore some of the competitiveness they had lost since September's devaluation of sterling.

On balance, the EMS realignments seem to have been caused by divergent economic performance among member countries, periods of dollar weakness and political events.

STRONG VERSUS WEAK CURRENCIES IN THE EMS

There are two groups of countries in the EMS: the strong group led by Germany, the Netherlands, Belgium/Luxembourg and the weak group consisting of the other EMS members. The two groups are broadly defined in terms of the movement of their currencies against the ECU since 1979 (see Ungerer et al. 1990, p. 12). Belgium/Luxembourg and the Netherlands move with Germany. They already keep their currencies within 1 per cent of the central rate against the Deutschmark, rather than exploiting the full official 2.25 per cent band. It appears, therefore, that some form of monetary union between the countries in the first group is possible.

Since Germany is the leading member of the EMS, the Deutschmark plays the role of the nominal anchor in the ERM. That is, the Bundesbank establishes the ERM rate of inflation while other member countries peg their exchange rate to the Deutschmark and allow their monetary policy to be determined by the exchange rate link. Some economists define an anchor currency as the currency of the country with the lowest interest rates. Others claim that an anchor currency is one with 'credibility' in financial markets, because of its anti-inflationary policies and monetary history. The Bundesbank has a consistent record in announcing and pursuing a credible low-inflation policy. Also, Germany has a sophisticated network of financial markets. In addition, the Deutschmark is a reserve currency.

On the other hand, Europe's weak currencies are characterized by 'thin' foreign exchange markets and thus are subject to persistent speculative expectations. Also, weak-currency countries maintain high interest rates to stave off a devaluation. Moreover, they often need to maintain capital and exchange controls; and this makes their currencies less attractive to investors. Within the EMS, assistance is given by the 'strong to the weak'. The 'weak' countries sacrifice part of their freedom to determine domestic economic policy in return for greater exchange stability.

SYSTEMIC AND FUNDAMENTAL PRESSURE

Experience shows that the EMS is subject to systemic as well as fundamental pressure. Systemic pressure arises because the EMS is a fixed-rate system dominated by the Deutschmark. The dominance of the Deutschmark causes the currencies within the system to be driven up or down by the movement of the Deutschmark against non-EMS currencies such as the dollar, regardless of the fundamental strength or weakness of the other currencies against the dollar. Appreciation of the Deutschmark against the dollar tends to push the currencies within the system up against the dollar, with the weaker currencies drifting to the bottom of their fluctuation margins. But a weak Deutschmark tends to depress the entire system, thereby easing the pressures caused within it by economic disparity among member countries. Thus, European currencies tend to weaken against the Deutschmark when the dollar is weak and vice versa.[6] This phenomenon is often termed the 'dollar–Deutschmark polarization'.[7] Giavazzi and Giovannini (1986) provide empirical evidence in support of this relationship. They find that the highest correlation was with those EMS currencies that had operated exchange controls – the French franc and the lira. The lowest correlation was with the guilder, which had no controls.

On the other hand, fundamental pressure arises because of divergent economic performance among member countries, and must ultimately cause adjustment of the member countries' bilateral exchange rates. Experience shows that countries with high inflation and big budget deficits are more likely to devalue their currencies than are countries with substantial current account deficits and growing foreign indebtedness. Although 'fundamentals' play an essential role in EMS realignments, the exact timing of realignments has often been determined by dollar crises, political events, and resource availability.

COMPETITIVENESS

The competitiveness view is that realignments have been justified with reference to underlying inflation rates so as to maintain purchasing power parity (competitiveness between member countries). In contrast, the discipline approach argues that the exchange rate adjustments only partially offset relative price changes.

Recall that the real exchange rate is defined as $q_t = e_t + p_t^* - p_t$, where e_t is the logarithm of the exchange rate index, p_t^* is the logarithm of the foreign price level, and p_t is that of the domestic price level, all taken at time t. An decrease in q_t represents a real appreciation; this is often called a loss of competitiveness. An increase in q_t represents a real depreciation. If a country has a higher inflation rate than its partners and its nominal exchange rate is constant, its real exchange rate is appreciating. To hold the central rate steady in real terms (thus maintaining external competitiveness), it must devalue in nominal terms – just enough to offset the inflation rate differential. In the past, high-inflation France has needed to devalue periodically to retain its cost competitiveness against low-inflation Germany. Between March 1979 and April 1986, prices in France rose much faster than those in Germany. However, a 31 per cent devaluation of the French franc against the Deutschmark over that period left the franc's real (inflation-adjusted) exchange rate more or less where it had been back in 1979.[8]

Another important point is the choice of a currency's central rate at the time of joining the ERM. Since the monetary authority does not know what would be a sustainable central rate, a currency's central parity is fixed closer to its market rate. As this may imply an overvalued currency in real terms because of high inflation, the country may experience pressures for realignment afterwards. This may have been an important factor in the devaluation of sterling in September 1992 and its subsequent suspension from the ERM.

CONCLUSION

History shows that between March 1979 and December 1994 systemic and fundamental pressures had been at work and caused severe exchange rate strains in the ERM. It appears, therefore, that the current system of fixed but adjustable exchange rates cannot survive frequent pressure and adjustment if there are destabilizing capital flows and divergent economic performances among member countries.

The September 1992 crisis has led to greater exchange rate flexibility in the ERM. The British pound and the Italian lira have left the system while most of the other EMS currencies have been permitted to fluctuate within 15 per cent of agreed central rates against the other members of the ERM. The exceptions are the Deutschmark and the guilder, which move in a 2.25 per cent band. However, given the postwar European institutions, particularly the common agricultural market, 'greater exchange rate flexibility is not a viable option in Europe today' (Giavazzi and Giovannini 1989). This leaves the EMS policy-makers with two options. First, they could go on operating the ERM in its present form but attempt to attain greater exchange rate stability through greater economic convergence (i.e. the weak-currency countries will have to reduce further their inflation differentials, budget deficits and current account deficits). However, for greater economic convergence to be achieved, EMS policy-makers would have to address unemployment and growth issues. Germany has a very low rate of unemployment as a result of which it is able to implement an orthodox policy of price stability. Other European countries have a more difficult social situation, and therefore need faster economic growth. This is obvious in the case of the UK and Italy. Now that sterling and the lira are out of the ERM, policy is focused more on growth than propping up the exchange rate. This basic asymmetry of the EMS may become a serious threat to the present system as the Bundesbank has proved more or less insensitive to the concerns of its ERM partners regarding unemployment and growth. The second option is to move on to a economic and monetary union (EMU) and a central bank, as outlined in the Maastricht Treaty. An EMU would demand fulfilment of the four convergence criteria laid down by the Maastricht Treaty.[9] It would also require Europe to establish political institutions that are able to form policies based on European economic cycles rather than national cycles. At present, the objectives of EMS countries differ significantly and therefore future developments in the exchange rate mechanism are difficult to predict.

NOTES

1. Giavazzi and Giovannini (1989, p. 1) give three reasons why Europeans dislike exchange rate fluctuations. First, they have relatively open economies. Second, many of them hold the floating rates of the 1920s and 1930s responsible for the ensuing collapse of national economies and of the international trading and monetary systems. Third, postwar European institutions — particularly the common agricultural market — depend for their success on exchange rate stability.
2. For example, the ECU central rates for the DM and the FFr imply that the bilateral central rate for the DM with respect to the FFr is FFr/DM and that the bilateral central rate of the FFr against the DM is DM/FFr. By linking together the ECU-related central rates we obtain for each currency participating in the ERM a series of bilateral central rates, the juxtaposition of which constitutes the parity grid.
3. Most of this section draws on the publications of the *Economist* that coincided with the dates of the realignments.
4. See *Economist*, 17 January 1987, p. 67.

5. 'The Bundesbank's Writ', *Economist*, 29 May 1993, p. 84. American short-term interest rates were only 3.4 per cent, while Germany's were at 9.9 per cent. That made staying in dollar assets expensive. See *Economist*, 29 August, 1992, p. 67.
6. When the US dollar is relatively weak, mobile international capital seeks alternative locations, and particularly tends to move to the Deutschmark and vice versa. Since currencies other than the Deutschmark play only a limited role as alternative reserve and investment currencies, there is a tendency for the Deutschmark to be strong against other European currencies when the dollar is weak, whether or not underlying economic developments dictate this. See Ungerer et al. (1983, p. 5; 1986, p. 11).
7. See 'G7 Currencies', in the 1993 Guide to Currencies, *Euromoney*, February 1993, p. 5.
8. See *Economist*, 17 January 1987, p. 67.
9. Since 1 January 1995, three more countries, Austria, Finland and Sweden, have been added to the list of the prospective economic and monetary union (EMU).

REFERENCES

Allen, Polly Reynolds (1990), 'The Private ECU Markets: What They Are, Why They Exist, and Where They May Go', *Journal of Banking and Finance*, **14** (November), 845–76.

Dixon, Joly H. (1977), 'The European Unit of Account', *Common Market Law Review*, **14** (May), 191–208.

Edison, Hali J. (1987), 'Is the ECU an Optimal Currency Basket?', in Richard M. Levich and Adrea Sommariva (eds), *The ECU Market: Current Developments and Future Prospects of the European Currency Unit*, Lexington, Mass.: Lexington Books, pp. 191–209.

Edison, Hali J. and Eric O'N. Fisher (1991), 'A Long-run View of the European Monetary System', *Journal of International Money and Finance*, **10** (May), 53–70.

Eichengreen, Barry and Charles Wyplosz (1993), 'The Unstable EMS', *Brookings Papers on Economic Activity*, **1**, 51–143.

Folkerts-Landau, D. and J.D. Mathieson (1989), 'The European Monetary System in the Context of European Financial Markets', Occasional Paper no. 66, Washington, DC: International Monetary Fund.

Giavazzi, Francesco (1989), 'The European Monetary System: Lessons from Europe and Perspectives in Europe', *The Economic and Social Review*, **20** (January), 73–90.

Giavazzi, Francesco and Alberto Giovannini (1986), 'The EMS and the Dollar', *Economic Policy*, April, 456–84.

Giavazzi, Francesco and Alberto Giovannini (1989), *Limiting Exchange Rate Flexibility: The European Monetary System*, Cambridge, Mass.: MIT Press.

Masera, Rainer S. (1987), *An Increasing Role for the ECU: A Character in Search of a Script*, Essays in International Finance no. 167, International Finance Section, Princeton, NJ: Princeton University.

Mundell, Robert A. (1973), 'A Plan for a European Currency', in Harry G. Johnson and Alexander K. Swoboda (eds), *The Economics of Common Currencies*, London: George Allen & Unwin, pp. 143–72.

O'Neill, T.J. (1984), 'Does Sterling Need the EMS?', *Euromoney*, November, 159–62.

Pozo, Susan (1987), 'The ECU as International Money', *Journal of International Money and Finance*, **6** (June), 195–206.

Taylor, Jon (1984), 'The Next Shake-Up in the EMS', *Euromoney*, March, 25–7.
Ungerer, Horst (1989), 'The European Monetary System and the International Monetary System', *Journal of Common Market Studies*, **27** (March), 231–48.
Ungerer, Horst, Owen Evans and Peter Nyberg (1983), 'The European Monetary System: The Experience, 1979–82', Occasional Paper no. 19, Washington, DC: International Monetary Fund, May.
Ungerer, Horst, Owen Evans, Thomas Mayer and Philip Young (1986), 'The European Monetary System: Recent Developments', Occasional Paper no. 48, Washington, DC: International Monetary Fund, December.
Ungerer, Horst, J. Jouko Hauvonen, Augusto Lopez-Claros and Thomas Mayer (1990), 'The European Monetary System: Developments and Perspectives', Occasional Paper no. 73, Washington, DC: International Monetary Fund, November.
Van Ypersele, Jacques and Claude Jean Koeune (1984), *The European Monetary System*, Cambridge, UK: Woodhead-Faulkner.
Von Hagen, Jürgen and Michele Fratianni (1990), 'German Dominance in the EMS: Evidence from Interest Rates', *Journal of International Money and Finance*, **9** (December), 358–75.

2. Flaws and omissions in the Maastricht process for European integration

Patrick M. Crowley and Robin Rowley

Do people want to rewrite the (Maastricht) criteria which have been accepted and voted on by the entire European Union? Either you fulfil those criteria or you don't.

Bertie Ahern, Irish Finance Minister, 6 September, 1994

INTRODUCTION

A strong imperative for European economic integration persists despite recent challenges. In this chapter, we address dynamic and practical aspects of economic and monetary union (EMU), assuming that past experience illuminates potential developments. We begin by discussing politics and EMU, dealing with basic approaches to integration, matters arising from the Werner Report of 1971, and the Delors Report of 1989. In the next section, we assess paths to EMU, currency issues, fiscal strains and new institutions to illuminate aspects of the unifying process. Then the relevance and determination of convergence are appraised before some alternatives to the Maastricht vision are considered. We close with a few general remarks.

PRIORITIES AND INTEGRATION PROCESSES

Historical origins of EMU can be traced to the aftermath of the Second World War when a Council of Europe was advocated and economic cooperation was viewed as more likely than political union. Neo-functionalists suggested that economic integration has a cumulative logic leading to political integration, and that supranational agencies attract additional responsibilities and weaken the inertial constraints of national autonomy. Some neo-functionalists believed that welfare issues could be delegated to bureaucrats and experts. Early treaties adopted by the European Community (EC) did not directly accept such notions but neo-functionalist elements are pervasive in the Werner and Delors Reports – the former arguing that, for assimilation of common interests within the community, EMU was a 'lever for the developments of political union, which in the long run it cannot do without'. Opponents of neo-functionalist ideas stress 'power politics' and resist the loss of political autonomy for national governments. Illustrations include de Gaulle's assertion that 'there is no European reality other than our nations and the states which are their expression' and the Bruges speech of Thatcher which railed against ceding economic and political autonomy to European authorities.

Early EMU plans also stimulated other divisions of views on appropriate actions and long-term mechanisms for greater integration. During negotiations of the Werner Group, strategies for attaining EMU separated 'monetarist' and 'economist' camps: the former label was attached to France, Belgium and Luxembourg; and the latter label identified with Germany, the Netherlands and Italy. 'Monetarists' usually argued along neo-functionalist lines that progress in the monetary field induced effective coordination of economic policies. They asserted that a narrowing of margins for exchange rate fluctuations were beneficial, and they sought an exchange stabilization fund to encourage adjustment to EMU. But monetarists also felt that monetary issues blurred distinctions between welfare and high politics, contending that the first priority for Europe was a common monetary 'face'. 'Economists' held that the harmonization of economic policies should take priority before a communal monetary policy was embedded in the emerging European system. Instead of a stabilization fund to protect intra-European parities, they argued that the burden of corrective adjustments should fall primarily on deficit countries.

The historical choices between alternative views of the integration processes demonstrate that evolutionary stages for economic and political union were controversial in Europe for more than four decades; the over-optimism which preceded the Maastricht Treaty masked long-standing differences in perceptions of fundamental dynamic processes and strategic priorities; and that progress towards united activity will never go unchecked. Transition processes remained unclear when the Maastricht Treaty was negotiated. Subsequent instabilities stimulated more awareness of strong obstacles to integration, without providing any obvious means of overcoming them. They signalled further delay and revised plans rather than an abandonment of the search for an effective union. After earlier attempts to forge greater integration, the Delors Report (Committee on the Study of Economic and Monetary Union, 1989) was a first sign that an integration process was again gaining momentum. Throughout the 1980s, active participation in the exchange rate mechanism (ERM) of the European monetary system (EMS) seemed to reduce monetary differences with regard to inflation and interest rates among most members of the Community. Such success encouraged adoption of a gradual approach to fuller monetary union in the plan recommended by the Delors Report, an approach which would lead through three stages to a wide circulation of the European currency unit (ECU). This unit, introduced in 1979, had been used for drawing up the EC budget and for conducting business by institutions. Significant opposition to the Delors Plan came from the UK government, the German government, and the Bundesbank. It involved resistance to a loss of monetary sovereignty, currency issues, participatory criteria, and control of the future European Central Bank. Loss of sovereignty to a European institution was of paramount concern to the UK government, which stressed Hayekian views on the benefits of competition among contemporaneously circulating currencies in a 'hard ECU' proposal. 'Economist' objections from the Bundesbank focused on strict national criteria to guide the process of monetary union, while the German government advocated more political integration so that the new European monetary institution would be answerable to the European Parliament. The 'hard ECU' proposal was unacceptable to most governments but German demands for national criteria could not be resisted without compromise. Thus, in December 1991, the Inter-Governmental Conference in Maastricht launched five convergence criteria to be attained before monetary union and permitted opt-out clauses for the UK and Denmark. Such expedient concessions clearly undermined the spirit of the Maastricht Treaty.

Optimistic scenarios for more convergence were dispatched by three events. First, German attention was redirected towards domestic concerns with the assimilation of East Germany. Public debt rose spectacularly, capital stock deficiencies emerged, East German consumption demand put pressure on inflation (and on interest rates which rose to contain the inflationary pressure), and unemployment grew. By the beginning of 1994, even the traditional targeting for monetary policy was in disarray. A second major blow came from weakened resistance to speculative attacks in 1992–93, which showed that the ERM was unsuitable for handling deregulated currency trading in a transition process, and produced withdrawals of the pound and lira from the EMS, currency realignments, and a widening of bands within the ERM. Finally, an economic downturn initiated widespread and persistent unemployment throughout Western Europe.

ECONOMICS AND THE EUROPEAN UNION

Recognition of the need for cohesion and a fostering of convergence in the early 1970s led to an identification of principles in the MacDougall Report (CEC 1977), assigning responsibilities to various levels of government within a multi-tiered structure. One principle recognized spillovers of benefits and costs, while a second accepted the view that some beneficial programmes could only be funded at the multinational level. Cohesion was associated with transfers of economic resources to less wealthy regions, and a principle of subsidiarity stressed local autonomy by keeping functions at disaggregated levels, unless clear advantage could be shown for governmental responsibility at a higher level. Such guides are interesting for several reasons. They indicate that sovereign governments should voluntarily surrender some power, subject to 'reasonable' grounds for delegation and to the perception that local autonomy is normally preferable. They also promote the view that political processes should not be left to short-term expediency. Finally, they indicate persistent roles for bureaucracies to reveal potential net benefits, monitor regional disparities, oversee multinational collaboration, and balance the conflicting pressures for harmonization and local autonomy.

EC members signed the Treaty on European Union in Maastricht (Council of the EC 1992) in 1991. The Treaty was ratified in 1992 and the Edinburgh Agreement seemed to settle the future evolution of the Community's budget, while the process continued with the establishment of the European Monetary Institute (EMI) at the beginning of 1994. The Maastricht path to monetary union envisaged three stages of adjustment. Before the end of 1993, capital controls were to be abolished and monetary cooperation among central banks strengthened. A second stage involved the EMI guiding transition to more fixed relationships. More independence of national central banks was expected, while achievement of convergence standards was monitored by the EMI and the European Commission. In a final stage, exchange rates among currencies would be irrevocably fixed, the European Central Bank (ECB) would begin operations, and the ECU would become the primary physical currency within the union, with the UK and Denmark being granted the right to opt out.

Clearly the Maastricht process involved a gradual transition to monetary union and the inclusion of members in the process is to a certain degree flexible, determined by the onset of the third stage or by the satisfaction of economic criteria as confirmed by the European Commission. There is a dispute as to the interpretation of the clause for the establishment of the third stage concerning, in particular, whether entering the third stage implies sole use of the ECU to replace each national currency. To some extent, this issue is moot, as the treaty can be modified or replaced at the Inter-Governmental Conference in 1996, before the third stage begins and before a majority of states satisfy the convergence criteria.

If the monetary union requires a single currency, free capital movements and a single market for financial services, the Maastricht path is not unique. There are alternative paths which could have been adopted. For example, some economists advocated a 'Hawaiian solution' (followed in German reunification) but the necessary institutions are insufficiently developed for this option to succeed. Further, political will to move quickly or surrender national autonomy was absent during the negotiations in 1991–92. Another alternative, the 'Hard ECU' approach, requires free choice among rival currencies. Hayek (1976a,b, 1984), who distrusted national monopolies in money supply, would argue that the EC should not reproduce monopolistic power by giving the sole control of ECUs to a new monetary institution. Instead currencies should coexist, with competitive pressures (Hayek argued) producing greater stability and restraining the abilities of individual national governments to increase their money supplies. The market-determined outcome might then not involve the ECU. Indeed, given the earlier process of the Deutschmark becoming the common currency in Europe, the case for supporting a 'Maastricht' role for the ECU may not be overwhelming.

Gradual paths to monetary union attract a host of questions. Should economic convergence accompany the creation of EMU? Would intertemporal stability of currencies come with EMU? How can national central banks be integrated into the system? What are their roles? To what extent will fiscal federalism develop during the transitional phase to deal with regional disparities and responsiveness to regional shocks? Should institutional innovations occur before EMU is finally established? The Maastricht path assumed a need for economic convergence and stability of national currencies, while promoting central bank independence. It also invoked minimal fiscal federalism and anticipated the need for new monetary institutions before the full implementation of EMU. As various sources have noted, the criteria for economic convergence are unlikely to be met by *any* of the member nations. By the end of 1993, no state met even four of the five Maastricht criteria, possibly because of recessionary difficulties, and there is no chance that the initial deadline for establishment of the monetary union (end of 1996, when a majority were to meet the criteria) will be met. Nor is it likely that the second deadline for a partial union (two years later, when some nations might meet the criteria) will persist. The Maastricht plan also set a goal of currency stabilization for states wishing to enter into EMU. The aftermath of the substantial exchange shocks in 1992, with wider margins of fluctuation introduced for most exchange rates, also suggests that the Maastricht blueprint is unlikely to remain unchanged.

Since a monetary union precludes countries from acting in isolation, the differential responsiveness of regional economies to major changes in economic conditions emerges as an obstacle to the widespread acceptability and efficiency of a communal policy. Simulations reported by Eichengreen and Bayoumi (1992) illustrate that the constituent nations may split into a core (Germany, France, Belgium, the Netherlands, Denmark), sharing correlated supply shocks, and a periphery exhibiting some different characteristics regarding magnitude and timing. Validation of regional differences would weaken the attractiveness of participation in any monetary union. The economic linkage of an optimum currency union with more regional cohesion is awkward for Europe's plans. As recognized by de la Dehesa and Krugman (1993), there are indeed regional conflicts here. Inevitably, the fundamental uncertainty in this context strengthens resistance to lower fiscal autonomy for the member states.

With respect to 'normal' bounds for fluctuations of exchange rates within the ERM, the Maastricht Treaty required members to observe them 'for at least two years, without devaluing against the currency of any other Member State'. The purpose of this requirement was to ensure that entry into EMU would be based on realistic levels, and that continuity in monetary stance would occur before and after entry. But achieving greater exchange rate stability might involve the imposition of short-term capital controls to offset undesirable speculative flows. The objective was not to impose *fixed* bounds for fluctuations, but rather to secure a reduction in short-term volatility. Here the use of the ERM to achieve monetary union seems to confuse an effective adjustable-peg system with a new process by which the EC moves towards the union. The two, however, could be mutually incompatible.

Various plans to address different regional responses to transitional shocks were woefully inadequate. Little was done to handle dynamic or transitional issues so it is difficult to assess whether disparities or asymmetries emerging during the transition can be adequately handled within an evolving federal structure. In most federations, subsidiarity and harmonization persistently conflict. For Europe, it seems sensible to ask whether the principle of subsidiarity confounds the attainment of EMU and distorts its impact. There are no formal mechanisms for applying the principle to allocate responsibilities across the European Union. Political compromises will interact with the implementation of subsidiarity in the intergovernmental negotiations in December 1996.

Fiscal sovereignty is important since it implies an ability to raise 'own resources' independent of the policies of member states. Any effective federal system provides sufficient governmental revenue to meet tasks given to various levels of government. With the Edinburgh Agreement as a guide, it is apparent that levels of European federal revenue envisaged for the run-up to EMU and thereafter are inadequate when compared to historical experiences elsewhere. In the MacDougall Report (CEC 1977), a range of 5–7 per cent of the Community's GDP was recommended as an adequate benchmark. However, the Edinburgh Agreement calls for a limit of 1.7 per cent! For Canadians, contemplating a corresponding value of almost a fifth of Canadian GDP, this seems to limit the scope of European fiscal policy.

Establishment of the EMI in 1994 signalled the beginning of the second stage of EMU. This transitory institution is vested with modest powers relative to those anticipated for the European Central Bank (ECB). As noted by Fratianni et al. (1992), the structural character of the EMI will be more 'federal' than that of the ECB since the third stage requires national central banks to give up some of their role in decision-making within the European System of Central Banks (ESCB). The EMI is charged with making recommendations to national authorities with regard to their conduct of monetary policy. It also inherited the EMS and operation of the ERM, took over the tasks of the European Monetary Cooperation Fund, and is expected to 'strengthen the coordination of the monetary policies of the Member States, with the aim of ensuring price stability'. The institute also oversees the ECU clearing system, stimulates the use of ECUs, and 'holds consultations concerning issues falling within the competence of the national central banks and affecting the stability of financial institutions and markets'. But the EMI is not the ECB, merely an instrument to encourage harmonization, provide a forum for debate on monetary matters, give wise advice, and prepare the ground for the third stage. The EMI will be dissolved once the final stage of the process of monetary union begins, and the ESCB will take its place with a new ECB sharing 'centre-stage' in a federal structure with national central banks, guided by principles of independence, subsidiarity and accountability, and by a commitment to price stability. Other objectives will include holding and managing foreign-exchange reserves of member states and smooth running of the payment system.

Other problems affect the institutions proposed for EMU. There is a lack of fiscal continuity whereby, as noted by Buiter et al. (1993), 'the sanction of exclusion from EMU seems a stronger incentive for fiscal discipline than the rather insipid sanctions proposed once the EMU is a fact'. Further, the ECB will enjoy little flexibility because of its commitment to price stability, although relevant indicators of such stability are not defined in the Maastricht Treaty itself. A third problem stems from the imprecise status of national central banks. The ECB Statute indicates that 'national central banks are an integral part of the ESCB and shall act in accordance with the guidelines and instructions of the ECB', but there is no unifying organizational structure and no provision for unilateral actions by a national central bank contravening ECB instructions. This omission leaves the national central banks with dual responsibilities both to their governments and to the ECB.

DISPARITIES AND CONVERGENCE

One hazard of a stage-wise transition to monetary union stems from the potential of states to benefit from 'end games', whereby 'participants know that a particular arrangement will stop at a certain time and that they can influence their relative wealth or income positions in the subsequent arrangement by taking certain actions under the current one' (Fratianni et al. 1992). End games are discouraged by ambiguous or unspecified timing of final transition and by strict entry conditions, represented in the Maastricht process by convergence criteria. The Maastricht Treaty indicates five conditions for admission based on price stability, average interest rates on long-term government bonds, national ratios of government deficits and overall debts to GDP, and respect for the bounds of normal fluctuations in the ERM (although the final condition was later effectively abandoned). All these criteria attracted much attention, but the fiscal standards especially so. In retrospect, the first two criteria (price stability, interest rates) were well specified. Given stable exchange rates, convergence of inflation rates in terms of tradable goods would be advantageous, while high capital mobility within the Community might imply that differentials in long-term interest rates simply reflect differences in default risk. The third and fourth criteria, however, were static and seemingly unrelated to the final objective of the process of integration. It is difficult to see them as sensible components for basic entry standards or as feasible by 1999. Requiring government deficits and debt levels to be no more than 3 and 60 per cent of national GDPs, respectively, is arbitrary, perverse and impractical. Excessive fiscal stringency, driven by state contingency and a contractionary fiscal bias, has no coherent rationale and the criteria are unlikely to be binding in practice. Calculations for sustainable fiscal policies by Buiter et al. (1993) clearly demonstrate their unrealistic nature. From simulations, they concluded that the criteria 'describe the economics of the lunatic asylum'. In similar vein, Bean (1992) pointed out that 'if the price of monetary union is the adoption of inappropriate fiscal policies then it is probably a price that is not worth paying'.

The need for numerical criteria for EMU was initially proposed by Lamfalussy (1989), who stressed the importance of an appropriate fiscal stance for the whole union, the avoidance of a disproportionate use of the Community savings by any country, and a possible bias toward fiscal profligacy. The EU budget is largely based on indirect taxes and does not involve direct taxation. Thus, at about 1.3 per cent of GDP, it has only a modest impact in determining overall fiscal stance. Also, policy coordination and intrafiscal jurisdiction give EC institutions little leeway through regional spillovers and other aspects. Most importantly, though, under Maastricht, the fiscal criteria are not only relevant to the period before the third stage of EMU is implemented, but are also applicable to national fiscal policies after entering into the final stage of EMU.

MAASTRICHT: ANY FEASIBLE ALTERNATIVES?

The Maastricht Treaty is reality but EMU is not. Entries in Table 2.1, derived from Emerson et al. (1992), provide a summary of major potential effects on fiscal policies and public finance from establishment of EMU. Quite why the architects of Maastricht chose their particular combination of objectives is unclear. Given the present situation, it is sensible to review alternatives to the Maastricht path in terms of potential amendments to the Treaty and in terms of replacing it.

Potential modifications to the Treaty are many but it seems appropriate to focus on a shortlist of options which might make the Treaty workable:

1. Drop fiscal criteria as entry and post-entry (stage 3) conditions.
2. Drop the debt entry condition, modify the budget-deficit entry condition, reassess or drop imposition of the fiscal post-entry (stage 3) conditions, and modestly increase the policy competences and budget of the European parliament.
3. Drop the debt entry condition, modify the budget-deficit criterion (for entry and post-entry conditions), and substantially increase the policy competences and budget of the European Parliament.

Table 2.1 Effects of EMU

	Monetary union	Economic union	Aggregate effect
Fiscal policy			
Need for autonomy	+	–	+
Need for discipline	+	neutral	+
Incentives to discipline[1]	+/–		
Need for coordination	+	+	+
Government income/expenditure			
Seigniorage revenues	–	–	–
Debt service	–	+/–	–
Tax revenues[2]	neutral	–	–
Provision of public goods[2]	+	+/–	+/–

Notes:
\+ increases
– decreases
[1] Incentives to discipline assuming no specific community budgetary rules
[2] Tax revenues and provision of public goods assuming no coordination.

In these cases, permanent alterations may enable the Maastricht plans to become operational – abandon narrow ERM bands as guides to entry or impose measures to allow the ERM to operate again under narrow bands (new capital controls or a tax on foreign exchange rate transactions), and change the EMU timetable. Option 1 would allow EMU to be realized while allowing increases in national fiscal autonomy and retaining current plans for a modest expansion of the EC budget. Option 2 would be more in line with the McDougall Report with regard to the EC budget but would recognize that fiscal adjustment is necessary in some states to prepare for entry into EMU. Fiscal conditions might not be in force after entry, depending on the extent or their reassessment. Option 3 goes much beyond the McDougall Report, but reflects the fiscal reality of most mature federations.

Economic options are well and good, but which options are politically feasible? The Bundesbank is highly influential so retention of post-entry conditions might be necessary for a political solution. On the other hand, the UK government is firmly opposed to federalist structures giving redistributive powers to Brussels. Thus options 1 and 3 are unlikely for a political solution, leaving only option 2 as a feasible compromise and assisted by the desire to give more credibility to the European Parliament and strengthen pan-European decision-making.

Dismissal of a gradual approach opens the way to other options in Europe. These include:

1. Abandon gradualism and pursue more political and economic integration before replacement of national currencies with the ECU.
2. Accept a competing currency or 'hard ECU' approach.
3. Reinstate the ERM as the principal mechanism towards attainment of a single currency, with adoption of measures to reduce the severity of speculative attacks.

The first option reflects the 'economist' view of integration, with economic and political integration foreshadowing monetary union. Here monetary integration evolves once other policy instruments are in place and after EC political institutions are already developed. The second option would not necessarily call for prior economic and political integration. Rather it would evolve in line with monetary preferences. EMU may never be completed as a process; more fiscal restraint might be encouraged while trade and cross-border transactions could be facilitated. Option 3 is clearly more controversial since it would involve a thorough review of recent adverse experiences with the ERM, as well as substantial reform of the defensive mechanisms embodied in the system. If a monetary authority, such as the EMI, were given complete and comprehensive control of the workings of the EMS, more prompt and appropriate adjustment might counteract speculative attacks. Once economic convergence is achieved, as determined by exchange rate stability and criteria defined by an independent EMI, members could replace national currencies by the ECU.

For political feasibility, only option 1 precludes the possibility of a 'two-speed' Europe. Given that legal tender provisions are in place for members, option 2 even removes timing of the decision to introduce EMU from the national governments. Option 3 would clearly be opposed by the current UK government but participation in the EMS is voluntary so its hands would not be tied. However, if opposition from the UK government were forthcoming, the UK would probably be pushed to the periphery of the integration process.

CONCLUSIONS

It would be improper to summarize the complexity of dynamic processes and the uncertainty of Europe's future in a few short sentences. Doubts concerning fiscal criteria for entry to a monetary union and the inadequate scope of fiscal activity in the Maastricht process have been stressed. Also notable is the loss of control over regional disparities and flexibility in dealing with asymmetric shocks when fiscal levers are underdeveloped at the community level. Somewhat understated here are problems in establishing both institutional autonomy and democratic responsibility in monetary policy. In the European context, these intertwined objectives require more clarification and definition. Optimistic scenarios for European integration have now disappeared in the face of recent developments. In the preceding section, a search for new or revised strategies is suggested to guide integration by indicating broad classes of realistic options. Both political and economic feasibility were seemingly absent in many features of the Maastricht plans. History need not repeat itself if sensible assessment of feasible options is undertaken before the Inter-Governmental Conference in 1996.

REFERENCES

Bean, C. (1992), 'Economic and Monetary Union in Europe', Discussion Paper no. 86, Centre for Economic Performance, London School of Economics.

Buiter, W., G. Corsetti and N. Roubini (1993), 'Excessive Deficits: Sense and Nonsense in the Treaty of Maastricht', *Economic Policy*, **16**, 58–100.

CEC (1977), *Report of the Study Group on the Role of Public Finance in European Integration* (The MacDougall Report), Brussels: CEC.

Committee on the Study of Economic and Monetary Union (The Delors Committee), (1989), *Report on Economic and Monetary Union in the European Community*, Luxembourg: Office for Official Publications of the EC.

Council of the EC (1992), *Treaty on European Union*, Luxembourg: Office for Official Publications of the EC.

De la Dehesa, G., and P. Krugman (1993), 'Monetary Union, Regional Cohesion and Regional Shocks', in G. de la Dehesa, et al. (eds), *The Monetary Future of Europe*, London: CEPR, chap. 9.

Eichengreen, B., and T. Bayoumi (1992), 'Shocking Aspects of European Monetary Unification', NBER Working Paper no. 3949.

Eichengreen, B., and C. Wyplosz (1993), 'The Unstable EMS', CEPR Discussion Paper no. 817.

Emerson. M., F. Gros, A. Italianer, J. Pisani-Ferry and H. Reichenbach (1992), *One Market, One Money*, Oxford: Oxford University Press.

Fratianni, M., J. von Hagen and C. Waller (1992), *The Maastricht Way to EMU*, Essays in International Finance no. 187, Princeton, NJ: Princeton University.

Hayek, F.A. von (1976a), 'Denationalization of Money', Hobart Paper no. 70, London: Institute of Economic Affairs.

Hayek, F.A. von (1976b), 'Choice in Currency', Occasional Paper no. 48, London: Institute of Economic Affairs.

Hayek, F.A. von (1984), 'The Future Unit of Value', in P. Salin (ed.), *Currency Competition and Monetary Union*, The Hague, Netherlands: Martinus Nijhoff.

Lamfalussy, A. (1989), 'Macro-coordination of Fiscal Policies in an Economic and Monetary Union in Europe', in *Collection of Papers Submitted to the Committee for the Study of Economic and Monetary Union*, Luxembourg: Office for Official Publications of the EC, pp. 91–125.

3. Cohesion in a stratified EU: development under integration

Arvind Jaggi

INTRODUCTION

Although the Single European Act (1986) strongly advocated engendering economic and social cohesion, recent studies claim that structural policies under the Delors Plan have failed to mitigate disparity.[1] Rather, inequality is likely to grow in the European Union (EU) as a consequence of unequal endowments of skills, capital, and wealth. Moreover the combined funding to the European Regional Development Fund (ERDF), the European Social Fund (ESF) and the European Investment Bank (EIB) is grossly inadequate (especially as compared to the Common Agricultural Policy – CAP), and the allocations from these funds have been misguided and disproportionately allotted in favour of the already prosperous regions in the EU's South (assumed to include Greece, Portugal and Spain).[2]

This chapter highlights the fact that market dynamics tend to accentuate inequality under integration and that elements of the North–South distinction provide an appropriate framework to analyse the integration of disparate regions. Consequently a case is made for a reformed regional/structural policy that fosters a sustained and broad-based development.

DEVELOPMENTAL IMBALANCES

In examining interregional economic inequality, it is useful to understand why the free market naturally spawns pockets of concentrated activity and a markedly uneven distribution of income and opportunities.

A historical overview of capitalism suggests that it has inherent tendencies toward developmental imbalances and endemic disparities in living standards. By causing 'capital and labor [to] concentrate together at privileged sites where significant increasing returns to scale are available' (Scott and Storper 1986), market processes create dense clusters of economic activity that are distinguished by: propulsive manufacturing industries prone to scale economies, technological spillovers, and extensive backward and forward linkages: a production mix biased toward income-elastic goods; a concentration of ancillary and auxiliary industries that enhance local content in production and hence magnify multiplier effects; and agglomerations of transportation systems and infrastructure facilities.

The Myrdal–Kaldor (Myrdal 1957; Kaldor 1981) conceptualization of 'cumulative causation' provides a useful explanation for the first two above. In this model the growth centre is the location of industries whose high-tech nature, capital intensity and cost structures ensure scale economies. Rising demand leads to falling average costs and hence higher profits which in turn induce heavier doses of investment and R&D expenditures. By interpreting the Myrdal–Kaldor model in an explicitly spatial context, Krugman (1991) provides insights into the last two factors above. Krugman's explanation rests on an interplay of scale economies and locational attributes like cheap intermediate inputs (because of proximity of related intermediate industries and ample provision of infrastructure), availability of skilled labour, lower transportation costs and a concentration of demand. High income elasticity of demand, and capital and skills intensities of modern manufactured goods imply both a rising share in consumer expenditure and continually rising efficiency due to scale economies. Additionally cost savings are realized due to lower transportation and information-gathering costs, the spillover of knowledge, and efficiency gains from ancillary and auxiliary industries.[3]

THE NORTH–SOUTH ANALYSIS

The neoclassical view prognosticates that unfettered markets accompanied by a heightened mobility of factors will ensure the convergence of factor prices and incomes. The persistence of spatial inequalities and of the South's relative backwardness are deemed only temporary and blamed chiefly on retarded technological development, and an immobile and rigid labour force. But with intra-EU disparities rising, especially with respect to peripheral territories in the South, it seems clear that these paradigmatic road-blocks tend to become permanent.

With respect to impact on indigenous industries in Greece, Portugal and Spain, accession exposed their technologically inferior firms to competition from their sophisticated Northern counterparts, damaged the prospects for infant industries to build market strength, and encouraged installation of foreign-owned production facilities leading to loss of market share. Together, these adverse developments penalized the already disadvantaged firms in the South.

Furthermore, the neoclassical viewpoint predicts falling wage differentials due to worker migration from the South and capital outflows from the North. However, significant labour mobility has occurred mostly within the South, as skilled and unskilled workers have migrated to the prosperous industrial and commercial centres like Athens, Lisbon and Madrid. This phenomenon has accentuated already wide disparities in income and living standards between the metropolitan areas and the outlying periphery: skills, higher incomes and jobs become concentrated in industrial regions of the three nations, thereby depriving the struggling regions of human resources, demand and a tax-base. Moreover the majority of foreign direct investment (FDI) has agglomerated in the increasingly wealthy regions of the South, thus having a limited impact on the overall economies.[4]

These observations suggest that market forces might plausibly work against the very objectives the South had hoped to attain through membership. The clear prospect of a two-tiered development in the EU warrants a search for a framework that accommodates the South's structural peculiarities.

Recent contributions to North–South analysis (Chichilnisky and Heal 1986; Stewart 1984) have asserted the unsuitability of free trade for developing economies since those among them 'that have achieved high and sustained growth via trade have done so by pursuing a blend of protectionism (and) industrial policies ...'.[5] They further stress that standard theoretical constructs like the Heckscher–Ohlin model were actually formulated to analyse trade between nations differentiated only by factor endowments. But there exist some fundamental North–South structural differences that are integral to rising disparities.[6] These differences relate to dissimilarities in the nature of factor markets, technologies, and the structure of demand.

Factor Markets

Developing economies have endemic shortages of capital and the majority of the workforce are ill educated and relatively unskilled. These features become manifest in low productivity growth and low value-added. Consequently free trade would surely lead to such economies specializing in primary and low-tech/labour-intensive goods.

There is also a contrast between how the Northern and Southern factor markets behave. According to Chichilnisky and Heal (1986), the presence of considerable unemployment and underemployment in developing nations makes their labour supply highly elastic to real wage changes. This implies that with limited and regionally concentrated employment opportunities, wages remain low. On the other hand capital is relatively unresponsive to changes in rates of return, which explains its chronic scarcity. These characteristics strengthen the long-term scenario of declining terms of trade, slow income growth, and low accumulation.

Technologies

The stark technological dualism in developing economies is typified by a small modern/urban industrial 'core' with advanced technology, extensive infrastructure, and modern communications networks coexisting with a large periphery using outdated techniques, aging machinery, and rudimentary transportation facilities. This spatial disparity not only prevents mutually gainful interaction between the two regions, but also propels them along divergent trajectories: the periphery stays mired in traditional activities and stagnant living standards, while the core experiences steadily rising incomes.

Structure of Demand

Lower GDP and the highly skewed income distributions in such countries imply that both the size and the structure of its demand constitute a disadvantage. First, the relatively low level of demand limits the scope of consumer markets and, therefore, hinders the Southern firms and industries from enjoying scale economies.[7] Second, even though the demand pattern of the opulent minority mimics that of the North, the inequitable income distribution generates overall consumption patterns biased toward food and simple manufactured products which are precisely the sectors not conducive to scale economies.

STRUCTURAL PROBLEMS

Despite some peculiarities in their development experiences, the post-accession records of Greece, Portugal and Spain exhibit several disturbing parallels, as indicated in Table 3.1. Although the fall of trade barriers led to an intensification of their relationships with Northern markets, as reflected by dramatic growth in exports to the EU, it also exposed these economies' deep-rooted structural problems. Consequently, exports have failed to keep pace with rapidly rising imports.

The promise exhibited by the Greek economy in the 1960s was frustrated by macroeconomic mismanagement which seriously damaged its potential for sustainable growth.[8] This is reflected in the retardation of growth and higher unemployment rates. In contrast, Portuguese and Spanish growth rates have improved substantially since accession. In large part, the steady flow of FDI has been a major impetus to both economies, contributing to rising

Table 3.1 *Basic macroeconomic statistics*

	1985	1988	1991
Greece			
% of exports to EU	54.9	64.8	63.7
Trade deficit ($m)	5614	6837	12810
GDP growth* (%)	1	2.1	1.7
Unemployment (%)	7.8	7.7	8.2
Portugal			
% of exports to EU	62.6	72.0	75.4
Trade deficit (bn escudos)	331	999	1485
GDP growth* (%)	1	2.7	4.6
Unemployment (%)	8.5	6.1	4.1
Spain			
% of exports to EU	52.1	65.6	70.9
Trade deficit (bn pesetas)	1007	2329	3446
GDP growth* (%)	1.4	3.6	4.5
Unemployment (%)	21.5	20.2	16.3

Note: * The GDP growth rates are five-year moving averages for the years 1985, 1988 and 1990.

Source: OECD, *Economic Surveys*.

incomes and production of semi-processed and finished goods for domestic and export markets. But, while Spain's economy has expanded at rates unseen in the EU, it is difficult to reconcile this with her chronically high unemployment rates. One possible explanation is that economic growth has been mostly a sectoral phenomenon: capacity creation and the infusion of FDI has favoured capital intensive industries where job creation is limited.

Table 3.2 reveals some important aspects of the three economies' structural profiles. Relative levels of GDP per capita in Greece and Portugal remain alarmingly below the EU average; while the relative levels in Portugal and Spain improved slightly in the four years after accession. Greece's position has worsened since 1981.[9] Tourism, a sector that supports low skills and underemployment, continues to be a significant portion of all three economies, reflecting a deficiency of manufacturing jobs. The relatively sparse road systems in all three countries indicate the gross inadequacy of transportation and infrastructural facilities. Beyond these struc-

Table 3.2 Structural indicators, 1989

	Greece	Portugal	Spain	EU 12
GDP per capita (1988)[a]	54.5	54.0	74.7	100
Tourism as % of exports[b]	15.3	17.5	20.6	8.0
Roads, km per 100 km^2	31.3	12.5	34.4	118.8

Notes:
[a] Figures are a percentage of the EU 12 average.
[b] Approximations.

Source: Eurostat (1991).

tural similarities, the following profiles detail individual characteristics and experiences.

Greece

According to Camagni (1992) progressive assimilation will most likely worsen Greece's relative standing in the EU. Since 1981, import penetration has effected a gradual contraction of emerging industries and forced indigenous business to retreat to the more traditional sectors like food processing, textiles and clothing (Tsoukalis 1993). These changes contribute to cementing an international division of labour that places the South, particularly Greece, in traditional labour-intensive activities. The structural weakness of the Greek economy has deterred capital inflows, resulting in relatively insubstantial magnitudes of FDI as compared to Portugal and Spain. Moreover the rather limited multinational activity is geographically concentrated in areas already rich in domestic industrial capacity, skilled workers, commercial facilities (banks, advertising, etc.) and transportation networks. Thus the development of industrial activity in regions outside areas like Attica has been hindered. While tourism and commerce do provide some employment in the peripheral regions, higher wages in the core regions are an impetus for the migration of workers, leading to the impoverishment of the peripheral economy.

Portugal

The most striking development in the Portuguese economy since accession has been a corroboration of the Kaldor–Myrdal–Krugman thesis. There is a distinct pattern of intensifying agglomeration of manufacturing activities around the Lisbon area, chiefly due to the presence of essential infrastructure. Adding to this bias is the increasingly mobile workforce: Camagni (1992) points to the disturbing tendency of a gradual process of 'desertification' of the peripheral regions as they lose the more productive element of their workforce; hence also demand and tax-bases.

Spain

In the decade preceding accession, Spain's government had pursued stringent stabilization policies, provided ample protection to industry, and injected massive doses of public investment expenditures. Additionally a strong cadre of educated and trained workers emerged. So, by 1985 the economy was fairly sophisticated, which explains its impressive growth rates and increasingly diverse industrial sector. The high growth of FDI and intra-industry trade reflect a pace of development much faster than that of Greece and Portugal (Tsoukalis 1993). Yet, there is clear indication of a two-speed development process in which improving living standards in the core areas are increasing their lead over those in the periphery. The centre and the south of Spain continue to be laggard regions as rates of unemployment and worker migration from these regions remain among the highest in the EU.[10]

The experiences of the three economies indicate a centripetal tendency that raises the concentration of industry, jobs and income in the prosperous and industrially mature regions.[11] Clearly, then, the appropriate structural policy for the South should envisage reversing the disturbing trends of increasing regional inequality. Such an effort should not only channel sizeable funds into the less advantaged regions and encourage FDI, but also stimulate indigenous entrepreneurship and productivity.

ECONOMIC DYNAMICS

The economic dynamics in three critical areas emphasize the need for an EU structural policy that targets geographical disparities in economic opportunities.

Labour

The claim by mainstream labour economists like Flanagan (1993) that North–South wage differentials within the EU are sufficient to induce labour mobility and erase income inequalities is unrealistic mainly because there are institutional and political obstacles in opposition to large-scale migration. Mass movement of workers within the EU neither was nor is a desired outcome of integration; the evidence shows that the share of migrant labour in the total EU labour force has consistently averaged around a mere 2 per cent.[12] Furthermore, blue-collar workers are the greatest component of the structurally unemployed in the North, and this serves as a powerful political deterrent to immigration from the South. Also, as Chichilnisky and Heal (1986) argue, wage equalization is implausible as long as there are wide differentials between the two regions' work skills, and as long as they are engaged in complementary production activities.

Camagni (1992) argues that preferential treatment of the urban industrial cores in all three economies, by both domestic governments and multinationals, has induced a growing migration of labour out of poorer regions. This mobility causes a 'desertification' of the peripheral regions through an erosion of local demand and tax revenues, thereby exacerbating unemployment and underemployment. In contrast, changes in the core regions have occurred faster than the labour market could accommodate them. The steady increase in unfilled openings reflects both a scarcity and a growing mismatch between workers' skills and firms' requirements. In Spain, unfilled jobs grew from 20 per cent in 1985 to 27 per cent in 1989 and a Ministry of Labour survey in 1991 reported that two-thirds of firms had expressed the need for better-trained employees (OECD 1991).

Under these circumstances, regionally balanced development warrants heavy investment in workforce improvement programmes through structural policy. Besides improving productivity and job opportunities in lagging areas, ERDF and ESF expenditures emphasizing job retraining, education, vocational institutes and so on would also contribute to insulating the South's employment from recessions in the North and temperamental capital flows.

Capital

Although accession stimulated traditional export industries and domestic investment in the South, trade creation and FDI have partially offset those gains. Domestic firms have lost market share to import penetration and multinationals, thus discouraging capital formation in the modern sector and even causing a slow contraction of entrepreneurial activity whose revival could be extremely protracted.[13]

In contrast to the pre-accession years, the establishment of offshore processing and production bases in the South are now motivated by the seduction of cheap labour.[14] Although capital flows from the North into Greece, Portugal and Spain have increased dramatically, there are some unsettling aspects of these investments. First, the bulk of foreign-owned subsidiaries and joint enterprises specialize in assembly and finishing activities which require unsophisticated skills and offer negligible scope for productivity growth. Furthermore, industries in which spatial specialization has gone the furthest due to intermediate processing by Southern subsidiaries, 'the employment effects were often small as (they were) accompanied by a more technology-intensive approach ...' (Buckley and Artisien 1987). Finally, most of the FDI has been concentrated in the core regions, that is Athens, Lisbon, Madrid and Barcelona, which strengthens the centripetal tendencies of regional agglomeration of employment, income and wealth. Therefore an abundance of cheap labour alone is insufficient to motivate FDI in disadvantaged regions; rather, as Lucas (1990) suggests, it is critical to have ample provision of infrastructure, modern technological and commercial support, and a significant demand base. This implies that without substantial involvement and contributions from Brussels, not only will capital, foreign and domestic, elude the South's periphery, but existing resources might even migrate to the core regions.

Technology

Historically, much of the R&D in developing countries has involved adapting imported technology to domestic needs. A survey by Stewart (1990) finds that FDI continues to dominate arrangements like joint ventures, licensing and franchising as the leading methods of technology transfer. Accordingly, foreign enterprises propagate technological knowhow and the accumulation of business acumen. However, the bulk of FDI is restricted to the small modern manufacturing sector that produces items for export to the North, luxury consumer goods, and sophisticated industrial equipment. Hence, the imported technology remains increasingly ill-suited to the broader needs of Southern economies because of the difficulty in adapting it to regional economies endowed with inadequate transportation, electric and communication networks, untrained workers, scant technical support, and 'thin' markets.

A REFORMED POLICY FRAMEWORK

Even though the EU doubled the budget for structural funds in 1988, prevailing structural and regional policy exhibits some worrying features. This section highlights some of the problems and recommends a reformed policy framework.

Table 3.3 indicates that despite its declining importance, primary sector employment remains significant in all three economies. Moreover the large employment shares relative to those in output suggest gross inefficiency and underemployment. Since rising agricultural productivity is a prerequisite for sustained development, European Agricultural Guidance and Guarantee Fund (EAGGF) assistance is imperative.

Musto (1982) claims that the size and composition of EU commitments to agriculture signify a bias against the South. The overwhelming expense of

Table 3.3 Relative importance of agriculture, forestry and fishing

	% share of employment		% share of GDP	
	1985	1990	1985	1990
Greece	29.0	27.0	17.3	15.8
Portugal	25.4	20.3	8.0	5.8
Spain	18.2	11.8	6.0	4.9

Source: OECD, *Economic Surveys*.

stabilizing agricultural markets reduces funding for policies targeted at struggling regions. This, according to Molle and Cappelin (1988) 'will not only undo some redistribution of wealth towards more developed regions, but may also negatively affect certain less developed regions'. Studies like those of Armstrong (1993), Tsoukalis (1993), and Molle and Cappelin (1988) concur that the CAP's price support programme favours richer countries because 'expenditure per farmer has been a function of farm size, productivity, and product specialization. Thus, the subsidy received by the average Dutch farmer is a multiple of the amount paid to his less fortunate colleagues in southern Europe.'[15] All this warrants both a re-evaluation of the agricultural policy and its alignment with the EU's structural programme.

Another policy that implicitly discriminates against the South is the recently instituted competition and technology initiative whose objective is to raise the competitiveness of EU firms against their American and Japanese rivals. Clearly large firms located in the North and core industrial districts will benefit most from this high-tech policy, worsening the relative position of smaller businesses in the periphery and furthering regional disparities.[16]

Some still maintain that regional policy expenditures under ERDF and ESF are mere transfer payments which are 'compensating the losers (in the process of integration) by means of redistribution policies (Molle 1990). This view is hazardous because it disregards the notions that regional disparities are symptomatic of fundamental structural imbalances, and that the long-term benefits of Southern prosperity will necessarily be EU-wide. Consequently, it yields myopic and static policies.

Instead, structural policy must be treated as a long-term development strategy that unclogs the channels of factor allocation, corrects for infrastructural imbalances, and ensures human-capital formation. One reformed policy framework that meets these criteria is a combination of the endogenous development, Keynesian approaches and heavy infrastructural investment.

The endogenous or 'bottom–up' development approach stresses raising of regional factor productivities through a more extensive and efficient utilization of local resources. The aim of policy is then to improve education and training facilities, encourage banking and commercial services, and foster the transfer of technology. The Keynesian or 'top–down' policy approach focuses on capital inflows and relies on rising regional exports of income-elastic goods; falling costs and high value-added associated with scale economies; and the Myrdal–Kaldor cumulative causation process. It is envisaged that infusion of funds due to ERDF and ESF and investment promotion schemes will catalyse domestic and multinational investment. Subsequently rising employment and incomes energize regional markets, thus stimulating local accumulation and FDI.

A recent study by Munnell (1990) finds that enhancing the public capital stock increases employment growth, rate of return to private capital, and productivity growth, thereby stimulating investment and output. This suggests that the inadequacy of public facilities does become an obstacle to private initiatives; hence the obvious justification for infrastructural development.

This discussion implies that supply-side measures like expanded infrastructure alone will be ineffective in mitigating inequalities; these must be accompanied by rising private investment and funding for education and training/apprentice schemes. In support of these recommendations, Louri (1989) finds that for Greece enlarged infrastructure and investment incentives are the chief regional policy instruments successful in attracting firms to its periphery. Growing domestic demand is the most consistent influence on capital formation in Greek manufacturing; and while investment incentives like accelerated depreciation and tax rebates are important in drawing firms into the consumer goods sector, urbanization and infrastructure provision are critical to capital goods industries.

CONCLUSION

This chapter uses the insights of North–South analysis to emphasize that not only is the market ineffective in smoothing out regional disparities, but reliance on it will definitely exacerbate them. With this understanding, Brussels must recognize the necessity of a long-term structural policy aimed at a sustained broad-based improvement in the less developed regions due to the deep-rooted nature of their problems. Accordingly, a meaningful structural/ regional programme for Greece, Portugal, and Spain must increase funding for infrastructure projects like power, transport and communications; negotiate structural unemployment and underemployment; stress job training, vocational and educational programmes; and promote the adaptation of technology through FDI and joint ventures.

NOTES

1. Using 1992 forecasts, Marques Mendes (1990) finds a tendency of increasing intra-EU inequality that the Delors Plan will not be able to offset.
2. The reason for focusing on these three nations is that they are the latest entrants into the EU. Correspondingly, the term 'North' signifies the remaining nine EU member nations.
3. The dynamics are such that firms tend to choose locations with large demand. But local demand is large precisely where there is a concentration of economic activity. 'Thus there is a circularity that tends to keep a manufacturing belt in existence once it is established' Krugman (1991), p. 15.
4. Cross-sectional regression analysis by Billet (1993) finds that FDI flows to richer, rather than poorer, developing countries/regions.
5. Chichilnisky and Heal (1986), p. 54.
6. It is reasonable to extend the North–South arguments from the international context to an intranational setting since there is inequality between the industrial core regions and the relatively poor and lagging regions of the South.
7. Firms experience *internal* scale economies that result from falling costs due to relatively high fixed cost. Industries, on the other hand, are attributed *external* scale economies which arise because of an agglomeration of firms in linked industries leading to lower transaction and transportation costs.
8. Tsoukalis (1993) blames the weak political will of successive Greek governments for the failure to impose austere adjustment policies after the oil shocks and inflationary budget deficits.
9. The corresponding figures at the respective accessions were Greece (1981): 56, Portugal (1985): 52, and Spain (1985): 72. These figures are based on market prices and purchasing power parities. See Eurostat (1989).
10. While Spain's average value-added in industry is 25.2 per cent, it is 19.1 per cent in the centre and a mere 17.5 per cent in the south. See Eurostat (1990).
11. Examples are the Barcelona–Malaga–Ebro Valley belt in Spain, the area north of Lisbon in Portugal, and the Athens–Salonica region in Greece. Ireland too shows a dualistic pattern in her manufacturing sector. The predominance of foreign-owned assembly and processing subsidiaries in modern capital-intensive industries has led to a withdrawal of most indigenous enterprise into less sophisticated and labour-intensive areas. While employment in traditional sectors is falling, the employment effects of the capital-intensive industries have been modest. As multinationals repatriate the bulk of the profits, there are negligible externalities for the economy at large. Camagni (1992), p. 363.
12. See Molle (1990) for a detailed analysis of the repressed migration that exists in the South. It is also possible to interpret the large flows of FDI into the South as an indirect emigration control strategy. In fact the movement of labour before the 1973 oil shock was far greater than that in the 1980s.
13. For example, the case of Italian Mezzogiorno, 'where this occurred extensively as a consequence of the location of large external firms, provides an important warning, especially to new member states' (Camagni 1992, p. 366).
14. Earlier, FDI was largely a substitute for Northern exports and 'many investments in the Southern EU in the 1970's were motivated by the need to penetrate a protected market' (Buckley and Artisien 1987, p. 151).
15. Tsoukalis (1993), p. 267.
16. Amin, Charles and Howells (1992) report that the overwhelming bulk of funding through the Framework Programme, operating under ESPRIT (European Strategic Programme for

Research and Development in Information Technology) and RACE (Research and Development in Advanced Communications for Europe), has gone to large firms in the North.

REFERENCES

Amin, A., D. Charles and J. Howells (1992), 'Corporate Restructuring and Cohesion in the New Europe', *Regional Studies*, **26** (4), 319–31.
Armstrong, H. (1993), 'Community Regional Policy', in J. Lodge (ed.), *The European Community and the Challenge of the Future*, 2nd edn, New York: St Martin's Press.
Billet, B. (1993), *Modernization Theory and Economic Development: Discontent in the Developing World*, Westport, Conn.: Praegar.
Buckley, P. and P. Artisien (1987), *North–South Direct Investment in the European Communities*, Riverside, Calif.: Macmillan.
Camagni, R. (1992), 'Development Scenarios and Policy Guidelines for the Lagging Regions in the 1990s', *Regional Studies*, **26** (4), 361–74.
Chichilnisky, G. and G. Heal (1986), *The Evolving International Economy*, Cambridge, New York: Cambridge University Press.
Eurostat (1989), *Basic Statistics of the Community* (1989), 26th edn, Brussels: Office for Official Publications of the EC.
Eurostat (1990), *Statistical Yearbook of Regions*, Luxembourg: Office for Official Publications of the EC.
Eurostat (1991), *A Community of Twelve: Key Figures,* 26th edn, Luxembourg: Office for Official Publications of the EC.
Flanagan, R. (1993), 'European Wage Equalization since the Treaty of Rome', in L. Ulman, B. Eichengreen and W. Dickens (eds), *Labor and an Integrated Europe*, Washington, DC.: Brookings Institution.
Kaldor, N. (1981), 'The Role of Increasing Returns, Technical Progress, and Cumulative Causation in the Theory of International Trade and Economic Growth', *Economic Appliquée*, no. 4.
Krugman, P. (1991), *Geography and Trade*, Cambridge, Mass.: MIT Press.
Louri, H. (1989), 'Regional Policy and Investment Behaviour: The Case of Greece, 1971–1982', *Regional Studies*, **23** (3), 231–9.
Lucas, R. (1990), 'Why Doesn't Capital Flow from Rich to Poor Countries?', *American Economic Review*, **80** (2), 92–6.
Marques Mendes, A. (1990), 'Economic Cohesion in Europe: The Impact of the Delors Plan', *Journal of Common Market Studies*, **29** (1), 17–36.
Molle, W. (1990), 'Will the Completion of the Internal Market Lead to Regional Divergence?' in H. Siebert (ed.), *The Completion of the Internal Market*, Boulder, Col.: Westview.
Molle, W. and R. Cappelin (eds) (1988), *Regional Impact of Community Policies in Europe*, Aldershot, UK: Avebury.
Munnell, A. (1990), 'Is There a Shortfall in Public Capital Investment? An Overview' in A. Munnell (ed.), *Is There a Shortfall in Public Capital Investment?*, Boston: Federal Reserve Bank of Boston.
Musto, S. (1982), 'Structural Implications', in D. Seers and C. Vaitsos (eds), *The Second Enlargement of the EEC: The Integration of Unequal Partners*, New York: St Martin's.

Myrdal, G. (1957), *Economic Theory and Underdeveloped Regions*, London: Duckworth.
OECD, *Economic Surveys: Greece, Portugal, and Spain, 1988–1993*, Paris: OECD.
Scott, A. and M. Storper (1986), 'Industrial Change and Territorial Organization: A Summing Up', in A. Scott and M. Storper (eds), *Production, Work, Territory: The Geographical Anatomy of Industrial Capitalism*, Boston: Allen & Unwin.
Stewart, F. (1984), 'Recent Theories of International Trade: Some Implications for the South', in H. Kierskowski (ed.), *Monopolistic Competition and International Trade*, Oxford: Oxford University Press.
Stewart, F. (1990), 'Technology Transfer for Development', in R. Evenson and G. Ranis (eds), *Science and Technology: Lessons for Development Policy*, Boulder, Col.: Westview.
Tsoukalis, L. (1993), *The New European Economy*, 2nd edn, New York: Oxford University Press.

4. 'Fortress' common markets: are they welfare-improving?

Constantinos Syropoulos and Elias Dinopoulos

INTRODUCTION

In the last decade, we have witnessed the proliferation of preferential trading arrangements in the form of free trade areas, customs unions, and common markets (e.g. NAFTA, MERCOSUR and the European Union). In addition to the substantial multilateral tariff cuts under the General Agreement on Tariffs and Trade (GATT) in the postwar era, two important dimensions of global economic integration have been: preferential reductions of trade barriers in product markets, and attempts to extend liberalization of factor flows within common markets (CMs). Perhaps the best known example of this latter type of integration scheme is 'Europe 1992'. Of course, the European attempts to integrate product and factor markets have not been met without suspicion in the rest of the world (ROW). Indeed one of the concerns of countries in the ROW has been that the EU may become a 'fortress' common market: that is, a trading bloc with high external tariffs that would divert trade flows and undermine access of outsiders into European markets.

The possibility of deepening economic integration through liberalization of factor flows within existing trading blocs raises several questions. What are the implications for global protection, national welfare and world efficiency? Under what conditions, if any, would a move from a customs union (CU) to a CM raise external tariffs? What would be the optimal response of the ROW? If, as a result of further integration, tariffs rise, will they necessarily hurt the ROW?

Although the literature on economic integration is extensive, the majority of the theoretical work in this area has been concerned with integration of product markets.[1,2] This chapter attempts to address the above questions, and thus represents a first step toward the analysis of factor market integration within a trading bloc. To that end, we develop a stylized general equilibrium model of three countries and three goods. Perfect competition prevails in all markets and two of the three countries are assumed to have formed a CU, which is labelled the 'home' trading bloc. The third country is the 'foreign' bloc. Both blocs levy tariffs on inter-bloc trade that are optimal in the Nash–Cournot sense. Factor movements can emerge within the home bloc because of cross-country productivity differences.

Our analysis generates several interesting findings. In general, integration of factor markets within the home bloc raises the bloc's productive capacity. The chapter shows that, depending on the nature of the bias in productive capacity, it is possible for the initial pattern of trade to change. On the one hand, if factor market integration results in inter-bloc trade expansion, then both blocs will raise their tariffs. However, despite this increase in tariffs, all countries will benefit from the deepening of integration; in other words, it is possible to have 'fortress' CMs which are Pareto welfare-improving. This possibility is more likely when there are large inter-country productivity differences within the home bloc. On the other hand, if the creation of a CM results in inter-bloc trade contraction, then both blocs will reduce their tariffs. However, in this case home bloc countries benefit from integration and the foreign bloc loses.

The basic elements of the model are presented in the next section, after which the Nash–Cournot tariffs are computed. Then the results of factor market integration are presented and conclusions are drawn. The Appendix contains the necessary algebra.

PREFERENCES, TECHNOLOGY AND TRADE PATTERNS

Consider a world that consists of three countries A, B and C. Each country produces three final goods labelled 1, 2 and 3. Perfect competition prevails in all product and factor markets. Countries A and B are assumed to have formed a CU, the home trading bloc. Similarly, country C can be viewed as another CU, the foreign bloc. The country members of each bloc trade freely with each other and adopt a common external tariff structure on inter-bloc trade. In each bloc a central planning authority is assumed to use the bloc's external tariffs to maximize joint welfare of bloc members. Intra-bloc transfers of income address intra-union distributional problems. Policy instruments (tariffs) are treated parametrically by agents throughout the world. These instruments are endogenously determined in a Nash–Cournot fashion.

Consumer preferences are identical across countries and assume the symmetric Cobb–Douglas form

$$U = \Pi_{j \in \mathrm{M}} (c_j)^{1/3} \tag{1}$$

where c_j is consumption of good j and $M \equiv \{1,2,3\}$. The production structure in each country takes an extremely simple form that allows us to study the effects of factor market integration without unduly complicating the analysis. Every country possesses three inelastically supplied factors of production, and each one is used only in the production of a single product. Table 4.1 summarizes the productivity levels and factor endowments (in parentheses) across goods and countries. To interpret the entries in Table 4.1 appropriately, consider the first row which specifies the production structure of country A. Country A's endowments of every industry-specific factor input are the same and equal to one-half. The (fixed) productivity levels for goods 1, 2 and 3 are α (≥ 1), 1 and β (≥ 1), respectively. Full employment of resources ensures that each country produces the maximum possible sectoral output, which can be found by multiplying the two numbers in each entry in Table 4.1.

*Table 4.1 Sector-specific factor endowments and productivity levels ($\alpha, \beta \geq 1$)**

	Good 1	Good 2	Good 3
Country A	α (1/2)	1 (1/2)	β (1/2)
Country B	1 (1/2)	α (1/2)	β (1/2)
Country C	1 (1)	1 (1)	1 (1)

Note: * The numbers in parentheses denote sector-specific factor endowments.

Table 4.1 imposes several strong restrictions for convenience; these restrictions could be readily relaxed without changing the basic results. First, the postulated specification of factor endowments ensures that the two blocs would be of equal size, and they would not trade with each other if productivity differences were absent, i.e. if $\alpha = \beta = 1$. Second, parameter α (≥ 1) captures the degree of cross-country productivity differences in industries 1 and 2 within the home bloc. Under a CU, the sector-specific wage rate in industry 1 is, therefore, larger in country A than the wage rate in the same industry in country B. Similarly, the wage rate in industry 2 is larger in country B than in country A. As a result, a larger value for parameter α translates into a larger incentive for factors to move across industries within the home bloc. Because the productivity of sector-specific factors is fixed, free intra-bloc factor mobility would result in country A (B) producing good 1 (2) for the home bloc. By construction, there are no incentives for factor movements within the home bloc in sector 3. Third, parameter a in relation to parameter β (> 1) captures the forces of comparative advantage which determine the pattern of inter-bloc trade. The two parameters also capture the size of the home bloc relative to the foreign bloc.

Table 4.2 depicts the effects of factor market integration on the maximum producible output in each bloc. Its entries can be derived from Table 4.1 as follows: Consider good 1 which corresponds to the first column of Table 4.2. If the home bloc remained a CU, then countries A and B would respectively produce $\alpha/2$ and $1/2$ units of good 1; hence total output of good 1 in the home bloc would equal $x_1 = (1 + \alpha)/2$ units. If the home bloc became a CM, then the specific factor in sector 1 would move from country B to country A, because of the latter country's superior technology, and the total output of good 1 would equal $x_1 = \alpha$ units. By construction, output of good 1 in the foreign bloc remains equal to unity. The remaining columns of Table 4.2 can be obtained from the corresponding columns of Table 4.1 by following a similar procedure.

A comparison of the first rows of Table 4.2 reveals the effects of factor market integration in the home bloc: there is a symmetric increase in the bloc's capacity to produce goods 1 and 2; the aggregate output of good 3 and production decisions in the foreign bloc remain unaffected. Although crude, this formalization captures what turns out to be a central force in the integration of factor markets: the nature of the bias in productive capacity which determines the impact on the volume of trade.

Table 4.2 Maximum producible output in each trading bloc[1]

		Good 1	Good 2	Good 3
Home bloc	CU	$x_1 = (\alpha + 1)/2$	$x_2 = (\alpha + 1)/2$	$x_3 = \beta$
(Countries A & B)	CM	$x_1 = \alpha$	$x_2 = \alpha$	$x_3 = \beta$
Foreign bloc	CU	$x_1^* = 1$	$x_2^* = 1$	$x_3^* = 1$
(Country C)	CM	$x_1^* = 1$	$x_2^* = 1$	$x_3^* = 1$

Note: [1] Asterisks denote variables of the foreign trading bloc.

In light of the symmetry in preferences, the pattern of inter-bloc trade will be determined by parameters α and β. We can infer this pattern of trade from Table 4.2. Supposing $\beta > 1$, first consider the case of a home CU (rows 1 and 3 in Table 4.2). For values of α between unity and $2\beta-1$, the home bloc exports good 3 and imports the other two products. For values of α greater than $2\beta-1$, the bloc exports goods 1 and 2 in return for imports of good 3. If α equals $2\beta-1$, then there is no inter-bloc trade. Now consider the case where the home bloc is a CM (rows 2 and 4 in Table 4.2). It can be easily verified that in this case trade patterns resemble the ones observed under a CU, except that now the value of α at which trade flows are reversed is equal to β. The move from a CU to a CM increases outputs of goods 1 and 2 in the home bloc. Clearly, this is equivalent to inter-bloc trade contraction (expansion) for low (high) values of α. The assumptions that $\alpha > 1$ and $\beta > 1$ imply that the home bloc is larger in size than the foreign bloc.

The above discussion can help illustrate how the formation of a CM may change the initial pattern of inter-bloc trade. To see this, consider the trivial case where $\alpha = 2\beta - 1 > 0$ which implies that $\alpha > \beta > 1$. The transformation of the home bloc into a CM changes the trade pattern from autarky to the one where the home bloc exports goods 1 and 2 in exchange for good 3.

OPTIMAL TARIFF STRUCTURES

We now utilize the special structure of the model to derive explicit solutions for the endogenous variables. Continue to adopt the convention that variables without (with) an asterisk are home (foreign) bloc variables. The solution to the consumer's optimization problem gives the following aggregate demand functions:

$$c_j = \frac{Y}{3p_j} \qquad \text{and} \qquad c_j^* = \frac{Y^*}{3p_j^*} \qquad \text{for } j \in \mathrm{M} \equiv \{1,2,3\} \tag{2}$$

where p_j (p_j^*) and Y (Y^*) respectively stand for the domestic price of good j and national income in the home (foreign) bloc.

The net import demand functions for every good $j \in \mathrm{M}$ are defined as $m_j \equiv c_j - x_j$ and $m_j^* \equiv c_j^* - x_j^*$. Denote with $\tau_j \equiv 1 + t_j$ ($\tau_j^* \equiv 1 + t_j^*$) the home (foreign) tariff factor on good j, where t_j (t_j^*) is the corresponding *ad valorem* tariff. Clearly, $p_j = \tau_j q_j$ and $p_j^* = \tau_j^* q_j$, where q_j is the world price of good j.[3]

National income of the home bloc is equal to the value of domestic production plus tariff revenues, i.e. $Y = \Sigma_{j\in \mathrm{M}} (p_j x_j + (\tau_j - 1) q_j m_j)$. Substituting m_j, c_j and p_j in this expression yields

$$Y = \frac{3}{\Sigma_{j\in \mathrm{M}}(1/\tau_j)}\left(\Sigma_{j\in \mathrm{M}} q_j x_j\right). \tag{3}$$

A similar expression can be derived for the national income Y^* of the foreign bloc.

Without loss of generality, let good 3 be the numeraire so that $q_3 = 1$. Moreover, let $T_k \equiv \tau_k/\tau_3$ ($T_k^* \equiv \tau_k^*/\tau_3^*$) be the relative tariff factor imposed on good $k = 1,2$ by the home (foreign) bloc. This normalization allows us to interpret the tariff factors as protective devices that raise the domestic price of imports independently of the pattern of trade.

In any tariff-distorted equilibrium, the following world market-clearing conditions must be satisfied:

$$m_j + m_j^* = 0, \quad \forall j \in \mathrm{M}. \tag{4}$$

Utilizing (4) and imposing symmetry in the tariff factors so that $T \equiv T_1 = T_2$ and $T^* \equiv T_1^* = T_2^*$, we can derive the following closed form solutions for equilibrium prices q_1 and q_2:[4]

$$q^{CU} \equiv q_1^{CU} = q_2^{CU} = \frac{(2+T^*)\beta + (2+T)}{T(2+T^*)\left(\frac{1+\alpha}{2}\right) + T^*(2+T)} \tag{5a}$$

$$q^{CM} \equiv q_1^{CM} = q_2^{CM} = \frac{(2+T^*)\beta + (2+T)}{T(2+T^*)\alpha + T^*(2+T)} \tag{5b}$$

where q^{CU} (q^{CM}) is the relative price of goods 1 and 2 when the home bloc is a CU (CM). Notice that $q^{CU} > q^{CM}$ because the formation of a CM raises the world supply for goods 1 and 2. *Ceteris paribus*, the difference between q^{CU} and q^{CM} increases with parameter α.

The world price under free trade can be found by setting $T = T^* = 1$ in (5a) and (5b) to obtain:

$$q_F^{CU} = \frac{2(\beta+1)}{\alpha+3} \tag{6a}$$

$$q_F^{CM} = \frac{\beta+1}{\alpha+1} \tag{6b}$$

where subscript F refers to free trade. Direct comparison of (6a) and (6b) reveals that $q_F^{CU} > q_F^{CM}$ for reasons that were already explained earlier.

The autarky prices for the home bloc are given by the relative productivity ratios

$$\overline{q}^{CU} = \frac{2\beta}{\alpha+1} \tag{7a}$$

$$\overline{q}^{CM} = \frac{\beta}{\alpha}. \tag{7b}$$

Comparing (7a) to (7b) we can establish once again that $\overline{q}^{CU} > \overline{q}^{CM}$ for $\alpha > 1$. The autarky prices of the foreign bloc equal unity.

The Appendix derives formally the Nash–Cournot tariffs under both integration schemes in the home bloc. The world prices of goods 1 and 2 in the non-cooperative tariff game are given by

$$q_N^{CU} = \left(\frac{2\beta}{\alpha+1} \right)^{1/2} \tag{8a}$$

$$q_N^{CM} = \left(\frac{\beta}{\alpha} \right)^{1/2} \tag{8b}$$

where subscript N denotes evaluation at the Nash–Cournot equilibrium. It is easy to verify that inter-bloc trade is not eliminated in this equilibrium. It should also be apparent from (8a) and (8b) that the integration of factor markets in the home bloc causes the relative prices for goods 1 and 2 to fall; this explains why the initial pattern of trade might be reversed. (See below for more details.)

PROTECTION AND WELFARE

We now illustrate how the move from a CU to a CM by the home bloc influences global tariffs and welfare outcomes. Relegating the more formal analysis to the Appendix, our discussion proceeds with the help of Figures 4.1a–4.2b. These figures are based on the supposition that $\beta > 1$ and $\alpha \geq 1$.

Consider Figure 4.1a which depicts the home bloc's import tariff rate t as a function of the productivity parameter α, under the assumption of no intervention in export markets. The solid curve refers to import tariffs under a CU regime and the dashed curve refers to import tariffs under a CM regime. (We adopt the same notational convention in the other figures.) In all cases considered, the level of protection is V-shaped under either regime. Under a CU, import tariffs fall with increases in α when $1 \leq \alpha < 2\beta - 1$; they reach a minimum at $\alpha = 2\beta - 1$ where there is no inter-bloc trade; and they rise with increases in α for $\alpha > 2\beta - 1$. Under a CM regime, import tariffs follow the same pattern but now the minimum is attained at $\alpha = \beta$. If α assumes a value in the range enclosed by the two vertical dotted lines, then the formation of the CM reverses the inter-bloc pattern of trade. For all other parameter values, the vertical distance between the tariff curves is the change in tariffs that is induced by the move to a CM. Notice that import tariffs fall if α is sufficiently low; exactly the opposite is true for sufficiently large α. Thus, depending on technology, the home bloc can become a 'fortress' CM. Figure

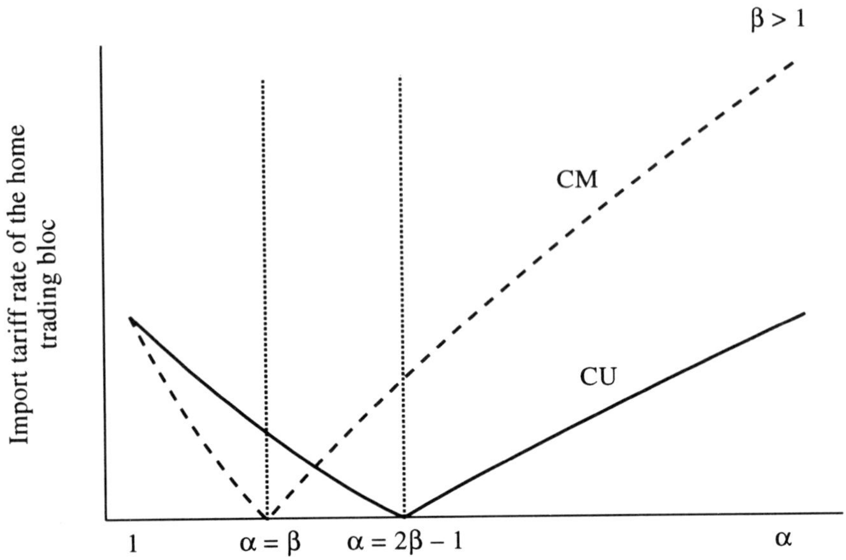

Figure 4.1a *Home bloc's import tariffs under CU and CM regimes*

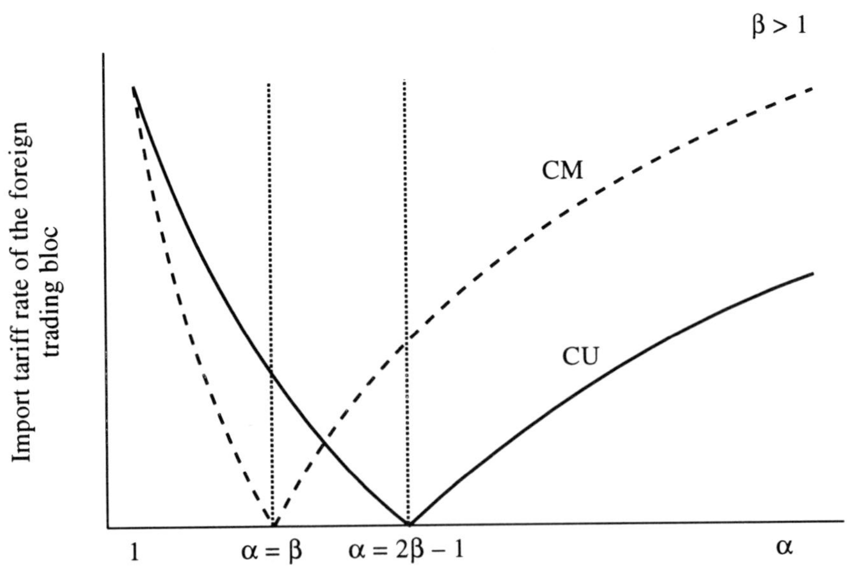

Figure 4.1b *Foreign bloc's import tariffs under CU and CM regimes*

4.1b depicts a similar relationship between the import tariff(s) of the foreign bloc and parameter α. In short, for large (small) values of α relative to β, integration of factor markets in the home bloc triggers higher (lower) protection both at home and abroad.

What is the economic intuition that underlies the above results? If α is small relative to β, the home bloc imports goods 1 and 2. An increase in α, or a move from a CU to a CM, corresponds to an expansion of output of the import sectors of the home bloc which reduces the volume of inter-bloc trade and takes each bloc closer to autarky. The reduction in the volume of trade renders the offer curves of both blocs more elastic and thus reduces their optimal tariffs. If α is large, the home bloc exports goods 1 and 2. Now an increase in α, or a move from a CU to a CM in the home bloc, corresponds to export-biased expansion which enlarges the volume of inter-bloc trade. In this case every trading bloc faces a less elastic offer curve and thus raises its optimal tariff.

Figures 4.2a and 4.2b illustrate how the welfare levels of the home and foreign blocs depend on parameters α and β parameters and the nature of the integration scheme. The home bloc's welfare level increases with α, regardless of the form that integration takes. Larger values of α improve the productive capacity of the home bloc and thus confer a direct benefit to its residents. This effect dominates any possibly adverse terms of trade and strategic tariff-response effects by the foreign bloc. Similar reasoning, applied to integration of factor markets, shows that the home bloc will indeed have an incentive to form a CM. Figure 4.2a shows that the welfare gains due to the deepening of integration in the home bloc increase with parameter α.

Figure 4.2b shows that the foreign bloc's welfare level is a U-shaped function of α with its minimum attained at $\alpha = \beta$ in the case of a CU, and at $\alpha = 2\beta-1$ in the case of a CM. In either case, the minimum corresponds to autarky for each bloc. Clearly the foreign bloc may gain or lose from the deepening of integration in the home bloc. Since, for α lower than β, the formation of the CM results in import substitution in the home bloc, the foreign bloc's terms of trade deteriorate and its volume of trade declines. This takes both blocs closer to autarky and, consequently, hurts the foreign bloc despite the fall in global tariffs. In the case of sufficiently large α, the integration of factor markets improves the foreign bloc's terms of trade and causes its volume of trade to expand. Despite the overall increase in protection, welfare of the foreign bloc rises. This corresponds to the case of welfare-improving 'fortress' common markets.

For large values of α, it is possible for the level of welfare of the home bloc to exceed the free trade welfare level. This is so because large values of α can make the home bloc sufficiently larger than the foreign bloc to win the tariff war.[5] This possibility suggests that, in the absence of inter-bloc transfers of

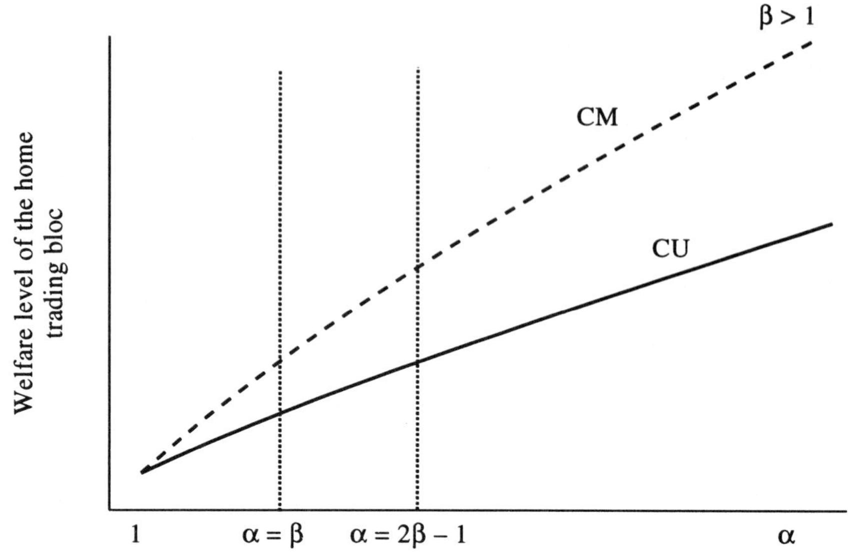

Figure 4.2a Home bloc's welfare level under CU and CM regimes

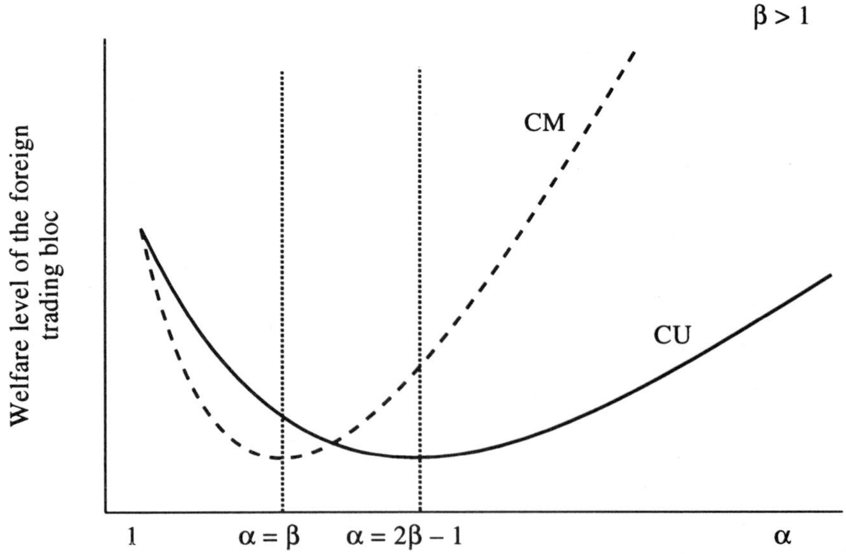

Figure 4.2b Foreign bloc's welfare level under CU and CM regimes

income, common markets may curtail multilateral negotiations to eliminate global trade barriers.

CONCLUSIONS

This chapter has developed a simple general equilibrium model to formally explore how the integration of factor markets within a trading bloc is likely to influence global protection and welfare. If the move to a CM by the home bloc results in inter-bloc trade contraction, then both blocs move toward autarky, equilibrium tariffs decline, and the foreign bloc is hurt. If integration results in inter-bloc trade expansion, then both blocs raise tariffs but their welfare increases. Consequently, it is possible to witness 'fortress', yet welfare-improving, common markets.

Our findings depend on what might appear to be a restrictive set of assumptions. However, one could easily relax the functional form of the utility, the sector specificity of factor inputs, the fixity of productivity coefficients, and the assumption of symmetry in technology across sectors. We claim that the economic intuition of our analysis – especially our distinction between import-biased and export-biased expansion of productive capacity – will remain intact in more general settings.

NOTES

1. Classic contributions include Viner (1950), Meade (1955), Lipsey (1960), Kemp and Wan (1976). Corden (1984) and Hine (1994) provide excellent surveys of the literature on international economic integration.
2. For recent studies on regional trade arrangements that rely on multi-commodity models see Lloyd (1982), Riezman (1985), Kennan and Riezman (1990), Krugman (1991), Bagwell and Staiger (1993a, 1993b), Bhagwati (1993), Bond and Syropoulos (1993, 1996), Bond, Syropoulos and Winters (1996), Dinopoulos and Syropoulos (1994a, 1994b), Srinivasan (1994) and Syropoulos (1993, 1994a, 1994b).
3. Notice that, if good j is imported (exported) by the home bloc, then $\tau_j > 1$ $(0 < \tau_j < 1)$ is an import (export) tax factor.
4. It can be shown (Syropoulos 1993) that the symmetric structure of the model ensures that optimal tariffs will obey the postulated condition of symmetry.
5. See Kennan and Riezman (1988) for an analysis of how size influences outcome of Nash–Cournot tariff games.

REFERENCES

Bagwell, K. and R.W. Staiger (1993a), 'Multilateral Tariff Cooperation During the Formation of Regional Free Trade Areas', NBER Working Paper no. 4364.

Bagwell, K. and R.W. Staiger (1993b), 'Multilateral Tariff Cooperation During the Formation of Customs Unions', NBER Working Paper no. 4543.
Bhagwati, J.N. (1993), 'Regionalism and Multilateralism: An Overview', in J. De Melo and A. Panagariya (eds), *New Dimensions in Regional Integration*, Cambridge, UK: Cambridge University Press.
Bond, E.W. and C. Syropoulos (1996), 'The Size of Trading Blocs: Market Power and World Welfare', *Journal of International Economics*, forthcoming.
Bond, E.W. and C. Syropoulos (1993), 'Trading Blocs and the Sustainability of Inter-Regional Cooperation', in M. Canzoneri, W.J. Ethier and V. Grilli (eds), *The New Transatlantic Economy*, London: Centre for Economic Policy Research (CEPR), forthcoming.
Bond, E.W., C. Syropoulos and L.A. Winters (1995), 'Deepening of Regional Integration and Multilateral Trade Agreements', mimeo, Pennsylvania State University.
Corden, W.M. (1984), 'The Normative Theory of International Trade', in R.W. Jones and P.B. Kenen (eds), *Handbook of International Economics*, vol. I, Amsterdam: North Holland.
Dinopoulos, E. and C. Syropoulos (1994a), 'Trade Liberalization and Schumpeterian Growth', mimeo, Pennsylvania State University.
Dinopoulos, E. and C. Syropoulos (1994b), 'Growth-Creating Trading Blocs', *The Canadian Economic Association Annual*, forthcoming.
Hine, R.C. (1994), 'International Economic Integration', in D. Greenaway and L.A. Winters (eds), *Surveys in International Trade*, Oxford: Blackwell.
Johnson, H.G. (1953–54), 'Optimum Tariffs and Retaliation', *Review of Economic Studies*, **21**, 142–53.
Kemp, M.C. and H. Wan, Jr (1976), 'An Elementary Proposition Concerning the Formation of Customs Unions', *Journal of International Economics*, **6**, 95–7.
Kennan, J. and R. Riezman (1988), 'Do Big Countries Win Tariff Wars?', *International Economic Review*, **29**, 81–5.
Kennan, J. and R. Riezman (1990), 'Optimal Tariff Equilibria with Customs Unions', *Canadian Journal of Economics*, **23**, 70–83.
Krugman, P.R. (1991), 'Is Bilateralism Bad?' in E. Helpman and A. Razin (eds), *International Trade and Trade Policy*, Cambridge, Mass.: MIT Press.
Lipsey, R.G. (1960), 'The Theory of Customs Unions: A General Survey', *The Economic Journal*, **70**, 496–513.
Lloyd, P.J. (1982), '3x3 Theory of Customs Unions', *Journal of International Economics*, **12**, 41–64.
Mayer, W. (1981), 'Theoretical Considerations of Negotiated Tariff Adjustments', *Oxford Economic Papers*, **33**, 135–53.
Meade, J. (1955), *The Theory of Customs Unions*, Amsterdam: North-Holland.
Riezman, R. (1985), 'Customs Unions and the Core', *Journal of International Economics*, **19**, 355–66.
Srinivasan, T.N. (1994), 'Preferential Trading Arrangements in South Asia: Theory, Empirics and Policy, ' Working Paper, Yale University.
Syropoulos, C. (1993), 'Customs Unions and Comparative Advantage', mimeo, Pennsylvania State University.
Syropoulos, C. (1994a), 'Pareto-Improving Free Trade Areas', mimeo, Pennsylvania State University.
Syropoulos, C. (1994b), 'Implications of Preferential Trade Arrangements for Policy and Market Access', *The Canadian Economic Association Annual*, forthcoming.

Viner, J. (1950), *The Customs Union Issue*, New York: Carnegie Endowment for International Peace.

APPENDIX

Consider the determination of the home bloc's external tariff structure. Substituting c_j from (2), Y from (3) and $p_j = \tau_j q_j$ into (1), we obtain the indirect utility function $V(q_1,q_2;\tau_1,\tau_2,\tau_3)$ of the home bloc. Maximizing $V(\cdot)$ with respect to world prices q_1 and q_2, we obtain the following first-order conditions for an interior solution:

$$-m_k^* + \Sigma_{j\in M}(\tau_j - 1)q_j(\partial m_j^* / \partial q_k) = 0, \qquad \text{for } k = 1,2 \qquad \text{(A1)}$$

Similarly, the first-order conditions for the foreign bloc can be derived from:

$$-m_k + \Sigma_{j\in M}(\tau_j^* - 1)q_j(\partial m_j / \partial q_k) = 0, \qquad \text{for } k = 1,2. \qquad \text{(A2)}$$

Recalling that $T_k \equiv \tau_k/\tau_3$ and $T_k^* \equiv \tau_k^*/\tau_3^*$, we can simplify (A1) and (A2) as follows:

$$T_k = T_k^* q_k (x_k^* / x_3^*), \qquad \text{for } k = 1,2 \qquad \text{(A3)}$$

$$T_k^* = T_k q_k (x_k / x_3), \qquad \text{for } k = 1,2 \qquad \text{(A4)}$$

respectively. The world prices in the non-cooperative policy equilibrium can be found from (A3) and (A4) to be

$$q_k = [(x_3^* x_3)/(x_k^* x_k)]^{1/2}, \qquad \text{for } k = 1,2. \qquad \text{(A5)}$$

Substituting (8a) into (5a) and (A5), the Nash equilibrium tariffs under a customs union regime can be calculated from:

$$\left(1 + \frac{\alpha+1}{2}\right)T^2 + \left(1 + \left[\frac{\beta(\alpha+1)}{2}\right]^{1/2}\right)T - 2(\beta+1) = 0 \qquad \text{(A6)}$$

$$\beta\left(1 + \frac{\alpha+1}{2}\right)T^{*2} + \left(\frac{\alpha+1}{2}\right)\left(\left[\frac{2\beta}{\alpha+1}\right]^{1/2} + \beta\right)T^* - (\beta+1)(\alpha+1) = 0. \qquad \text{(A7)}$$

Similarly, the equilibrium tariffs under a common market can be found from:

$$(\alpha+1)T^2+[(\beta\alpha)^{1/2}+\beta\alpha]T-2(\beta+1)=0 \tag{A8}$$

$$\beta(\alpha+1)T^{*2}+[(\beta\alpha)^{1/2}+\beta\alpha]T^*-2\alpha(\beta+1)=0 \tag{A9}$$

Equations (A6)–(A9) are plotted in Figures 4.1a and 4.1b. Substituting the equilibrium tariffs and q_k from (A5) into the indirect utility functions of the home and foreign blocs, one can obtain the welfare levels for the two blocs which are depicted in Figures 4.2a and 4.2b.

5. Are there political cycles in the member countries of the EU? An empirical investigation

Andreas A. Andrikopoulos and Kyprianos Prodromidis*

INTRODUCTION

In the political cycles literature, governments act in favour of their own political interests and/or the interests of particular pressure groups. As a consequence, their actual policies can give rise to political cycles distinguished into electoral cycles (EC), defined as persistent cyclical patterns of key policy and target variables across electoral terms, regardless of the political party in power, and partisan cycles (PC), i.e. persistent differences in such patterns conditional upon the ideology of the party in power (Haynes and Stone 1990). Both the EC and PC approaches, which presume democratically elected governments, a two-party system and a predetermined timing of elections, have been criticized on the grounds of superficiality (Alt and Chrystal 1983, pp. 125, 242) and the lack of supporting or inconclusive empirical evidence (McCallum 1978; Hibbs 1977, 1987; Soh 1986, Van der Ploeg 1987; Alesina 1987, 1989; Alesina and Sachs 1988. The outcome of those criticisms was the development of the rational electoral and rational partisan cycle theories (REC and RPC), respectively. These theories assume a forward-looking private sector rationally anticipating future political and economic developments.

The objective of this chapter is to detect electoral or partisan cycle patterns in the 12 member countries of the European Union (EU). The chapter is organized as follows: The next section discusses our methodological approach. The data used and their sources are then discussed. After that the empirical results are reported. The last section summarizes the main findings and conclusions.

*Revised version. The paper was completed while the second author was on leave at the University of Cyprus.

METHODOLOGY

The modern theories of political cycles include the EC, PC, REC and RPC approaches. From a theoretical point of view, the EC models emphasize the incumbent political party's intent and policy actions to secure re-election by maximizing its expected vote share at the next election. To accomplish that objective, the EC models hypothesize a backward-looking private sector judging the government by its past track record, and a short-sighted government (systematically) fooling a myopic electorate, by judiciously exploiting a short-run Phillips curve trade-off during its term in office.[1] Thus, the testable EC hypothesis is stated as: the government, regardless of ideology or partisanship, adopts contractionary (expansionary) policies in the early (late) years of its term in office in order to depress (reduce) the expected rate of inflation (rate of unemployment). This short-sighted attitude of the incumbent government de-emphasizes the economic problems associated with it and accumulated in the aftermath of elections. On the contrary, the PC models stress that incumbents pursue partisan macroeconomic policies.[2] Since the parties at issue represent different pressure groups, they take account of the different preferences, incentives and objectives of the competing parties by assigning different weights to inflation and unemployment. However, they switch to electoral policies if their re-election is in jeoparty (Frey and Schneider 1978, 1988). The testable PC hypothesis is that, before the election, left-wing or 'socialist' parties give greater weight to high employment and less to low inflation than right-wing or 'conservative' parties. The former adopt expansionary and the latter deflationary policies after they have won the election; they often maintain these policies for their entire term in office.[3]

On the other hand, the REC hypothesis emphasizes the role of temporary information asymmetries in explaining electoral cycles in macroeconomic policy instruments (taxes, transfers, government consumption spending, money growth) rather than in indicators of economic performance (Rogoff and Sibert 1988 and Rogoff 1990). Based on information advantages the incumbent party has an incentive to try to signal, before elections, that it is competent. To accomplish that it manipulates the policy instruments, thus fooling the public and creating cycles in the policy variables.

Finally, the RPC models consider two ideologically different parties, 'socialists' vs 'conservatives', with objectives and incentives known to the public, as well as rational and informed voters. In the context of the inflation–unemployment paradigm 'socialists' have been relatively more averse to unemployment and less averse to inflation than 'conservatives'. In such a framework, rational voters (wage-setters) anticipate the incentives of the alternative policy-makers and form their expectations accordingly. As a result, the RPC hypothesis predicts a transitory expansion (recession) at the beginning of a 'socialist' ('conservative') administration, whereas differences in output and unemployment between governments taper off in the later part of their term in office with inflation being higher during 'socialist' administrations (Alesina and Sachs 1988; Alesina 1989). In general, proponents of electoral and partisan cycles (rational or not) argue that incumbent governments manipulate a number of policy instruments during the election year and/or the preceding one in order to influence in time a number of key target variables so that they can impress the electorate and enhance their chances of re-election.

From the empirical point of view, and in searching for EC and PC regularities in the European Union countries, we have utilized the so-called 'ratios' approach. This approach, which can be applied for each individual variable (controlled or policy, and non-controlled or target, variable)[4] in each country of the EU, is based on two alternative economic indicators given by:

$$R_1 = (\overline{X}_1 / \overline{X}_2), \quad R_1 \gtrless 1 \tag{1}$$

and

$$R_2 = (\overline{Y}_1 / \overline{Y}_2), \quad R_2 \gtrless 1 \tag{2}$$

where R_1 is the ratio of the mean value of the annual rates of change of the ith variable realized in the election years ($\overline{X}_1$) to the mean value of the annual rate of change of the same variable in the non-election years ($\overline{X}_2$). Similarly, R_2 gives the ratio of the mean value of the annual rate of change of the variable involved in the election years plus one year before the election ($\overline{Y}_1$) to the mean value of the same variable ($\overline{Y}_2$) in the remaining years of the sample.[5] We interpret the values of the R_1 and R_2 ratios in the following manner. Depending on the nature of the variables in question, a value of R_1 or R_2 greater than or less than one is taken as a signal of the government's action to please voters in election years and/or in years immediately preceding the election years. For instance, a value of R_i, $i = 1,2$ greater (less) than one for government consumption and investment expenditure, government transfer payments and monetary base (direct taxes and indirect taxes) indicates the conscientious effort of the party in power to attract the confidence of the electorate and, hence, its desire to win the upcoming election.

THE DATA

The empirical analysis concerns the 12 EU member countries and it is based on a sample of 31 observations (1960–90).[6] The variables considered in this

Table 5.1 *Election years and elected governments in the 12 EU countries*

	Belgium	Denmark	France	West Germany	Greece	Ireland	Italy	Luxembourg	Netherlands	Portugal	Spain	UK
1957	–	SOC	–	CON	–	FFF	–	–	–	–	–	–
1958	COL	–	CON	–	CON	–	COL	–	–	–	–	–
1959	–	–	–	–	–	–	–	COL	COL	–	–	CON
1960	–	SOC	–	–	–	–	–	–	–	–	–	–
1961	COL	–	–	CON	CON	FFF	–	–	–	–	–	–
1962	–	–	CON	–	–	–	–	–	–	–	–	–
1963	–	–	–		SOC	–	COL	–	–	–	–	–
1964	–	SOC	–	–	SOC	–	–	COL	COL	–	–	LAB
1965	COL	–	–	COL	–	FFF	–	–	–	–	–	–
1966	–	CON	–	–	–	–	–	–	–	–	–	LAB
1967	–	–	CON	–	–	–	–	–	–	–	–	–
1968	COL	CON	CON	–	–	–	COL	COL	COL	–	–	–
1969	–	–	–	SOC	–	FFF	–	–	–	–	–	–
1970	–	–	–	SOC	–	–	–	–	–	–	–	CON
1971	COL	MIN	–	–	–	–	–	–	COL	–	–	–
1972	–	–	–	SOC	–	–	COL	–	COL	–	–	–
1973	–	MIN	CON	–	–	FGL	–	–	–	–	–	–
1974	COL	–	–	–	COD	–	–	COL	–	–	–	LAB
1975	–	SOC	–	–	–	–	–	–	–	SOC	–	–
1976	–	–	–	SOC	–	–	COL	–	–	SOC	–	–
1977	COL	SOC	–	–	CON	FFF	–	–	COL	–	COD	–

1978	COL	–	CON	–	–	–	–	–	–	–	–	–
1979	–	SOC	–	–	–	–	COL	COL	–	SPD	–	CON
1980	–	–	–	SOC	–	–	–	–	–	SPD	COD	–
1981	COL	SOC	SOC	–	SOC	FGL	–	–	COL	–	–	–
1982	–	–	–	–	–	FFF	–	–	COL	–	–	–
1983	–	–	–	CON	–	–	COL	–	–	SOC	SOC	CON
1984	–	CON	–	–	–	–	–	COL	–	–	–	–
1985	COL	–	–	–	SOC	–	–	–	–	–	–	–
1986	–	–	COP	–	–	–	–	–	COL	SPD	–	–
1987	COL	CON	–	CON	–	FFF	COL	–	–	–	SOC	CON
1988	–	CON	SOC	–	–	–	–	–	–	SPD	–	–
1989	–	–	–	–	COL	FGL	–	COL	COL	–	SOC	–
1990	–	CON	–	CON	CON	–	–	–	–	–	–	–

Notes:
In Ireland (1982) and the UK (1974) two elections took place, in which FFF and FGL won the elections in Ireland and LAB in the UK.
COL = Coalition government
SOC = Socialist government
CON = Conservative government
MIN = Minority government
COP = Conservative government – socialist president
FFF = Fianna Fail government
FGL = Fine Gael government
SPD = Social democratic party government
LAB = Labour government
– = National elections were not held in this year.

investigation are classified into two categories: target variables, which include gross domestic product (GDP), disposable income (YD), private consumption deflator (PC) and unemployment rate (u); and policy variables, which include government consumption spending (GC), government investment spending (GI), direct (DT) and indirect (IT) taxes, government transfer payments to the private sector (GTP), and monetary base (MB). The variables GDP, YD, GC and GI are expressed in levels and real terms, variables PC and u are in percentages, and the remaining variables are in levels and nominal terms. All data come from various issues of OECD (*Annual National Accounts*), IMF (*International Financial Statistics*) and European Commission (*European Economy*) publications.

Table 5.1 gives the years of the parliamentary elections in the 12 EU member countries and the political party that won the elections and formed a government. Two sorts of information are provided in Table 5.1: first, a variety of coalition governments have been formed in Belgium, Italy Luxembourg and the Netherlands.[7] Second, in the remaining countries of our sample, we have witnessed an interchange of two parties in power, broadly characterized as 'conservatives' and 'socialists'. Two exceptions have been observed: in Ireland, where both political parties (i.e. Fianna Fail and Fine Gael–Labour party) have been non-socialist; and in Portugal, where both political parties may be classified as non-conservative (i.e. Socialist and Social Democratic Party).[8]

EMPIRICAL RESULTS

In view of the election results and the nature of the governments formed in the 12 EU member countries (Table 5.1), we searched for: electoral cycle patterns, both in the policy and target variables (Tables 5.2 and 5.3) in each EU member country; and partisan cycle patterns (Tables 5.4 and 5.5) in the eight countries with a two-party, 'conservative' vs 'socialist', system.

Electoral Cycle Patterns

Policy variables

Tables 5.2 and 5.3 present empirical evidence for electoral cycles in policy and target variables, respectively. Although the evidence does not seem to be entirely conclusive, there are strong indications supporting the REC and EC hypotheses relative to the RPC and PC hypotheses. In particular, the incumbent parties appear to have manipulated the policy instruments in the election year and/or the year before the election year. This argument is supported by the fact that the values of R_1, R_2 or both are greater than one in a relatively

Table 5.2 Evidence for electoral cycles in policy variables

	Belgium	Denmark	France	Germany	Greece	Ireland	Italy	Luxembourg	Netherlands	Portugal	Spain	UK
R_1 – ratios of election year: non-election year means of:												
1. GC	0.93	0.23	1.26	1.00	1.35	0.49	1.25	0.83	1.01	0.88	1.20	0.97
2. GI	–	–	1.95	0.56	–	–	0.75	0.32	–	–	2.30	–
3. GTP	1.02	1.04	0.77	0.83	1.25	—	1.05	1.04	1.16	—	—	0.83
4. DT	1.18	0.94	0.65	0.38	0.55	0.87	1.00	1.08	0.99	1.47	0.81	1.30
5. IT	1.01	0.83	0.86	1.53	0.87	1.16	0.75	0.73	1.10	1.14	1.08	1.16
6. MB	1.11	1.09	0.85	2.46	0.29	1.34	1.46	n.a.	0.86	0.78	1.01	0.92
R_2 – ratios of election year plus one year before election means: other years' means of:												
1. GC	0.90	0.64	1.11	0.65	1.32	0.50	1.30	0.70	1.14	0.97	1.17	1.00
2. GI	–	–	1.26	1.47	–	–	0.30	0.31	–	13.39	2.38	–
3. GTP	0.88	1.32	0.78	0.88	1.17	—	1.17	0.76	0.84	—	—	0.88
4. DT	1.21	0.52	0.59	5.21	1.00	1.19	0.99	2.18	0.88	3.88	0.84	1.00
5. IT	1.07	0.84	0.87	1.56	0.83	1.83	0.71	1.51	1.04	1.17	1.01	1.06
6. MB	1.21	0.23	2.07	0.70	0.14	1.29	1.34	n.a.	1.08	0.70	0.56	1.01

Notes:
– Meaningless (the numerator or the denominator of the ratio has a negative value).
n.a. Not available.
— Insufficient observations.

Table 5.3 Evidence for electoral cycles in target variables

	Belgium	Denmark	France	Germany	Greece	Ireland	Italy	Luxembourg	Netherlands	Portugal	Spain	UK
	R_1 – ratios of election year: non-election year means of:											
1. GDP	0.68	0.78	1.11	1.44	0.86	1.20	1.21	1.91	0.82	1.27	0.95	1.15
2. YD	0.64	0.83	1.00	1.46	0.80	1.19	1.39	1.20	0.98	1.98*	1.04	1.19
3. PC	1.21	1.08	0.83	1.02	1.10	1.05	1.00	1.08	1.04	1.62	1.28	0.98
4. u	0.99	1.17	1.07	0.76	0.97	1.06	1.01	1.26	1.19	1.12	0.88	0.96
	R_2 – ratios of election year plus one year before election means: other years' means of:											
1. GDP	1.05	0.44	1.01	1.26	0.91	1.07	0.87	2.04	0.88	0.62	0.89	1.68
2. YD	1.12	0.50	0.91	1.39	1.10	0.89	0.93	1.14	1.11	0.56*	0.88	2.01
3. PC	1.08	1.32	0.81	0.60	1.29	1.35	1.01	0.94	0.86	23.43**	1.50	0.80
4. u	0.93	1.41	1.14	1.04	0.95	4.44	0.96	1.30	1.16	1.17	0.62	0.98

Notes:
* An extreme observation for 1985 has been omitted.
** This estimate should be interpreted with care in view of the small number of observations available.

large number of policy variables. More specifically, the figures in Table 5.2 indicate that the incumbent parties have stimulated: government consumption spending in France, Greece, Italy, the Netherlands and Spain; government investment spending in France, Germany, Portugal and Spain; government transfer payments to the private sector in Denmark, Greece, Italy, Belgium, Luxembourg and the Netherlands; and with the exception of Greece, Luxembourg and Portugal, the monetary base. In addition, the incumbent parties have depressed: both the direct and indirect taxes in Denmark, France, Greece and Italy; indirect taxes in Luxembourg and direct taxes in Germany, Ireland, the Netherlands and Spain.

Target variables

The evidence for electoral cycle regularities in the target variables is given in Table 5.3. As shown in this table, the R_1 ratio is greater than one: for all target variables in Ireland, Luxembourg and Portugal; for variables PC and u in Denmark and the Netherlands; for variable PC in Belgium, Germany, Greece and Spain; for variables GDP and YD in Italy and the UK; for variables GDP and u in France; and for variables u and YD in Italy and Spain, respectively. A roughly similar picture is displayed by the values of the R_2 coefficients. Twenty-six out of 48 R_2 coefficients concerning the non-tax variables have exhibited values greater than unity.

Even though it is quite difficult to detect electoral cycles, rational or not, in the target variables,[9] the findings lead us to the following conclusions. First there are indications of an acceleration of GDP and YD growth in the election *vis-à-vis* the pre-election years. This is suggested by the higher R_1 relative to the R_2 values in seven out of the 12 member countries.[10] Second, short-run Phillips curve phenomena seem to have taken place in Belgium, Greece, Germany and Spain. This argument is supported by the fact that increases in the inflation rates and decreases in the unemployment rates, during the election years and/or the years before the election years relative to the other years, have been recorded in the above-mentioned four countries; and an increase in the inflation rate in Denmark, Ireland, Portugal, Luxembourg and the Netherlands and a decrease in the unemployment rate in the UK have also been observed (Table 5.3).

Partisan Cycle Patterns

Policy variables

Table 5.4 reports the evidence concerning the partisan cycle regularities for the policy variables in the eight member countries only.[11] The evidence cited in this table is rather mixed and not entirely conclusive. Based on the distinction between 'socialist' and 'conservative' administrations and the values of

Table 5.4 Evidence for partisan cycles in policy instruments

			Denmark	France	Germany	Greece	Ireland[1]	Portugal[2]	Spain	UK
			R_1 – ratios of election year: non-election year means of:							
1.	GC	C	0.31	1.51	1.24	1.51	1.01	1.19	1.44	1.51
		S	1.10	0.88	0.66	1.25	0.45	1.04	0.83	1.09
2.	GI	C	–	1.02	1.53	4.93	3.81	0.17	3.70	–
		S	–	3.26	0.20	0.18	23.10	0.09	0.37	–
3.	GTP	C	1.84	0.73	0.53	0.87	—	—	—	0.63
		S	0.54	0.97	0.98	1.43	—	—	—	1.47
4.	DT	C	0.92	0.61	0.14	0.82	1.16	0.71	0.56	1.29
		S	1.00	0.73	0.70	0.19	0.76	1.59	1.48	1.07
5.	IT	C	0.63	0.95	1.18	0.69	1.12	1.04	1.18	1.28
		S	1.06	0.82	1.21	0.91	1.41	1.25	1.27	0.97
6.	MB	C	1.52	1.27	1.83	0.23	1.32	0.58	0.70	1.05
		S	0.94	0.25	2.47	0.28	1.21	0.79	1.48	0.45

R_2 – ratios of election year plus one year before election means to other years' means of:

1.	GC	C	0.31	1.35	0.76	1.39	0.89	1.13	1.04	0.93
		S	1.21	0.59	0.76	0.97	0.62	1.44	1.10	1.42
2.	GI	C	–	–	4.43	0.08	1.01	0.13	68.90*	–
		S	–	3.36	0.49	1.28	2.98	–	–	–
3.	GTP	C	2.06	0.51	0.52	0.87	—	—	—	0.82
		S	0.50	1.03	1.24	1.28	—	—	—	1.09
4.	DT	C	1.39	0.65	0.40	1.33	1.61	0.69	0.48	0.76
		S	0.23	0.79	0.60	0.75	0.92	1.40	1.76	1.07
5.	IT	C	0.71	0.90	1.14	0.74	1.66	1.15	1.07	1.05
		S	1.18	0.97	1.09	0.75	1.22	1.02	1.13	0.81
6.	MB	C	0.43	2.02	2.07	0.03	1.21	0.64	0.42	1.55
		S	0.62	1.03	2.44	0.27	1.21	1.23	1.26	1.21

Notes:

C Conservative; S Socialist.

1 In Ireland's two-party system both parties are non-socialist. However, just for the sake of presentation of our results FF has been classified in the conservative group and FG–LP in the socialist group.

2 In Portugal's two-party system the AD–PPD/PSD governments have been classified in the conservative group.

– Meaningless (the numerator or the denominator of the ratio has a negative value).

— Insufficient observations or not available.

* This estimate should be interpreted with care in view of a small number of observations available.

the R_1 and R_2 coefficients, we observed that 25 out of 45 R_1 values exceed one in the case of conservative governments and the remaining 20 in the case of socialist governments. The reverse finding applies to the R_2 ratio (Table 5.4). However, the greater than one values of R_1 and R_2 are not, both in terms of magnitude and intensity, identical for all member countries examined in this investigation. For instance, the figures in the table indicate two main findings.

First, regardless of differences in their ideology, both conservative and socialist governments in the above countries have: increased government consumption spending in Greece (R_1>1), Portugal (R_1>1 and R_2>1), Spain (R_2 >1) and the UK (R_2 >1); increased government investment spending in France (R_1>1) and Ireland (R_1>1 and R_2>1),[12] and the monetary base in France (R_2>1), Germany (R_1>1 and R_2>1), Ireland (R_1>1 and R_2>1) and the UK (R_1>1); and decreased direct taxes in France, Germany and Greece and indirect taxes in France and Greece. Notice that six out of the 12 values of the above R_1 coefficient and four out of the ten values of the R_2 coefficients are greater in the case of socialist than in the case of conservative governments.

Second, regardless of ideology, socialists and conservatives in the remaining countries of the EU have used the same policy instruments in the election year and/or the preceding to the election year *vis-à-vis* the remaining years in order to attract voters. For instance, conservatives have increased GC in France, Spain, Germany and Ireland (R_1>1), GI in Germany, Spain and Greece (R_1>1), and GTP and MB in Denmark; and reduced DT in Portugal, Spain and Denmark, and IT in Denmark. On the other hand, socialists have: increased GC in Denmark, Portugal and the UK, GTP in France, Germany, Greece and the UK and MB in Portugal and Spain; and reduced DT in Denmark and IT in the UK.

Target variables

Table 5.5 presents empirical evidence for partisan cycles in the target variables. The evidence appears to support both the EC and REC hypotheses. In particular, higher GDP growth rates in election and pre-election years relative to the remaining years of our sample have been observed under both administrations in most of the countries under examination. More specifically, under conservative administrations GDP growth increased in five (France, Germany, Ireland, Portugal and the UK) out of eight countries (both R_1 and R_2 are greater than one). More or less similar results have been recorded for YD. That is, in the same years and under conservative administrations, higher growth rates have been observed in Ireland, Portugal, the UK, France and Germany. Under socialist administrations, on the other hand, the countries that experienced higher growth rates in GDP include Greece, Spain, the UK, France and Germany. The evidence for short-run Phillips curves is scanty for conservative administrations and has been recorded for Portugal and the UK;

Table 5.5 Evidence for partisan cycles in target variables

			Denmark	France	Germany	Greece	Ireland	Portugal	Spain	UK
			R_1 – ratios of election year: non-election year means of:							
1.	GDP	C	0.92	1.39	1.67	0.82	1.15	2.61	0.54	1.41
		S	0.83	0.65	1.01	1.35	3.64	0.26	1.31	0.73
2.	YD	C	0.85	1.07	1.11	0.76	1.11	8.02	0.41	1.71
		S	0.60	0.87	1.11	1.33	1.13	–	2.70	0.55
3.	PC	C	0.61	0.77	0.94	0.94	0.98	1.00	1.06	0.91
		S	1.43	1.14	0.97	0.83	1.42	0.88	0.78	1.06
4.	u	C	1.56	0.55	1.06	0.73	1.15	1.15	0.43	1.28
		S	1.04	2.07	1.21	1.13	1.80	0.53	1.64	0.29
			R_2 – ratios of election year plus one year before election means: other years' means of:							
1.	GDP	C	0.75	1.14	1.41	0.96	1.11	3.54	0.70	1.35
		S	0.65	0.54	0.63	0.90	1.17	0.06	1.19	1.39
2.	YD	C	0.86	0.99	1.43	0.95	1.00	1.06*	0.61	1.69
		S	0.51	0.97	0.61	1.77	0.98	–	1.29	1.38
3.	PC	C	5.43	1.23	0.71	0.96	1.31	1.03	2.04	1.55
		S	1.50	1.44	1.00	0.89	1.32	1.12	0.69	0.78
4.	u	C	1.74	0.48	1.09	–	1.38	1.27	0.36	1.76
		S	1.08	1.92	1.16	0.78	1.96	0.59	1.24	0.30

Notes:
C Conservative; S Socialist.
– Meaningless (the numerator or the denominator of the ratio has a negative value).
* Extreme values for years 1975 and 1990 have been omitted.

as well as for socialist administrations in Portugal and the UK. Other things being equal, this implies that the higher inflation rates that have been observed in the election and pre-election years relative to the other years in certain countries, such as Denmark (both administrations) and Ireland, have not been compensated for lower unemployment rates.

SUMMARY AND CONCLUSIONS

The purpose of this chapter was to detect electoral or partisan cycle regularities in six policy and four target variables in the 12 EU member countries. To this end, we have employed the 'ratio approach' which relies on two alternative indices, labelled as R_1 and R_2. R_1 is the ratio of the mean value of the annual rates of change of the *i*th variable involved in the election years and the mean value of the annual rate of change of the same variable in the non-election years. Similarly, R_2 is the ratio of the mean values of the annual rate of change in the *i*th variable in the election years plus one year before election and the other years' mean.

The empirical analysis, based on time-series data, led to the following basic results. First, the incumbent parties in power, taken jointly (i.e. regardless of their ideology) or separately (i.e. conservatives vs socialists), appear, on the average, to have manipulated the policy variables in the same direction. This finding is consistent with the REC hypothesis which predicts that the incumbent party, based on information advantages, has an incentive to try to signal, before elections, that it is competent. To accomplish that, it manipulates the policy instruments, thus attempting to fool the public and create cycles in the policy variables. Second, the evidence does not support the RPC hypothesis stating that 'socialists' have been relatively more averse to unemployment and less averse to inflation than 'conservatives'. Third, regardless of individual countries, the two political parties have not exhibited consistent partisan policies during their terms in office. Even though this finding is not in full agreement with those reported elsewhere (Soh 1986), it appears to be in line with the proposition that political parties switch to electoral cycles if their re-election seems threatened (Frey and Schneider 1978, 1988).

In general, the empirical evidence provides significant support for electoral cycles in policy instruments and economic outcomes. It does not, however, provide strong support in favour of partisan cycles in policy and target variables. Other things being equal, this finding may be due to differences in cultural and institutional structures, size of the public sector, time span and personal characteristics of the individual politicians.

NOTES

1. See Nordhaus (1975), MacRay (1977) Van der Ploeg (1984), and Alt and Chrystal (1983, ch. 5).
2. See Hibbs (1977, 1987), and the majority of the papers in Hibbs and Fassbender (1981), Alesina (1987), the literature cited in Alesina and Sachs (1988, p. 65).
3. A practical difficulty lies with coalition governments, which may behave quite differently from single party governments. See Alesina (1989, p. 65). For instance, two heterogeneous coalition governments (a right-wing–communist party, July–October 1989, and a right-wing–communist party–socialist party, (November 1989 – April 1990) in Greece failed to design a non-partisan economic policy in order to provide a check to the deteriorating state of the economy since the early 1980s.
4. For the variables involved in this investigation and their classification between 'policy' and 'target' variables, see below.
5. For a similar approach see Soh (1986).
6. It should be noted here that although the time span for this investigation covers the period 1969–90, the time period for certain variables is not uniform in all countries of our sample. Specifically, the variables GDP, YD, PC, u, GC, IT and MB cover the period 1961–90 and the variables GI, DT and GTP the period 1971–90. Certain exceptions have been observed for a number of variables which include: GDP in Belgium (1971–90); u in Greece, Portugal and Spain (1964–90); GI in Denmark (1972–90), Ireland (1975–90), Portugal (1978–90) and Spain (1974–90); DT in Denmark (1972–90) and Portugal (1978–90); GTP in Denmark (1972–90), Greece (1974–90), and France, Italy, Luxembourg and the Netherlands (1970–90). Data on MB in Luxembourg and GTP in Ireland and Portugal are not available. In addition, the period 1967–73 for Greece and the pre-1978 and pre-1977 ones for Portugal and Spain, respectively, were not considered due to these countries' dictatorial regimes in those periods.
7. The composition of the coalition governments and the characteristics of the parties in power are given in an appendix provided upon request.
8. It should be noted that the smallness of our sample size and the unequal data periods for a number of series in certain countries have prevented us from using more sophisticated statistical techniques, notably testing for unit roots in the autoregressive representations of the individual time series and cointegration.
9. This is due, among other things, to the fact that the target variables are jointly dependent variables. That is, they are not only affected by the government-controlled policy instruments, but also by the working of the entire economic system. This implies that they are affected by the non-controlled exogenous variables and the remaining endogenous variables of the economic system, provided the latter are not decomposable.
10. The seven countries are Denmark, France, Germany, Ireland, Italy, Portugal and Spain.
11. Note that in four countries (Belgium, Italy, Luxembourg and the Netherlands) partisan cycles cannot be detected due to their coalition governments.
12. Note that both parties that came to power in Ireland are non-socialist.

REFERENCES

Alesina, A. (1987), 'Macroeconomic Policy in a Two-Party System as a Repeated Game', *Quarterly Journal of Economics*, **102**, 651–78.

Alesina, A. (1989), 'Politics', *Economic Policy*, April, 55–98.

Alesina, A. and J. Sachs (1988), 'Political Parties and the Business Cycle in the United States, 1948–1984', *Journal of Money, Credit and Banking*, **20** (1) (February), 63–82.

Alt, J.E. and K.A. Chrystal (1983), *Political Economics*, Berkeley: University of California Press.
Frey, B. and F. Schneider (1978), 'An Empirical Study of Politico-Economic Integration in the United States', *The Review of Economics and Statistics*, **60** (May), 191–206.
Frey, B.S. and F. Schneider (1988), 'Politico-Economic Models of Macroeconomic Policy: A Review of the Empirical Evidence' in T.D. Willet (ed.), *Political Business Cycles: The Political Economy of Money, Inflation and Unemployment*, Durham, NC: Duke University Press, pp. 239–75.
Haynes, S.E. and J.A. Stone (1990), 'Political Models of the Business Cycle should be Revived', *Economic Inquiry*, **28** (July), 442–65.
Hibbs, D.A. Jr (1977), 'Political Parties and Macroeconomic Policy', *American Political Science Review*, **71** (December), 1467–87.
Hibbs, D.A. Jr (1987), *The American Political Economy*, Cambridge, UK: Cambridge University Press.
Hibbs, D.A. Jr and H. Fassbender (1981), *Contemporary Political Economy, Studies on the Interdependence of Politics and Economics*, Amsterdam: North-Holland.
MacRay, D. (1977), 'A Political Model of the Business Cycle', *Journal of Political Economy*, **85** (April), 239–64.
McCallum, B.T. (1978), 'The Political Business Cycle. An Empirical Test', *Southern Economic Journal*, **4** (3), (January), 504–15.
Nordhaus, W.D. (1975), 'The Political Business Cycle', *Review of Economic Studies*, **42** (April), 169–90.
Ploeg, F. van der (1984), 'Government ideology and Re-election Efforts', *Oxford Economic Papers*, **36**, 213–31.
Ploeg, F. van der (1987), 'Optimal Government Policy in a Small Open Economy with Rational Expectations and Uncertain Election Outcomes', *International Economic Review*, **28** (2) (June), 469–91.
Rogoff, K. (1990), 'Equilibrium Political Budget Cycles', *American Economic Review*, **80** (1) (March), 21–36.
Rogoff, K. and A. Sibert (1988), 'Elections and Macroeconomic Policy Cycles', *Review of Economic Studies*, **55**, 1–16.
Soh, B.H. (1986), 'Political Business Cycles in Industrialized Dynamic Countries', *Kyklos*, **39** (1), 31–46.

PART II

Empirical and Theoretical Analyses of Monetary Union

6. Convergence issues in the emerging European economic and monetary union

Apostolos Serletis and Panos Afxentiou

INTRODUCTION: THE ISSUES

As a hypothesis, convergence suggests that the growth rates of countries are inversely related to their absolute levels of productivity or real per capita incomes, and infers that through this process absolute as well as relative levels of poverty are reduced as laggard countries catch up with the leading ones. This hypothesis is based on the premise that economic leaders will tend to grow more slowly than laggards, resulting from a rearrangement in competitive advantage whereby industrial dynamism passes from leading countries to laggards. Whether a never-ending interchangeability between laggards and leaders will become a permanent feature of the economic scene is not discussed in the literature. And, even if such interchangeability is assumed, it is likely to have only a marginal effect on economic well-being, as per capita income would then be fluctuating within a relatively narrow range.

Convergence has enormous welfare ramifications. These emanate from the homogenizing forces which it involves. Homogenization is strengthened by global competition, which compels domestic firms to adopt modern practices,[1] and is accelerated by imaginative social engineering strategies, which transform the domestic infrastructural conditions and enhance the movement of capital from capital-rich to capital-poor countries in consonance with the neoclassical tenet of diminishing marginal productivity of capital.[2] Competition, both international and domestic, punishes inefficiency. It encourages technological transplants by putting pressures on producers to invest in the most advanced industrial processes. These investments, which replace more outdated capital stocks in lagging countries with capital embodying the most advanced technology, are largely responsible for the growth rate differences among countries (Abramovitz 1986). Technological transfers are common nowadays, as important technological secrets tend to become disseminated in a universe of expanding knowledge and information. This occurs despite the fact that command of a technology requires major investments of many kinds, particularly in labour force retraining organization, and management (Nelson and Wright 1994, p. 158). Such investments are prerequisites for successful social engineering.[3]

From a reactive process in its original stages, convergence evolves into an interactive process as productivity and real per capita income among countries narrow and as technological leadership shifts from sector to sector and from country to country. If it is to promote learning it requires an efficient system of dissemination and absorption of new knowledge. Accompanied by this assumption, the concept was known to Gerschenkron (1952) in his treatment of late industrialization, to Kuznets (1973) in his statistical examination of the patterns of growth, and to Abramovitz (1986) in his historical analysis of industrial leadership. The insights of these pioneers stimulated an interest in convergence and its measurement, and in growth studies that focus on the identification of those factors which are responsible for convergence.

A statistically significant inverse relationship between initial productivity levels and subsequent productivity growth across countries is taken as validation of convergence – see Abramovitz (1986) and Baumol (1986). In more elaborate treatments, analysts have emphasized the contribution of both economic factors, such as the rate of capital formation, scale economies, openness to international competition, and industrial structure, as well as the contribution of a multiplicity of social and political factors described by Abramovitz (1986, 1990) as social capability, and approximated by Baumol (1994) as ancillary variables, which though important do not play a direct role in the convergence process.

The importance of the economic factors was statistically shown by Alam (1993) for 16 developed countries in the postwar period. However, Bernard and Durlauf (1995) rejected the convergence hypothesis in a study of 15 OECD countries for the longer 1900–87 period. Similar results or tendencies for divergence were reported for larger samples of countries by DeLong (1988), Baumol et al. (1989), Alam and Naseer (1992); mixed results were also reported by Dollar and Wolff (1988) and by Dowrick and Nguyen (1989). In a sample of 21 high-income and 88 developing countries Ingram (1994) using the Summers–Heston purchasing parity per capita real income data from 1960–85 found little evidence of convergence of per capita GDP growth and levels among developing countries or between developing countries and developed countries.

With regard to the 'social capability' factor,[4] most of its multidimensional attributes which characterize people, their attitudes toward cooperation, competition, trust and respect for institutions are unquantifiable, while other attributes like levels of education and government stability can only be roughly defined and imperfectly measured. Baumol et al. (1989) and Ram (1991) found that education has a positive impact on convergence, while Barro (1991) and Barro and Lee (1994), found, also in addition to the positive impact of education, a statistically significant negative impact of government instability on convergence. Abramovitz (1994) argued that the collapse of the Bretton Woods regime of fixed exchange rates introduced a high degree of instability in the international monetary system that will prove inimical to future convergence. In the light of this diagnosis, he viewed the convergence of the 1950s and 1960s as a transitory phenomenon.[5]

Before turning to methodological issues of measurement, it should be borne in mind that convergence is likely to be a normal growth process in countries with similar environments, in which cooperation is close, the exchange of information is free, technological transfers are unimpeded, factor mobility is free, institutions and human capital are similar, and in which convergent economic policies are pursued. Economic policies as facilitators of convergence, unless coordinated, may lead to contradictory objectives if not to totally divergent paths (see Maddison 1994). The European Union (EU) as a collectivity of countries cannot be considered as a natural homogeneous group either in terms of resources, geography or culture, yet by adopting the appropriate monetary and fiscal policies it is expected that through free mobility of persons, commodities and capital it will foster homogenization leading finally to the creation of a well integrated economic, and perhaps political, entity.

The EU is now a reality with an expansive potential. Its present membership of 15 will probably grow further as future members, especially from Eastern Europe, wait anxiously to join this prestigious club. As membership grows the degree of heterogeneity will increase causing problems with integration to intensify. Following the analysis of the various convergence issues covered thus far, in the next section we examine briefly the methods used in measuring convergence and, based on the most rigorous method, we test for the convergence of nominal exchange rates that is used as a proxy for the outcome of monetary policies.

CONCEPTS OF CONVERGENCE AND THEIR MEASUREMENT

In the absence of unanimity as to what convergence stands for, it is natural that the measurements of one concept of convergence will differ from those of another, and that for each concept more than one method of measurement might be used.[6] Problems arise because researchers sometimes concentrate on the behaviour of a single variable to the exclusion of others. On other occasions they may be concerned more with the explanatory value of growth variables than with the overall ultimate convergence *per se*, and on still other occasions they may analyse more the statistical properties of their results than the operationality of their findings. Thus tests vary depending on whether a simple convergence criterion is satisfied or, further to the satisfaction of one criterion, whether statistical explanations of convergence are sought in strategic variables, or whether the unexplained residuals follow prescribed statistical rules.

Some of the empirical studies test for gross convergence of a certain variable without correcting for the influence exercised by other pertinent variables. Some test for explained convergence by evaluating the role of pertinent and measurable variables that reasonably affect the time path and degree of convergence. Others test for residual convergence in that they examine the convergence behaviour of the unexplained residuals of the dependent variables, while still others test for cross-sectional dispersion by looking at the decline of standard deviations of logarithms of variables under study over time as a proof of convergence (for an application of these approaches see Baumol 1986; Dowrick and Nguyen 1989; and Barro 1991). Of all the methods employed in testing convergence two are statistically the most rigorous: the first is based on cointegration analysis; the second is based on the Haldane and Hall (1981) time-varying/Kalman filter.

The Cointegration Methodology

Cointegration is designed to deal explicitly with the analysis of the relationship between non-stationary time series. In particular, it allows individual time series to be integrated of order one or I(1), in the terminology of Engle and Granger 1987, but requires that a linear combination of these series be I(0). Therefore, the basic idea behind cointegration is to search for linear combinations of individually non-stationary time series that are themselves stationary.

Several methods have been proposed in the literature for the estimate of cointegrating vectors; see, for example, Gonzalo (1994). The most frequently used is that of Engle and Granger (1987) which, after it has arbitrarily selected a normalization procedure, then regresses one variable on the others to obtain the ordinary least squares (OLS) regression residuals $\hat{e}$. A test of the null hypothesis of no cointegration is based on testing for a unit root in the regression residuals $\hat{e}$ using the ADF (Augmented Dickey-Fuller) test (and the simulated critical values reported in Engle and Yoo 1987, Table 2, which correctly take into account the number of variables in the cointegrating regression). This approach, however, does not distinguish between the existence of one or more cointegrating vectors and as a consequence is best suited for the bivariate case which can have at most one cointegrating vector.

Johansen's (1988) maximum likelihood extension of Engle and Granger's (1987) cointegration approach is superior to the simple Engle and Granger regression-based technique, because it fully captures the underlying time-series properties of the data, provides estimates of all the cointegrating relations among a given set of variables, offers a test statistic for the number of cointegrating vectors, and allows direct hypothesis tests on the elements of the cointegrating vectors; see, for example, Johansen and Juselius (1992). This multivariate approach to the estimation of the number of linearly independent cointegrating vectors for a vector-autoregressive process, $X_{i,}$ of order k involves regressing ΔX_t on $\Delta X_{t-1}, \ldots, \Delta X_{t-k=l}$; regressing X_{t-k} on the same set of regressors; and performing a canonical correlation analysis of the residuals of these two regressions – see Serletis and Krichel (1992) for an application of Johansen's approach in investigating the degree of shared output trends among European countries.

Cointegration analysis, however, cannot in principle detect convergence, because it fails to take account of the fact that convergence is a gradual and ongoing process, which implies that statistical tests should lead to the rejection of the null hypothesis of no-cointegration only when convergence has already taken place; see, for example, Bernard (1991). In other words, while cointegration tests are tests for convergence over the whole period under consideration, these tests are not tests of a move from non-convergence to convergence. Similarly, cointegration techniques are inappropriate for investigating whether the degree of convergence has changed over time.

The Haldane and Hall (1991) Methodology

A proper test of convergence has been proposed by Haldane and Hall (1991) based on the use of time-varying parameter (Kalman filter) analysis. The Kalman filter estimation method is typically used to estimate regression-type models where the coefficients follow a random process over time. As such, Kalman filter estimation is highly useful in investigating structural change in parameters and, hence, in describing the process of structural change both in terms of degree and timing. In what follows, we apply the Haldane and Hall (1991) test to measure the degree of nominal exchange rate convergence in Europe.

The importance of this test should be seen in the context of the European monetary system (EMS) which in the first place has established a system of almost fixed exchange rates, and has as its ultimate objective by the end of the decade an evolution toward economic and monetary union (EMU) in the EU where the free movement of people, goods, services and capital will lead to a full integration of financial markets and to irreversibly fixed exchange rates, or perhaps to a single currency. Based on the Delors Report, the transition to EMU is designed to follow a gradualist strategy so that after progressive convergence in inflation rates and in strategic macroeconomic variables, accompanied by harmonized monetary and fiscal policies, the ultimate goal of fully converged EU countries will be to render monetary unification feasible and relatively painless.[7] This strategy is consistent with the optimal currency approach, as set forth by Mundell (1961), according to which sufficient mobility of commodities and production factors is a precondition for monetary unification.

Some nominal convergence of declining inflation rates, of short-term rates, and primary budget deficits has been observed in the EU, along with an increasing divergence of relative price levels which, as argued by Froot and Rogoff (1991), will be highly destabilizing as the monetary union draws closer. Because nominal convergence is a necessary condition for the success of European monetary unification, we focus in this section on the degree of convergence of nominal exchange rates, which embrace and reflect various aspects of monetary policies pursued by the sampled countries.

In particular, we regress the log of Deutschmark (DM) bilateral rates with European monetary system (EMS) currencies on the log of the DM/US dollar exchange rate, as in the following equation (in the case of sterling):

$$\log\left[\frac{DM}{£}\right](t)=\alpha(t)+\beta(t)\log\left[\frac{DM}{\$}\right](t)+\varepsilon(t) \tag{1}$$

Note that the levels formulation appears useful both as an economic and as an econometric matter: economically, such as to enable an equilibrium to be defined; econometrically, such as to allow the detection of potential shared stochastic trends in the data.

The $\alpha(t)$ parameter is a stochastic constant which partials out all systematic influences upon the DM/£ exchange rate other than those resulting from movements in the DM/$ rate. The potentially time-varying parameter $\beta(t)$ measures the temporal relationship of sterling with the DM and the dollar. For example, if sterling were fixed against the dollar, then DM/£ and DM/$ would be perfectly correlated and we would therefore expect the restriction $\beta = 1$ to be satisfied. Hence the requirement for convergence is that $\alpha(t)$ tends to a constant and ß(t) tends to zero.

Using quarterly (end-of-period) exchange rate data from the OECD-Main Economic Indicators covering the period 1974:1–1992:1, we present in Figures 6.1 and 6.2 the $\beta(t)$ coefficient for each of nine countries – Ireland and Luxembourg are excluded. Clearly, except for the Dutch guilder all other currency rates have not only converged but the link between the other EMS currencies and the DM has strengthened over the whole period; a definite tendency for the coefficients to move towards zero is visible in the figures.

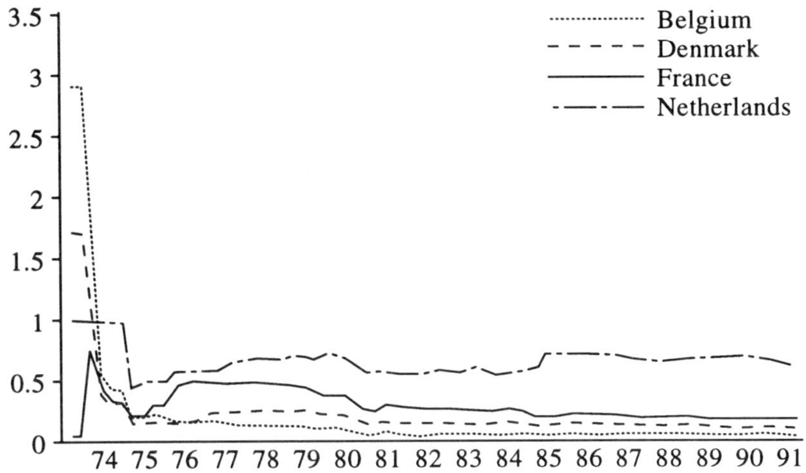

Note: Quarterly data: 1974:1–1992:1.

Figure 6.1 *Nominal exchange rate differentials, Belgium, Denmark, France and the Netherlands: DM differentials versus DM/US dollar differentials*

These results are consistent with those of Giavazzi and Giovannini (1990) who also found that the sensitivity of exchange rate mechanism (ERM) bilateral rates to dollar perturbations had declined markedly since the inception of the EMS.

The Haldane and Hall (1991) methodology can also be used to investigate convergence in general, for example in nominal convergence (concerned with inflation rates and nominal interest rates), which is a requirement for EMU, as well as real convergence (concerned with growth, real interest rates and real exchange rates). Regarding nominal convergence, the original members of the ERM (Belgium, Denmark, France, Germany, Ireland, Italy, Luxembourg and the Netherlands) have succeeded in achieving convergence in inflation rates, except for Italy, although the process of inflation convergence has taken some time; see, for example, Froot and Rogoff 1991. Also, the recent high-inflation entrants into the ERM (Portugal, Spain and the UK) have made significant steps towards reducing their inflation rates, but rates in these countries are still significantly higher than the average across the original ERM countries.

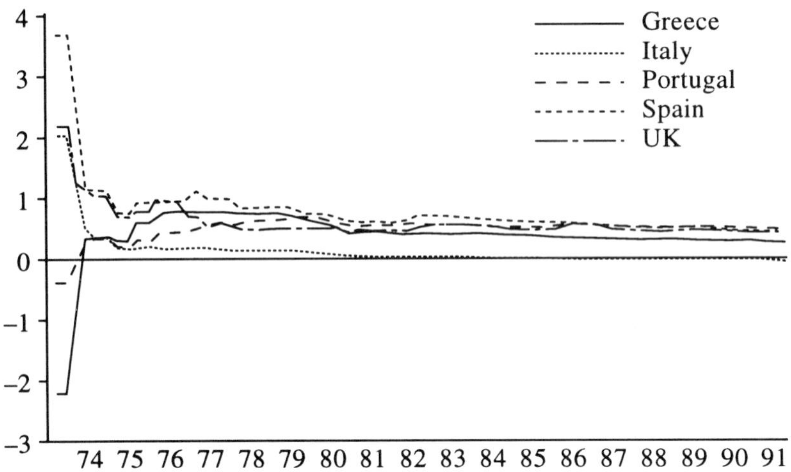

Note: Quarterly data: 1974:1–1992:1.

Figure 6.2 Nominal exchange rate differentials, Greece, Italy, Portugal, Spain and the UK: DM differentials versus DM/US dollar differentials

CONCLUSIONS

Concomitantly with the creation of the EU steps were taken for the implementation of monetary unification with the ultimate purpose of establishing a European central bank and perhaps a single currency. The movement toward fixed exchange rates will be the culmination of a series of measures designed to secure free mobility of people, commodities and capital in an environment where the transmission of information is almost instantaneous and technological transfers relatively unimpeded. At the core of the measures taken was the intention to foster a convergence of the European countries that is more likely to be reached in rather homogeneous socioeconomic conditions.

Our emphasis on convergence is based on the realization that it represents a precondition for monetary unification. After an appraisal of the various concepts of convergence, we finally selected the statistically more rigorous method of the measurement of convergence, namely the time-varying parameter technique proposed by Haldane and Hall (1991) and applied it to the nominal exchange rates of the European countries. Our results strongly suggest that the link between the EMS currencies and the DM has been strengthening, suggesting that the transition to European monetary union would be easier than if these currencies were still primarily linked to the dollar.

NOTES

1. Investment in general is an important determinant of growth, but more important as a determinant of per capita GDP growth, according to DeLong and Summers (1990), is investment in machinery and equipment that embody the most recent technological advances.
2. The risks of uncritically accepting the neoclassical tenet of capital mobility have been highlighted by Lucas (1990). As pointed out by the author, unless other conditions are satisfied, particularly human investment, the higher marginal productivity of capital in poor countries turns out to be untenable.
3. There are difficulties in modelling advanced knowledge and technical progress, but there is no disagreement among economists that these two forces exert their principal impact when embodied in human and physical capital, and can thus be considered as major engines of growth (see Maddison 1994).
4. Originally the term was used by Ohkawa and Rosovsky (1973).
5. In the modern era technological breakthroughs and industrial restructuring increase economic instability, widen the social capability gap between developed and developing countries and render convergence more problematic. Under these conditions the cumulative development process, which permeates the work of Gunnar Myrdal, becomes more evident, and the disquieting repercussions of increased income inequalities become more ominous.
6. For a summary of seven convergent concepts and their measurement see Baumol et al. (1994).
7. See Serletis (1994) for a historical background and appraisal of the Delors Plan for European monetary unification.

REFERENCES

Abramovitz, Moses (1986), 'Catching-Up, Forging Ahead, and Falling Behind', *Journal of Economic History*, **46**, 385–406.

Abramovitz, Moses (1990), 'The Catch-Up Factor in Postwar Economic Growth', *Economic Enquiry*, **28**, 1–18.

Abramovitz, Moses (1994), 'Catch-Up and Convergence in the Postwar Growth Boom and After' in W.J. Baumol, R.R. Nelson and E.N. Wolff (eds), *Convergence of Productivity*, Oxford: Oxford University Press, 86–125.

Alam, M. Shahid (1993), 'Convergence in Developed Countries: An Empirical Investigation', *Weltwirtschaftliches Archiv*, 189–201.

Alam, M. Shahid and A. Naseer (1992), 'Convergence and Polarization: Testing for an Inverted-U Relation Between Growth Rates and GDP Per Capita', *Applied Economics*, **24**, 363–6.

Baumol, William J. (1986), 'Productivity Growth, Convergence, and Welfare: What the Long Run Data Show', *American Economic Review*, **76**, 1072–85.

Baumol, William J. (1994), 'Multivariate Growth Patterns: Contagion and Common Forces as Possible Sources of Convergence', in W.J. Baumol, R.R. Nelson, and E.N. Wolff (eds), *Convergence and Productivity*, Oxford: Oxford University Press, pp. 62–85.

Barro, Robert J. (1991), 'Economic Growth in a Cross Section of Countries', *Quarterly Journal of Economics*, **106**, 407–43.

Barro, Robert J. and Jong-Wha Lee (1994), 'Losers and Winners in Economic Growth' in M. Bruno and B. Pleskovic (eds), *Proceedings of the World Bank Annual Conference on Development Economics 1993*, Washington, DC, World Bank, pp. 267–97.

Baumol, W.J., S.A.B. Blackman, and E.N. Wolff (1989), *Productivity and American Leadership: The Long View*, Cambridge, Mass.: MIT Press.

Baumol, W.J., R.R. Nelson, and E.N. Wolff (1994), 'Introduction: The Convergence of Productivity, Its Significance, and Its Varied Connotations' in W.J. Baumol, R.R. Nelson, and E.N. Wolff (eds), *Convergence and Productivity*, Oxford: Oxford University Press, pp. 3–19.

Bernard, Andrew B. (1991), 'Empirical Implications of the Convergence Hypothesis', Centre for Economic Policy Research (CEPR), Stanford University, CEPR Publication no. 239, January.

Bernard, A.B. and S.N. Durlauf (1995), 'Convergence of International Output', *Journal of Applied Econometrics*, **10**, 97–108.

DeLong, J. Bradford (1988), 'Productivity Growth, Convergence, and Welfare: Comment', *American Economic Review*, **78**, 1138–54.

DeLong, J.B. and L.H. Summers (1990), 'Equipment Investment and Economic Growth', Working Paper no. 3515, Cambridge, Mass.: National Bureau of Economic Research.

Dollar, David and Edward N. Wolff (1988), 'Convergence of Industry Labour Productivity Among Advanced Economies, 1963–1982', *Review of Economics and Statistics*, **79**, 549–58.

Dowrick, S. and D. Nguyen (1989), 'OECD Comparative Economic Growth 1950–85: Catch-up and Convergence', *American Economic Review*, **79**, 1010–30.

Engle, Robert F. and Clive W. Granger (1987), 'Cointegration and Error Correction: Representation, Estimation and Testing', *Econometrica*, **55**, 251–76.

Engle, Robert F. and Byung Sam Yoo (1987), 'Forecasting and Testing in Cointegrated Systems', *Journal of Econometrics*, **35**, 143–59.

Froot, Kenneth A., and Kenneth Rogoff (1991), 'The EMS, the EMU, and the transition to a Common Currency', *NBER Macroeconomics Annual*, **6**, 269–317.

Gerschenkron, Alexander (1952), 'Economic Backwardness in Historical Perspective' in Bert F. Hoselitz (ed.), *The Progress of Underdeveloped Areas*, Chicago: University of Chicago Press, pp. 3–29.

Giavazzi, Francesco and Giovanni, Alberto (1990), Limiting Flexibility: The European Monetary System, Cambridge, Mass.: MIT Press.

Gonzalo, Jesus (1994), 'Five Alternative Methods of Estimating Long-Run Equilibrium Relationships', *Journal of Econometrics*, **60**, 203–33.

Haldane, A.G. and S.G. Hall (1991), 'Sterling's Relationship with the Dollar and the Deutschemark: 1976–89', *The Economic Journal*, **101**, 436–43.

Ingram, Gregory K. (1994), 'Social Indicators and Productivity Convergence in Developing Countries', in W.J. Baumol, R.R. Nelson and E.N. Wolff (eds), *Convergence and Productivity*, Oxford: Oxford University Press, pp. 316–33.

Johansen, Soren (1988), 'Statistical Analysis of Cointegration Vectors', *Journal of Economic Dynamics and Control*, **12**, 231–54.

Johansen, Soren and Katarina Juselius (1992), 'Some Structural Hypotheses in a Multivariate Cointegration Analysis of the PPP and the UIP for the U.K.', *Journal of Econometrics*, **53**, 211–44.

Kuznets, Simon (1973), *Population, Capital, and Growth: Selected Essays*, New York: Norton.

Lucas, Robert E. Jr (1990), 'Why Doesn't Capital Flow from Rich to Poor Countries?', *American Economic Review*, **80** (May), 92–6.

Maddison, Angus (1994), 'Explaining the Economic Performance of Nations, 1820–1989', in W.J. Baumol, R.R. Nelson, and E.N. Wolff (eds), *Convergence and Productivity*, Oxford: Oxford University Press, pp. 20–61.

Mundell, Robert A. (1961), 'A Theory of Optimum Currency Areas', *American Economic Review*, **51**, 657–65.

Nelson, Richard R. and Gavin Wright (1994), 'The Erosion of U.S. Technological Leadership as a Factor in Postwar Economic Convergence' in W.J. Baumol, R.R. Nelson, and E.N. Wolff (eds), Oxford: Oxford University Press, pp. 129–163.

Ohkawa, Kazushi and Henry Rosovsky (1973), *Japanese Economic Growth: Trend Acceleration in the Twentieth Century*, Stanford: Stanford University Press.

Ram, Rati (1991), 'Education and Convergence Hypothesis: Additional Cross-Country Evidence', *Economica Internazionale*, **44**, 224–53.

Serletis, Apostolos (1994), 'Economic and Monetary Union in Europe: Progress and Prospects' in Gretchen M. MacMillan (ed.), *The European Community, Canada and 1992*, The Faculty of Social Sciences, The University of Calgary.

Serlestis, Apostolos, and Thomas Krichel (1992), 'Output Trends in EC Countries and the Implications for Transition to Monetary Union', *Economics Letters*, **40**, 211–16.

7. The politics and economics of exchange rate intervention

Richard Jankowski

In recent decades the economic interdependence of nations has substantially increased. A general decline in trade barriers coupled with technological innovations in communications have promoted an unprecedented flow of goods, money, and credit between nations. As a consequence, fiscal policy has become less effective because of 'fiscal leakage'.

In addition to increased economic interdependence, the break-up of the Bretton Woods agreement in May 1973 marked a crucial transformation of the international economic system. The transformation took the form of a shift from fixed-managed to flexible exchange rates. With the shift to flexible exchange rates, fiscal policy becomes even less effective in stabilizing the business cycle. In this sense, a government-induced increase in aggregate demand leads to an increase in interest rates and an appreciation of the currency. This change in the exchange rate, in turn, reduces exports and increases imports, thereby exacerbating the fiscal leakage problem. Monetary policy is a substitute for fiscal policy under a free-floating currency regime, however. Monetary expansion reduces the real interest rate, which in turn induces capital outflows, both of which depreciate a currency. A lower exchange rate, then, raises demand for domestic output. Monetary policy is enhanced by a flexible exchange regime. However, it is not a substitute for fiscal policy because monetary policy is frequently targeted at inflation. A single policy instrument cannot simultaneously control two targets, such as inflation and unemployment.

The combination of increased economic interdependence and the shift to a flexible exchange rate system has required a substantial rethinking of macroeconomic policy. Exchange rate intervention is a potential alternative macroeconomic policy instrument in an interdependent world economy. As fiscal policy appears to lose some or most of its effectiveness, economists have shifted to a study of exchange rate intervention as a macroeconomic stabilization instrument. Indeed, a number of economists now consider exchange rate policy as a third independent instrument of macroeconomic stabilization (e.g. Dominguez and Frankel 1993; Branson 1977; Henderson 1979); that is, in addition to fiscal and monetary policy. Moreover, even economists who argue that exchange rate policy is not an independent policy instrument do not claim that exchange rates are free-floating, favouring the terms 'dirty' or 'managed' to describe the current system.

While there is theoretical justification for intervention and much anecdotal evidence of such intervention, there are no quantitative studies that explicitly address both the political and economic determinants of exchange rates in the wake of Bretton Woods. In this chapter I retest the Nordhaus–MacRae political business cycle hypothesis and Hibbs's partisan cycle hypothesis with exchange rate intervention as the macroeconomic policy instrument. I undertake a reaction model test to determine whether exchange rate policy is targeted at unemployment, inflation, or exchange rate movements; and for electoral, partisan or purely stabilization reasons.

EXCHANGE RATE INTERVENTION AS A MACROECONOMIC STABILIZATION POLICY

Economists have proposed a number of alternative explanations of how exchange rate intervention can function as a third macroeconomic instrument for policy-makers. Specifically, it is argued that governments can affect the net holding of foreign and domestic securities and foreign and domestic currencies; control capital movements (Argy 1982); jawbone exchange rates (Cooper 1986); and employ announcement effects to intervene in exchange rate markets. I focus upon government net holding currencies because this instrument is under direct government control. Measuring jawboning, announcement effects, and capital controls is much more difficult as they are discrete acts which are not amenable to a cardinal measure.

Central banks have one instrument of exchange rate intervention which is directly under their control: central bank holdings of foreign currency.[1] Changes in holdings of foreign currencies are a well-known method of affecting the exchange rate of the home currency. The price of one currency in terms of another can be thought of as the price of that currency. Hence, the purchase or sale of either currency will affect the price of that currency.

Assume that the supply of currencies is fixed. A central bank desiring to depreciate (appreciate) its currency would buy (sell) foreign currencies. Increasing its demand for a foreign currency has the effect of increasing the price of that foreign currency. As the price of the foreign currency increases, the home currency depreciates in value relative to the foreign currency. Hence, central banks increase (decrease) foreign currency holdings in order to depreciate (appreciate) the domestic currency relative to the foreign currencies. A recent example of the use of this familiar instrument was central bank intervention to maintain the European rate mechanism of exchange rates. The Bundesbank alone bought $35 billion worth of French francs during the last week of July 1993 in an attempt to keep the franc from depreciating. In addition, the French central bank bought nearly $55 billion worth of francs on the international market (*Wall Street Journal*, 16 August 1993).[2]

I test below whether the monetary authorities manipulate their holdings of foreign currencies as a substitute for fiscal policy. I do not test whether exchange rate intervention is an effective instrument. The standard interpretation is that exchange rate intervention is not effective. This view dates back at least to the Jurgeson Report commissioned by the Group of Five in 1982 to study the effectiveness of exchange rate intervention. However, Dominguez and Frankel (1993) have provided copious evidence that exchange rate intervention is effective, even when it is totally sterilized. In this chapter, I focus on the reasons for government intervention in exchange rate markets.

The literature suggests several alternative targets of exchange rate intervention. It has been argued by different authors that intervention is used to stabilize employment, fight inflation, or stabilize exchange rates. Henderson (1984) argues that exchange rate intervention is the primary instrument to fight unemployment, given the growing ineffectiveness of fiscal policy. By depreciating the home currency, foreign purchase of exports is promoted; hence aggregate demand increases, with the result that employment increases.

Alternatively, exchange rate intervention can fight inflation (Niehans 1984). Lastly, a number of authors, e.g. Grubel (1977), have argued that the primary purpose of exchange rate intervention is to stabilize exchange rates.

In theory, exchange rate intervention can be used (though not simultaneously) to fight all these problems. Only through empirical analysis can we determine which targets are in practice chosen by the monetary authorities. This chapter reports the results of this test.

THE POLITICS OF EXCHANGE RATE POLICY

In addition to using exchange rate intervention for economic goals, governments often have political goals. The Nordhaus–MacRae political business cycle (PBC) and Hibbs's (1977) partisan policy hypotheses are the two dominant political interpretations of macroeconomic policy.

Nordhaus (1975) and MacRae (1977) argue that elected government officials manipulate the economy to enhance their chances of re-election. In contrast to Nordhaus and MacRae, Hibbs (1977) proposes a partisan business cycle in which left and right political parties have different partisan goals with regard to the economy. He argues that there is a partisan policy effect such that the left promotes low unemployment at the expense of higher inflation, while the right prefers low inflation even at the expense of high unemployment. For Hibbs, parties and politicians are not opportunistic but ideological. Left parties favour workers, right parties capitalists.

A REACTION FUNCTION TEST OF THE HYPOTHESES

This study employs a reaction function approach in testing the determinants of macroeconomic policy behaviour. Reaction function models are regression models which utilize the policy instruments as the dependent variables. The policy targets and political determinants of the instruments are independent variables. Reaction function models try to determine empirically the policy objectives of policy-makers. Instead of relying on the stated goals of policy-makers, reaction action models examine what policy-makers do in response to changes in the economy and politics. Hence, this chapter presents an empirical test of the determinants of policy; not a test of competing macroeconomic theories nor the effectiveness of these policies.

Economic theory does not directly help us in specifying the economic constraints on foreign exchange holdings. In the economic literature there is no argument that economic factors drive central bank holding of foreign assets and currency in a system of floating exchange rates. Yet the evidence is overwhelming that central banks have extensive foreign exchange holdings, and engage in buying and selling substantial amounts of these holdings. For example, as noted above, in a recent episode the Bundesbank bought $35 billion worth of French francs in one week. Downes (1989) notes that governments hold foreign assets and currency for the sole purpose of exchange rate market intervention.

Hence, I employ two economic constraints which are implied by more general economic constraints. First, the domestic nominal interest rate is viewed as a constraint on holding foreign currency. Following standard liquidity theory, the interest rate should affect holdings of currency. The higher the interest rate, the greater the opportunity cost of holding non-interest-bearing assets such as currency. Hence, we would expect that as interest rates increase, holdings of currency decrease.

Second, the measure of foreign exchange holdings is in terms of their value in the domestic currency. Hence, as the value of the domestic currency increases, foreign currencies are depreciated – the value of foreign currency holdings should decrease. The MERM (Multilateral Exchange Rate Model) rate, which is an index of the value of the domestic currency relative to a basket of foreign currencies, should therefore be negatively related to the value of foreign currency holdings.[3]

In addition, a measure of the economic openness (or interdependence) is used to control for the amount of fiscal leakage for each country. I do not argue that fiscal policy is abandoned *in toto* as national economies become interdependent. Rather, some economies which are relatively closed, e.g. the US and Japan, continue to rely on fiscal policy for stabilization purposes. Even very open economies might continue to use fiscal policy instruments, but at a reduced rate, and in conjunction with exchange rate policy.

The regression equation has the following specific variables:

$$\text{FOREIGN-EXCHANGE HOLDINGS}_t = B_0 + B_1\ \text{UNEMPLOYMENT}_{t-1} + B_2\ \text{INFLATION}_{t-1} + B_3\ \text{MERM}_{t-1} + B_4\ \text{OPENNESS}_{t-1} + B_5\ \text{INTEREST RATE}_t + B_6\ \text{MERM}_t + B_7\ \text{ELECTION}_{t+j} + B_8\ \text{PARTY}_t + e_t$$

(See the data appendix for further discussion of the variables used in the analysis.)

It has been hypothesized here that exchange rate intervention is a substitute for fiscal policy, but that both instruments could be used simultaneously or alternately to stabilize employment. Fiscal policy has not lost all its effectiveness in all countries. Hence, I must test exchange rate and fiscal policy simultaneously in determining either's effect on unemployment. For example, monetary authorities might not pursue exchange rate intervention if they perceive that fiscal stimulation is sufficient. Fiscal and exchange rate policies, thus, are linked. Therefore, the statistical test required is a simultaneous equation estimate of exchange rate and fiscal policy.

The fiscal policy reaction function which I use parallels the exchange rate reaction function. Government surplus or deficit expenditure is the standard Keynesian instrument for affecting unemployment. Hence, it is the dependent variable in a reaction function test. (For a complete specification of the equation see Jankowski 1994.)

The statistical tests used to estimate these two equations are two-stage least squares. In the text, I report only the foreign-exchange equation estimates from the simultaneous equations. (The fiscal policy estimates are available from the author on request.)

EMPIRICAL FINDINGS

The political and economic hypotheses described above are empirically tested using a group of 12 OECD countries. Following Keohane (1985), the full emergence of flexible exchange rates is designated as beginning in the second quarter of 1973. A transition period of mixed fixed and flexible exchange rates – the Smithsonian Agreement – existed from the third quarter of 1971 to the first quarter of 1973. As such, the initial analysis is confined to the period between the second quarter of 1973 and the fourth quarter of 1984.[4]

Table 7.1 presents the results of the two-stage least squares regression analysis for a pooled, cross-sectional statistical analysis for the 12 countries, with foreign currency holdings of the monetary authorities as the policy instrument. Because I use a pooled analysis of 12 countries, a correction for fixed effects is employed.

Table 7.1 Foreign exchange holdings of central bank (1973: 2–1983: 4)

	F-Exchange	(Standard error)
Intercept	–928.33***	(298.40)
Unemp.	40.06***	(10.95)
Inf.	–27.78	(20.76)
MERM-lag	–162.30**	(62.94)
Interest rate	68.06***	(10.64)
Openness	7.92***	(2.98)
MERM	207.87***	(64.70)
Left–right	–131.56***	(46.97)
Election	4.08	(43.99)
Australia	–38.34	(100.50)
Austria	–149.44	(177.26)
Belgium	–884.14***	(287.90)
Canada	–330.05***	(123.67)
France	742.98***	(117.39)
Germany	2393.93***	(320.82)
Italy	316.45**	(134.65)
Japan	1690.42***	(129.45)
Netherlands	–322.46	(247.78)
Sweden	–941.81**	(427.64)
UK	516.15***	(124.04)
Total $R^{2\dagger}$	0.749	

Notes:
* = 0.10 level of significance.
** = 0.05 level of significance.
*** = 0.01 level of significance.
† The simultaneous equations estimates only allow an R^2 for both equations, i.e. of both the foreign exchange and fiscal regression equations.

It is clear that exchange rate policy is targeted at unemployment. The positive correlation for unemployment indicates that as unemployment increases, governments increase their holdings of foreign currency in an effort to depreciate their home currency. A depreciated currency promotes exports, and hence reduces unemployment. Governments use exchange rate intervention as a countercyclical employment stabilization policy. There is no support for the proposition that exchange rate intervention is targeted at inflation, since the estimate is insignificant.

The most common alternative interpretation of exchange rate intervention is that it is used to stabilize the exchange rate. MERM-lagged is statistically significant but it has the wrong sign. When governments attempt to stabilize the exchange rate of their domestic currency, they should counter changes in their exchange rate by depreciating their currency after appreciating it. Hence, foreign exchange holdings should be positively correlated with the MERM measure of the exchange rate. However, the estimate is significantly negative. There is no explanation for this finding in the literature.

Alternatively, some authors claim that exchange rate intervention is targeted at inflation. However, the inflation measure is neither statistically significant nor does it have the right sign if used to fight inflation. A central bank would appreciate its currency in response to inflation, if it desired to reduce the inflation rate.

Of the economy controls, only openness exhibits the hypothesized relation. More open economies tend to hold larger amounts of foreign exchange. Hence, they are more likely to depreciate their currency to fight unemployment. The other two economic controls are significantly related to the dependent variable, but they have the wrong hypothesized sign. The interest rate is found to be positively associated with foreign currency holdings. This means that as the opportunity costs of holding non-interest-bearing assets (foreign money) increase, central banks increase their holdings. Likewise, as the domestic currency appreciates and foreign currencies depreciate in value, the value of foreign currency holdings is increasing in value. These findings suggest that movements in foreign exchange holdings are not driven by economic forces but are controlled by government officials.

Lastly, of the two political interpretations of macroeconomic policy formation, only Hibbs's partisan difference hypothesis is supported. Left governments tend to depreciate their domestic currency and spur employment, while right governments tend to appreciate the value of the domestic currency.

The empirical findings presented in Table 7.1 reveal substantial sources of exchange rate intervention since the break-up of the Bretton Woods agreement for employment stabilization. The analysis strongly suggests that unemployment forms an important target of exchange rate manipulation, as indicated by the very reliable positive coefficient.

A natural question given these findings is: did the break-up of the Bretton Woods system permit governments to use exchange rate intervention as a stabilization instrument? During the period of fixed exchange rates under Bretton Woods, did governments also target exchange rate intervention for domestic economic purposes? This is an important question because exchange rate manipulation is a 'beggar-thy-neighbour' policy, and may explain recent attempts at re-establishing a system of fixed exchange rates as witnessed with the European monetary system and European monetary integration.

To answer this question, I re-estimated the same policy reaction function for the period of the Bretton Woods agreement. There is not the slightest hint that exchange rate intervention was used as a policy instrument during the Bretton Woods period. (The tables from this analysis are available from the author on request.)

DISCUSSION: EUROPEAN MONETARY INTEGRATION AND EXCHANGE RATE INTERVENTION

The evidence presented above indicates that in the wake of Bretton Woods, exchange rate intervention has been used for employment stabilization and for partisan political purposes. However, it was not used to fight inflation or stabilize exchange rates, as suggested by a number of authors. Under the Bretton Woods system governments were much more constrained in their control of exchange rates. The evidence indicates that exchange rate intervention was not used as a policy instrument. The findings of systematic countercyclical and partisan manipulation since the break-up of the Bretton Woods system explain the recent calls for greater constraints on and/or coordination of macroeconomic policies (Cooper 1986; Kenen 1988). Exchange rate intervention is a 'beggar-thy-neighbour policy': if other countries do not respond to the lowering of the home country's exchange rate, they will suffer. If other countries respond to the initial depreciation, all countries may suffer as a result, because volatility of exchange rates reduces international trade in the process. If all depreciations are matched, no one gains a relative advantage, but everyone suffers from the increased volatility of exchange rates. Moreover, the incentive structure is that of a prisoner's dilemma, because one country is better off depreciating its currency to fight unemployment, irrespective of what other countries do. Hence, a free-floating exchange rate system is not politically feasible. (For a more extensive discussion of the possible solutions see Jankowski 1994.)

APPENDIX: DATA SOURCES

(All data are from IMF's International Financial Statistics, unless otherwise indicated.)

Inflation rate: a moving average of the inflation rate in the previous four quarters; the percentage change in the consumer price index computed from monthly data drawn from the *Monthly Bulletin of Statistics*, Statistical Office of the United Nations, 1973–84.

Interest rate: the nominal interest rate in each country.[5]

MERM (contemporaneous and lagged one quarter): the IMF's MERM effective exchange rate, a measure of each country's exchange rate relative to a basket of 23 different currencies, which is indexed so that 1980 = 100 for each country. (An increase in the index indicates an appreciation of the currency.)

OPENNESS: the average ratio between the sum of total exports and imports and GDP in the previous four quarters.

PARTY: the ideological position of the governing party, with 1=Right and 0=Left (based on Alt. 1985).

SUM-ELECTION: a dichotomous dummy variable taking on the value of 1 in pre-election quarters and 0 in the other quarters;[6] from the *International Almanac of Electoral History*, edited by Thomas T. Mackie and Richard Rose, New York: Facts on File, Inc.; updated using the *Europa Year Book 1984*.

Unemployment rate: a moving average of the unemployment rate in the previous four quarters;[7] computed from monthly data drawn from the *Monthly Bulletin of Statistics*, Statistical Office of the United Nations, 1973–84.

NOTES

1. The other possible instrument is holdings of foreign assets. Henderson (1979) and Branson (1977) have argued for a portfolio-balance model of exchange rate intervention. I tested this instrument for exchange rate intervention, but the tests consistently showed no manipulation of the instrument.
2. France was attempting to preserve the EMS at the time. Hence it was ignoring domestic economic problems (high unemployment) by appreciating its currency in the face of market pressures to depreciate.
3. A third economic control was also employed in some of the tests. It was assumed that the balance of payments would affect foreign currency holdings by the central bank. For example, a country experiencing a balance of payments surplus might receive payments for its goods in terms of foreign currency. Hence, foreign exchange holdings might increase as

a result of a surplus in the balance of payments. This control was never statistically significant, and the results are not reported here.

4. The empirical tests cover only the period through 1984. An empirical analysis of the more recent developments are needed. The analysis presented here must be updated through 1993. However, not all the measures needed for the analysis are available. In particular, the left–right measure is now available only through 1984. Once it is updated to the present an extensive analysis of the EMS, the effects of the Plaza and Louvre agreements, and the recent ERM crisis experienced by EMU can be undertaken. This task must be left to the experts in the area, as defining left or right dominance in coalition governments, and when parties are in flux, is complicated.
5. The real interest rate was also tested in the regression analysis. The results did not differ markedly between nominal and real interest rates; thus, I report only the estimates with the nominal interest rate.
6. The estimates reported are based on three quarters, the quarter of the election and the two immediately prior quarters. This length is suggested by Lewis-Beck (1986) who presents evidence that this is the appropriate reference period for voters.
7. A moving average over four quarters is used to avoid complications stemming from simultaneity and multicollinearity. Due to high levels of multicollinearity, in particular, the signs of the estimates varied continuously when separate lagged versions of the independent variables were incorporated into the regression equations.

REFERENCES

Alt, James E. (1985), 'Political Parties, World Demand, and Unemployment: Domestic and International Sources of Economic Activity', *American Political Science Review*, **79**, 1016–40.

Alt, James E. (1986), 'Party Strategies, World Demand and Unemployment: The Political Economy of Economic Activity in Western Industrial Nations', *American Economic Review*, **76**, 57–61.

Argy, Victor (1982), *Exchange-Rate Management in Theory and Practice*, Princeton, NJ: Princeton University Press.

Branson, William (1977), 'Asset Markets and Relative Prices in Exchange Rate Determination', *Sozialwissenschaftliche Annalen*, **1**, 69–89.

Cooper, Richard (1986), 'Macroeconomics in an Open Economy', *Science*, September 12, 1155–9.

Dominguez, Kathryn and Jeffrey Frankel (1993), *Does Foreign Exchange Intervention Work?,* Washington, DC: Institute for International Economics.

Downes, Patrick (1989), 'Managing Foreign Exchange Reserves', *Finance and Development*, **24**, 558–77.

Grubel, H.G. (1977), 'How Important is Control over International Reserves?' in R.A. Mundell and J.J. Polak (eds), *The New International Monetary System*, New York: Columbia University Press.

Henderson, Dale (1979), 'Financial Policies in Open Economies', *American Economics Review*, **69**, 232–9.

Henderson, Dale (1984), 'Exchange Market Intervention Operations: Their Role in Financial Policy and Their Effects' in John Bilson and Richard Marston (eds), *Exchange Rate Theory and Practice*, Chicago: University of Chicago Press.

Hibbs, Douglas, Jr (1977), 'Political Parties and Macroeconomic Policy', *American Political Science Review*, **71**, 1467–87.

Jankowski, Richard (1994), 'Exchange-Rate Intervention and European Monetary

Integration'. Paper presented at the York University International Conference on Economic Integration and Public Policy.
Kenen, Peter (1988), *Managing Exchange Rates*, New York: Council on Foreign Relations Press.
Keohane, Robert O. (1985), 'The International Politics of Inflation', in Leon N. Lindberg and Charles S. Maier (eds), *The Politics of Inflation and Economic Stagnation*, Washington, DC: Brookings Institution.
Lewis-Beck, Michael (1986), 'Economic Voting, "Yes"; Political Business Cycle, "No"', University of Iowa Occasional Paper no. 22.
MacRae, G.D. (1977), 'A Political Model of the Business Cycle', *Journal of Political Economy*, **85**, 59–72.
Niehans, Jurg (1984), *International Monetary Economics*, Baltimore: Johns Hopkins University Press.
Nordhaus, William G. (1975), 'The Political Business Cycle', *Review of Economic Studies*, **42**, 169–90.

8. Empirical issues of the sterling–Deutschmark exchange rate behaviour before and after the September 1992 crisis

Dimitris Georgoutsos and Nicolaos Karamouzis

INTRODUCTION

The Exchange rate mechanism (ERM) of the European monetary system (EMS) had long been considered the cornerstone of the European Union's policy towards a full-fledged monetary union. The ERM had performed relatively well, without realignments, between January 1987 and mid-1992, although some of its critics attributed its stability to the existence of capital controls.

The first major crisis in the ERM broke out in mid-September 1992 and led to the 'temporary' suspension of the UK pound and the Italian lira from the system. It is now widely accepted that this crisis should be mainly attributed to two factors.

First, the US dollar had reached record low levels against the Deutschmark, DM, by late August 1992. Despite the repeated interventions by the central banks, on 25 August one US dollar was trading at DM1.40, down 20 per cent from its level of a year before. This had come as a result of the record high level that the short-term interest rate differential of those two currencies had reached at that time. US short-term interest rates were 3.4 per cent, their lowest level for 30 years, while Germany's were at 9.9 per cent, their highest for about 60 years. As investors were rushing out of US dollars into DM, immense pressure was put on the two weakest currencies of the ERM, i.e. the UK pound and the Italian lira, which were forced to trade at the lower limits of the ERM band. When the Bundesbank, on 14 September 1992, decided to trim its interest rates by a considerably smaller amount than the market had anticipated (the Lombard rate fell by one-quarter of a point) the final blow to the UK pound had been struck. Speculators had interpreted that move by the Bundesbank as a refusal to support the UK pound and the lira.

The second reason for the outbreak of the crisis was related to the uncertainty on the outcome of the French referendum on the Maastricht Treaty, scheduled for 20 September 1992, following the rejection of the Treaty by Danish voters on 7 June 1992. A negative vote would have meant the end of the Maastricht Treaty and the drive for economic and monetary union. The market had perceived this Treaty as an external constraint on countries with macroeconomic imbalances which pursued stabilization policies in order to meet the convergence criteria. Many investors thought that rejection of the Treaty by the French voters would have inevitably led to an ERM realignment.

During the UK's membership in the ERM an issue which was frequently discussed was whether the pound had entered the mechanism at a central rate *vis-à-vis* the DM, which could harm the competitiveness of UK exports. It is by now widely accepted that the appreciation of the pound in the early 1980s, and the higher inflation experienced by the UK, led the current account deficit to deteriorate steadily after a peak in 1981 and put the trade balance in the red. The rate of DM 2.95/£ (central rate in the ERM) was effectively the rate which the monetary authorities had experimented with during the 'shadowing the DM' period of 1986–88. Critics claim that this central rate was not justifiable and depreciation expectations were built in for the pound. This explains why, when interest rates in the UK increased dramatically in the late 1980s the DM/£ exchange rate remained almost at its previous level. In December 1989 the three months' borrowing rate in the UK was standing at 15.06 per cent compared to 7.85 per cent in Germany while the DM/£ exchange rate was at 2.92. This state of affairs implied that substantial exchange rate risk premia had been built into the UK interest rates and that the market was expecting a depreciation of the pound.

This chapter attempts to shed light on three issues: first, to investigate the credibility of the exchange rate band for the DM/£ parity in the ERM; second, to study the variability of the DM/£ exchange rate changes during sterling's participation in the ERM and after its suspension from it; and third, to identify the main Granger-causal factors of the DM/£ changes during the two sub-periods.

TESTING THE CREDIBILITY OF THE TARGET ZONE BAND

A target zone for the exchange rate implies certain limits to the rate of return of foreign interest rates, denominated in the domestic currency. If domestic interest rates lie outside those limits then arbitrage is completely safe and the exchange rate band cannot be credible. For example, if an investor who borrowed Deutschmarks for three months and invested the proceeds, for an equal period, in pounds, was 100 per cent certain he would make a profit, we could claim that the target zone band was not credible to survive. This would happen if domestic interest rates exceeded the sum of foreign interest rates plus the maximum allowed depreciation of domestic currency by the band. Therefore, a necessary condition for the exchange rate band to be credible is that the following inequality holds (Svensson 1991; Caramazza 1993):

$$\left[(1+i_t^*)\left(\frac{S^L}{S}\right)_t^{1/m}-1\right]\leq i_t \leq\left[(1+i_t^*)\left(\frac{S^U}{S}\right)_t^{1/m}-1\right] \qquad (1)$$

where i^* and i denote interest rates of the same maturity, m, and default risk for foreign currency (DM), and home currency (£), respectively. Interest rates, i, are annualized rates of return and maturity, m, is expressed in years. S represents the price of the home currency per unit of the foreign one, £/DM, and the superscripts L and U stand for the lower and upper bound of the ERM band for the £/DM. In the case we examine, the upper limit was 0.3599 (£/DM) and the lower one 0.3192 (£/DM).

The width of the rate-of-return band in (1) above is inversely related to the maturity of the investment. A certain change of the exchange rate of a currency from its present level to the limits of the band will be translated to smaller annualized percentage changes the longer the period of the investment. For long-term investments, the validity of the testing procedure, as exemplified in (1) above, still applies although the interpretation is that 'the exchange rate depreciates/appreciates gradually, so that to reach the edge of its band at maturity' (Svensson 1991).

We have applied the above test on daily observations of the £/DM exchange rate, three months' inter-bank borrowing rates quoted in London, for £, and in Frankfurt, for DM, and the yields on ten years' government bonds of those two currencies. The data are daily and cover the period from 1 January 1992 to 20 October 1993. They have been obtained from the data bank of Bloomberg Financial Services.

Figure 8.1 depicts the rate-of-return bounds, calculated as in (1) above, for the case of a three-month period and for the period 1 January 1992 to 15 September 1992. As is clear from the figure, the domestic, UK, interest rate was always within the two critical bounds. The only two exceptions were 1 and 15 September 1992 when the domestic interest rate exceeded the upper bound. However, it is clear from the graph that by the end of August 1992 the credibility of the system had started to become problematic.

In Figure 8.2 the same analysis is conducted based on the rate of return of ten years' bonds. The picture here is entirely different from the previous one. The domestic interest rate has been above the upper bound throughout the

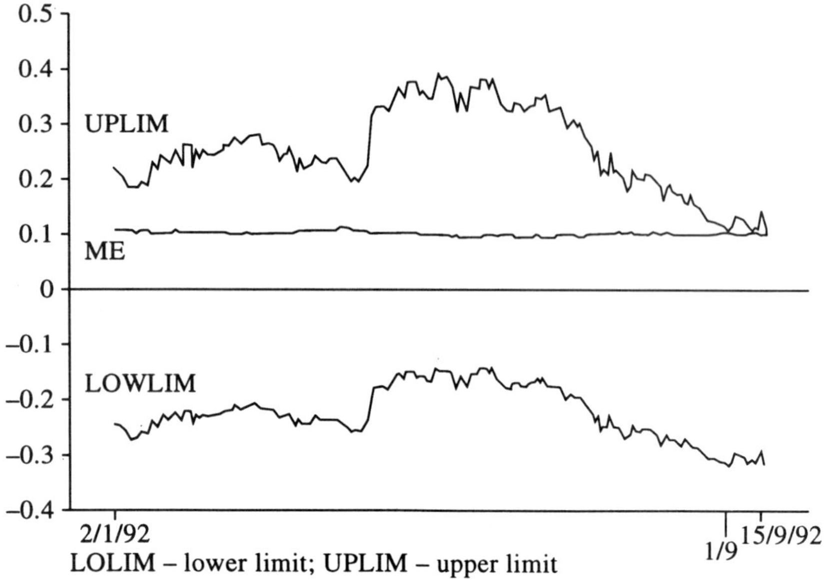

Figure 8.1 Three months' London inter-bank rate-of-return bounds

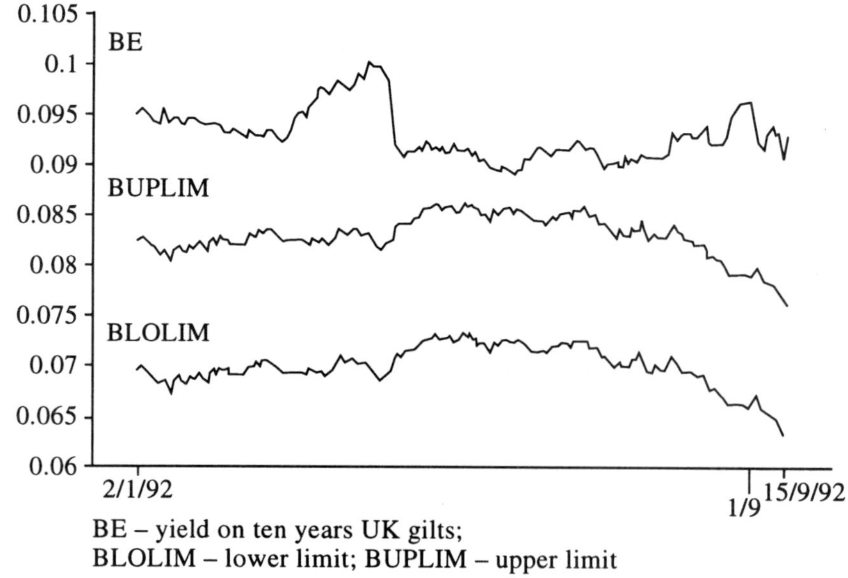

Figure 8.2 Yields on ten years' UK gilts

period examined. This piece of evidence casts in doubt the long-run sustainability of the £/DM band in the ERM. It should be emphasized, however, that the interpretation of the results concerning the long-term rates should be done with caution because of the risk premia which are embedded in the interest rates.

The general conclusion which can be drawn from this section is that despite the criticism which was often heard on the chosen level of the £/DM parity for the UK's entry in the ERM, the market participants' behaviour showed no indication that they were expecting a devaluation. It was only in the very few days before the development of the crisis that there were signs that uncertainty for the future of the system was mounting.

TESTING THE CONDITIONAL VARIANCE OF EXCHANGE RATE CHANGES

One of the arguments supporting sterling's entry in the ERM was that it would stabilize the fluctuation of its exchange rate against the currencies of its major trade partners. However, stability of the exchange rate meant different things to different people. To some of them it meant that the competitiveness of UK products would be preserved; to others that the variability of the nominal exchange rate changes would be diminished, which is the issue explored in the present section.

Table 8.1 presents some evidence on the variability of the £/DM parity changes over the two regimes, i.e. fixed exchange rate regime under the ERM and the floating one prevailing after 16 September 1992. The standard deviations of the changes have been considerably lower under the ERM regime, although when we look at the coefficients of variations the variability appears to have remained stable. It is interesting, however, to note that the ratio of the coefficients of variation of the £/DM changes to the DM/$ changes had been considerably smaller during the first period. This seems to contradict the view that the pound would be better insulated from the DM/$ fluctuations under a floating rate regime.

The standard deviation is a good measure of the variability if the variable under examination follows the normal distribution. As Table 8.1 shows, this is not the case with the £/DM changes. The coefficient of kurtosis indicates that this variable deviates considerably from the normal distribution in both periods. In other words, the distribution of the £/DM changes exhibits a leptokurtotic behaviour. This is not surprising since this is a well known behaviour of assets' return. Leptokurtosis can be attributed to two factors. The first may be that the variable is not normally distributed. The second is that the conditional variance of the variable (i.e. the prediction errors' vari-

Table 8.1 *Descriptive statistics on nominal £/DM and DM/$ changes*

	C.V.	S.D.	Kurtosis (–3)	Skewness
		Sample period: 1/1/92–15/9/92		
Δ(£/DM)	22.61	0.47E–4	1.75	–0.31
Δ(DM/$)	64.55	0.012	0.98	0.70
		Sample period: 17/9/92–20/10/93		
Δ(£/DM)	18.75	0.002	1.68	0.28
Δ(DM/$)	27.71	0.012	0.62	–0.03

Notes:
C.V. = coefficient of variation.
S.D. = standard deviation.

Skewness to the right (left) of the distribution is indicated by positive (negative) values of the coefficient. The value for a normal distribution should be zero.

The *kurtosis* coefficient is centred to 3 and measures the curvature of the distribution. Positive (negative) values indicate that the tails of the distribution are thicker (thinner) than those of the normal one.

ance) follows a heteroscedastic pattern. All this means is that volatility is clustered, that is, rates of return tend to be more volatile when they have just been so. This kind of behaviour can be generated by investors' reactions to each other's guesses, thus generating self-fulfilling prophecies.

Preliminary tests have shown that the log (£/DM) changes exhibited a low-order autoregressive pattern. For both periods examined lagged terms were significant only at the first order. The autocorrelation pattern of the squared log (£/DM) changes was however entirely different. We were unable to reject, in both periods, that the squared lagged terms, even of an order 12, were not significant. There was therefore compelling evidence that the conditional variance was characterized by Generalized Auto-Regressive Conditional Heteroscedasticity (GARCH) (Mills 1993).

Modelling the conditional variation of the exchange rates is of greater importance than the variation itself, since what investors are worried about is the unanticipated changes of the exchange rates. Given the results from our preliminary tests we estimated the following GARCH-in-mean model on the rate of change of the exchange rate. ΔS (Bollerslev, Engle and Wooldridge 1988):

$$\Delta S_t = a_0 + a_1 \Delta S_{t-1} + a_2 h_t + e_t \tag{2}$$

$$e_t / \Omega_{t-1} \sim N(0, h_t) \tag{3}$$

$$h_t = c_0 + c_1 h_{t-1} + c_2 + e_{t-1}^2 \tag{4}$$

The structure of the model implies that the exchange rate percentage changes are related to the conditional variance of the forecast errors, h. Moreover, a lagged term of the conditional variance has been included in equation (4) in order to account for the autocorrelated pattern of the squared £/DM changes we referred to above.

The model has been estimated by maximum likelihood estimation and the results appear in Table 8.2. There is a striking difference in the structure of the model, as emerges from the significance of the estimated coefficients. However the most important result is that the standard deviations and the coefficients of variation of the prediction errors were substantially smaller during the ERM period. This implies that the nominal exchange rate changes were more predictable during that period.

Table 8.2 Maximum likelihood GARCH-in-mean estimates for the ERM (1/1/92–15/9/91) and the post-ERM (17/9/92–20/10/93) periods (The model is given by eqs (3) to (5)

Coefficients	ERM		post-ERM	
a_0	0.60E–3	(0.72)	–0.10E–4	(–0.29E–1)
a_1	0.12	(–1.0)	–0.088	(–1.30)
a_2	–6.45	(–2.7)	0.002	(0.0008)
c_0	0.31E–4	(2.11)	0.56E–5	(1.07)
c_1	0.32	(2.97)	0.517	(17.34)
c_2	1.64	(2.81)	0.064	(1.43)
S.D.	0.0029		0.0060	
C.V.	18.11		65.86	

Notes:
Numbers in parentheses show t ratios.

S.D. and C.V. stand for the standard deviation and the coefficient of variation of the residuals of eq. (3).

SEARCHING FOR THE DETERMINANTS OF EXCHANGE RATE CHANGES

An interesting question which is often asked is whether the pound was better insulated outside or inside the ERM from the wide fluctuations of both the DM/$ exchange rate and the volatility of the German interest rates. To answer this question we estimated, for the two sub-periods, a vector autoregressive model (VAR) and we conducted Granger causality tests.

In order to determine the correct specification of the VAR model, in levels or in first differences, one must first determine the unit root properties of the variables. The results from those tests appear in Table 8.3. The most striking difference between the two sub-periods was that both the level of log (£/DM) and of the UK interest rates exhibited a mean reverting behaviour only under the post-ERM period. This finding concerning the exchange rate behaviour is surprising since one would expect that when the exchange rate fluctuates within a band it is likely to be mean-stationary. Two explanations can be given for this finding. The first is that our data set spans a very short period of time which does not allow the series to show its true properties. The second is that investors were expecting a realignment of the system so that any shock to the nominal exchange rate had permanent effects on its level. For the ERM

Table 8.3 Unit root tests

	log (£/DM)	log (DM/$)	i	i^*
		Period: 1/1/92–15/9/92		
A.D.F.	–0.57	–1.10	–2.19	–2.12
	–0.89	–1.36	–1.74	–2.04
P.P.	–0.68	–1.01	–2.84	–1.68
		Period: 17/9/92–20/10.93		
A.D.F.	–3.92†	–1.95	–6.36†	–0.68
	–4.07†	–1.94	–6.58†	–0.64
P.P.	–3.63†	–2.17	–5.49†	–0.66

Notes:
Critical values at 5% = –2.88; † denotes significance at that level.

A.D.F. = Augmented Dickey-Fuller test with 5 lags (1st row) and 12 lags (2nd row).
P.P. = Non-parametric Phillips and Perron (1988) test.
i (i^*) = 3 months' London (Frankfurt) inter-bank borrowing rates.

period where the existence of a unit root in each one of the variables mentioned above could not be rejected, we tested for the existence of a long-run equilibrium relationship between the variables, i.e. we tested for cointegration. We applied Johansen's maximum likelihood estimation technique and it was interesting to find that although we experimented with various lag structures we could not reject that no cointegration existed. To this piece of evidence could be given the same interpretation as the one on the unit roots results above, i.e. either the time period our data span is too short for this kind of test or the ERM lacked credibility.

The tests reported above allowed us to specify the VAR models in the first difference of the series. Table 8.4 reports the Granger causality tests derived from a five-lags structure which gave us good specification test results. It is clear from those results that the £/DM exchange rate gained its independence in the post-ERM period. At the 5 per cent significance level the DM/$ percentage changes appear to be the main determinant of the £/DM percentage changes, during the ERM period. This result disappears when we look at the post-ERM period where £/DM changes exhibit an independent behaviour. Another noteworthy piece of evidence is that exchange rate considerations used to be an important determinant of money rate changes, in the UK, for

Table 8.4 Granger-causality tests from a VAR model (consisting of the first differences of the variables: log (£/DM), log (DM/$), i *and* i**)*[1]

Dependent variable	Δlog (£/DM)	Δlog (DM/$)	Δi	Δi^*
		Period: 1/1/92–15/9/92		
Δlog (£/DM)	0.081	0.046	0.31	0.60
Δlog (DM/$)	0.058	0.572	0.12	0.67
Δi	0.002	0.315	0.04	0.87
Δi^*	0.710	0.606	0.17	0.17
		Period: 17/9/92–20/10/93		
Δlog (£DM)	0.384	0.317	0.338	0.156
Δlog (DM/$)	0.062	0.970	0.955	0.263
Δ_i	0.8E–4	0.085	0.316	0.218
Δi^*	0.53	0.009	0.089	0.026

Note: [1] The VAR model has been estimated with five lags of the endogenous variables. Marginal significance levels are reported.

both the ERM and the post-ERM period. Finally, the lack of any Granger-causal relationship between the German interest rates and both the domestic rates and the exchange rate seems to imply that monetary authorities sterilized their impact through an intervention policy in both the foreign exchange and the money markets.

CONCLUDING REMARKS

The UK's participation in the ERM had received a serious amount of criticism on the grounds that the pound was overvalued at the DM2.95 parity. In this chapter we have tested for the credibility of the £/DM ERM band by examining whether domestic interest rates fall inside the rate-of-return bands for different terms. We have shown that within a three-month horizon, investors behaved as if they did not expect any realignment to take place. It is however evident from our results that the degree of confidence to the ERM target zone had been diminishing after mid-August 1992. However, the results derived from the ten years' long bond rates indicates that the market had doubts concerning the medium-term credibility of the £/DM band throughout the period under investigation. This finding should be read with caution due to the substantial risk premia which might have been built in long-term interest rates.

The second issue addressed in this chapter was the variability of the DM/£ changes over the ERM and the post-ERM, floating rates, regime. A GARCH-in-mean model was estimated and it was shown that the volatility of the DM/£ exchange rate prediction errors was smaller during the ERM period. This seems to imply that the predictability of the DM/£ exchange rate changes deteriorated after the pound's suspension from the ERM. In the last section we have tried to identify some of the determinants of the DM/£ changes. We conducted Granger-causality tests and our main result was that the statistical dependence of DM/£ parity changes from the DM/$ ones, during the ERM period, disappeared after the pound's suspension from the ERM. Moreover, there is indirect evidence of the exercise of a substantial intervention policy which sterilized the impact of German interest rate changes on both the exchange rate and the domestic rates.

REFERENCES

Artis, M. (1992), 'Counter-inflationary Policy in the Framework of the EMS', CEPR Discussion paper no. 649.

Bollerslev, T., Engle, R.F. and Wooldridge, J.M. (1988), 'A Capital Asset Pricing

Model with Time-Varying Covariances', *Journal of Political Economy*, **96**, 116–31.

Caramazza, F. (1993), 'French–German Interest Rate Differentials and Time-Varying Realignment Risk', *IMF Staff Papers*, **40** (3).

Johansen, S. and K. Juselius (1990), 'Maximum Likelihood Estimation and Inference on Cointegration – with Applications to the Demand for Money', *Oxford Bulletin of Economics and Statistics*, **52**, 169–210.

Miller, M. and A. Sutherland (1990), 'Monetary and Exchange Rate Targets, and After: A Stochastic "Hard Landing" for Sterling?' in V. Argy and P. De Grauwe (eds), *Choosing an Exchange Rate Regime*, Washington, DC: International Monetary Fund.

Mills, T. (1993), *The Econometric Modelling of Financial Time Series*, Cambridge, UK: Cambridge University Press.

Pesaran, B. and G. Robinson (1993), 'The European Exchange Rate Mechanism and the Volatility of the Sterling-Deutschemark Exchange Rate', *The Economic Journal*, **103**, 1418–31.

Phillips, P. and P. Perron (1988), 'Testing for a Unit Root in Time Series Regression', *Biometrica*, **75**, 461–71.

Svensson, Lars E.O. (1991), 'The Simplest Test of Target Zone Credibility', *IMF Staff Papers*, **38** (3).

9. The real interest rate differential in an economic union

Leo Michelis*

INTRODUCTION

The relationship among real interest rates across countries is of central importance to our understanding of open economy macroeconomics as well as of the effectiveness of stabilization policies by governments. Movements in the real interest rate affect the consumption–savings decision and hence capital formation, economic growth and productivity. If real interest rates are completely equal internationally, the ability of a country's monetary policy to influence its own real rate would be limited to the extent that it could influence the world rate. Consequently, international real rate inequality is a necessary condition for monetary policy to influence the domestic economy through the real interest rate.

In a world of free trade in goods and assets, costless international arbitrage in goods and financial assets should equalize *ex-ante* real returns of comparable securities across different countries, thereby reducing the power of domestic authorities to control economic fluctuations. Clearly, the decision of a country to join a 'free trade area' such as the recent NAFTA or the more 'mature' European Union should depend critically on the effect of their membership on the relative autonomy of its monetary policies.

Economists have studied extensively the international linkages among *ex-ante* real rates – often referred to simply as real rates in this chapter. Simple arbitrage models (eg. Frenkel 1976; Bilson 1978) predict the international equality of real rates provided that two international parity conditions are satisfied: uncovered interest parity (UIP) and expected relative purchasing power parity (PPP) (see below). Violations of either UIP or PPP or both lead to real rate inequality across countries. There are several factors that can cause violations of PPP. Among them, a well known example is the existence

*I am grateful to Professor C.C. Paraskevopoulos for encouragement and guidance. Helpful comments from Professors Arman Mansoorian and John Paschakis are also gratefully acknowledged. All remaining errors are my responsibility.

of market imperfections that lead to price stickiness in the short run. The majority of literature of exchange rates (eg. Dornbush 1976; Buiter and Miller 1982) predicts that the real rate differential between two countries is equal to the expected rate of change of the real exchange rate.

As to the UIP condition, it can be violated provided that international investors are assumed to be risk-averse. Risk aversion and the associated risk premium suffices to drive a wedge between nominal rates of return adjusted for expectations of depreciation. There are many theoretical models relating the risk premium to market fundamentals (eg. Frankel 1979; Hodrick 1981; Solnik 1973; Stulz 1981). A particularly interesting and general way of modelling risk premia is the representative agent consumption-based capital asset pricing model (CCAPM) of Lucas (1978, 1982) and Breeden (1979). In CCAPM models the representative consumer/investor is assumed to maximize discounted expected utility defined over consumption subject to sequential budget constraints. The first-order condition for a maximum, when properly manipulated, gives rise to a risk premium which is expressible as a function of the covariation of the return on a risky asset with the intertemporal marginal rate of substitution in consumption. Thus, one is able to study the time-series properties of risk premia derived from a theoretically consistent dynamic economic framework. (See, for instance, Hansen and Hodrick 1983 and the recent survey by Hodrick 1987).

In this chapter we examine the linkages among real interest rates across different countries in an economic union with fully integrated economic policies. The economic union consists of *n* member states with identical consumers but with technologies that are subject to state-specific random shocks. We also assume that the economic union (or federation) is endowed with a central authority responsible for maximizing the expected utility of the representative consumer and for the optimal allocation of resources within the federation. Using this simple general equilibrium framework, inspired by the work of Craine (1989), we derive the real rate differential between any pair of states in the economic union and show that it depends on the relevant risk premium differential. Our analysis is different from existing literature in that it is cast in a general equilibrium framework. Existing financial CCAPM models may be viewed as partial equilibrium in the sense that they assume an exogenous distribution of asset returns (i.e. dividends).

The rest of the chapter is organized as follows. We next give a brief overview of related literature on the relationship of real interest rates across countries. Both basic definitions and econometric issues of estimation and testing are discussed. Then we specify the general equilibrium framework and derive the relationship between *ex-ante* real rates in an economic union. A final section concludes.

OVERVIEW OF RELATED LITERATURE

In this section we specify the basic definitions and briefly review the empirical literature intended to test the equality of real rates across countries. Well known among these are the papers by Cumby and Obstfeld (1984), Mishkin (1984a and b), Mark (1985), Merrick and Saunders (1988), Cumby and Mishkin (1986), Frankel and MacArthur (1988) and Johnson (1992).

Definitions

For simplicity, consider only two countries (domestic and foreign) and let the superscript * denote foreign variables. At time $t + k$ the domestic k-period *ex-post* real interest rate, $r_{t,k}$, is defined to be

$$r_{t,k} \equiv R_{t,k} - \Pi_{t,k} \tag{1}$$

where $R_{t,k}$ is the nominal yield on a k-period domestic bond that matures at time $t + k$ and $\Pi_{t,k}$ is the domestic rate of inflation from t to $t + k$.

At time t, investors make forecasts about the *ex-post* real rate that will prevail at time $t + k$, based on the information set Ω_t, available at t. Taking expectations on both sides of (1), we obtain the *ex-ante* real rate at time t,

$$E_t(r_{t,k}) = R_{t,k} - E_t\Pi_{t,k} \tag{2}$$

where E_t denotes mathematical expectation conditional on the information set Ω_t. Similarly, the foreign *ex ante* real rate is defined by

$$E_t(r^*_{t,k}) = R^*_{t,k} - E_t\Pi^*_{t,k} \tag{3}$$

Domestic and foreign *ex-ante* real rates can be hypothesized to be equal under the conditions of UIP and expected PPP. These two conditions can be stated respectively as

$$R_{t,k} - R^*_{t,k} = E_t(s_{t,k} - s_t) \tag{4}$$

and

$$E_t(\Pi_{t,k} - \Pi^*_{t,k}) = E_t(s_{t,k} - s_t) \tag{5}$$

where s_t is the logarithm of the spot exchange rate at time t, defined as the domestic currency price of one unit of foreign exchange. UIP is the equilibrium condition that expected returns on domestic and foreign assets of similar risk be equal. Expected PPP requires that the expected inflation differential between the domestic and foreign country equals the anticipated rate of change of the exchange rate. It is easy to see that UIP and PPP imply the equality of real rates across countries. Substituting (5) into (4) and rearranging we obtain

$$0 = E_t(r_{t,k} - r^*_{t,k}) = (R_{t,k} - E_t\Pi_{t,k}) - (R^*_{t,k} - E_t\Pi^*_{t,k}). \qquad (6)$$

Testing for Real Rate Equality

Testing for real rate equality across countries can be done in several ways. Notice that (2) and (3) imply

$$\Pi_{t,k} - \Pi^*_{t,k} = E_t(r_{t,k} - r^*_{t,k}) + (R_{t,k} - R^*_{t,k}) + u_{t,k} \qquad (7)$$

where $u_{t,k} = \Pi_{t,k} - \Pi^*_{t,k} - E_t(\Pi_{t,k} - \Pi^*_{t,k})$. Cumby and Obstfeld (1984) regress the inflation differential on a constant and the nominal yield differential and perform a (0, 1) joint test on the coefficients of this regression. Using data on Euro-rates, they are able to reject the equality hypothesis.

Mishkin (1984a and b) uses a different methodology. He combines (1) and (2) to arrive at the relation

$$r_{t,k} = E_t(r_{t,k}) - \varepsilon_{t,k} \qquad (8)$$

where $\varepsilon_{t,k} = \Pi_{t,k} - E_t\Pi_{t,k}$. Since $E_t(r_{t,k})$ is not observable, he replaces it with its best linear prediction based on X_t, an observable subset of Ω_t. Letting this projection be $X_t\beta$, the *ex-ante* real rate can be written as

$$E_t(r_{t,k}) = X_t\beta + \eta_{t,k} \qquad (9)$$

where $\eta_{t,k}$ is the linear least-squares prediction error. Substituting (9) into (8) yields

$$r_{t,k} = X_t\beta + (\eta_{t,k} - \varepsilon_{t,k}). \qquad (10)$$

Mishkin uses a constant and a fourth-order polynomial in time as the components of X_t. In both his studies the balance of evidence is against the null hypothesis of real rate equality.

Mark (1985) uses dynamic empirical models to test the real rate equality hypothesis. In one specification the *ex-post* real rate differential is regressed on its own lagged values, and in another specification it is regressed on lagged values of domestic and foreign money growth and inflation rates.

Under the null hypothesis, the regressors in either specification should be statistically insignificant. In the majority of cases considered, the null hypothesis is rejected.

Merrick and Saunders (1986) regress the *ex-post* real rate of a particular country on a cross-sectional mean of several OECD countries. Under the null hypothesis of real rate equality across countries, the estimated cross-sectional mean is an unbiased estimator of the corresponding population mean and hence the regression coefficient in the above regression should be unity. These authors find significant but less than perfect association between real rates.

Cumby and Mishkin (1986) estimate the effect of changes in the US real rate on the real rates of a number of European countries. Using instrumental variable techniques, these authors also find a statistically significant but less than perfect connection between European and US real rates. Based on this evidence, they conclude that it is still possible for European monetary policy to influence domestic economic activity.

Frankel and MacArthur (1988) examine political and currency premia in international real rate differentials. In their cross-section study of forward rates from 24 countries, they find that 'currency factors' due to exchange rate variability are a larger contributor to the failure of real interest parity than are capital controls across different political jurisdictions.

Frankel and MacArthur provide an interesting decomposition of the *ex-ante* real rate differential as follows:

$$\begin{aligned} E_t(r_{t,k}) - E_t(r^*_{t,k}) = & [R_{t,k} - R^*_{t,k} - (f_{t,k} - s_t)] \\ & + [(f_{t,k} - s_t) - E_t(s_{t,k} - s_t)] \\ & + [E_t(s_{t,k} - s_t) - E_t(\Pi_{t,k} - \Pi^*_{t,k})] \end{aligned} \tag{11}$$

where, in addition to other variables defined above, $f_{t,k}$ is the logarithm of the forward exchange rate for the end of period $t + k$ as of the end of period t. The three terms on the right-hand side of (11) are easily identifiable. The first term is the covered interest differential. Covered interest parity has been tested in Eurocurrency markets and has been found to hold (eg. see Frenkel and Levich 1977, 1981). The second term is simply $f_{t,k} - E_t(s_{t,k})$, so that it is an exchange risk premium. The third term is the expected rate of change in the real exchange rate between periods t and $t + k$.

The second and third terms are what Frankel and MacArthur label 'currency factors' in creating a gap between real rates across different countries. Johnson (1992) uses the decomposition (11) to examine both real and nominal return differentials between Canada and the US under both fixed and flexible exchange rate regimes. He finds that *ex-ante* return differentials are stable across the two exchange rate regimes.

In summary, much of the empirical evidence, provided by well known empirical studies, indicates that the hypothesis of international real rate parity is unlikely to hold in actual economies. The existence of risk premia may be a likely cause for the failure of real rate parity, but risk premia are derived from definitional relations (eg. (11) above) rather than a coherent economic model such as the CCAPM. In the following section we accomplish this task in the framework of simple general equilibrium CCAPM. We turn to this discussion next.

THE REAL RATE DIFFERENTIAL IN AN ECONOMIC UNION

In this section we analyse the real rate differential in the context of an economic union using a simple general equilibrium CCAPM. The economic union consists of n member states with identical consumers and production processes that are subject to state-specific random shocks or 'states of nature'. Since, by definition (see Ethier 1988, ch. 12), an economic union consists of countries with fully integrated economic policies, we imagine that there exists a central planning authority that maximizes the expected utility of the representative consumer subject to the aggregate resource constraints of the whole economic union (or federation). In what follows we first specify the structure of preferences, technologies and resource constraints in the economic union. Second, we characterize the central planning optimal solution in terms of the relevant first-order necessary conditions or Euler equations. Third, using the Euler equation for capital, we show that the *ex-ante* real rate differential between any pair of states is expressible as a function of the risk differential in the two states. Finally, we compare the general equilibrium results to the partial equilibrium results.

Preferences, Technologies and Resource Constraints

The infinitely lived representative household wishes to maximize total discounted expected utility defined over consumption and leisure,

$$\sum_{j=0}^{\infty} \delta^j E_t U(C_{t+j}, H_{t+j}\ s_{t+j}) \tag{12}$$

where $\delta (0 < \delta < 1)$ is the household's discount factor, E_t is mathematical expectation conditional on the information set Φ_t, C is consumption, $H(0 < \mathrm{H} < 1)$ is leisure, $L = 1 - H$ is labour and s is an independently and identically distributed random shock. The household's instantaneous utility function $U(\cdot)$ is assumed to be concave in consumption and leisure.

The economic union consists of n states each producing a single commodity that can be either consumed or added to productive capital. The production function of each state is defined over inputs capital and labour,

$$y_{it} = f^i(k_{it}, \ell_{it}, s_{it}), \quad i = 1, \ldots n \tag{13}$$

where s_{it} is a state-specific random shock and $f^i(\cdot)$ is linearly homogeneous in the factor inputs of which labour is variable and capital is predetermined.

The economic union's resource constraint limit aggregate current consumption C_t and investment, I_t, to aggregate current production

$$Y_t = C_t + I_t \tag{14}$$

where

$$Y_t = \sum_{i=1}^{n} y_{it} \tag{15}$$

$$I_t = K_{t+1} - K_t \tag{16}$$

$$K_{t+1} = \sum_{i=1}^{n} k_{it+1} \tag{17}$$

and also

$$L_t = \sum_{i=1}^{n} \ell_{it}. \tag{18}$$

The Central Planning Solution

The central planner chooses a sequence of capital and labour $\{k_{it+1+j}, \ell_{it+j}\}$ to maximize the household's expected utility (12) subject to the resource constraints (14) to (18). Assuming that a solution exists, it is a Pareto-optimal competitive equilibrium characterized by the following necessary conditions (Euler equations) with respect to labour and capital respectively,

$$f^i_{\ell t} = U_{Ht} / U_{ct} \equiv w_t, \quad i = 1, \ldots, n \tag{19}$$

and

$$U_{ct} = \beta E_t[U_{ct+1}(f^i_{kt+1} + 1)], \quad i = 1,\ldots,n. \tag{20}$$

where f^i_ℓ is the marginal product of labour and U_x denotes the partial derivative of $U(\cdot)$ with respect to x. The optimality conditions (19) and (20) are easy to interpret. The relation (19) states that in the optimal solution labour is allocated so that its marginal product in each state equals the 'shadow' real wage w_t. Since w_t is the same in all states, (19) is equivalent to free labour mobility among states, a condition which is necessary for the existence of an economic union.

The Euler equation for capital says that, at a maximum, capital is allocated to each state so that the marginal utility of a unit of current consumption forgone equals the expected discounted utility of the return from investing that unit of the consumption good. Notice that capital is an asset that can be used to transfer consumption between time periods and to diversify risk across different states. It is also a risky asset, since capital accumulation adds to the next period's production and so capital must be chosen before the realization of the random shock.

Ex-Ante Real Rate Differential

Let

$$r^i_{t+1} \equiv 1 + f^i_{kt+1} \tag{21}$$

be the gross real rate of return to capital in the ith state of the economic union, and let

$$q_{t+1} \equiv \beta U_{ct+1} / U_{ct} \tag{22}$$

denote the representative household's intertemporal marginal rate of substitution. Then, since U_{ct} is an element of the information set Φ_t, (20) can be written more compactly as

$$E_t(q_{t+1} r^i_{t+1}) = 1. \tag{23}$$

Further, using the fact that for any two random variables x and y: $E(xy) = E(x)E(y) + \mathrm{Cov}(x, y)$, (23) can be rewritten as

$$E_t(r^i_{t+1}) = r^f_{t+1}[1 - \mathrm{Cov}_t(q_{t+1}, r^i_{t+1})] \tag{24}$$

in which

$$r_{t+1}^{f} \equiv 1 / E_t(q_{t+1}) \tag{25}$$

is the risk-free rate that obtains directly from (23) under the assumption that capital is a riskless asset. Equation (24) states that the expected return to capital in the ith state only deviates from the risk-free rate to the extent of the covariance of that return and q_{t+1}. Comparing (24) with the case of risk neutrality, it is clear that the risk premium is a function of the covariance term.

Define capital's 'beta' in state i as

$$\beta_{t+1}^{i} \equiv \text{Cov}_t(q_{t+1}, r_{t+1}^{i}), \quad i = 1,\ldots,n. \tag{26}$$

Substituting (26) in (24), using it twice for two states i and j, $i \neq j$, and taking the difference gives

$$E(r_{t+1}^{i}) - E(r_{t+1}^{j}) = r_{t+1}^{f}\,(\beta_{t+1}^{j} - \beta_{t+1}^{i}). \tag{27}$$

This equation makes clear that the *ex-ante* real rate differential between any pair of states i and j is proportional to the difference of the riskiness of capital in the two states. Only if $\beta^i = \beta^j$ does *ex-ante* real rate equality obtain across states.

Notice also that equation (24) indicates two potential sources of variation in the *ex-ante* real rate differential: movements in the conditional covariance and movements in the risk-free rate of return. This information may be useful in empirical studies of the time-series properties of the real rate differential.

Comparison with Partial Equilibrium Models

The analysis in this chapter involves a CCAPM in a general equilibrium framework. In general equilibrium, output, consumption, investment and asset payoffs (i.e. dividends or profits) are interdependent endogenous variables that respond jointly to exogenous shocks. For instance, a mean-preserving spread in the distribution of a random shock, s_i, increases the risk of capital and implies a different allocation of resources in the economic union. This, in turn, implies a new distribution of asset payoffs.

By contrast, partial equilibrium CCAPMs value assets assuming an exogenous distribution of asset payoffs (i.e. dividends) (see Sargent 1987, ch. 3). A mean-preserving spread in the dividend process increases an asset's risk but, by definition, it does not alter the expected value of dividends. Clearly, the assumption of exogenous distribution of dividends is not tenable from a general equilibrium point of view.

As a related point, a general equilibrium view may help in empirical investigations of CCAPMs. In particular, since q_{t+1} and r_{t+1} are interdependent endogenous variables, an applied econometrician may search for conditioning variables that improve the explanatory power of CCAPMs. In the present context, this means that business cycle variables (recessions or expansions) or exogenous events, such as the recent removal of exchange controls in Greece, may help explain the time-series properties of real rate differentials in the European Union.

CONCLUSION

In this chapter we reviewed the main evidence relating to real interest rate equality across countries. Overall, the balance of the empirical evidence rejects the null hypothesis of international real rate parity, thereby leaving open the possibility that monetary policy in a country can affect the real rate and therefore economic fluctuations.

In search of an explanation for the real rate differential, we employed a general equilibrium capital asset pricing model in the context of an economic union with fully integrated economic policies. Our results indicate that the real rate differential is related to differences in the risk of capital across different member states in the economic union. Also, the general equilibrium results point to a plausible set of variables that may help explain real rate differentials across countries. An econometric investigation of this issue is an interesting topic for future research.

REFERENCES

Bilson, J.F.O. (1978), 'Rational Expectations and the Exchange Rate', in J.A. Frenkel and H.G. Johnson (eds), *The Economics of Exchange Rates: Selected Studies*, Reading, Mass.: Addison-Wesley.

Breeden, D. (1979), 'An Intertemporal Asset Pricing Model with Stochastic Consumption and Investment Opportunities', *Journal of Financial Economics*, 265–96.

Buiter, W.H. and M. Miller (1982), 'Real Exchange Rate Overshooting and the Output Cost of Bringing Down Inflation', *European Economic Review*, **18** (1), 85–123.

Craine, R. (1989), 'Risky Business: The Allocation of Capital', *Journal of Monetary Economics*, **23**, 201–18.

Cumby, R.E. and F.S. Mishkin (1986), 'The International Linkages of Real Interest Rates: The European–U.S. Connection', *Journal of International Money and Finance*, **5** (1), 5–23.

Cumby, R.E. and M. Obstfeld (1984), 'International Interest-Rate and Price-Level Linkages under Flexible Exchange Rates: A Review of Recent Evidence', in J.F.O.

Bilson and R. Marston (eds), *Exchange Rates: Theory and Practice*, Chicago: University of Chicago Press for the NBER.
Dornbusch, R. (1976), 'Expectations and Exchange Rate Dynamics', *Journal of Political Economy*, **84** (December), 1161–76.
Ethier, W.J. (1988), *Modern International Economics*, 2nd edn, New York: Norton.
Frankel, J.A. (1979), 'On the Mark: A Theory of Flating Exchange Rates Based on Real Interest Differentials', *American Economic Review*, **69** (September), 610–22.
Frankel, J. and Alan T. MacArthur (1988), 'Political vs. Currency Premia in International Real Interest Rate Differentials: A Study of Forward Rates for 24 Countries', *European Economic* Review, **32** (June), 1083–114.
Frenkel, J.A. (1976), 'A Monetary Approach to the Exchange Rate: Doctrinal Aspects and Empirical Evidence', *Scandinavian Journal of Economics*, **78** (May), 200–24.
Frenkel, J.A. and Richard Levich (1977), 'Transactions Costs and Interest Arbitrage: Tranquil vs. Turbulent Periods', *Journal of Political Economy*, **85** (December), 1209–26.
Frenkel, J.A. and Richard Levich (1981), 'Covered Interest Arbitrage in the 1970's', *Economics Letters*, **8** (3), 267–74.
Hansen, L.P. and R.J. Hodrick (1983), 'Risk Averse Speculation in the Forward Foreign Exchange Market: An Econometric Analysis of Linear Models', in J.A. Frenkel (ed.), *Exchange Rates and International Macroeconomics*, Chicago: University of Chicago Press.
Hodrick, R.J. (1981), 'Intertemporal Asset Pricing with Time-Varying Risk Premia', *Journal of International Economics*, **11**, 573–87.
Hodrick, R. (1987), 'The Empirical Evidence of the Efficiency of Forward and Futures Foreign Exchange Markets', New York: Harwood Academic Publishers.
Johnson, D.R. (1992), 'International Interest Rate Linkages and the Exchange Rate Regime', *Journal of International Money and Finance*, **11**, 340–65.
Lucas, R.E. Jr (1978), 'Asset Prices in an Exchange Economy', *Econometrica*, **46**, 1429–45.
Lucas, R.E. Jr (1982), 'Interest Rates and Currency Prices in a Two-Country World', *Journal of Monetary Economics*, **10**, 335–60.
Mark, N.C. (1985), 'Some Evidence on the International Inequality of Real Interest Rates', *Journal of International Money and Finance*, **4** (June), 189–208.
Merrick, John J. and Anthony Saunders (1986), 'International Expected Real Interest Rates: New Tests of the Parity Hypothesis and U.S. Fiscal Policy Effects', *Journal of Monetary Economics*, **18**, 313–22.
Mishkin, F.S. (1984a), 'The Real Interest Rate: A Multicountry Empirical Study', *Canadian Journal of Economics*, **17** (May), 283–311.
Mishkin, F.S. (1984b), 'Are Real Interest Rates Equal Across Countries: An Empirical Investigation of International Parity Conditions', *Journal of Finance*, **39** (December), 1345–57.
Sargent, T.J. (1987), *Dynamic Macroeconomic Theory*, Cambridge, Mass.: Harvard University Press.
Solnik, B. (1973), *European Capital Markets: Toward a General Theory of International Investment*, Lexington, Mass.: Lexington Books.
Stulz, R. (1981), 'A Model of International Asset Pricing', *Journal of Financial Economics*, **9** (December), 383–406.

10. Industry- versus nation-specific shocks in the EU: evidence from industry data

Bernd Kempa*

INTRODUCTION

The degree of internal real exchange rate variability within the borders of a prospective common currency area can be regarded as the single most important measure of the desirability of monetary unification (Vaubel 1978). At the time of writing, the degree of real exchange rate variability within the European Union (EU) appears to be too high to recommend the implementation of the proposed European economic and monetary union (EMU) (Eichengreen 1990, 1992; von Hagen and Neumann 1992; De Grauwe and Vanhaverbeke 1993).

The incidence of real shocks within the EU is a crucial factor in determining the variability of the real exchange rate. It is useful to distinguish between two types of real shocks: symmetric shocks and asymmetric shocks. Whereas symmetric shocks leave relative prices between regions (countries) or industries within a currency union unchanged, asymmetric shocks affect these relative prices and call for an adjustment of the national real exchange rates. Hence the incidence of asymmetric shocks within the EU is an important piece of information in determining the economic desirability of EMU. The first study to measure the magnitude of asymmetric shocks within the EU is Cohen and Wyplosz (1989). They compare the behaviour of GDP, the GDP deflator, real wages and current account balances for German and French data by transforming all variables into sums and differences, interpreting sums as symmetric shocks and differences as asymmetric shocks. Cohen and Wyplosz find mostly symmetric behaviour for these two countries. Weber (1990) applies the same approach to all original member countries of the exchange rate mechanism (ERM)[1] and finds that rates of inflation, as well as domestic demand and supply shocks, display symmetric behaviour. Real wages and employment, on the other hand, tend to be dominated by asymmetric shocks.

*This chapter was written while the author was a PhD student at the University of Toronto. Gordon Anderson, John Floyd, Allan Hynes, Peter Pauly and Birgitta Weitz provided helpful comments and suggestions.

Bayoumi and Eichengreen (1993) use a VAR decomposition to extract information on underlying demand and supply disturbances for 11 EU member nations and four US regions. They find that the underlying shocks are significantly more idiosyncratic across EU countries than across US regions. Moreover, they identify a core of EU countries consisting of Belgium, Denmark, France, Germany, Luxembourg and the Netherlands, which is characterized by relatively small and mainly symmetric supply shocks. The remaining EU countries form an 'EU periphery' which exhibits bigger and more asymmetric shocks. Performing a principal components analysis on output innovations in EU countries, Caporale (1993) is able to confirm Bayoumi and Eichengreen's findings that asymmetric shocks account for a sizeable percentage of GDP fluctuations in the EU. However, he cannot confirm the existence of an EU 'core' and 'periphery'.

All the above papers provide insights into the magnitude of asymmetric shocks currently observed at the EU level. Due to their aggregate nature, however, they cannot identify the sources of these disturbances. This chapter investigates the incidence of asymmetric shocks at the industry level by applying an analysis of variance (ANOVA) procedure to sectoral output fluctuations across six EU countries.[2] The focus is twofold: to determine the relative importance of symmetric versus asymmetric shocks within the EU; and to analyse the different sources of asymmetric shocks. The results may shed additional light on the question whether or not the countries of the EU or a subset thereof are ready for monetary unification.

The next section discusses a typology of various shocks and their effects on the real exchange rate, after which the data set is described. Then a statistical model is developed, which can be used to disaggregate the total variability in the data into its component parts. The results of the empirical analysis follow. A final section summarizes the findings.

A TYPOLOGY OF SHOCKS

This section provides an overview of the different categories of shocks analysed in the chapter. Shocks may be classified with respect to their source into shocks originating at the industry level and shocks originating at the national level. Moreover, shocks must be distinguished with regard to their effect on the real exchange rate into symmetric and asymmetric shocks. The above categorization results in four different types of shocks:

1. *Symmetric shocks at the national level (global shocks).* These include coordinated government policies or technology and demand shocks that affect all industries in all member countries symmetrically.

2. *Symmetric shocks at the industry level (sectoral shocks).* This category consists of technology shocks, demand shocks or input price shocks that affect a subset of industries symmetrically across all countries.
3. *Asymmetric shocks at the national level (national shocks).* These shocks come in the form of discretionary fiscal and monetary policies or technology and demand shocks with differential impacts on member countries.
4. *Asymmetric shocks at the industry level (idiosyncratic shocks).* These include asymmetric technology or demand shocks originating in one or more industries and symmetric industry-specific shocks with differential impacts across member countries.

By definition, symmetric shocks at both the national and the industry levels do not affect relative prices and are therefore neutral with respect to the real exchange rates among the member countries of the union. Asymmetric shocks, on the contrary, affect both relative prices and real exchange rates and thus constitute the main cost of monetary unification.

THE DATA

Data come from the OECD International Sectoral Databank, which currently contains annual data for seven EU countries across approximately thirty industries covering the period 1970–90. Data are given in 1985 constant local currency prices. The largest data set that could be constructed from this databank consists of 14 industries[3] across six EU countries (Belgium, Denmark, France, Germany, the UK and Italy) and 20 time periods (1971–90), resulting in a total of 1680 observations in the panel. Panel observations are ordered first by industry, then by country, and finally by time. In the remainder of the chapter, industries are denoted by i (i = 1,…,I), countries are referred to as n (n = 1,…,N), and time periods are denoted by t (t = 1,…,T).

THE STATISTICAL MODEL

This section presents a statistical model which separates the total variation in the growth rates of industrial output into components corresponding to the typology of shocks discussed earlier. The following regression is used:

$$\mathbf{Y} = D_{IN}\,\mathbf{b_1} + D_T\,\mathbf{b_2} + D_{IT}\,\mathbf{b_3} + D_{NT}\,\mathbf{b_4} + \mathbf{e} \qquad (1)$$

where **y** is a vector containing all INT observations in the panel with typical element Y_{int}, capturing the change in the log of industrial output of industry *i* in country *n* at time *t*. D_{IN}, D_T, D_{IT} and D_{NT} are matrices of dummy variables with dimensions INTxIN, INTxT, INTxIT and INTxNT, respectively; $\mathbf{b}_i$, i = {1,...,4}, are vectors of coefficients estimating the share of total variability that can be ascribed to each set of dummy variables, and **e** is a vector of residuals, assumed to be i.i.d., with typical element e_{int}.

The right-hand side of regression (1) is made up of different sets of dummy variables, where each set is associated with the identification of one particular type of shock. $D_{IN}\mathbf{b}_1$ is the constant term of the regression and measures the variability across the IN different time-averaged growth rates of **y**. Each of these time-averaged growth rates, denoted by y_{in}, is obtained by summing the original observations in the panel over all time periods:

$$y_{in} = \frac{1}{t}\sum_t y_{int} \text{ for all } i\ (i = 1,\ldots,I) \text{ and } n\ (n = 1,\ldots,N) \qquad (2)$$

The matrix D_T consists of T different dummy variables, one for each time period *t* (*t* = 1,...,T). $D_T\mathbf{b}_2$ identifies the time component in the data set that is common to observations across all industries and all countries. The term measures that part of the total variation in **y** which is neither industry- nor country-specific, and is thus associated with global EU-wide shocks. The fraction of the total variance captured by the term $D_T\mathbf{b}_2$ is obtained by first marginalizing out the various industries and countries in the panel and then measuring the variation over the T marginal components

$$y_t = \frac{1}{in}\sum_i \sum_n y_{int} \text{ for all } t\ (t = 1,\ldots,T) \qquad (3)$$

D_{IT} contains a total of IT dummy variables, one for every combination of time period *t* (*t* = 1,...,T) and industry *i* (*i* = 1,...,I). $D_{IT}\mathbf{b}_3$ captures the variation of the dependent variable that is due to the interaction of industry and time effects while ignoring variation arising at the national level, thus measuring sectoral shocks. The pertaining marginal components are given by

$$y_{it} = \frac{1}{n}\sum_n y_{int} \text{ for all } i\ (i = 1,\ldots,I) \text{ and } t\ (t = 1,\ldots,T) \qquad (4)$$

$D_{NT}\mathbf{b}_4$ captures national shocks over time while ignoring differences across industries. The typical marginal component is given by

$$y_{nt} = \frac{1}{i}\sum_i y_{int} \text{ for all } n\ (n = 1,\ldots,N) \text{ and } t\ (t = 1,\ldots,T) \qquad (5)$$

Finally, the residual vector **e** consists of idiosyncratic shocks which are unique to a particular industry i in a specific nation n. Therefore, e measures asymmetric shocks at the industry level.

By construction, the estimated $\hat{\mathbf{y}}$ captures all possible sources of variation in **y** except for idiosyncratic disturbances picked up by the residual $\hat{\mathbf{e}}$. From the total sum of squares (SSQ) of the regression, the share associated with the intercept is subtracted to arrive at a corrected SSQ, reflecting only those components of variation which are functions of time. After subtracting the variation of the intercept, the R^2 of the regression (1) can be interpreted as the share of total variation which is not accounted for by idiosyncratic shocks. Conversely, $1–R^2$ is the share of idiosyncratic disturbances in the total variation of industry production.

In order to eliminate perfect collinearity in the regression, some of the dummy variables have to be set equal to zero. This can be done by choosing one time period t^* as a base period, one country n^* as a reference country and one industry i^* as a reference industry. The estimated coefficients of all other industries, nations and time periods are then expressed relative to the ones chosen to be zero. The particular choice of reference is of no consequence to the empirical analysis in the next section.

Since real shocks cannot be observed directly, an endogenous variable must be used as a proxy. The present chapter reports estimates of regression (1) for the growth rate of industrial output. Since both supply and demand disturbances have a direct impact on output, this proxy should closely mirror the actual variability of the underlying exogenous shocks.[4]

REGRESSION RESULTS

Table 10.1 summarizes the results.[5] All the F-statistics and regression coefficients turn out to be highly significant. Part (a) of the table reports the analysis of variance (ANOVA) table for output variability for the time period 1971–90. We find that 40.77 per cent of the corrected output variability is due to symmetric shocks while the remaining 59.23 per cent can be attributed to asymmetric shocks. A total of 9.18 per cent are asymmetric shocks arising at the national level while 50.05 per cent are industry-specific (idiosyncratic) shocks. As discussed earlier, asymmetric shocks at the national level are generally due to discretionary monetary and fiscal policies. The part of this variability which is due to discretionary policies in the EU member countries is likely to be reduced with the implementation of EMU. Idiosyncratic shocks,

Table 10.1 Analysis of variance for annual quantity data

Regressor		SSQ	F	p	%*
(a) 1971–90, 1680 obs., $R^2 = 0.5413$, F: 3.28, p: 0.0001 Total SSQ: 6.359391, Corrected SSQ** : 5.827647					
Intercept	$(D_{IN}\hat{\mathbf{b}}_1)$	0.531744	2.71	0.0001	–
Symmetric national shock	$(D_T\hat{\mathbf{b}}_2)$	1.003718	22.37	0.0001	17.22
Symmetric industry shock	$(D_{IT}\hat{\mathbf{b}}_3)$	1.372473	2.35	0.0001	23.55
Asymmetric national shock	$(D_{NT}\hat{\mathbf{b}}_4)$	0.534945	2.38	0.0001	9.18
Asymmetric industry shock	$(\hat{\mathbf{e}})$	2.916511	–	–	50.05
(b) 1971–80, 840 obs., $R^2 = 0.5955$, F: 3.39, p: 0.0001 Total SSQ: 3.966902, Corrected SSQ**: 3.422363					
Intercept	$(D_{IN}\hat{\mathbf{b}}_1)$	0.544538	2.39	0.0001	–
Symmetric national shock	$(D_T\hat{\mathbf{b}}_2)$	0.761508	30.85	0.0001	22.25
Symmetric industry shock	$(D_{IT}\hat{\mathbf{b}}_3)$	0.785830	2.45	0.0001	22.96
Asymmetric national shock	$(D_{NT}\hat{\mathbf{b}}_4)$	0.270331	2.19	0.0001	7.90
Asymmetric industry shock	$(\hat{\mathbf{e}})$	1.604695	–	–	46.89
(c) 1981–90, 840 obs., $R^2 = 0.5183$, F: 2.48, p: 0.0001 Total SSQ: 2.363989, Corrected SSQ**: 2.074611					
Intercept	$(D_{IN}\hat{\mathbf{b}}_1)$	0.289378	1.79	0.0001	–
Symmetric national shock	$(D_T\hat{\mathbf{b}}_2)$	0.213711	12.20	0.0001	10.30
Symmetric industry shock	$(D_{IT}\hat{\mathbf{b}}_3)$	0.519582	2.28	0.0001	25.05
Asymmetric national shock	$(D_{NT}\hat{\mathbf{b}}_4)$	0.202709	2.31	0.0001	9.77
Asymmetric industry shock	$(\hat{\mathbf{e}})$	1.138608	–	–	54.88

Notes:
* percentage share of corrected sum of squares.
** Total sum of squares minus sum of squares of the intercept.

on the other hand, cannot be expected to disappear with monetary unification, yet these shocks constitute roughly 50 per cent of the total real exchange rate variability within the six EU countries in the sample.

In order to determine whether idiosyncratic shocks had a tendency to increase or decrease over time, parts (b) and (c) of Table 10.1 break down the data set into two time periods, the first ranging from 1971 to 1980 and the second ranging from 1981 to 1990.[6]

Comparing parts (b) and (c), it can be seen that the sum of squares of both symmetric and asymmetric shocks is about 40 per cent lower in the 1980s than in the 1970s. However, the reduction in overall output variability is largely due to a decline in symmetric disturbances. While symmetric variability as a share of overall variability fell from 45.21 per cent in the 1970s to 35.35 per cent in the 1980s, asymmetric shocks at the national level increased

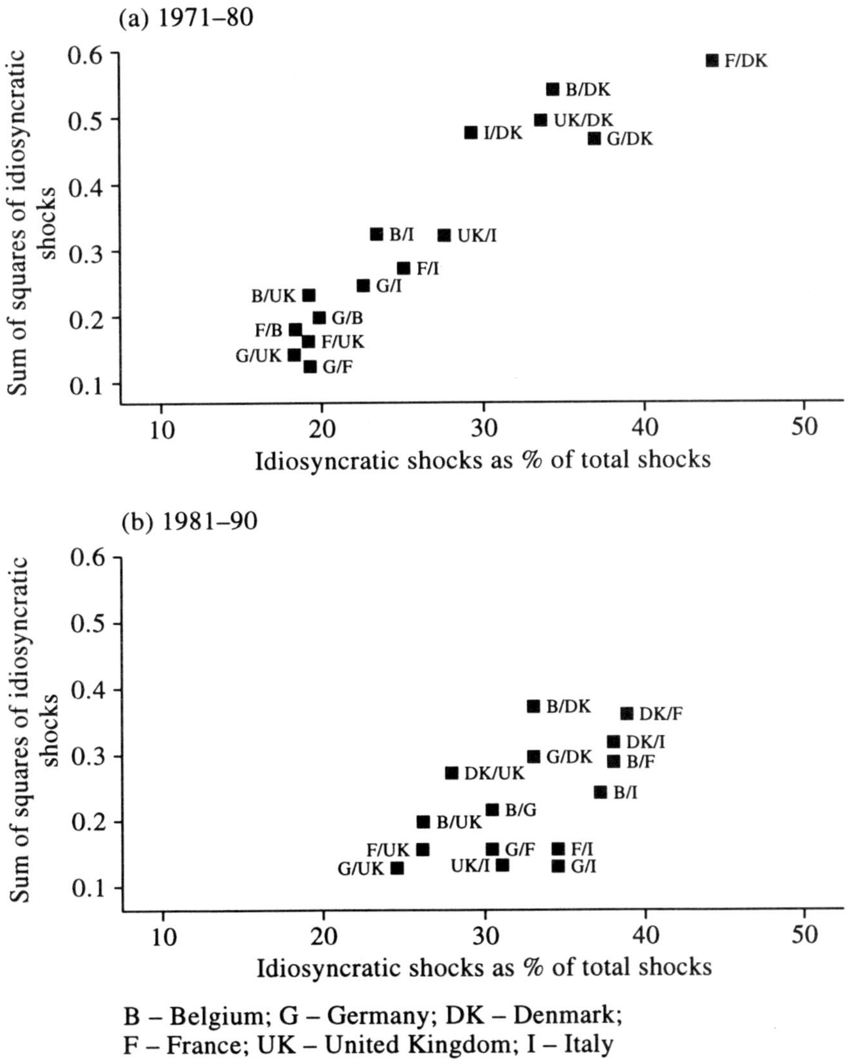

Figure 10.1 Industry-specific idiosyncratic shocks for pairs of countries

from 7.90 per cent in the 1970s to 9.77 per cent in the 1980s and idiosyncratic shocks increased from 46.89 per cent to 54.88 per cent. Although idiosyncratic shocks were the dominant source of output variability in the 1980s, their total variability (sum of squares of $D_{NT}\hat{\mathbf{b}}_4$ plus the residual) decreased by roughly 30 per cent when compared to their 1970s level.

After having discussed the breakdown of total variability for the whole sample, we now turn to the question whether our data can identify a core–periphery distinction with respect to the incidence of asymmetric shocks in the EU. To test for the presence of a core, regression (1) is run separately for all pairs of countries that could be constructed from the six countries in the sample. The absolute and relative levels of idiosyncratic shocks obtained from these 15 regressions were summarized in Table 10.1.

Figure 10.1(a) displays an identifiable core–periphery distinction. Belgium, France, Germany and the UK are characterized by the mutually lowest degrees of asymmetric shocks, whereas country combinations involving Denmark or Italy display stronger asymmetries. Figure 10.1(b) shows that for the 1980s, the spread between the highest and lowest observation is reduced for all groups of countries, eliminating the core–periphery distinction. Mutual variability for Belgium, France and Germany increases, whereas variability for groups of countries involving Denmark, the UK or Italy decreases.

CONCLUSION

This chapter has investigated the sources of real exchange rate variability within the European Union. An analysis of variance (ANOVA) approach was used to decompose annual growth rates of industrial output for 14 industries across six EU countries into components that are specific to industries but common to nations, components that are specific to nations but common to industries, and idiosyncratic components.

For the time period 1971–90, roughly half of the total variability is found to be due to asymmetric disturbances. Total variability declines in the 1980s as compared to 1970 levels. However, the decline in total variability is largely due to a decrease in symmetric shocks, whereas the share of idiosyncratic shocks increases.

For the period 1971–80, the chapter identifies a core of countries consisting of Belgium, France, Germany and the UK which is characterized by relatively low degrees of idiosyncratic variability, while a periphery consisting of Italy and Denmark shows relatively higher degrees of idiosyncratic variability. The distinction becomes less clear-cut for the period 1981–90, as idiosyncratic variability increases for the core countries and decreases for the periphery. However, this result does not necessarily reflect a convergence of the EU countries in the sample. Whereas the 1970s witnessed enormous real disturbances in the form of the two oil price shocks, those disturbances were absent in the 1980s. It is left to future research to ascertain the impacts of the 'shock' of German unification on the incidence of asymmetric shocks in the EU.

Although asymmetric shocks are lower in the 1980s for the entire sample, Belgium, France and Germany, the countries generally considered to be the most likely to establish a successful monetary union, experienced an increase in idiosyncratic variability.

Our results suggest that the degree of real exchange rate variability currently observed at the EU level cannot be expected to be significantly reduced after monetary unification. Moreover, we are unable to identify a core–periphery distinction among the countries in the sample. Our analysis suggests that the implementation of EMU at the present time cannot be endorsed on the basis of the real exchange rate criterion either for the EU as a whole or for any group of core countries.

NOTES

1. The original members were Belgium, Denmark, France, Germany, Ireland, Italy and the Netherlands.
2. Stockman (1988) uses a similar approach to investigate different issues.
3. Data on the following industries were used: agriculture; food, beverages and tobacco; textiles; paper, printing and publishing; chemicals; non-metallic mineral products; basic metal products; machinery and equipment; other manufactured products; electricity, gas and water; construction; wholesale trade, retail trade, restaurants and hotels; transport, storage and communication; community, social and personnel services.
4. Regression (1) has also been estimated for the rate of change of industry *prices*. This alternative proxy provides a direct measure of the relative price effects of the underlying shocks. The regression yielded similar results to the ones presented in the chapter and is not reported here.
5. Tests for serial correlation of the residuals did not turn out to be statistically significant.
6. We restrict the analysis to these two time periods in order to maintain a sufficiently large number of degrees of freedom.
7. Regressions have also been run for all groups of three, four and five countries. However, these regressions are not reported since the first yielded results similar to the ones reported in Table 10.1, while the latter two necessarily mix both core and periphery countries and thus cannot discriminate between them. Detailed results of all regressions can be obtained from the author on request.

REFERENCES

Bayoumi, T. and B. Eichengreen (1993), 'Shocking aspects of monetary unification', in F. Torres and F. Giavazzi (eds), *Adjustment and growth in the European monetary system*, Cambridge, UK: Cambridge University Press, pp. 193–229.

Caporale, G.M. (1993), 'Is Europe an optimum currency area? Symmetric versus asymmetric shocks in the EC', *National Institute Economic Review*, **144**, 95–103.

Cohen, D. and C. Wyplosz (1989), 'The European monetary union: An agnostic evaluation', in R.C. Bryant, D.A. Currie, J.A. Frenkel, P.R. Masson and R. Portes (eds), *Macroeconomic Policies in an interdependent world*, Washington, DC: International Monetary Fund, pp. 311–37.

De Grauwe, P. and W. Vanhaverbeke (1993), 'Is Europe an optimum currency area?: Evidence from regional data', in P.R. Masson and M.P. Taylor (eds), *Policy issues in the operation of currency unions*, Cambridge, UK: Cambridge University Press, pp. 111–29.

Eichengreen, B. (1990), 'One money for Europe? Lessons from the U.S. currency and customs union', *Economic Policy*, **10**, 117–87.

Eichengreen, B. (1992), 'Is Europe an optimum currency area?' in S. Borner and H. Grubel (eds), *The European Community after 1992: Perspectives from the outside*, Basingstoke: Macmillan, pp. 138–61.

Stockman, A.C. (1988), 'Sectoral and national aggregate disturbances to industrial output in seven European countries', *Journal of Monetary Economics*, **21**, 387–409.

Vaubel, R. (1978), 'Real exchange rate changes in the European community. A new approach to the determination of optimum currency areas', *Journal of International Economics*, **8**, 319–39.

Von Hagen, J. and M.J.M. Neumann (1992), 'Real exchange rates within and between currency areas: How far away is EMU?', CEPR Discussion Paper no. 660.

Weber, A.A. (1990), 'Asymmetries and adjustment problems: Some empirical evidence', in *European Economy – The Economics of EMU*, special issue.

PART III

Social Policy Reform and Social Union

11. Economic integration and social policy reform

Christos C. Paraskevopoulos

INTRODUCTION

Nations are contemplating taking part in various integration schemes for a purpose. They anticipate some discernible improvements in the well-being of their citizens – that is, a rise in their living standards – resulting from a closer economic integration. However, such an improvement in the standard of living, as measured by the level and growth of real income per person, has been perceived to be rather ambivalent, to say the least.

With the onset of the 1990s, both the developed and less developed nations are having to come to grips with the new trends and realities of a highly integrated global or regional trading environment. They must face issues and problems of economic adjustment to the changing forces of demography, the environment, social and political transformation, technological advances and trade. The long postwar boom, that enabled governments to provide for ever-expanding public services, came to an end in the 1970s, mainly due to a combination of demographic changes and sluggish growth. The persistence, however, of high unemployment rates, especially in the European Union (EU), and slow productivity growth, coupled with mounting deficits (fiscal and current account/trade), have placed an inordinate strain on the maintenance of social programmes and the defence of declining living standards for vast segments of the world's population. Countries are now groping to find ways to protect the living standards of, and provide adequate protection for, their citizens.

While the processes and implications of recent developments are not yet fully understood, they do point, nevertheless, to the necessity of building a new consensus around the substantive content of the successful economic policy reforms that are needed for an economy to enter the modern era. To a large extent such a consensus exists in some areas, such as fiscal discipline, microeconomic liberalization and participation in the global economy, but there is much less consensus on other issues, including social policy reform, the appropriate exchange rate regime and the political conditions necessary to sustain meaningful economic reform.[1]

Given the above general considerations for both developed and less developed countries, this chapter will focus on the impact of a closer economic integration and the call for social policy reform on both social protection and living standards by examining and evaluating the European and the North American experience. The experience and effectiveness, therefore, of these two polar systems (models), namely, the European and the American, chiefly the US system, will be analysed in the context of social policy reform.

Accordingly, we proceed with a brief comparison of the European and American models: the real per capita income as a measure of standards of living, and its sources of change; the labour productivity growth, the key factor for improving living standards; social policy reform and trade flows in a global and regional economy; and the impact of cuts in services on cost-shifting, hidden taxation, and regional and social cohesion.

THE EUROPEAN AND AMERICAN MODELS COMPARED

Countries in the European model have defended their high standards of living by placing greater reliance on *equity* (redistribution) considerations (mainly government intervention through rather comprehensive social protection policies and income redistribution schemes) and to a lesser extent on *market efficiency*. At the other extreme, the American model with its chief – perhaps only – representative the US, is placing greater reliance on *market efficiency* and less on *equity* considerations, by advocating minimum government intervention in defending living standards and providing social protection.

The outcome of the two approaches may have been persistently high unemployment rates[2] now averaging 12 per cent, throughout the European Union, and in some other countries, like Canada, with a strong social protection system in place. In contrast, in the US, although lower unemployment rates – now 6 per cent – are observed, the number of 'working poor' – those whose income is below the poverty line – rose to around 15 per cent of the workforce, as most of the newly created jobs are low-skill jobs paying low wages. It is worth noting that the Organization for Economic Cooperation and Development (OECD), in its most recent report[3] (1994), identified the most politically explosive question facing many Western European governments as: how to reduce 'structural' unemployment without eroding living standards and slashing welfare and other social benefits? Thus, urgent calls for social policy reform dominate the socioeconomic and political agenda.

DESCRIPTION

This is an ex-library book and may have the usual library/used-book markings inside.This book has hardback covers. In good all round condition. No dust jacket.

ORDER NUMBER

PO NYAATP08

BOOK NUMBER

5586676

BAY NUMBER

2584-5

AUTHOR	Grinspun, R
TITLE	Economic Integration and Public Policy in the European Union

REAL PER CAPITA INCOME AND ITS DETERMINANTS

In this study we suggest using the level and rate of growth of real income per person in order to: facilitate the identification of the sources of improvement in our standards of living; help illustrate the available choices to management and policy-makers; and assist in evaluating the effectiveness of social protection programmes and social policy reform proposals, both in terms of equity and market efficiency.

Despite its shortcomings, real per capita income is the universally accepted standard for measuring the living standards between nations. Real per capita income (GNP/P) is a measure of average performance (productivity) of a nation. It is a ratio of real gross national product (GNP) and population (P). The disparity in income per person among regions and social groups is generally accepted as the key indicator of cohesion.

Per capita income will rise if the rate of growth of GNP outpaces that of population. In the last 25 years, however, the growth in real income has dramatically declined. This suggests that the growth in GNP did not keep pace with population increases. To assess how to reverse that trend or avert an erosion in the standards of living we decompose the determinants of per capita income into the components (factors) indicated in the following:

$$(GNP/P) = (GNP/GDP)\,(LE)\,(E/P)\,(GDP/L)\ldots \qquad (1)$$

where:

GNP = real gross national product
P = population
GDP = real gross domestic product
L = person hours worked
E = employment

Hence equation (1), in an interactive[4] manner, identifies the sources of improvement in the standards of living. Therefore, from equation (1) changes in real per capita income (GNP/P) depend – other things being equal – on changes in the foreign indebtedness and international competitiveness (GNP/GDP); average hours worked per employee (LE); the employment participation rate (E/P); and labour productivity (GDP/L – output per hour).

Per capita improvements, however, in the standards of living can be attained in at least four ways:

1. *International competitiveness* – increased international competitiveness through improvements in the 'terms of trade' and reduction in foreign

indebtedness (GNP/GDP). In the short to medium term, an improvement in international competitiveness could increase exports and decrease imports, improve the trade balance, and increase output, employment and real wages. The terms of trade, in the long run, will have a positive effect on rate of growth of living standards through its influence on real GDP.

2. *Hours worked per employee* – increased amount of work being done (L/E) by people working longer hours: lengthen the work week and work year; extend part-time work to full-time; and lower the total weeks of unemployment.
3. *Employment participation* – increased amount of work being done by more people working (E/P) by increasing labour force participation (reverse early retirement for men, increase women's participation, and increase variety of work arrangements and schedules); raising the level of migration; improving labour market functioning; and linking increased support to work.
4. *Labour productivity* – increased levels of labour productivity (GDP/L – output per worker hour) by increases in: capital investment;[5] human resource investment (training, education); R&D, technological advance; and the quality of resource management.

The discussion so far suggests that the goal of improving living standards (GNP/P) is inextricably linked to labour productivity growth (GDP/L) as the key factor. Productivity growth is by far the most important factor determining the growth in real wages. To capture its impact, productivity studies have employed methods for identifying and measuring economic growth and technical progress through the use of a non-parametric framework based on Solow's (1957) general index of disembodied technological change or through more advanced parametric studies, such as the translog model. Both the parametric and non-parametric studies, however, are dealing almost exclusively with the manufacturing sector and not the service sector, due to the difficulty of measuring services, although services comprise almost two-thirds of the economy.

In the long run the terms of trade and labor productivity are expected to have a positive effect on real per capital income.

SOCIAL POLICY REFORM AND TRADE FLOWS

The strategy of the EU is import substitution and trade creation. In North America, however, where we have only a free trade arrangement, through NAFTA, trade is favourably affected by trade deflection,[6] which in turn is counterbalanced by the imposition of country rules of origin. Trade deflection, according to Balassa (1987) 'will affect the distribution of welfare between member and non-member countries by reducing the terms of trade gain (loss) for the former (latter)'.

Closer economic integration is expected to increase the standards of living through import substitution and trade creation, and in the case of free trade to improve trade through trade deflection. In an increasingly integrated (global, regional) world, without a doubt, social policy reform has emerged as the single most important issue of public policy in the Western industrial countries. Social policy reform – within the framework of market-oriented economies – is exploring specific instruments and policies which are designed to incorporate all sectors of economic growth as efficiently as possible and in a manner that will ensure prosperity for as many as possible. In an increasingly integrated (global, regional) world, social policy reform is affecting trade flows. How much it does so, however, will depend on the extent of government involvement in financing the cost of social programmes out of general taxation. The greater the financing of social programmes in this way, the greater the effect on international trade flows. As Balassa (1987) pointed out, 'The case is equivalent to a wage subsidy that favors labor-intensive activities' (p. 46).

SOCIAL POLICY REFORM: COST SHIFTING VS HIDDEN TAXATION

During the long postwar growth period, Western nations enjoyed an unprecedented expansion of the public service sector. This was achieved without government having to impose especially heavy taxes. This happy era eventually came to an end by 1973, the first oil crisis. A combination of sluggish growth and demographic changes led to the deterioration of living standards throughout the industrialized countries. Governments now find themselves in the politically uncomfortable and highly unpopular position of having to raise taxes or cut services. That choice, as it was more recently put by *The Economist*[7] (1995), 'is only going to grow more urgent, and more unpalatable' (p. 53).

The 1970s and 1980s are now referred to as the 'malaise' and 'lost' decades respectively. With the onset of the 1990s, however, both developed and less developed countries are having to come to grips with the new trends and realities of a highly integrated global or regional trading environment. It is quite clear, and for the reasons mentioned earlier (high unemployment rates, low productivity growth, mounting deficits), that the welfare state and social 'safety nets' – on both sides of the Atlantic – cannot be sustained as we have known them. Hence the urgent calls for social policy reform. We are now turning to these calls for social policy reform that have dominated the socio-economic and political agenda in both Europe and North America.

Article 130a of the Single European Act, confirmed by the Treaty on the European Union (Maastricht) states:

> In order to promote its overall harmonious development, the Community shall develop and pursue its actions leading to the strengthening of its economic and social cohesion. In particular, the Community shall aim at reducing disparities between the levels of development of the various regions and the backwardness of the least favoured regions, including rural areas.

In the EU, therefore, redistribution has become a statutory obligation, and cohesion – with its regional and social dimension – whether it is achieved or not, is largely a political question. As far as social policy is concerned, the EU has created the European Social Fund (ESF), articles 123, 125, 126, as an important instrument for the fight against *unemployment* and against *social dumping* by the harmonization of a variety of labour market regulations. According to Molle (1994), 'Evaluations of the effectiveness of both policies are fairly critical; although then distribution effect in budgetary terms is certain, the contribution to growth and efficiency appears to be unsatisfactory' (p. 448). In the EU, unemployment overshadows any other social problem today. One reason is that the European economies are unable to create jobs at the rate that the American economy does. It has been argued (OECD 1994) that the many market rigidities in the European economies, coupled with long-ingrained public attitudes, makes job creation very difficult. A proposed reform, for example, is to encourage the creation of part-time jobs – without traditional full benefits – something of which most Europeans (governments, and labour unions) have taken a dim view up to now.

CONCLUDING REMARKS

Given the budgetary constraints, other market considerations and the irresistible pressures of re-election politics, social policy reform often leads to curbing spending or cutting services in the most popular and politically sensitive benefits programmes, including medicare, medicaid, welfare, health care and pensions. The desire to balance the budget within a certain time – as it currently unfolds in the US – or place the budget deficit on a steady reduction path – of no more than 3 per cent of GDP, as required by the EU – has been the driving force behind many social policy reform efforts. However, spending cuts or cuts in services often leads to 'cost-shifting' and, if there is no real excess capacity or waste in the system, to a 'hidden tax'. This phenomenon is likely to increase the disparity in income per person among regions and social groups, hence adversely affecting economic and social cohesion.

NOTES

1. For more on this subject see Williamson (1994).
2. Economists disagree about the causes of high unemployment. Some of the most common causes suggested are: competition from low-wage countries and labour market rigidities; product market barriers, and low-inflation monetary policy.
3. The OECD study focuses only on the labour market conditions. It blames Western Europe's high unemployment rate on minimum wages, restrictive employment protection laws, and generous unemployment benefits.
4. If we take the rates of growth of equation (1) we can identify the sources of increase, in an additive manner, of real per capita income as follows:

$$(gnp - p) = (gnp - gdp) + (l - e) + (e - p) + (gdp - p)$$

   where: gnp, p, gdp, l, and e are the annual rates of growth of GNP, P, GDP, L, and E respectively.
5. Capital investments increase labour productivity through substitution of capital for labour and scale economies that raise productivity for both capital and labour.
6. There will be trade deflection, according to Balassa (1987), 'if imports enter the free trade area via the member country which applies the lowest tariff' (p. 45).
7. See *The Economist*, 10 June 1995, p. 53.

REFERENCES

Advisory Council on Adjustment (1989), *Adjusting to Win: Report of the Advisory Council on Adjustment*, Ottawa: Advisory Council on Adjustment.

Balassa, Bala (1987), 'Economic Integration', in J. Eatwell, M. Milgate and P. Newman (eds), *The New Palgrave: A Dictionary of Economics*, vol. 2, London: Macmillan Press, pp. 43–7.

Baltagi, B.H. and J.M. Griffith (1988), 'A General Index of Technical Change', *Journal of Political Economy*, **98** (1), 20–40.

Economic Council of Canada (1992), 'Pulling Together Productivity, Innovation and Trade', EC22-180/1992E.

Economic Council of Canada (1988), *Managing Adjustment: Policies for Trade-Sensitive Industries*, Ottawa: Canadian Government Publishing Centre.

Georgakopoulos, T., C. Paraskevopoulos, and J. Smithin (eds) (1994), *Economic Integration Between Unequal Partners*, Aldershot, UK: Edward Elgar.

Hufbauer, Gary Clyde, and Jeffrey I. Schott (1992), *North American Free Trade: Issues and Recommendations*, Washington: Institute for International Economics.

Ma, Barry K., and Christos C. Paraskevopoulos (1992), 'Economic Growth of Canadian Total Manufacturing by Regions: An Econometric Analysis', mimeo, York University.

McCleery, Robert, and Clark Reynolds (1991), 'A Study of the Impact of a US–Mexico Free Trade Agreement on Medium-Term Employment, Wages, and Production in the United States: Are New Labor Market Policies Needed?', Stanford: Americas Program, Stanford University.

Molle, Willem (1994), *The Economics of European Integration*, 2nd edn, Aldershot, UK: Dartmouth.

OECD (1994), *The OECD Jobs Study: Evidence and Explanations*, vols I & II, Paris: OECD.

Pacolet, Jozef (ed.) (1995), *Social Protection and the European Economic and Monetary Union*, Aldershot, UK: Avebury.

Paraskevopoulos, Christos C. (1994), 'Competitiveness and Productivity Growth Between Canadian and U.S. Manufacturing Industries', in T. Georgakopoulos, Christos C. Paraskevopoulos and John Smithin (eds), *Economic Integration Between Unequal Partners*, Aldershot, UK: Edward Elgar.

Solow, R.M. (1957), 'Technical Change and the Aggregate Production Function', *Review of Economics and Statistics*, **39**, 312–20.

Williamson, John (ed.) (1994), *The Political Economy of Policy Reform*, Washington, DC: Institute for International Economics.

12. Economic integration and social security: experiences in federal states and in the EU

Steven Vansteenkiste

INTRODUCTION

The funding treaties of the European Communities, as well as the recent Treaty on European Union, reflect a fairly negative answer to the question as to whether the creation of an economic – and eventually monetary – union should be accompanied by measures in the social field. However a growing number of scholars and politicians is strongly critical of the Community's lack of powers in the social field, including social security law.

In this chapter we shall not attempt to repeat all the arguments in favour of a genuine European 'social dimension', but rather try to add a new perspective to the debate. We shall compare the distribution of competences in matters of social security in a number of federal – or otherwise composed – states with the one in the European Community.

For the purpose of this chapter we shall follow a rather pragmatic path and only consider as social security schemes those which are classified as such by the ILO Convention 102 or by EC Regulation 1408/71. Thus we include schemes dealing with the following: medical care, sickness and maternity benefits, professional injuries and occupational diseases, invalidity benefits, old age benefits, survivors' benefits, benefits in case of death, unemployment benefits and family allowances. To this list we add social assistance benefits aimed at providing a general subsistence minimum when the risk 'need' occurs.

SOCIAL SECURITY IN FEDERAL STATES

Belgium

Since 1970 the formerly unitarian Belgium has gradually been transformed into a genuine federal state. The latest – but probably not the last – constitutional reform dates from 1993. In Belgium powers are distributed between the federal state, three 'regions', and three so-called 'communities'. The latter are based on a linguistic or cultural criterion rather than on a territorial one and, as such, they partly overlap the regions.

The competences of the regions and the communities are enumerated in the Constitution and in a large amount of special majority legislation. In principle the Belgian system does not recognize concurrent powers. All powers are attributed exclusively to the state, the regions or the communities. The residual competence is with the federal government, although this should be reversed in the future (Belgian Constitution, article 35).

As far as social security is concerned, the distribution of competences is quite simple. In its narrow sense, as we have defined it above, social security is in Belgium an exclusive competence of the federal state. The regions and communities do not play any role: neither in its legislation, in its financing, nor in its administration.

Canada

Of course the British North America (BNA) Act could not in 1867 have prescribed any allocation of powers in the field of social insurance. Other forms of social policy, which would only later on be included in the broad concept of social security, such as health care and (social) assistance, were not considered to be of great importance and consequently entrusted to the realm of the provinces. The original BNA Act included only very minor federal competences that were in any way linked with today's notion of social security (article 91, sections 8 and 11).

The federal government gained some control over social insurance when, in 1940, article 91 2A was added to the BNA Act, making unemployment insurance an exclusive power of the federation. By 1951 article 94A was added to the BNA Act by which a concurrent competence was created, allowing both levels of government to legislate in the field of old age pensions and supplementary benefits. Remarkably, provincial legislation in these fields is superior to federal legislation. In spite of the superiority of provincial law, however, provinces did not take much legislative action in the field of old age pensions – the Quebec old age pension being the main exception in this respect. Next to this a number of provinces have created additional benefits to those of the federal programmes.

The fact that the provinces did not undertake much action in the field of old age pensions seems to be explained mainly by general federal 'spending power', which allows the federal government to subsidize provincial programmes. These grants are largely conditional and therefore reduce the provincial margin for decision making. It is with the use of this 'spending power' that the Canadian government has also realized a major harmonization in other branches of social security. This has been the case, for instance, with medical insurance, the Canada Assistance Plan and the family allowance benefit plan.

Spain

The 1978 Spanish Constitution introduced a new constitutional concept and reality with the creation of so-called autonomous communities (*comunidades autónomas*). In doing this the Constitution does not define a complete regional structure, nor does it define a list of competences with which regional authorities are endowed. Rather it lists the competences with which the communities *can* be endowed. Therefore, the competences of the autonomous communities can only be derived from a combined reading of the Constitution and the statutes of the autonomous communities.

As far as social security is concerned, the Constitution does not provide much possibility for autonomous competence. It does, however, allow the exclusive and complete competence of the autonomous communities in the sphere of social assistance (article 148.1, 20°). This is a provision of which all the autonomous communities have made use. As far as social insurance is concerned, the cornerstone of the distribution of powers between state and autonomous communities is to be found in article 149.1.17 of the Constitution, which grants as exclusive competence to the Spanish state over the basic legislation and economic regime of social security, leaving the execution of federal legislation in the hands of the autonomous communities.

The problem here is of course how to define exactly the notions 'basic legislation' and 'economic regime'. The Spanish Constitutional Court has given a broad interpretation of federal competence to draft basic legislation in matters of social security. According to the Court's rulings every type of legislation would be within the federal competence, excepting only the competence of the communities to draw up administrative regulations.

Switzerland

The Swiss Constitution dates from 1874 and at the outset did not include any provision dealing with social security. Since the federation has only enumerated powers, all competences in matters of social security were originally entrusted with the cantons.

A series of constitutional amendments have gradually shifted competences in the field of social security to the Confederation. This was the case in matters of health insurance as early as 1890 (article 34bis). Later on, in 1925, the Swiss Confederation acquired competences in the fields of old age, survivors and invalidity insurance (article 34quater). In 1945 the Confederation acquired competences in the field of family allowances and maternity insurance (article 34quinquies) and in 1947 in the field of unemployment insurance. However, the latter did not allow the Confederation to introduce a compulsory unemployment insurance. This situation was altered in 1976 with a new constitutional amendment (article 34novies).

In spite of the broad competences of the Confederation, the cantons still play an important role, as a consequence of their concurrent powers, which allow them to create additional legislation to the federal legislation when this is not exhaustive. First, there is important supplementary cantonal legislation as far as health insurance and old age, survivors and invalidity pensions are concerned. Second, the Confederation has made only a very limited use of its competence in matters of family allowances, leaving the bulk of legislation in that field to the cantons. Third, the federal legislation only provides unemployment benefits for a limited period of time. The cantons have set up a number of programmes supplementing federal unemployment insurance by providing benefits for the long-term unemployed.

United States

Federal powers are mainly enumerated in article 1, section 8 of the US Constitution, which has remained unaltered since the Constitution came into force. Evidently, social security or similar concepts are not mentioned in this disposition, which is over two hundred years old. The federation has in principle only enumerated powers, the residual power being with the separate states. However since 1935, with the introduction of the Social Security Act, the federation has taken major legislative initiatives in the field of social security. These initiatives are inevitably based on constitutional powers that are only indirectly linked with social security.

In general, federal social policy in the US has been mainly based on three constitutional provisions: the competence to collect taxes and to spend for the general welfare of the US (article 1, section 8, 1), the 'commerce power' (article 1, 8, 3), and the 'necessary and proper clause' which mandates Congress to make all laws which are necessary and proper for executing the powers which are vested in the federal authorities (article 1, section 8, 18). The 'necessary and proper clause' has been at the basis of the very broad implicit powers of the federation, as a result of the Congress's and Supreme Court's interpretation.

Although some states had set up some rather modest social security programmes, the real breakthrough in social security in the US is dated 1935, when, as a part of Roosevelt's New Deal, the Social Security Act (SSA) was passed. The SSA was based on a broad interpretation of federal powers through the 'necessary and proper' clause and on Congress's general spending power. The SSA includes a distribution of responsibilities and powers between the federation and the states. The SSA realized two major goals: the introduction of federal old age insurance and a federal harmonization of the unemployment insurance programmes of the separate states through the use of conditioned grants. Next to this, federal subventions for a number of social assistance programmes could be provided. Since then, after a number of crucial judgements of the Supreme Court, this distribution of responsibilities in matters of social security has been widely accepted.

In spite of the fact that the federation has no explicit powers in the field, its role in social security has been of great importance. The federal old age insurance was based on the federation's power to tax and spend for the general welfare. So were the many cases in which the federation subsidizes states' programmes. Moreover, through the use of conditional grants the federation has realized a certain harmonization of states' social security legislation.

EUROPEAN COMMUNITY COMPETENCES IN SOCIAL SECURITY

The European Community Treaty

The legislative competence of the European Community is based on the powers expressly granted to it by the EC Treaty. Although generally accepted, the principle of enumerated powers was not expressly stated in the EC Treaty until the coming into force of the Treaty on European Union. Now the first part of article 3b of the EC Treaty reads: 'The Community shall act within the limits of the powers conferred upon it by this Treaty and of the objectives assigned to it therein'. As we shall show, the significance of the principle of enumerated powers is diminished by the use of article 235 of the Treaty.

The Treaty on European Union also introduced the so-called 'subsidiarity principle' in the new article 3b:

> In areas which do not fall within its exclusive competence, the Community shall take action, in accordance with the principle of subsidiarity, only if and in so far as the objectives of the proposed action cannot be sufficiently achieved by the Member States and can therefore, by reason of the scale or effects of the proposed action, be better achieved by the Community. Any action by the Community, shall not go beyond what is necessary to achieve the objectives of this Treaty.

It is hard to assess the juridical impact of the subsidiarity principle. *If* the Court accords any legal force to the provision, how will it then appreciate the words 'not sufficiently' or 'better'? The Court will of course have the last word. Until then one can probably assume that the Court's intervention will be limited and that the Court will not venture into the hazardous mission of checking the practice of Community initiative.

Article 2 of the EC Treaty establishes the general goals of the European Community. In its new wording it also says that the Community shall have as its task, among others, to promote 'a high level of employment and of social protection, the raising of the standard of living and quality of life, and economic and social cohesion and solidarity among Member States'. The new wording, more than the previous version, provides an argument for the thesis that a certain harmonization of social policy, including social security, is among the goals of the Community. However, article 2 itself does not provide any basis for Community action. Concrete competences of the Community have to be searched for in the rest of the Treaty. As far as social security is concerned, only a rather limited number of provisions are of direct or indirect importance.

To begin with, article 51 of the Treaty mandates the Council of Ministers to elaborate, unanimously, a regulation that deals with the coordination of national social security schemes. Shortly thereafter, the Council adopted a number of such coordination regulations in the field of social security. These regulations are ruled by four main principles. First, coordination is aimed at indicating one, and only one, applicable legislation, which is generally the legislation of the country of employment. Second, the regulations prohibit any form of discrimination on grounds of nationality. Third, for the purpose of acquiring and retaining the right to benefit and of calculating the amount of the benefit, all periods taken into account under national law are aggregated. Fourth, benefits are paid to persons resident in any one of the member states, which makes the benefits exportable from one member state to the other. Article 51 of the Treaty has without any doubt provided the Community with an important competence, and the regulations based on it play an important role in safeguarding the free movement of labour. Let us stress however that article 51 only seems to mandate the Council to coordinate national social security law. Thus it does not give any power to the Community to actually interfere in the content of national law, or to harmonize.

Under the heading 'social policy' we find some further dispositions referring directly or indirectly to social security. In the first part of article 117 the 'Member States agree upon the need to promote improved working conditions and an improved standard of living for workers, so as to make possible their harmonization while the improvement is being maintained'. There is ample room for discussion on the question whether article 117 expresses the member states' conviction that in the field of social security some harmonization is also needed. But whatever bells the wording of the first part of article

117 may ring, it is clear that the second part of the article reveals that no effective competences are rendered to Community institutions. It is said there that the member states believe that such a development will ensue not only from the functioning of the common market, which will favour the harmonization of social systems, but also from the procedures provided for in this Treaty and from the approximation of provisions laid down by law, regulation or administrative action. In other words, the member states believe that a harmonization of social policy will ensue from the mere working of the market. If not, they believe that the competences already given to the Community should suffice. The conclusion can be brief: whatever political statement article 117 may contain, it does not give any new competences to the European Community institutions.

Article 118 of the Treaty charges the Commission with the task of promoting close cooperation between member states in the social field. However, no legislative competence whatsoever can be derived from the disposition. The same can be said of article 118B on the basis of which the Commission should endeavour to develop a dialogue between management and labour at European level.

Finally, there is article 119. Although article 119 of the Treaty does not deal with social security as such, it has been the single disposition of the Treaty that has brought about a certain harmonization of social security law. Article 119 establishes the principle of equal treatment between men and women as far as equal pay for equal work is concerned. The Court of Justice has gradually enlarged the interpretation of the notion of 'pay' in this context, so that finally even contributions and benefits in non-statutory, or occupational, social security schemes are included. In that manner the principle of equal treatment is also applicable to occupational social security schemes, and therefore a form of harmonization of national social security law. Next to article 119 the Council has issued a number of directives. The so-called 'third directive', on the progressive implementation of the principle of equal treatment for men and women in matters of social security, has had a considerable impact on social security legislation in the member states. Noteworthy is the fact that the third directive was based on article 235 of the Treaty.

This survey of the Treaty may be rather disappointing when specific Community competences in the field of social security are being sought. It should not be ruled out, therefore, that action in the field of social security could be based on one or both of the provisions which confer a more general competence to the Community. These are articles 100 and 235 of the Treaty.

Article 100 mandates the Council to issue directives for the approximation of such laws, regulations or administrative provisions of the member states as directly affect the establishment or functioning of the common market. It should be noted here that the Council is allowed, or obliged, to harmonize such national legislation that is a hindrance to the *establishment* of the common market, or that hinders the *functioning* of the common market. In the latter case we might think of national provisions which do not forbid entry to the common market as such, but which might negatively influence fair competition in that market. Until now article 100 was only used in combination with article 235 for harmonization in the field of social security, and only as far as equal treatment of men and women was concerned. It should not be ruled out, however, that in the future the Community will acknowledge a growing influence of social security legislation on fair competition. In that case it seems that article 100 could contain great potential for certain harmonization initiatives in the field of social policy in general. It does not seem very likely that this will happen in the near future, since the use of article 100 has to be based on unanimity. Unanimity is not required for the use of article 100A, which equally allows the Council to take harmonization measures, directives as well as regulations, with an eye toward establishing and securing the functioning common market. But the use of article 100A in matters of social security has been expressly excluded.

It is without any doubt that article 235 gives the broadest competence to the Community:

> If action by the Community should prove necessary to attain, in the course of the operation of the common market, one of the objectives of the Community and this Treaty has not provided the necessary powers, the Council shall, acting unanimously on a proposal from the Commission and after consulting the Assembly, take the appropriate measures.

Legal doctrine has always assumed the position that the Community may only exercise power which is granted to it by the Treaty, which is now formally confirmed by the new article 3b.

Article 235 seems to give less explicit powers for the determination of various issues, which are necessary in the course of the operation of the common market, to attain any of the objectives of the Community. In this way the principle of enumerated powers is to a certain extent weakened. Article 235 has been compared with the 'necessary and proper' clause in the US Constitution. Until now, however, neither the Council nor the Court has ever given such a broad interpretation. What is certain is that it was always ruled out that article 235 could be considered as the expression of 'Kompetenz-Kompetenz'. Article 225 only offers the opportunity to take decisions which are closely related to existing powers, that is, those which contain a supplement to existing powers. We shall not deal extensively with the fierce debate on the interpretation of article 235 here. It suffices to point out that there is a broad view that the Council may rely on article 235 each time the Treaty grants Community competence but either no express legislative power or only insufficient legislative power.

If we now look at the goals of the Community, expressed in article 2 and eventually in article 117, and the powers vested in the Community on the basis of article 100, we might have a strong case to argue that article 235, perhaps in combination with article 100, could lead to Community action in the field of social security.

The Protocol and the Agreement on Social Policy

With the Treaty on European Union, a protocol on social policy was annexed to the Treaty establishing the European Community, in which the 12 member states agreed that 11 of them (excluding the UK) should be authorized 'to have recourse to the institutions, procedures and mechanisms of the Treaty for the purposes of taking among themselves and applying as far as they are concerned the acts and decisions required for giving effect' to an Agreement that the 11 have adopted among them.

The 11 member states are consequently mandated by their agreement on social policy to take social policy measures among themselves, some of them even with a qualified majority. In a number of provisions the agreement does, moreover, give broader competences to the 11 states than the Treaty gives to the 12. As far as social security is concerned, however, decisions of the 11, based on the agreement, still need unanimity.

The legal force of the protocol, of the agreement and of legal instruments that would be based on the agreement, is controversial, to say the least. Some authors consider that the agreement is of a merely intergovernmental nature. If they are right, the juridical consequences are rather dramatic, since both the agreement on social policy and all further decisions based on it would be no more than traditional international agreements. Each new decision would hence need the ratification of all member states concerned. Other interpretations attribute more sense to the protocol and the agreement as integrating parts of the Community legal order. Indeed, according to article 239 of the EC Treaty, the protocol constitutes an integral part of the Treaty. The fact that the agreement has only been concluded between 11 member states should not diminish this, since the protocol, as an integral part of the Treaty, is making exactly that possible. But, even if the Court of Justice were to follow the latter interpretation, a heap of practical questions would remain unanswered. We shall not deal further with these juridical questions here, since it seems rather unlikely that the construction of the protocol and the agreement will ever be used.

SOME CONCLUSIONS AND SOME QUESTIONS

Generally, in all federations the federal authority plays the main role in the shaping of social security legislation, although the constituent entities are not completely without power. The contents and nature of federal power in matters of social security, however, are quite divergent from country to country. Sometimes the federation has an exclusive competence, sometimes it has only concurrent powers. Sometimes the federal power is based on constitutional provisions explicitly dealing with social security, and sometimes it has been based on a broad interpretation of federal power to tax and to spend for the general welfare.

In spite of the diversity some general trends in the distribution of social security competences between federal states and their constituent entities can be discerned. A distinction can be made between three types of social security arrangements: social assistance schemes; income replacement schemes; and cost compensating schemes. With income replacement schemes we mean social insurance schemes which aim to replacing lost labour income because of unemployment, sickness, old age, invalidity and so on. With cost compensating schemes we mean social insurance schemes which aim at totally or partly compensating some specific costs, such as those for medical care, specific to having children, and so on.

The role of the constituent entities in federal states is the largest as far as *social assistance* is concerned. Except for Belgium, in each of the countries studied the constituent entities have exclusive competence in this field. If the federal government plays any role it is in subsidizing these programmes. This is of course not very surprising. In unitarian states the local government's role is mostly in regulating and financing social assistance schemes. As far as *cost compensating schemes* are concerned, most of the federal systems seem to allow a wide margin for proper policy by the constituent entities. They have either exclusive or concurrent competence to legislate in matters of family allowances and health insurance. The role of the federation is mostly limited to a certain harmonization, either through basic legislation or through conditioned subventions. In the last category – *income replacement schemes* – federal intervention tends to be much stronger. Unemployment and old age insurance are either exclusive federal competences or are very much controlled by the federation.

Unlike the federal states the Community does not have extensive competences in the field of social security, nor has it recourse to a general taxing and spending power to influence the social policy of the member states. We shall not venture reasons for this sharp contrast of situations here. However, most economists would probably have little difficulty in explaining the necessities of federal involvement in social security programmes of several types. They would probably also acknowledge that such involvement is mainly wanted in the case of income replacement schemes, for reasons of scale effects and fair competition. Similar economic arguments have indeed been used to plead for European action in the field of security.

Until now it seems that participants in the European debate (on the social dimension of the Community) have not spent much energy in studying the federal experience, at least not as far as social security is concerned. Nevertheless, it is our strong conviction that an analysis of the rationale behind the evolution of the distribution of social security competences in federal states will provide important feedback to the European debate on that same question. We hope that this chapter has made a modest contribution to formulating the questions. Finding the answers will require the continued and combined effort of economists, lawyers and social policy analysts.

13. The relative welfare position of older persons in the member states of the EU: evidence and policy implications

Panos Tsakloglou*

INTRODUCTION

In 1990 one in seven citizens of the European Union (EU) was aged over 64. By 2020 this ratio is expected to rise to one in five (CEC 1991). The greying of the population has imposed a great burden on the already overstretched social security systems of all EU member states. In many countries, the resulting deficits of the social security systems are among the top contributors to the budget deficits. Several policies have been recommended to tackle these problems. The impact of some recommendations on the welfare of the elderly is not expected to be dramatic (for example, policies intended to reverse the trend towards early retirement, to raise the retirement age, to devise systems combining full or partial provision of pensions and payment of salaries with or without payment of social insurance contributions for workers employed beyond their retirement threshold, to encourage and support private pension schemes, etc.). Some of these recommendations have already been adopted in a number of EU countries. A different approach to the problem of social security deficits recommends cuts in pensions and other social security benefits targeted towards the elderly. As the experience of some EU members shows, implementation of such policies is likely to affect adversely the living standards of large segments of the elderly population. The latter recommendations are frequently accompanied by the claim that the elderly are better off than the rest of the population. This claim is supported by some empirical

*This chapter is based on a longer report (Tsakloglou 1994) written in the context of a contract with the Institute of Social Studies Advisory Service (ISSAS) for the Statistical Service of the European Union (Eurostat). The views expressed here are those of the author and should not be attributed to Eurostat or ISSAS. Helpful comments were received from the late Aldi Hagenaars, Klaas de Vos, Asghar Zaidi, Bernard van Praag, Robert Flik, Deo Ramprakash and seminar participants at the Athens University of Economics and Business, the University of Frankfurt, York University and the 23rd General Conference of the International Association for Research in Income and Wealth in St Andrews, Canada.

studies in the case of the US (see Hurd 1990 and the references cited there) but the evidence for Europe is, at best, mixed (see CEC 1991, 1993). A number of empirical investigations of the living conditions of the elderly in individual EU member states can be found in the literature but there exists no corresponding comparative study applying the same methodology to all EU countries. This chapter attempts, first, to examine the relative welfare position of the elderly *vis-à-vis* the rest of the population (non-elderly) in all EU member states using the consumption expenditure data of Household Budget Surveys (HBSs) carried out in the late 1980s and, second, to examine the economic status of particular sub-groups of elderly persons. The policy implications of the empirical findings are spelt out briefly in the concluding section.

METHODOLOGICAL ISSUES

For Belgium (1987), Greece (1988), Spain (1988), France (1989), Italy (1988), Luxembourg (1987), the Netherlands (1988) and the UK (1988) the results presented below were obtained using the micro-data sets of the corresponding HBSs, whereas for Denmark (1988), Germany, excluding former East Germany (1987), Ireland (1987) and Portugal (1990) they were derived from the estimates reported in Hagenaars et al. (1993). Since no micro-data were available in the case of the four latter countries, the corresponding results are not as detailed as those concerning the eight former countries. Even though the consumption expenditure data of most HBSs are of reasonably high quality, differences in information collection methods, enumeration periods and institutional arrangements make them not strictly comparable across countries. Hence the chapter focuses on differences between the elderly and the non-elderly within individual countries rather than on cross-country comparisons.

Since the objective of the chapter is to compare the welfare levels of the elderly and the non-elderly, the distributions used are distributions of persons, not households. In line with several EU studies (Eurostat 1990; CEC 1991, 1993; Hagenaars et al. 1993), persons aged over 64 are classified as 'elderly' and persons below this threshold as 'non-elderly'. The distributions of equivalent consumption expenditure were derived by dividing the total consumption expenditure of each household by the number of equivalent adults living in it and assigning the resulting figure to each household member. Hence, it is implicitly assumed that the distribution of resources within the household is equitable. Although this is a common assumption in distributional studies, there may be grounds to suspect that it is not necessarily correct (see Haddad and Kanbur 1990; Thomas 1990; and Jenkins 1991). The equivalence scales utilized are the so-called 'modified OECD scales' (see Hagenaars et al. 1993), which assign weights of 1, 0.5 and 0.3 to the household head, each subsequent adult and each child, respectively (a child is defined as a person aged below 15). Even though there is no consensus regarding the size of the 'correct' household equivalence scales, these scales lie somewhere in the middle of the range of such scales used in the literature (see Buhmann et al. 1988; Hagenaars et al. 1993). It should be noted that the quantitative results of our analysis are sensitive with respect to the choice of a particular set of equivalence scales. In most EU member states over two-thirds of the elderly live either alone or with their spouses. Therefore, the larger the economies of scale implied by the set of equivalence scales used in the analysis, the more likely it is to find more elderly persons located closer to the bottom of the distribution of equivalent consumption expenditure. The data used to derive the estimates reported below were weighted either by the sample weights provided by the National Statistical Institutes or – in case no weights were provided – by weights calculated by the author using the detailed grouped data of the Labour Force Surveys of the countries in question.

The elderly may be under-represented in the samples of some HBSs since the HBSs cover only the non-institutional households and a disproportionately large number of elderly persons live in institutional households (nursing homes). Moreover, there is evidence that the non-cooperation of the elderly households with the enumerators of the HBSs is higher than that of the rest of the population. This under-representation is mitigated by the use of sample weights, but even in the weighted samples the elderly are still slightly under-represented in most countries. Since in our analysis the welfare indicators of the elderly are expressed as fractions of the corresponding indicators of the non-elderly, this under representation would not affect the results seriously if the elderly included in the samples of the HBSs were representative of all the elderly in the population. Unfortunately, though, this is not always the case. In most samples the very elderly (those aged over 74) are relatively more under-represented in the weighted samples of the HBSs than the less elderly (those aged 65–74). Since, as demonstrated below, the very elderly persons enjoy a substantially lower welfare level than the relatively less elderly persons, it may be plausible to argue that, from this point of view, in most cases, the 'true' relative status of the elderly is lower than that implied by the estimates reported below.

For a number of theoretical and practical reasons, an individual's consumption is usually considered as a good approximation of his/her permanent or life-cycle income and, hence, of his/her welfare level (see Sen 1976; Deaton 1980) and has been used as a welfare indicator in several empirical studies. However, HBSs collect data on consumption expenditure which is just an approximation to an individual's consumption. Apart from purchased goods and services, the concept of 'consumption expenditure' used here includes consumption of own production (including imputed rent) and benefits in kind provided by the employer (for those countries for which no information on imputed rent was available, it was calculated using the estimates of 'hedonic' regressions). Therefore, this concept of 'consumption expenditure' is broader than pure 'expenditure' but narrower than 'consumption' since it does not include the value of goods and services provided free of charge by the state or other organizations (e.g. education, health and medical care, housing, public transport services, etc.). The latter may have some serious implications for our results, if the elderly are heavier/lighter users than the non-elderly of the subsidized or freely provided goods and services. The situation is likely to vary considerably across countries, depending on their institutional arrangements. For example, the elderly are heavier users of health and medical services than the rest of the population. Hence, if in a particular country these services are heavily subsidized or provided free of charge by the state then the 'true' relative welfare of the elderly is higher than that depicted by their recorded expenditures. Exactly the opposite is the situation regarding educational services. Smeeding et al. (1993) examine the distributional impact of non-cash transfers from the government to the population in the areas of health, education and housing in a number of countries – among them Germany, France, the Netherlands and the UK. Their results suggest that, on the aggregate, the relative position of elderly and non-elderly is not affected significantly by such transfers. However, these transfers have a more progressively redistributive impact within the group of the elderly than within the group of the non-elderly and, hence, after the transfers inequality and poverty decline more in the former group. Nevertheless, in the case of the elderly these results are driven by the impact of transfers in the areas of health and medical services. It is questionable whether health and medical expenditures should be included in our welfare indicator since it can be reasonably argued that the relevant services are, simply, used to bring their users to a physical state similar to that of the rest of the population.

Another problem arises in the case of durable goods since, on the one hand, expenditure on durables cannot be identified with consumption in the same period and, on the other hand, many households enjoy the flow of services of durable goods purchased outside the enumeration period of the HBSs. Due to life-cycle reasons, the elderly are likely to own an accumulated stock of durables and, hence, they are less likely than the rest of the population to purchase them during that period. Therefore, the fact that the HBSs record expenditures on durables rather than the value of services derived from them may result in an underestimation of the 'true' relative welfare position of the elderly. Even though this argument is correct, Tsakloglou (1994) demonstrates that in all EU member states the households of the elderly are less well equipped with durables than the rest of the households, sometimes substantially so. Hence, proper treatment of the value of the flow of services derived from their use would have a rather marginal impact on our results.

WELFARE COMPARISONS OF ELDERLY AND NON-ELDERLY

Table 13.1 reports estimates related to the consumption expenditures of elderly and non-elderly persons. Line (1) reports the population shares of the elderly and line (2) reports the mean equivalent expenditure of the elderly as a percentage of the mean equivalent expenditure of the non-elderly. In all EU member states the mean equivalent expenditure of the elderly is lower than that of the non-elderly although, as demonstrated in Figure 13.1, in quantitative terms the situation varies considerably across countries. In some countries (Belgium, Luxembourg) the mean equivalent expenditure of the elderly is only slightly lower than that of the non-elderly, whereas in others it is substantially lower (Greece, Portugal, the UK). However, average figures do not reveal too much. Several studies suggest that the level of inequality among the elderly is higher than the level of inequality of the entire population (see, for instance, EC 1991, 1993). A comparison of the levels of inequality of the two groups is presented in lines (3) and (4) of Table 13.1 using the second Theil index of inequality. In all countries for which we were able to estimate such indices, inequality among the elderly is higher than inequality among the non-elderly (inequality indices could not be estimated for the countries for which micro-data were not available). Nevertheless, the quantitative differences are quite substantial across countries. The difference in the levels of inequality of elderly and non-elderly is most profound in Greece, the UK and the Netherlands (although in the latter the levels of inequality are relatively low for both groups) and least so in Luxembourg. The second Theil index is utilized instead of other more commonly used measures of inequality because it is 'strictly additively decomposable', that is, it decomposes exactly aggregate inequality into inequality 'within groups' and inequality 'between groups' and thus allows the quantification of the contribution of each particular population group to aggregate inequality (see Bourguignon 1979). The percentage contribution of the elderly to aggregate inequality is shown in line (5) of Table 13.1. Comparison of these estimates with the estimates of line (1) suggests that the contribution of the elderly to aggregate inequality is higher than their population share in all EU member states examined there.

Tsakloglou (1994) shows that elderly are disproportionately concentrated at the bottom deciles of the distribution of equivalent consumption expendi-

Table 13.1 Relative welfare position of the elderly in the countries of the EU

Line no.	Variable	Country B	DK*	D	GR	E	F	IRL	I	L	NL	P	UK
1	Population share of the elderly (% of total population)	13.8	14.0	16.6	14.5	14.9	13.0	10.0	13.1	12.0	10.7	14.6	15.2
2	Mean equivalent expenditure of elderly (% of non-elderly)	98.4	80.1	92.4	70.5	93.3	92.3	90.2	80.5	95.7	90.9	70.7	73.6
3	Theil index of inequality of elderly	0.101	n.a.	n.a.	0.199	0.139	0.153	n.a.	0.221	0.114	0.091	n.a.	0.218
4	Theil index of inequality of non-elderly	0.092	n.a.	n.a.	0.160	0.121	0.130	n.a.	0.200	0.111	0.066	n.a.	0.186
5	Contribution of elderly to aggregate inequality (%)	15.0	n.a.	n.a.	16.7	16.8	14.9	n.a.	14.1	12.3	14.7	n.a.	16.9
6	Poverty rate of elderly (%)	7.9	7.5	17.4	37.4	17.9	18.2	20.0	33.1	11.4	11.7	42.9	36.8
7	Poverty rate of non-elderly (%)	7.0	3.3	9.6	14.5	11.4	11.8	15.2	19.0	10.0	3.4	21.4	13.3
8	Contribution of elderly to aggregate poverty rate (%)	15.4	27.1	26.3	30.5	21.7	18.8	12.7	20.7	13.4	29.1	25.6	33.2
9	Poverty gap of elderly (%)	12.4	14.3	21.4	32.8	20.8	22.6	23.4	28.7	15.5	15.8	34.0	27.2
10	Poverty gap of non-elderly (%)	16.9	15.8	18.2	25.1	22.6	19.9	21.2	24.2	18.9	11.6	29.1	20.9
11	FGT index of poverty of elderly (×10)	0.021	0.028	0.122	0.546	0.118	0.140	0.169	0.393	0.046	0.052	0.687	0.401
12	FGT index of poverty of non-elderly (×10)	0.032	0.014	0.051	0.135	0.087	0.072	0.099	0.168	0.054	0.010	0.278	0.088
13	Contribution of elderly to aggregate poverty according to the FGT index (%)	9.7	24.2	32.3	40.8	19.4	22.5	15.7	26.0	10.3	39.7	29.7	45.1

Notes:
n.a. Not available.
* Estimates derived from the report of Hagenaars et al. (1993).
B: Belgium; DK: Denmark; D: West Germany; GR: Greece; E: Spain; F: France; IRL: Ireland; I: Italy; L: Luxembourg; NL: Netherlands; P: Portugal.
FGT: Foster, Greer and Thorbecke.

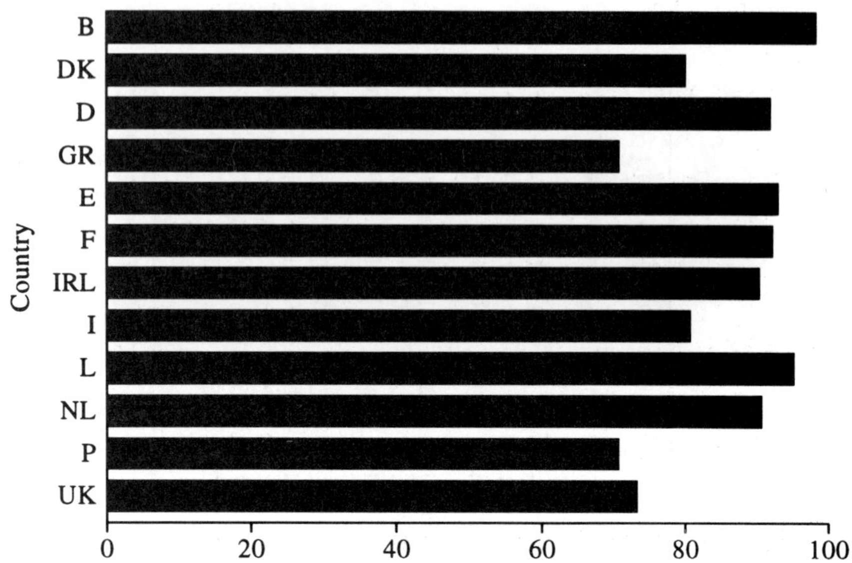

Figure 13.1 Mean equivalent expenditure of elderly persons in the countries of the EU (non-elderly: 100.00)

ture, implying that the poverty rates of the elderly should be higher than the poverty rates of the non-elderly. Defining as the poverty line one half of the mean equivalent expenditure, a relativistic approach to social exclusion commonly used by the EU (Eurostat 1990; Hagenaars et al. 1993), we derive the poverty rates for the elderly and the non-elderly which are reported in lines (6) and (7). The contributions of the elderly to the aggregate poverty rate are reported in line (8). In all EU member states the poverty rate of the elderly is higher than the poverty rate of the non-elderly; this pattern is illustrated vividly in Figure 13.2. However, considerable cross-country differences are also evident. In some countries the differences in the poverty rates of the two groups are insignificant (Belgium, Luxembourg), whilst in others they are very large (Portugal, Greece, the UK, the Netherlands and Denmark, even though in the last two the poverty rates are pretty low for both groups). Comparison of the figures in lines (1) and (8) of Table 13.1 reveals that the contribution of the elderly to the aggregate poverty rate is substantially higher than their population share in all EU member states.

Poverty rates alone do not convey a great deal of information. Two groups may have the same poverty rate and still in the first group the poor may be clustered close to the poverty line whereas in the second group they may be close to absolute destitution. Hence, it may be interesting to look at the

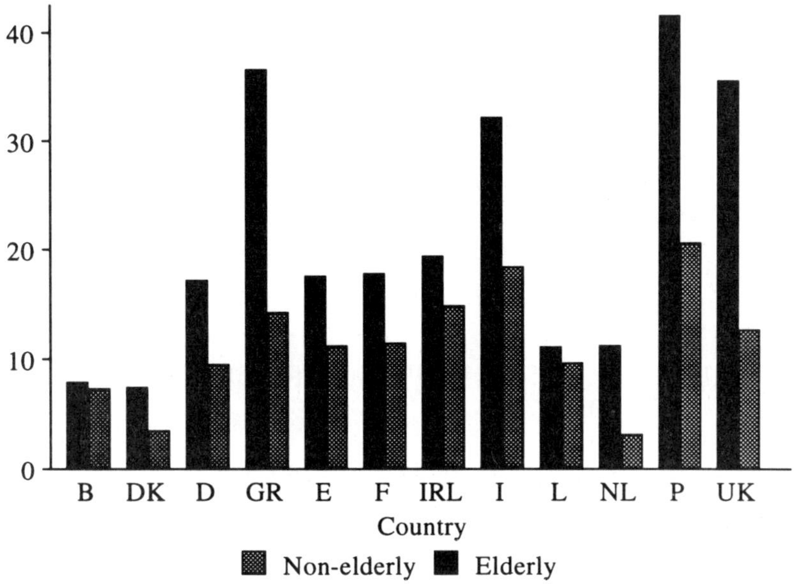

Figure 13.2 Poverty rates of elderly and non-elderly persons in the countries of the EU

average shortfall of a poor person's expenditure from the poverty line expressed as a proportion of the poverty line; the 'poverty gap'. The poverty gaps of the elderly and the non-elderly are reported in lines (11) and (12). This time the pattern is not uniform across countries. Although in most countries the poverty gap of the elderly is larger than the poverty gap of the non-elderly, in four countries (Belgium, Denmark, Luxembourg and Spain) the mean consumption expenditure of a poor elderly person is higher than that of a poor non-elderly person.

Even if two groups have the same poverty rate and the same poverty gap, they may differ with respect to the distribution of expenditure among the poor. Therefore, it may be preferable to use indices which take into account the poverty rate, the poverty gap and the degree of inequality within the group of the poor persons, such as the index of Foster, Greer and Thorbecke (1984). This index is also 'additively decomposable'; that is, it allows the exact quantification of the contribution of each particular group to aggregate poverty. Estimates of the FGT for the elderly and the non-elderly are reported in lines (13) and (14) (in line with most empirical studies which use this index, the value of 2 is assigned to its 'poverty aversion' parameter). The corresponding percentage contributions of the elderly to the aggregate poverty are shown in line (15). Considerable cross-country qualitative and quantitative differences can be observed. In two countries (Belgium and Luxembourg) the values of the index are higher for the group of the non-elderly, while in others (Greece, Portugal, and the UK) the values of the FGT indices of the elderly are substantially higher than those of the non-elderly in absolute terms. As a result, the contribution of the elderly to the aggregate poverty according to FGT in Belgium and Luxembourg is lower than their population share, whereas in most countries it is between almost two and four times larger than that share (Germany, Greece, Ireland, Italy, the Netherlands, Portugal and the UK).

WELFARE COMPARISONS OF SUB-GROUPS OF ELDERLY PERSONS

Earlier the elderly were treated as a homogeneous group. This section attempts a more elaborate examination of the living standards of sub-groups of elderly in those EU countries for which micro-data were available. The group of elderly is subdivided into relatively homogeneous sub-groups and the living standards of each sub-group are examined in detail. The sub-groups are formed by splitting the elderly using three alternative criteria: sex ('male' and 'female'), age ('65–74' and 'over 74') and household type ('single male', 'single female', 'elderly couple' and 'other household type' – an elderly couple is defined as a couple with at least one member aged over 64). In some countries a number of the reported sub-group estimates have been derived from a relatively small number of observations and hence should be interpreted with caution. The quantitative evidence for the detailed examination of the living standards of the sub-groups of elderly persons is reported in Table 13.2.

When the elderly are subdivided by sex, the estimates of the first two columns of Table 13.2 show that, as one would anticipate, the population share of elderly females is higher than that of elderly males. In all countries the mean equivalent expenditure of the elderly males is higher than that of the elderly females. However, in some countries the difference between the two sub-groups is marginal (Belgium, Spain), whereas in others it is substantial (France, the Netherlands). No uniform pattern emerges regarding the levels of inequality of the two sub-groups. In most countries inequality is higher among elderly males, but the reverse can be observed in Greece and the Netherlands and there is a tie in the UK. As a result of the small differences in the mean expenditures of the two sub-groups and the more unequal distribution of expenditure among elderly males, the poverty rate of elderly males is marginally higher than that of elderly females in Belgium, Spain and Luxembourg, while the poverty rates of the elderly females are higher than those of the elderly males in the remaining countries. The poverty gap of the poor elderly females is higher than that of the poor elderly males in all countries apart from Spain and, similarly, the value of the FGT index is higher in the former sub-group in all countries apart from Spain and Belgium. In conclusion, it can be argued that in most EU member states the elderly males are better off than the elderly females but the differences between the two sub-groups are not important.

In the next two columns of Table 13.2 the elderly are subdivided by age. In all countries the less elderly (those aged 65–74) are more numerous than the very elderly (those aged over 74). In all countries but Luxembourg the mean equivalent expenditure of the younger elderly is at least 10 per cent higher than that of the older elderly and in some cases the difference is substantial (the UK, France, Italy). In fact, in Belgium and France the less elderly enjoy an expenditure level higher than that of their non-elderly compatriots. Furthermore, inequality is higher among the very elderly in all countries apart from Luxembourg, the UK and Italy and the poverty rates of the very elderly are considerably higher than those of the less elderly in all countries except Luxembourg. On average, the mean equivalent expenditure of poor persons aged 65–74 is higher than the mean equivalent expenditure of poor persons aged over 74 in all countries apart from Luxembourg, Spain and the Netherlands. The picture painted by the FGT index is in line with the rest of the findings of this part of Table 13.2. In all countries apart from Luxembourg the FGT is higher for the sub-group of very old elderly and in some cases the differences in the estimates are enormous (Belgium, France, the UK).

The last four columns of Table 13.2, where the elderly are split according to household type, contain the potentially most relevant information for policy purposes. Probably due to their differential life expectancies, in all countries the population share of single elderly females is higher than the population share of single elderly males. In most cases the difference in these population shares is considerable and the population share of the latter sub-group is very small (therefore, the corresponding estimates should be interpreted with caution). In all countries apart from Spain and Luxembourg most of the elderly live with their spouses, whereas in Spain and Luxembourg the (relative) majority of the elderly live with other family members. This situation appears to be very common in Greece and Italy, too. No clear pattern is evident regarding the mean expenditure of the various sub-groups. However, it is worth noting that in some countries a few sub-groups of elderly have higher mean equivalent consumption expenditure than the non-elderly (elderly living alone in Belgium and Luxembourg, single elderly males in Spain and France, elderly living with other family members in the Netherlands). On the other extreme, the mean equivalent consumption expenditure enjoyed by a number of sub-groups of elderly in Greece and the UK is barely above 60 per

Table 13.2 *Welfare position of sub-groups of elderly in eight EU countries*

Line no.	Variable	Sex of elderly		Age of elderly		Household type of elderly			
		Male	Female	65–74	Over 74	Single male	Single female	Elderly couple	Other
	Belgium								
1	Population share (% of total popul.)	6.8	7.0	10.1	3.7	2.1	3.4	6.4	2.0
2	Mean equiv. expenditure (% of non-elderly)	98.9	98.3	101.7	90.2	101.1	101.5	98.7	91.8
3	Theil index of inequality	0.105	0.098	0.094	0.115	0.126	0.098	0.098	0.087
4	Poverty rate	8.2	7.5	5.1	15.3	8.5	6.9	7.1	11.4
5	Poverty gap	12.2	12.7	10.6	14.1	13.9*	13.7*	11.1	12.6*
6	FGT index of poverty (×10)	0.023	0.020	0.009	0.056	0.038	0.021	0.014	0.029
	Greece								
1	Population share (% of total popul.)	6.6	7.9	8.2	6.3	0.5	2.3	6.0	5.7
2	Mean expenditure (% of non-elderly)	72.9	68.5	74.3	65.6	78.9	62.7	62.4	81.7
3	Theil index of inequality	0.191	0.204	0.190	0.205	0.211	0.230	0.188	0.173
4	Poverty rate	35.2	39.2	33.8	42.0	33.1	45.5	44.6	26.7
5	Poverty gap	31.4	33.9	30.2	35.5	30.0	37.4	33.5	28.6
6	FGT index of poverty (×10)	0.473	0.606	0.431	0.695	0.437	0.855	0.657	0.310
	Spain								
1	Population share (% of total popul.)	6.2	8.7	8.9	6.0	0.3	1.5	4.9	8.2
2	Mean equiv. expenditure (% of non-elderly)	94.1	92.7	97.9	86.9	115.1	96.7	93.5	91.6
3	Theil index of inequality	0.149	0.131	0.133	0.142	0.276	0.160	0.129	0.133
4	Poverty rate	18.3	17.3	14.7	22.6	16.2	18.5	16.0	19.1
5	Poverty gap	22.4	19.5	21.7	19.9	30.3*	26.1	19.6	20.1
6	FGT index of poverty (×10)	0.139	0.103	0.108	0.131	0.154	0.159	0.096	0.120
	France								
1	Population share (% of total popul.)	5.3	7.7	6.8	6.2	0.8	3.3	6.3	2.6
2	Mean equiv. expenditure (% of non-elderly)	99.8	88.7	102.1	83.3	104.2	79.8	99.8	91.9
3	Theil index of inequality	0.159	0.145	0.145	0.150	0.244	0.145	0.141	0.136

4	Poverty rate	16.1	19.6	12.7	24.1	25.8	26.5	13.6	16.2
5	Poverty gap	22.3	22.8	21.2	23.4	24.8*	23.8	21.6	21.2
6	FGT index of poverty (×10)	0.118	0.156	0.089	0.197	0.233	0.228	0.092	0.117
	Italy								
1	Population share (% of total popul.)	5.7	7.4	8.0	5.1	0.7	2.7	5.2	4.5
2	Mean equiv. expenditure (% of non-elderly)	83.1	78.4	86.3	71.2	76.3	72.8	78.4	88.1
3	Theil index of inequality	0.222	0.219	0.221	0.208	0.231	0.230	0.223	0.203
4	Poverty rate	31.7	34.2	29.1	39.4	36.1	39.4	35.6	26.0
5	Poverty gap	27.8	29.3	26.7	40.0	30.3	30.9	28.4	26.6
6	FGT index of poverty (×10)	0.359	0.419	0.305	0.531	0.488	0.525	0.414	0.274
	Luxembourg								
1	Population share (% of total popul.)	5.0	7.0	8.1	3.9	0.7	3.2	3.9	4.2
2	Mean equiv. expenditure (% of non-elderly)	98.3	94.6	97.0	94.4	128.1	100.4	96.7	86.7
3	Theil index of inequality	0.122	0.108	0.123	0.095	0.200	0.111	0.094	0.111
4	Poverty rate	11.5	11.3	11.6	10.9	17.6	9.8	7.6	15.0
5	Poverty gap	14.2	16.4	18.0	9.9	14.3*	16.6	20.0*	13.0
6	FGT index of poverty (×10)	0.043	0.048	0.059	0.019	0.060	0.035	0.050	0.048
	The Netherlands								
1	Population share (% of total popul.)	5.1	5.7	8.1	2.7	0.8	2.4	6.7	0.8
2	Mean equiv. expenditure (% of non-elderly)	95.0	87.3	93.2	84.1	94.8	79.6	93.1	102.4
3	Theil index of inequality	0.086	0.094	0.088	0.097	0.099	0.091	0.087	0.078
4	Poverty rate	9.5	13.7	9.7	18.0	18.1	17.4	9.7	4.4
5	Poverty gap	10.9	18.8	16.6	14.6	9.7*	22.0*	11.6	45.2*
6	FGT index of poverty (×10)	0.022	0.079	0.043	0.080	0.018	0.114	0.030	0.090
	U.K.								
1	Population share (% of total popul.)	6.6	8.6	9.2	6.0	1.6	4.0	7.0	2.6
2	Mean equiv. expenditure (% of non-elderly)	77.1	71.0	80.3	63.5	60.4	61.3	79.2	85.2
3	Theil index of inequality	0.217	0.217	0.216	0.205	0.168	0.209	0.238	0.154
4	Poverty rate	32.9	39.7	29.8	47.3	45.0	50.3	33.4	20.4
5	Poverty gap	26.2	27.8	25.3	29.0	31.1	30.2	24.4	23.0
6	FGT index of poverty (×10)	0.327	0.457	0.287	0.572	0.575	0.675	0.306	0.157

Note: * Estimate derived from less than 25 observations.

cent of that of their non-elderly compatriots (elderly living alone in the UK, single elderly females and elderly couples in Greece). In all countries apart from the UK inequality is highest among elderly living alone (particularly single elderly males) and in all countries except Spain and Luxembourg inequality is at its lowest in the sub-group of elderly living in 'other household types'. No clear cross-country pattern is observed with respect to the high-risk poverty sub-groups. In some countries the poverty rates of elderly living alone are clearly higher than those of the rest of the elderly (France, the Netherlands, the UK) whereas in Italy and, to a lesser extent, Greece elderly living with their spouses can also be considered as high-risk poverty groups. No systematic pattern becomes evident in the remaining countries. Finally, the FGT index suggests that in most countries the most acute poverty is experienced by elderly living alone. When poverty is measured by this index, it appears to be at its highest among single elderly females and its second highest among single elderly males in Greece, Spain, Italy and the UK and in reverse order in France. Furthermore, the FGT index takes its highest value in the sub-group of single elderly males in Belgium and Luxembourg and in the sub-group of single elderly females in the Netherlands.

CONCLUSIONS

The principal conclusion of this chapter is that many qualitative similarities and quantitative differences can be observed in the EU countries with respect to the relative welfare position of their senior citizens. On the side of similarities, the results show that in all EU countries the non-elderly are better off than the elderly. The elderly have lower mean equivalent consumption expenditure than their non-elderly fellow citizens, proportionally more of them fall below the poverty line and inequality is higher among them than among the non-elderly. On the side of differences, in some countries the gap in the living standards of elderly and non-elderly is marginal, whereas in others it is very considerable. This gap tends to be larger in the southern EU member states (with the exception of Spain) whose welfare systems are less developed than those of the rest of the EU and smaller in the northern EU countries (with the exception of the UK). Furthermore, in most EU countries the elderly are not a homogeneous group. As a general pattern, elderly males are better off than elderly females, the less elderly substantially better off than the very elderly, whereas no clear conclusion can be reached regarding the sub-division of the elderly according to their household type. In most cases, elderly living alone are at higher risk than the rest of the elderly of falling below the poverty line, even though in several instances the mean equivalent consumption expenditure of their group is relatively high.

Although this chapter is mostly descriptive, some interesting policy implications can be derived from its results. As noted in the introduction, in most EU countries the deficits of the social security systems are among the top contributors to the budget deficits and sooner or later they will have to be eliminated or, at least, reduced drastically. Certainly, one of the groups that will be affected by the reform of the social security systems is the elderly. Among the recommended policies for the reduction of the social security deficits which affect the elderly, those which are likely to be most effective in reducing the deficit in the short term are those which rely heavily on substantial cuts in pensions and other social security benefits targeted towards the elderly. Since the results indicate that the elderly are already less well off than the rest of the population, such a policy reform is likely to increase the distance between the elderly and the non-elderly and raise inequality and poverty both within the group of elderly and nationally. The elderly of today belong to a generation with lower productivity than that of those currently employed and, hence, there may be an argument to justify their lower living standards. However, if the policy-makers are really interested in achieving social cohesion and intergenerational solidarity along with economic efficiency, as many of them proclaim (it should be mentioned that 1993 was designated at the 'European year of the elderly and solidarity between the generations', even though this was almost completely forgotten in the turmoil of the financial markets), it may be preferable to promote alternative policies for the elimination of the social security deficits. Among these policies are those mentioned earlier (reversal of the trend towards early retirement, increase in the retirement age thresholds, marginal increases in contributions, support of supplementary private pension schemes, etc.). These policies are likely to have a slower impact on the budget deficits than cuts in social security pensions, but they are not expected to affect adversely the gap between the living standards of elderly and non-elderly. Moreover, although the elderly are over-represented among the poor, Tsakloglou (1994) demonstrates that in all EU countries a fairly large proportion of them belong to the top deciles of the distribution of equivalent consumption expenditure and a number of elderly sub-groups enjoy welfare levels higher than the rest of the population. Hence, there may be strong grounds to argue for a redistribution within the group of elderly and a better targeting of the limited resources of the social security systems towards the most needy of them. In spite of this, it is fair to say that in the EU countries where policies intended to redistribute resources within the group of the elderly were introduced, there was fierce reaction from groups of older persons.

REFERENCES

Bourguignon, F. (1979), 'Decomposable income inequality measures', *Econometrica*, **47**.

Buhmann, B., L. Rainwater, L.G. Schmaus and T. Smeeding (1988), 'Equivalence scales, well-being, inequality and poverty: Estimates across ten countries using the LIS database', *Review of Income and Wealth*, **34**.

CEC (1991), *Social and economic policies and older people: First annual report of the European Community Observatory*, Brussels, CEC.

CEC (1993), *Older people in Europe: Social and economic policies. The 1993 report of the European Observatory*, Brussels, CEC.

Deaton, A.S. (1980), 'Measurement of welfare: theory and practical guidelines', World Bank Living Standards Measurement Study Working Paper no 7.

Eurostat (1990), *Poverty in figures: Europe in the early 1980s*, Luxembourg: Eurostat, Theme 3, Series C.

Foster, J.E., J. Greer and E. Thorbecke (1984), 'A class of decomposable poverty measures', *Econometrica*, **52**.

Haddad, L. and S.M.R. Kanbur (1990), 'How serious is the neglect of intra-household inequality?', *Economic Journal*, **100**.

Hagenaars, A.J.M., K. de Vos and M.A. Zaidi (1993), 'Research on poverty statistics based on micro-data for the Member States of the European Community', Department of Economic Sociology and Psychology, Erasmus University, Rotterdam.

Hurd, M.D. (1990), 'Research on the elderly: Economic status, retirement and consumption and saving', *Journal of Economic Literature*, **28**.

Jenkins, S.P. (1991), 'Poverty measurement and the within-household distribution: agenda for action', *Journal of Social Policy*, **20**.

Sen, A.K. (1976), 'Real national income', *Review of Economic Studies*, **43**.

Smeeding, T.M., P. Saunders, J. Coder, S. Jenkins, J. Fritzell, A.J.M. Hagenaars, R. Hauser and M. Wolfson (1993), 'Poverty, inequality and living standard impacts across seven nations: the effects of non-cash subsidies for health, education and housing', *Review of Income and Wealth*, **39**.

Thomas, D. (1990), 'Intrahousehold resource allocation', *Journal of Human Resources*, **25**.

Tsakloglou, P. (1994), 'Living conditions of the elderly in EC countries on the eve of the single market', Report to the Statistical Office of the EC.

PART IV

Public Finance in the European Union

14. Fiscal policy in European economic and monetary union

George Demopoulos and Kyprianos Prodromidis*

INTRODUCTION

The Treaty on the European Union (1992) has envisaged economic and monetary union (EMU) for Europe as an objective to be accomplished in three stages.[1] The Treaty has been ratified through a national referendum process or through the process of a majority parliamentary vote in all member states of the Union.

To participate in EMU, the member states have to satisfy a number of nominal convergence criteria, and respect the timetable when adopting them. These convergence criteria refer to inflation rates, a sustainable budgetary position, exchange rate stability, and nominal long-term interest rate convergence.[2] In addition to these criteria and the long-run benefits arising from them, the Treaty also focuses on the real convergence of the economies of the member states to the Community's average performance. This can be effectuated via specifically designed structural and cohesion funds (see next section).

Serious questions have been raised about the processes adopted for accomplishing EMU as well as for the speed of adjustment of national monetary and government policies to meet the agreed objectives.[3] The debate has gone beyond the simple criticism of the appropriateness of the convergence criteria, whether the approach to monetary union is the proper strategy, or whether the Treaty's axioms on the process of monetary union have disrupted the workings of the European monetary system. Certainly, the Treaty suffers from a notable weakness, i.e. it does not make any provision for the creation of a (strong) federal institution to help the conduct of national fiscal policies.

The purpose of this chapter is to explore the question of how national fiscal policies could be conducted in EMU as it is envisaged by the Treaty. Specifically, it addresses the following questions:

*Financial support by the Research Centre of the Athens University of Economics and Business is gratefully acknowledged. This chapter draws heavily on Demopoulos and Prodromidis (1994).

1. What does the theory of optimum currency areas say about the conduct of national fiscal policies in a monetary union?
2. Would the desirable EMU lead to the sustainability of the national public debt of the member states?
3. How do national fiscal policies relate to EMU?
4. What is meant by fiscal discipline in EMU?[4]

The chapter is organized as follows. The following section touches on the major structural changes expected to shape the European Union's (EU) new economic environment by the end of the century. Next, a brief discussion of some of the problems associated with the theory of optimum currency areas and the conduct of national fiscal policies in a monetary union is presented. The chapter moves on to explain the debt sustainability issue in the context of monetary union, after which a section is devoted to a discussion of the determinants of debt dynamics. The concern thereafter is with the interpretation of the restrictions imposed on fiscal policies by the Maastricht Treaty. Finally, concluding comments are offered.

EMU: A NEW ECONOMIC ENVIRONMENT FOR THE EU

The birth of EMU, by the end of the century, is expected to bring with it significant (direct and indirect) changes in the working of the economies of the member states.[5] The most important of these changes appear to be the following:

1. *Economic efficiency gains*. These will arise in the private sector due to the disappearance of exchange rate related conversion, transaction, and other banking costs.
2. *Relative price stability and reduction of anticipated inflation*. These outcomes are expected to take place thanks to the complete independence of the European Central Bank (ECB)'s monetary policy from the policies of the national governments and the European Commission, and from the adherence of ECB to price stability.
3. *Elimination of exchange rate uncertainty and reduction of price uncertainty for investors*. These developments will help reduce the risk premiums firms have to pay on equity and thus increase their investment opportunities.
4. *Exploitation of potential, union-wide, external effects or economies of scale*. These will result from the creation of the single market, and are characterized by the free movement of goods, capital and persons. (The

latter is expected to take place at a lower pace than the movements of goods and capital due to linguistic and cultural barriers.)

In addition to these points should be mentioned the impact of the structural and cohesion funds on the restructuring and stimulation of the economies of the member states in the transition period. The structural funds are oriented toward the development and structural adjustment of regions and/or countries of the Union lagging behind 75 per cent of the Community average. The cohesion funds are directed toward the improvement of environment and trans-European networks in member states with per capita GDP of less than 90 per cent of the Community average. By directing structural and cohesion funds to the poorest areas and countries of the EU, the European Commission emphasizes its intention and will to help increase their infrastructure (transportation networks, ports and airports, information networks) and improve the quality of their human capital (training programmes), thus enabling them to stimulate their economic activity proportionately more, and enhance their labour and physical capital, respectively. The outcome, desired and expected, from such EU economic policy actions is to direct these areas and countries into higher growth paths of rising per capita income, thus enabling them to close the gap between their per capita income and the corresponding EU average. More formally, the eventual outcome expected of such economic policy actions is to take, via the externalities so created, the poorer areas and countries of the EU on board a production technology which exhibits increasing returns to scale.[6]

Put another way, the purpose of the structural and cohesion funds is to enable the member states to improve their longer-term performance and achieve real convergence at the EU average per capita GDP. This would increase their labour productivity, narrow differences in their per capita real income, increase employment opportunities and reduce their unemployment rates by creating improved supply conditions and establishing favourable and lasting business expectations concerning a competitive real rate of return on capital.

THE THEORY OF OPTIMUM CURRENCY AREAS AND THE CONDUCT OF NATIONAL FISCAL POLICIES IN A MONETARY UNION

This chapter does not discuss whether EU is an optimum currency area.[7] Nor does it deal with the weaknesses of the theory of optimum currency areas. Rather, it reviews the insights of that theory in order to draw the relevant implications concerning the conduct of national fiscal policies in a monetary union.[8]

Mundell's (1961) celebrated article on optimum currency areas emphasizes three important aspects that are of great interest in analysing the conduct of national fiscal policies in a monetary union. The first refers to the explicit assumption of money illusion and wage stickiness; the second focuses on the implications of an asymmetric real demand shock; and the third deals with the assumption of labour mobility.

Consider a monetary union consisting of countries A and B. The interpretation of the theory of optimum currency areas where country A is hit by an asymmetric demand shock, while country B is favoured by an increase in aggregate demand, is the centralization of the national government budgets for monetary union in order to neutralize the negative social consequences of the asymmetric shock.[9] The reasoning is as follows. With centralized national budgets in a monetary union, social security systems and income taxes are under the control of the central (federal) government. An asymmetric demand shock in country A produces the following effects: it decreases output and increases unemployment. As a consequence, income taxes collected by the central government in country A decline, while unemployment payments increase. The opposite effects take place in country B, which was favoured by the increase in the aggregate demand. With centralized national budgets there would be a redistribution of income from country B to country A, thereby softening the unfavourable social consequences in the latter, which was hit by the negative asymmetric demand shock.

With decentralized national budgets, the scenario of an asymmetric demand shock would increase country A's payments to the unemployed and decrease its tax receipts, thereby increasing its budget deficit. Since there would be no automatic system to redistribute income, country A would have to increase its domestic and/or foreign borrowing. Hence, fiscal policies in a monetary union with decentralized national budgets should allow country A to have the *autonomy* and *flexibility* to let its budget deficit increase so as to absorb the ill-effects of the negative shock. In the spirit of the theory of optimum currency areas, the indicated autonomy and flexibility of national fiscal policies do not lead to unsustainable budget deficits. We deal with this question in the next section.

MONETARY UNION AND DEBT SUSTAINABILITY

In relation to the conclusion on the autonomy and flexibility of national fiscal policies in a monetary union with decentralized (limited degree of centralization) national government budgets, an influential argument has developed. According to this argument the systematic use of fiscal policy leads to problems of sustainability, which force countries to run budget surpluses for a number of years (De Grawe 1992).

The view is supported by empirical evidence from EU countries, which have experienced large budget deficits during the 1980s and the early 1990s. Table 14.1 presents data on general government budget deficits, interest payments, and gross public debt, all as percentages of GDP. Two main findings emerge from this table. First, all four countries presented have experienced large budget deficit during the late 1980s. At the end of 1990, Belgium and the Netherlands were successful in stabilizing their debt:GDP ratio by running large primary budget surpluses. In contrast, Greece and Italy had not been successful in stabilizing their debt:GDP ratio since they did not run the

Table 14.1 Government deficits, interest payments and gross public debt (as percentages of GDP)

Variable/country	1988	1989	1990	1991	1992	1993
Government deficit						
Belgium	–6.6	–6.7	–5.7	–6.6	–6.9	–6.2
Greece	–13.8	–17.7	–18.6	–15.2	–13.4	–9.8
Italy	–10.7	–9.7	–10.9	–10.2	–10.5	–10.2
Netherlands	–4.6	–4.7	–4.9	–2.5	–3.5	–3.5
Interest payments						
Belgium	10.3	10.6	10.9	10.6	10.9	10.3
Greece	7.9	8.2	11.9	12.8	14.6	14.5
Italy	8.1	8.9	9.6	10.2	11.5	12.6
Netherlands	6.3	6.0	6.0	6.2	6.2	6.2
Primary balance (a+b)						
Belgium	3.7	3.9	5.2	4.0	4.0	4.1
Greece	–5.8	–9.5	–6.7	–2.4	1.2	4.7
Italy	–2.6	–1.0	–1.3	0.0	1.0	2.4
Netherlands	1.7	1.3	1.1	3.7	2.7	2.7
Public debt						
Belgium	131.9	127.9	128.3	130.1	132.2	134.3
Greece	80.2	85.9	95.3	100.9	105.6	106.0
Italy	92.6	95.5	97.8	101.3	106.8	112.2
Netherlands	78.8	78.8	78.8	78.3	79.8	81.7

Source: CEC (1993).

required primary budget surpluses. Second, the empirical evidence of the early 1990s emphasizes the great effort made by these countries to restrain their explosive debt due to their fiscal policies of the 1980s: they were forced to run primary budget surpluses.

In brief, the evidence does not lend support to the view of the theory of optimum currency areas that national fiscal policies can create deficits to absorb the negative effects of adverse shocks without leading to problems of sustainability of these deficits. On this question the Delors Report (Committee for the Study of Economic and Monetary Union 1989) emphasizes that a national government budget deficit in a monetary union should be bound by explicit rules. This issue is further explored below.

NATIONAL FISCAL POLICY IN THE EMU

The (consolidated) budget constraint of a national government states that, in a given period of time, the primary deficit (i.e. the excess of government spending, G, over tax receipts, T) plus debt service must be financed either by base money creation or sales of debt or by running down foreign-exchange reserves or by any combination of them. The sources of government funds may be supplemented by revenues from public asset sales and by net income from the exploitation of public assets. The government budget identity is written as,

$$Z + iB = \dot{M} + \dot{B} + \dot{F} + S \tag{1}$$

where $Z = G - T$ = primary balance (deficit if $G > T$ and surplus if $G < T$); G = government consumption spending plus net investment plus replacement investment, and T = total tax plus other current receipts. Transfer payments are subsumed in T as negative taxes;

B = interest-bearing government debt outstanding. Bonds of all maturities are included;

M = monetary base;

F = foreign-exchange reserves in nominal currency;

S = net income on public assets plus revenue from sales of public assets;

i = average nominal rate of interest on government debt.

The dots over variables B, M and F denote respective time derivatives. For simplicity, no distinction has been made between short-term and long-term government bonds and, hence, between short and long interest rates. The latter can be interrelated through the expectations hypothesis of the term structure. Foreign assets and liabilities, and government revenues from sales or the exploitation of public assets, are omitted from the rest of the analysis for simplicity.

By setting $Z = zpy, B = bpy$ and $\dot{B} = (b\dot{p}y)$, dividing both sides of the resulting expression by the nominal GDP = py, where p = GDP deflator and y = real GDP, and d and b denote real primary balance and real debt, respectively, performing a few algebraic manipulations and arranging the terms, we obtain:

$$z + (r - g)b = \frac{\dot{M}}{py} + \dot{b} \tag{2}$$

where $r = i - \dot{p}/p$ and $g = \dot{y}/y$. The loss of seigniorage as a source of government revenue in EMU implies that $\dot{M}/py = 0$. Hence, equation (2) becomes the dynamic constraint,

$$\dot{b} = -z + (r - g)b \tag{3}$$

where all variables are ratios to real GDP, and $-z$ stands for the primary budget surplus. For $\dot{b}$ to be negative r must be no greater than g.

The government's intertemporal budget constraint is the integral of (3):

$$b(t) \leq -E_t \int_t^{\infty} z(t) e^{-(r-g)t} dt \tag{4}$$

Expression (4) turns into a solvency constraint if $r < n$. Equation (4) states that, in the case of a strict equality, the current level of the net government debt must be equal to the present discounted value of the expected primary surpluses. This condition rules out the possibility of Ponzi games, where additional borrowing is needed to pay the interest on the existing debt. The government's fiscal policy is sustainable (Haan and Zelhorts 1990).

However, if the above condition is violated, i.e. $r > n$, the public debt could grow without bounds and a debt crisis could be imminent. This suggests that the budgetary policies should be changed and may have to be supplemented by public asset sales and the depletion of the country's foreign-exchange reserves. This is the reason why the Treaty advises the member countries to avoid running 'excessive' deficits after their entry into EMU.

FISCAL DISCIPLINE IN EMU

There have been considerable criticisms of the application of strict rules for the conduct of fiscal policies in the economic and monetary union proposed by the Delors Committee. As a consequence the Treaty on the European Union provides for:

1. Explicit rules on the public finances of the individual member countries of the EU as a necessary condition for their entry into the monetary union.
2. After their entry, the member states retain fiscal flexibility for stabilization and adjustment purposes, but as public debt monetization is ruled out, they should avoid excessive deficits leading to unsustainable fiscal positions.

Countries experiencing excessive deficits have to undergo adjustment programmes or be subject to penalties. These penalties range from (a) simple (internal) recommendations made by the Council of the EU to member states to bring that situation to an end within a given period of time to (b) a chain of more severe punishments in case of no compliance. That is, the recommendations under (a) will be made public; the European Investment Bank will reconsider its lending policy toward those states; the member states involved will make non-interest bearing deposits of an appropriate order with the Union until the excessive deficit has been corrected; and, finally the states in such a disorder will pay appropriate fines.

The statutory restraints on fiscal policies imposed under the Treaty in conjunction with the free movement of capital and labour and the loss of seigniorage revenues render the individual member states of the EU less autonomous than before as regards their ability to conduct their fiscal policies. However, the fear of a complete loss of fiscal autonomy is unfounded. For, although capital is freely mobile, labour is not. Cultural and linguistic heterogeneity among the member states (Bean 1992) suggests that labour mobility would be lower in the EU in the foreseeable future than it is in the US. Hence, national governments should have some leverage in varying their income tax rates without the fear of eroding the tax base of their countries due to labour's potential migration to lower-tax countries within the Union. However, it remains an open question whether national governments can raise sufficient funds in the intra- and inter-European financial markets to cover their potential deficits.

CONCLUDING COMMENTS

The tentative conclusion emerging from the preceding discussion is that the creation of EMU will be associated with smaller size national government sectors, thus indirectly contributing to greater fiscal discipline among the participating states.

On the other hand, the Treaty does not provide for any significant centralization of the national government budgets in EMU. This implies that there will not be any explicit automatic transfer mechanism redistributing income, thereby softening the social consequences on the member states hit by asymmetric demand shocks.

Under these conditions, the national governments would push for higher transfer payments from the budget of the EU. To avoid such political pressures it might be necessary to examine the creation of a federal-type fiscal authority empowered to alleviate more chronic fiscal difficulties of member states provided that they do not incur excessive deficits as measured by some divergence indicator operating within specified bands.

NOTES

1. The main features of the three EMU stages (1 July 1990–31 December 1993; 1 January 1994–31 December 1996 or 1998; 1 January 1997 or 1999 onward) are briefly summarized as follows. First, the economic features. These are: (a) completion of the internal market; (b) strengthened competition policy; (c) structural reform via structural funds; (d) enhanced coordination and surveillance; (e) budgetary adjustments in high deficit-debt countries: (f) evaluation and adaptation of preceding policies; (g) review of national macroeconomic adjustments; (h) a definitive budgetary coordination system; and (i) strengthening of structural and regional policies. Second, the monetary features. These are: (a) capital market liberalization; (b) enhanced monetary and exchange rate coordination; (c) currency realignments (limited possibilities); (d) participation of all EU currencies in the narrow band (±2.25 per cent) of the exchange rate mechanism (ERM); (e) extended use of the European currency unit (ECU); (f) establishment of the European Central Bank (ECB); (g) narrowing of the ERM bands; (h) ECB in charge of monetary policy, and (i) adoption of a single currency, the ECU. Features (a) to (e), (f), (g), and (h) and (i), under both economic and monetary features, refer to stages I, II and III, respectively. Details are given in: CEC (1990) and Council of the European Communities (1992).
2. The specific convergence criteria are: (a) the average rate of CPI inflation over the preceding 12 months must not exceed the inflation rates of the three lowest-inflation member states by more than 1.5 per cent; (b) a country's long-term interest rates over the preceding 12 months must have been no more than 2 per cent above those of the three best performing member states in terms of inflation; (c) a country's nominal exchange rates must have been within the normal ERM fluctuation bands of ±2.25 per cent for two years before entering the monetary union; (d) budget deficits should be no larger than 3 per cent of GDP, and gross public debts no larger than 60 per cent of GDP. At this point the following qualification is in order: excessive deficits (debts) exist if the deficit:GDP (debt:GDP) ratio exceeds 3 per cent (60 per cent) and if in addition it has not declined substantially and approached the 3 per cent (60 per cent) threshold at a satisfactory pace.
3. See for example Eichengreen (1992), Fratianni et al. (1992), Minford et al. (1992) and De Grauwe (1993).
4. For an elaboration of these questions see also De Grauwe (1992).
5. See note 1.
6. See Romer (1986), Lucas (1988), and Azariadis (1993, chap. 14).
7. See De Grauwe and Vanhaverbeke (1991), and Eichengreen (1990).
8. Recent contributions in the theory of optimum currency areas include: Eichengreen (1990), Melitz (1991), Bayoumi and Eichengreen (1992), De Grauwe (1992), von Hagen and Neumann (1992), and Bini Smaghi and Vori (1993).

9. The analysis that follows is heavily based on De Grauwe (1992, chap. 8).

REFERENCES

Azariadis, C. (1993), *Intertemporal Macroeconomics,* Oxford: Blackwell.

Bayoumi, T. and B. Eichengreen (1992), 'Shocking Aspects of European Monetary Integration', CEPR Discussion Paper Series no. 643.

Bini Smaghi, L. and S. Vori (1993), 'Rating the EC as an Optimal Currency Area', Banca d'Italia, Temi di Discussione, no. 187, January.

CEC (1990), *European Economy*, no. 44, Luxembourg: Office for Official Publications of the EC.

CEC (1993), *European Economy*, no. 54, Luxembourg: Office for Official Publications of the EC.

Committee for the Study of Economic and Monetary Union (the Delors Report) (1989), *Report on Economic and Monetary Union in the European Community,* Luxembourg: Office for Official Publications of the EC.

Council of the European Communities (1992), *Treaty on European Union*, Luxembourg.

De Grauwe, P. (1992), *The Economics of Monetary Integration*, Oxford: Oxford University Press.

De Grauwe, P. (1993), 'The Maastricht Treaty as an Obstacle to Monetary Union', Katholieke Universiteit Leuven, Discussion Paper no. 94.

De Grauwe, P. and W. Vanhaverbeke (1991), 'Is Europe an Optimum Currency Area? Evidence from Regional Data', CEPR Discussion Paper Series no. 55.

De Haan, J. and D. Zelhorst (1990), 'The Impact of Government Deficits on Money Growth in Developing Countries', *Journal of International Money and Finance*, **9**, 455–69.

Demopoulos, G.D. and K.P. Prodromidis (1994), 'Fiscal Discipline in the European Monetary Union', *Atlantic Economic Journal*, **22** (3), September.

Eichengreen, B. (1990), 'Is Europe an Optimum Currency Area?', CEPR Discussion Paper Series no. 478.

Eichengreen, B. (1992), 'Should the Maastricht Treaty be Saved?' *Essays in International Finance*, **74**, Princeton, December.

Fratianni M., J. Von Hagen and C. Waller (1992), 'The Maastricht Way to EMU', *Essays in International Finance*, **187**, Princeton, June.

Lucas, R.E. Jr (1988), 'On the Mechanics of Economic Development', *Journal of Monetary Economics*, **22**, 3–42.

Melitz, J. (1991), 'A Suggested Reformulation of the Theory of Optimal Currency Areas', CEPR Discussion Paper Series no. 590.

Minford, P. et al. (1992), 'The Price of EMU Revisited', CEPR Discussion Paper Series no. 656.

Mundell, R. (1961), 'A Theory of Optimum Currency Areas', *American Economic Review*, **51**, 657–65.

Romer, P.M. (1986), 'Increasing Returns and Long-Run Growth', *Journal of Political Economy*, **94**, 1002–37.

Von Hagen, J. and M.J.M. Neumann (1992), 'Real Exchange Rates within and between Currency Areas: How far away is EMU?', CEPR Discussion Paper Series no. 660.

15. Taxing intra-union trade in the EU: the hybrid destination/origin principle

Theodore Georgakopoulos and Theodore Hitiris

INTRODUCTION

The taxation of intra-union trade, after the abolition of fiscal controls in an economic union, is an important issue that has attracted the interest of both theorists and tax practitioners in the European Union.[1] The issue was first raised in the 1950s and 1960s by the Tinbergen and the Neumark Committees and has since been the subject of analysis by many investigators. The basic question is whether the destination principle should continue to apply after the abolition of fiscal controls on intra-union trade and how it should be administered or whether there should be a shift to the origin principle. Three separate questions have been raised that form the core of the issues under discussion:

1. What are the allocative efficiency and the inter-country redistributional effects of each of these principles?
2. Under what conditions are the two principles equivalent?
3. What are the administrative problems of applying each principle in practice?

In the late 1980s the Commission of the European Community presented several proposals in support of the introduction of the origin principle (CEC 1987, 1989). But the Council confirmed instead a hybrid destination/origin principle as a transitory system to apply until 1996 when a decision on a definitive system based on the origin principle is to be reached. According to this system, trade by agents subject to VAT is taxed according to the destination principle (with the tax effectively applied following the import stage), whereas trade by VAT-exempt traders, mail and border-crossing consumers is taxed according to the origin principle.[2]

This chapter analyses the allocative and inter-country redistributional effects of this hybrid destination/origin principle for a general VAT and compares them with those of the origin principle. For this, a special model is set up which allows explicitly for two routes of intra-union trade: trade carried out by VAT-registered traders (trade via route 1), which is taxed according to the destination principle; and trade by final consumers or VAT-exempt traders (trade via route 2) where the origin principle applies. The model applies to three commodities X, Y and Z, and three countries: the high-tax home country H, the low-tax partner country L, and the rest of the world, W. All three commodities are produced in each country. Production and utility functions are well behaved. Under free trade, perfect competition and no distortions, comparative advantage considerations determine that country H exports X and imports the other two commodities, country L exports Y and imports the other two commodities, while country W exports Z and imports the other two commodities, as shown in Figure 15.1. Trade flows can, however, change if market conditions make it profitable. International prices are determined by country W, that is countries H and L are price-takers both before and after the change in the tax principle. We assume flexible prices and wages and fixed exchange rates, but consider later wage–price rigidity and exchange rate flexibility. We assume perfect inter-industry factor mobility within a country and immobility across borders, but we also discuss how the results are modified for intra-union factor mobility.

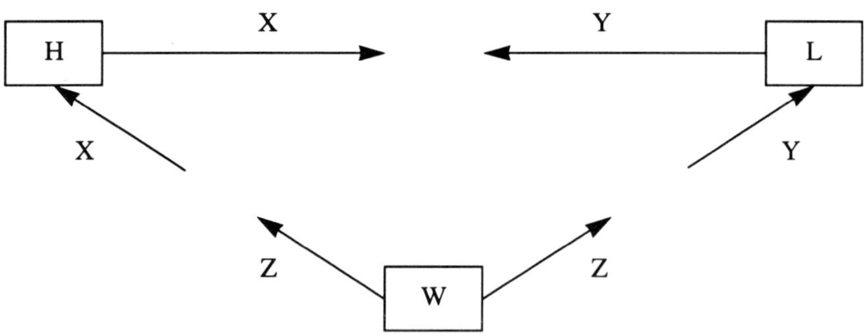

Figure 15.1 Trade flows under free trade

THE HYBRID DESTINATION/ORIGIN PRINCIPLE AND PARETO EFFICIENCY WITH COSTLESS DEFLECTION

Assume there are no other distortions but a general product tax which is levied at rates t_h and t_l in the two member countries with $t_h > t_l$. Under the destination principle, arbitrage secures that producer prices equal world prices, whereas consumer prices are higher by each country's tax (see Table 15.1,

Table 15.1 *Prices under the destination and the hybrid destination/origin principle with a general VAT and costless deflection*

Tax regime/prices	Country H	Country L
A. Destination principle with tax rates $t_h > t_\ell$		
Consumer prices	$P_i(1 + t_h)$	$P_i(1 + t_\ell)$
Producer prices	P_i	P_i
B. Hybrid destination/origin principle with costless deflection		
Consumer prices	$P_i(1 + t_\ell)$	$P_i(1 + t_\ell)$
Producer prices	P_i	P_i

Note: P_i is the world price of product i, t_h and t_ℓ are the general VAT rates levied in H and L, respectively.

Part A). Suppose now that the hybrid destination/origin regime is adopted, so that intra-union traded products are taxed at different rates according to the route they take, as Figure 15.2 shows. Adopting this new regime results in discrimination of the tax on imports by VAT-registered traders in country H, which are now taxed at t_h. In contrast, imports by border-crossing consumers and VAT-exempt traders are taxed at L's lower tax rate, t_l. If consumers' trade deflection is costless, that is the cost of importing goods by either route is identical, consumers will import all products directly from L or from W via L, using route 2. In this way, they will pay the world price increased by the low-tax rate (see Table 15.1, Part B) so that absolute consumer prices will fall, but relative prices will remain unaffected. Therefore, no consumption

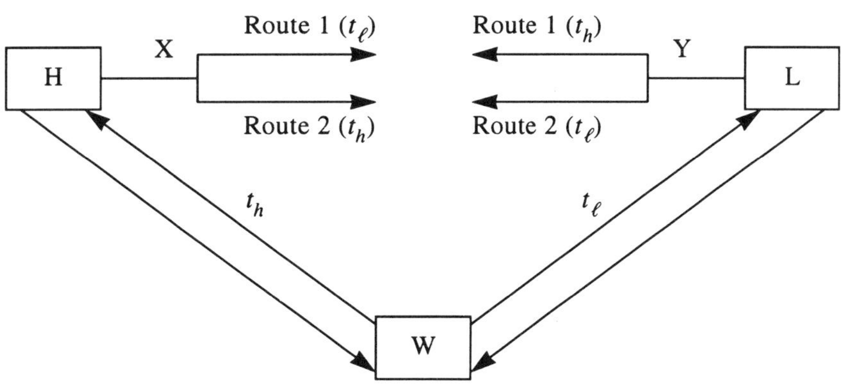

Figure 15.2 *Tax burdens under the hybrid destination/origin principle*

effects will follow. Producers in H will also be able to deflect trade and either sell in L via route 1 or simply export all three products to W, realizing the world prices, so no production effects occur in H[3]. In country L the new tax regime discriminates against imports by border-crossing consumers or VAT-exempt traders and favours imports by VAT-registered traders. Therefore, consumers will import product X via route 2, paying the world price increased by L's tax rate, so both absolute and relative prices remain unaffected and no consumption effects follow the change in principle. Moreover, absolute and relative producer prices in L remain unaffected, so again no production effects take place. These results are similar to those holding for the complete switch to the origin principle (Georgakopoulos and Hitiris 1992).

THE HYBRID DESTINATION/ORIGIN PRINCIPLE WITH DEFLECTION COSTS

Suppose now that trade deflection is not costless, as will probably be the case in practice. Assume consumers' excess costs in H amount to λ_i, when they import product *i* via route 2 rather than route 1, while deflection by producers is costless. If λ_i is larger than the tax difference, consumers in H will continue to buy the product *i* as before, paying the world price increased by H's tax rate. But if λ_i is smaller than the tax difference, consumers will import the product from L, or from W via L by route 2, paying the world price increased by L's tax rate *plus* deflection costs (see Table 15.2, Part A). Therefore, if the deflection costs are higher than the tax difference for all products, consumer prices in H remain unaffected and no consumption effects follow the change in principle. If, however, for some products the deflection costs are lower than the tax difference, the new principle causes consumption effects, which from the welfare point of view are negative because under the destination principle the situation was optimal.[4] Producers in H, however, can sell in either L via route 1 or W, realizing the world price, so producer prices remain unaffected and no production effects are present. The situation in L is different. Consumers in L can buy the products from all three sources (from H via route 1), paying the world price increased by L's tax rate, whereas producers can sell in all three markets (to H via route 2), realizing the same price as before. So, neither consumption nor production effects occur in this country.

Assume now that producers' deflection is costly, the percentage cost for product *i* being μ_i, but consumers' deflection is costless. Consumers in H could import all three products from L via route 2, paying the world prices increased by L's tax rate, so no consumption effects follow the change in principle (see Table 15.2, Part B). However, production effects may occur

Table 15.2 Prices under the hybrid destination/origin principle with deflection costs

Tax regime/prices	Country H	Country L
A. Hybrid destination/origin principle with consumers' deflection costs amounting to λ_i		
Consumer prices		
$\lambda_i > (t_h - t_\ell)$	$P_i(1 + t_h)$	$P_i(1 + t_\ell)$
$\lambda_i < (t_h - t_\ell)$	$P_i(1 + t_\ell)(1 + \lambda_i)$	$P_i(1 + t_\ell)$
Producer prices	P_i	P_i
B. Hybrid destination/origin principle with producers' deflection costs amounting to μ_i		
Consumer prices	$P_i(1 + t_\ell)$	$P_i(1 + t_\ell)$
Producer prices		
$\mu_i > (t_h - t_\ell)$		
$D_i^u < S_i^h$	$P_i(1 + t_\ell)/(1 + t_h)$	P_i
$D_i^u < S_i^h$	$P_i/(1 + \mu_i)$	P_i
$\mu_i < (t_h - t_\ell)$	$P_i/(1 + \mu_i)$	P_i

Note: D_i^u stands for the union's demand for product i whereas S_i^h stands for H's supply of product i.

which, of course, will have a negative welfare impact, since the situation under the destination principle was optimal. If producers' deflection cost for a product is higher than the tax difference, H's producers will sell in the union market, if union demand can absorb their total supply.[5] Thus, they will realize net prices equal to the world prices but reduced by the tax differences. Absolute producer prices fall but relative prices remain unaffected, so no production effects follow this change in principle. If, however, union demand cannot absorb H's total supply of same products, H's producers would sell in W, realizing a lower price. Therefore, relative producer prices change, and the new principle brings about production effects. It will also cause production effects, if for same or all products the deflection costs are lower than the tax difference. If this occurs, H's producers will sell in W, realizing the world price reduced by the deflection costs.[6]

EQUALIZING DOMESTIC TAX RATES OR RATES OF BORDER TAX ADJUSTMENTS

If tax rates are equal in the member countries, introducing the hybrid destination/origin principle leaves consumer and producer prices unaffected (see Table 15.3, Part A) and causes neither trade deflection nor Pareto-type effects, just as for a complete switch to the origin principle (Georgakopoulos and Hitiris 1992). However, though sufficient, rate equalization is not necessary for these results. Just as under the origin principle (Shibata 1967; Johnson and Krauss 1970; Georgakopoulos and Hitiris 1992), under the hybrid destination/origin principle member countries can simply make the rates of border tax adjustments equal with those of W and thus avoid both deflection and Pareto-type inefficiencies. If the member countries adopt a common rate of border tax adjustments ξ, equal to W's, neither consumers nor producers will have any cause to deflect trade. This is so because consumers will in any case pay a price equal to the world price increased by the common rate of border tax adjustments, whereas producers will realize a net price equal to the consumers' price reduced by each country's tax rate (see Table 15.3, Part B). Absolute consumer and producer prices can change in both member countries (if $\xi \neq t_h \neq t_l$) but relative prices remain unaffected, so neither consumption nor production effects will follow in either country.

Table 15.3 Prices under the hybrid destination/origin principle with domestic rates or rates of border tax adjustments equal

Tax regime/prices	Country H	Country L
A. Domestic rates equal $t_h = t_\ell = t$		
Consumer prices	$P_i(1 + t_h)$	$P_i(1 + t_\ell)$
Producer prices	P_i	P_i
B. Border tax adjustment rates equal to ξ and $t_h > t_l$		
Consumer prices	$P_i(1 + \xi)$	$P_i(1 + \xi)$
Producer prices	$P_i(1 + \xi)/(1 + t_h)$	$P_i(1 + \xi)/(1 + t_l)$

DISTRIBUTIONAL ASPECTS AND THE QUESTION OF EQUIVALENCE

Consider now the problem of inter-country income transfers and the question of equivalence. Even if it is neutral on Pareto-efficiency grounds, the hybrid destination/origin principle transfers income between the member countries and thus it can be non-equivalent to the destination principle. Indeed, when deflection is costless, Pareto efficiency is obtained at the expense of income redistribution from L to H by the latter losing tax revenues to the former. Therefore, in this case the two principles cannot be equivalent. Similarly, the two principles are not equivalent when deflection is costly and takes place only for some products, causing both Pareto-type inefficiencies and inter-country tax revenue transfers. The two principles can, however, became equivalent if trade deflection is prevented by equalization of either tax rates or border tax rate adjustments or by high costs. The conditions for equivalence are that: in the first two cases the initial trade of partners by border-crossing consumers and by VAT-exempt traders is in equilibrium; and in the latter case tax rates in the member countries are set in inverse relation to the initial value of bilateral trade via route 2 (Georgakopoulos 1994). The difference between the two cases arises because in the first, the redistribution of income per unit of trade (the tax rate or the rate of rebate) is the same in the two member countries, and thus equalization of income flows also requires equalization of the trade flows that cause this redistribution; and in the second, it differs and therefore trade flows must be in inverse relation to tax rates. These conditions are different from, though parallel to, the corresponding conditions which hold for a complete switch to the origin principle, where these relations must hold for total intra-union trade, not only for border-crossing consumers and VAT-exempt traders. Obviously, the difference between them arises because for the complete origin principle it is total intra-community trade that causes redistribution, whereas in the case considered here, it is only trade by border-crossing consumers or VAT-exempt traders that causes the redistribution.

THE HYBRID DESTINATION/ORIGIN AND THE ORIGIN PRINCIPLES COMPARED

Consider now a shift from the current EU regime to the complete origin principle applied to intra-union trade via both routes, which is the scheme the EU recommends for the longer-run harmonization of the tax principle. Since importers will be allowed to claim the tax levied by exporters against their tax liability on domestic sales, the change in principle will not affect the final tax burden on products traded via route 1. These products will continue to carry the burden levied in the importing country, as is the case of the hybrid destination/origin principle. So, the new principle will not affect relative producer or consumer prices and will cause neither production nor consumption effects. Therefore, on efficiency grounds the complete origin principle and the hybrid destination/origin principles are equivalent, provided, of course, the VAT is levied according to the credit method and importers are allowed to set the tax collected on their imports by the exporters against their VAT liability on domestic sales.

Nevertheless, since the origin-principle redistributes revenues via H's total intra-community imports, the two principles can have different redistributional effects. The question, therefore, is whether and under what conditions the two principles are fully equivalent in the sense of both efficiency and inter-country tax revenue transfers. The preceding analysis suggests that the redistributional effects of the two principles are identical and, therefore, they are fully equivalent when complete trade deflection via route 2 occurs under the hybrid destination/origin principle. This comes about when the deflection costs are lower than the tax difference or, of course, when deflection is costless. In all other cases the inter-country revenue redistribution from H to L is necessarily larger. Therefore, on this facet alone the origin principle could be considered as inferior.

CONCLUSIONS

Just as for the switch from the destination to the complete origin principle, the shift to the hybrid destination/origin principle, currently in use in the EU, can cause trade deflection and/or Pareto-type reallocation effects and income redistribution among the member countries. In a first-best world, as used in this study, the efficiency effects are always negative because the destination principle is optimal. But in a second-best world, these effects can be positive, just as for the complete origin principle.

In particular, we have found that the hybrid destination/origin principle is free of efficiency effects when deflection is costless, but it redistributes income from the high-tax to the low-tax member country and thus it is not equivalent to the destination principle. Efficiency effects are also absent when deflection is prevented by either high costs or by equalization of domestic tax rates or border tax adjustment rates. In the former case, the hybrid destination/origin principle is equivalent to the destination principle when tax rates are set in inverse relation to the bilateral balance of trade by VAT-exempt traders and final consumers. In contrast, in the latter two cases equivalence is reached when trade is bilaterally balanced. For value-added tax implemented according to the credit method, the hybrid destination/origin and the origin principles are equivalent on efficiency grounds, but their redistributional effects may differ.

These results remain valid even if the assumption of fixed exchange rates is replaced by flexible ones which would provide a general adjustment mechanism to correct price level changes as in the case of wage and price flexibility.

But such a mechanism does not account for area discriminatory tax changes, because of exchange rate interdependence. Similarly, nothing will change in the model if the EU sets up economic and monetary union with member countries' exchange rates irrevocably fixed to each other but floating in unison relative to non-union currencies. However, our results might change if intra-union factor mobility is allowed. In this case, changes in relative commodity prices would lead to factor price changes which could give rise to factor movements between the member countries, causing resource allocation.

NOTES

1. For a selection of relevant studies, see especially: Berglas (1981); Dosser (1967); CEC (1963, 1987, 1989); Georgakopoulos (1989, 1992); Georgakopoulos and Hitiris (1991, 1992); Shibata (1967); and Whalley (1979).
2. For distant sales, the origin principle applies if total annual sales of an agent are below a certain limit, whereas for VAT-exempt agents, such as hospitals, banks, insurance companies etc., the origin principle applies if their annual purchases are below a certain limit.
3. Notice that producers in L can also deflect exports to W via H, thus gaining from the higher rebates, a type of 'export deflection' which would lead to 'revolving equilibrium' (Shibata 1967, p. 223). This could lead to L's imports from W being re-exported via H to get the same benefit. So an endless redistribution from H to L would emerge with no equilibrium in sight, unless some constraint is introduced. But this sort of deflection can be checked by H's authorities and is assumed away.
4. Note also that consumption effects will be absent if the deflection costs are common for all products and are lower than the tax difference.
5. Union demand absorbs H's total supply for products Y and Z, which are H's importable commodities, but it may not absorb H's total production of X, unless H's exports to W are lower than L's domestic production of this same product.
6. Production effects are not present, if deflection costs are common for all products and are lower than the tax difference. Then, producers sell in the world market, realizing the world price reduced by the common deflection costs, so absolute prices fall but relative prices remain unaffected.

REFERENCES

Berglas, E. (1981), 'Harmonization of commodity taxes: destination, origin and restricted origin principles', *Journal of Public Economics*, **16**, 377–87.

CEC (1963), *Report of the Fiscal and Financial Committee* (The Neumark Report), Brussels: CEC.

CEC (1987), 'Proposal for a Council Directive Supplementing the Common System of Value-Added Tax and Amending Directive 77/388/EEC – Approximation of VAT Rates', COM(87) 321, final.

CEC (1987a), 'Proposal for a Council Directive Completing and Amending Directive 77/388/EEC – Removal of Fiscal Frontiers', COM(87) 322, final/2.

CEC (1987b), 'Commission Communication on the Completing the Internal Market:

The Introduction of a VAT Clearing Mechanism for Intra-Community Sales', COM(87) 323, final/2.
CEC (1989), Commission Announcement to the Council and the Parliament: Completion of the Internal Market and Approximation of Indirect Taxes', COM(89), 260, final.
Cnossen, S. (1983), 'Harmonization of indirect taxes in the EEC', in C. McLure Jr (ed.), *Tax Assignment in Federal Countries*, Canberra: The Australian National University.
Cnossen, S. and C.S. Shoup (1987), 'Coordination of value-added taxes', in S. Cnossen (ed.), *Tax Coordination in the European Community*, Deventer: Kluwer.
Dosser, D. (1967), 'Economic analysis of tax harmonisation', in C.S. Shoup (ed.), *Fiscal Harmonisation in Common Markets*, New York: Columbia University Press.
Georgakopoulos, T. (1989), 'Harmonisation of commodity taxes: the restricted origin principle-comment', *Journal of Public Economics*, **39**, 137–9.
Georgakopoulos, T. (1992), 'Trade deflection, trade distortions and Pareto inefficiencies under the restricted origin principle', *Journal of Public Economics*, **47**.
Georgakopoulos, T. (1994), 'Tax harmonisation in the European Union: The hybrid destination/origin principle', Athens University of Economics and Business, Discussion Paper no. 5.
Georgakopoulos, T. and T. Hitiris (1991), 'On the equivalence of the destination and the origin principles of taxation in the case of non-general product taxes', *Osaka Economic Papers*, **39** (3–4), 331–5.
Georgakopoulos, T. and T. Hitiris (1992), 'On the superiority of the destination over the origin principle of taxation for intra-union trade', *The Economic Journal*, **102**.
Johnson, H.G. and M. Krauss (1970), 'Border taxes, border tax adjustments, comparative advantage, and the balance of payments', *The Canadian Journal of Economics*, **3**, 595–602.
Shibata, H. (1967), 'The theory of economic unions', in C.S. Shoup (ed.), *Fiscal Harmonisation in Common Markets*, New York: Columbia University Press.
Whalley, J. (1979), 'Uniform domestic tax rates, trade distortions and economic integration', *Journal of Public Economics*, **11**, 13–21.

PART V

European Union: Policies and Accession

16. The Common Agricultural Policy of the EU and developing countries

Bala Batavia and A.G. Malliaris

INTRODUCTION

Ever since the Second World War, numerous less developed countries have attempted to accelerate their economic development by following various strategies. Among such strategies, industrialization via import substitution or export promotion has played an important role. Other strategies included economic planning when significant market failures existed, external borrowing or foreign aid when internal financing was limited, transfer of technology when education, science and technology were at low levels, as well as others.

Kondonassis and Malliaris (1991) evaluate several such policies and conclude that after four decades of developmental experiences, the actual record suggests that industrialization was overemphasized at the expense of agricultural development. This chapter wishes to go a little further by documenting the substantial effort that agricultural issues commanded for the European Union (EU) whose purpose was to accelerate its economic growth via the formation of a customs union. Thus, with trade creation at the core of the EU strategy, it becomes instructive to enumerate the remarkable efforts invested in agricultural issues. Such efforts by the EU could serve developing countries well; the majority of those countries have neglected their agriculture.

The chapter begins by discussing in some detail the Common Agricultural Policy (CAP) of the EU as it evolved from 1957 to 1993. After presenting the evolution of the CAP in the first five sections, we proceed to analyse agricultural policies in less developed countries. Finally, we compare and contrast the experiences of the EU and those of the developing countries, to offer possible guidelines for agricultural world trade.

BIRTH OF THE CAP

In March 1957, six countries of Western Europe took the unprecedented step of setting up a common market designed to lead to eventual economic and political union. This experiment was intended to stimulate economic growth based on a large home market and to establish an influence on the world scene to rival that of the US.

It was clear that agricultural markets could not be excluded from the process of integration. Existing national support systems were not compatible with a common market in agricultural products, but continued support to farmers was a political necessity. In fact, in the 1950s all the prospective member states of the EU had increased the degree of government intervention in agriculture in order to support farm incomes. The purpose of these policies was both to prevent prices from being depressed by a rapid rise in output and to enable farm incomes to keep pace with other incomes because of the relatively low income elasticity of demand for agricultural products.

Given the desire to bring agriculture within the common market and to maintain a degree of government intervention in this sector, there was no alternative but to adopt a common policy so as to avoid the distortions that might result from a continuation of separate national agricultural policies. The CAP was thought necessary to manage the integrated European market for farm goods.

The Treaty of Rome, which established the EU, explicitly mandated such a policy, and set up the machinery to put it in place. However, since the founder members of the Union each had a complex set of agricultural policies, it was argued by Buckwell et al. (1982, p. 10) that the Treaty of Rome was able to outline a common plan for agriculture only in very broad terms.

The objectives and the main features of the CAP were stated in articles 39 and 40 of the Treaty of Rome. Five objectives were adopted:

1. Raising productivity.
2. Ensuring a fair standard of living for the agricultural community.
3. Stabilizing markets.
4. Food security.
5. Reasonable prices for consumers.

Depending on the product, the CAP would entail common rules on competition and compulsory coordination of the various national market organizations.

Hill (1984, p. 21) explains that the Treaty of Rome had envisaged a three-stage progression towards a common policy. In the first stage, for which three years were allotted, policies were to be formulated and agreed. In the second stage, to last until 1970, these policies were to be introduced. The last stage was to be the full operation of the policy in a unified market.

In 1958 over 15 million people – more than 20 per cent of the working population – were occupied in agriculture in the six member countries. The 6.5 million holdings were small and fragmented. Despite existing national support policies, agricultural incomes were generally about half those in the non-agricultural sector. The geographical areas of these six were differentiated by variations in climatic conditions. At the same time they also had different policy instruments and attitudes, from relatively free trade in Italy to generous price supports and subsidies in Germany. Given the diversity of economic, political and geographical situations of the six member states, forging a common agricultural policy was not an easy task.

We propose to study the CAP as it evolved historically. Its development can be roughly separated into three time periods: up to 1968; the years 1968–80; and from 1981 onward. For an extensive presentation see Moyer and Josling (1990, pp. 59–61).

CAP DURING 1957–68

The first period was a time when unified markets and policies were established. This was an era of significant changes in EU agriculture. At the beginning in 1958, the Commission convened a conference in Stresa, Italy, hoping to prepare the ground for the CAP. The conference expanded on the objectives set by the Treaty of Rome and indicated in general terms how they should be pursued. European agriculture was to be reformed and made competitive but without prejudicing the family character of the farm unit. Common agricultural prices, which were to be established progressively and expected to settle slightly above world market prices, were to remunerate farmers adequately without encouraging overproduction.

The Union's agricultural policy could not be based on self-sufficiency, but rather on protection against unfair foreign competition. Building on the conclusions of the Stresa conference, the Commission in early 1960 prepared detailed operational proposals for the CAP which underwent several amendments.

The policy which emerged and came into force in January 1962 embodied three major components: markets and prices, external relations and structure. The three principles of the CAP were: a unified market implying common prices and free circulation of goods; Union preference, which was to protect the unified market from imports and price fluctuations in world markets by subjecting imports to levies that would ensure that their prices exceeded Union prices; and financial solidarity, whereby funding would be transferred from the national to the community level through the European Agricultural Guidance and Guarantee Fund (FEOGA). By 1962, the new CAP began to replace the plethora of support schemes used in the six member states.

The goal of the CAP was for common prices to rule throughout the community in accordance with the principles of a customs union. National prices were too disparate initially for member states to move immediately to common price levels because of potential disruptions to production and markets. Although the principles of the CAP had been agreed, the member states were reluctant to consider their application, clinging instead to their existing national policies.

During the first two years of the CAP there was little progress in reducing the wide divergence between the national prices. Therefore, early in 1964, the Commission proposed that common price levels should be established for cereals, pigmeat, poultrymeat and eggs for the 1964/65 harvest year. There was a serious argument over the price levels because of differences in national interests. Since an easy compromise could not be found quickly, the unified prices did not come into force until 1 July 1967.

In July 1966, the Council of Ministers agreed on prices for fruit and vegetables effective from 1 July 1967, and for other major products, effective from 1 July 1968. Hill (1984, p. 24) argues that the high prices agreed on for cereals necessarily set the tone for other products, and the Commission was forced to propose rather high price levels for beef and veal, milk and dairy products, sugar, olive oil and oil seeds. Eventually, the Council adopted even higher prices for milk, sugar, olive oil and oil seeds than those proposed by the Commission.

CAP DURING 1968–77

During the second period of the CAP, disruptive factors began to reassert themselves and, in some cases, actually emerged as consequence of the very policies that were designed to promote further European unification. The combination of high and guaranteed prices for unlimited amounts of production, stringent protection against imports and technical progress was bound to lead to overproduction. Common financing ensured that the financial consequences of overproduction were not met directly by the member states responsible for them.

As a result, the second decade of EU history witnessed the inconsistencies of the CAP. Developments since the late 1960s indicated that the essential preconditions for a successful continuation of the CAP did not exist and the initial political momentum, which in some instances was enough to overcome economic conflicts, seemed to have evaporated. The major development within the agricultural sector was the steady growth in supply, which tended to surpass that of demand.

When the EU introduced common policies, it adopted a unit of account (UA) to denominate its financial transactions. A UA was introduced, defined in terms of gold and made conveniently equivalent in value to the US dollar, which at that time was convertible into gold. Under the Bretton Woods system of currency exchange rates then operating, national currencies exchanged for one another at fixed rates. All agricultural prices were set in terms of UAs. Thus the CAP would achieve common prices within a common market despite the existence of different national currencies, but the EU-level decisions would be in terms of its own supranational currency. In the late 1960s, strains within the EU became apparent when a weakness of the French franc and a strength of the German Mark materialized.

The CAP's price-support system had developed during a time of fixed exchange rates and assumed the continuation of such stability. Floating rates necessitated the continuous revisions of agricultural prices in terms of national currencies. When during 1969 exchange rates among the member countries began to change, the governments concerned were unwilling to adjust domestic farm prices according to the rules of the common policy. In the absence of offsetting measures, breaches of price unity would unavoidably lead to major trade distortions. These would be all the greater because farmers in countries with devalued currencies would be in a position to sell unlimited quantities to intervention agencies of countries with revalued currencies. To avoid this, trade was made subject to the monetary compensatory amounts (MCAs). These served as import levies and export subsidies for countries with revalued currencies, where domestic proceeds exceeded the common price level, and they served as import subsidies and export levies for countries with devalued currencies, where domestic prices were below the common price level. MCAs permitted agricultural commodities to be traded between the countries as though common prices existed. However, the single market, one of the three basic principles of the CAP, was no more than a fiction created and maintained by MCAs.

The enlargement of the EU in 1973 to include Denmark, Ireland and the UK altered the balance within the EU because of the various patterns of economic performance and the different potentials of these new members as producers of and markets for agricultural products. Thus, following the Smithsonian Agreement in December 1971, when floating exchange rates replaced fixed parities, the underlying economic disparities between member countries showed up more clearly. The 1973 enlargement of the Union complicated matters. Denmark and Ireland, as small countries that were net agricultural exporters, integrated comfortably into the CAP. The UK, on the other hand, like Germany, was a large net importer but, unlike Germany, had neither the political incentive nor the economic means to contribute sizeably to the cost of the CAP. Hill (1984, p. 10) explains how the UK had previously maintained farm income through direct payments to farmers rather than through price support, so that the CAP entailed unwelcome rises in consumer prices. The UK's problems were temporarily alleviated by MCAs and by transitional arrangements which ensured that the UK did not feel the full impact of the cost of the CAP until 1979.

CAP AFTER 1981

The third period of the CAP, which is from 1981 onward, has been one of growing realization of the inevitability of change. The economic pressures for agricultural policy reform in the EU at present come largely from the high financial costs. The recent escalation of CAP costs, relative to the resources available for all common policies, provides the most urgent signal that change is necessary. In the early years, expenditures increased in part as a result of the transfer of spending obligations to the EU from national budgets and later as a consequence of the 1972 enlargement to include the UK, Denmark and Ireland. The problem of CAP expenditures became more severe in the 1980s. Spending has doubled between 1980 and 1986, largely because of increasing costs for market intervention, storage and surplus disposal.

Intervention becomes expensive as producers unload their output on intervention agencies instead of finding a market. Producer subsidies become significant budget items, even for commodities that account for a small share of agricultural output. High import levies and export subsidies arouse the displeasure of exporting countries and promote the search for alternative sources of inputs into food and feed processing industries. Disharmonies arise between supported sectors and unsupported ones, and between agricultural and non-agricultural industries. Generous price awards in 1981 and 1982 ensured an upward trend in production, just as world markets became saturated. The debt problem and slower world growth halted the growth in world trade that had characterized the previous decade. Surpluses in other countries exacerbated the situation.

As early as the beginning of 1980, the Commission was asked by the Council to consider the range of agricultural and budgetary problems and to lay out its suggestions for their resolution – the so-called Mandate of 30 May 1980. The response to this request started a chain of events leading to a more radical set of CAP adjustments that continues to the present.

In response to the Council's Mandate, the Commission published three documents: *Reflections on the Common Agricultural Policy* (December, 1980); *Report on the Mandate* (June, 1981); *A New Impetus for the Common Poli-*

cies (April, 1982). Throughout the three documents, the 'three principles' of the CAP are emphasized. The solutions to the CAP's problems are set out in *Reflections* and expanded in the other two documents. They relate to three areas: the adjustment of market organizations, a new approach to export policy and the adaptation of structural policy.

Reform in the CAP proceeded from general notions to specific commodity applications. The EU took different reform policies to deal with the two crises in the 1980s. On 31 March 1984, the Council of Agriculture Ministers approved the establishment of dairy quotas to check burgeoning milk production. In 1986, it was found that the dairy quotas were not the solution to the budget cost problem. In July 1987, the Commission submitted a package of agricultural stabilizers designed to penalize farmers for overproduction, by imposing automatic price cuts if production thresholds were exceeded. After heated discussion, a stabilizer's package along with set-asides was approved by the European Council in February 1988. This package established a system of budget stabilizers for agricultural commodity programmes designed to keep them within budgetary targets and to prevent overproduction.

The second CAP reform, adopted in June 1992, relied heavily on the abolition of the price–volume support mechanism in favour of direct income subsidies to the agricultural producers with policies aimed at production ceilings and favourable treatment to farmers who have been able to diversify their overcapacity into non-farm production.

THE AGRICULTURAL SECTOR IN LDCs

Having outlined the great emphasis placed by the EU on the CAP, we next make a radical shift in our analysis by focusing on developing economies and their policies towards agriculture. From 1950 to 1975, real output for both developed and developing countries grew at high rates. A major reason for these rates was the increased liberalization and integration of the global economy. Several rounds of negotiation under GATT resulted in sharp reductions in the protection of most manufactured goods by the developed countries; increases in the speed and reductions in the cost of transportation and communications resulted in the greater interdependence and integration of developed countries. Most of the expansion of world trade came about due to increased growth of exports of manufactured products compared to agricultural products. An important factor for these differences is that although trade in manufactured goods was made freer, over the last few decades there had been increasing restrictions to trade in agriculture.

In the 1950s and 1960s, almost all developing countries had economies with agriculture as a major proportion of their GDP, and primary commodities constituted the bulk of their exports. Most of these developing economies isolated themselves from the international economy and focused on costly domestic production, mostly of manufactured goods. In the 1970s some countries rejected the earlier policies and began to pursue export-oriented policies resulting in high rates of economic growth for them. By the 1980s, differences between the developing countries grew further, and many other countries undertook the difficult task of integrating their economies into the international economy.

For developing countries, agriculture is a primary economic activity. It employs 40–50 per cent of the labour force in middle-income developing countries and 70–80 per cent in low-income countries. For low-income countries, it also accounts for 35–40 per cent of the GDP. The share of agriculture in national income declines in the long run as income levels rise, because people spend a decreasing portion of their incomes on food as their incomes rise, and also due to increased productivity of land and labour. However, developing countries should not force this decline of the share of agriculture; it should occur gradually as their income levels rise. For many developing countries, their balance of payments position depends heavily on earnings from exports of agricultural products. Thus, success in agriculture is important for these countries' development over the long run.

Developing countries' economic policies have in general produced a bias against agriculture (Bautista and Valdes 1993; Schiff and Valdes 1992). Two broad set of policies have produced this bias: sectoral and trade policies and economy-wide macroeconomics policies. The impact of each of these is now dealt with in more detail.

TRADE AND SECTORAL POLICIES AGAINST AGRICULTURE IN LDCs

Trade policies in developing countries have often discriminated against agriculture. Tariffs and quotas were used to provide substantial protection to import-substituting manufacturers relative to agriculture. This was typically done to foster economic development, and was meant to be temporary. However, these restrictions were continued for far longer than necessary. This protection has had a substantial effect on agriculture because it reduced incentives for non-protected traded goods (usually agricultural exports) relative to those for protected and non-traded goods. The higher prices of protected goods encouraged a shift in demand towards non-traded goods and less protected traded goods. For example, in the Philippines, a policy of heavy protection of industrial consumer goods was estimated to have reduced the prices of agricultural exports relative to those of protected goods by between

44–71 per cent (depending on the category), and 33–5 per cent relative to the price of the non-traded goods over the period 1950–80 (Chhibber and Wilton 1986). Many developing countries, in addition, have taxes on agricultural exports and subsidies and special import promotion schemes for exports of manufactured goods, further distorting the prices of agricultural goods relative to other goods. This has led to significant decreases in the growth rates of the agricultural sector of the economy, and also the overall economy.

Apart from trade taxes and subsidies, farmers face many sectoral taxes and subsidies. Agricultural output is often taxed to raise revenues, especially through export taxes. Export taxes of 50 per cent or more have been common in many countries, especially in Africa, as reported by Ray (1986). Also, import-competing food crops are excessively taxed, depressing incentives and domestic supplies, and bringing about a greater dependence on imports.

Many developing countries provide generous subsidies and allocate a fair proportion of government expenditure to investment in the agricultural sector. The subsidies are typically provided on farm imports such as seeds, chemical fertilizer, machinery, pesticides, and credit. The main beneficiaries of these subsidies tend to be the larger and affluent farmers. The input subsidies cause distortions in the choice of crops and farming techniques, compounding the adverse effects of output taxes.

In many countries, where balanced pricing policies have been followed, and where considerable public expenditures have been used to support and subsidize research and extension services, irrigation, electricity, rural education, and health services, the agricultural sector has grown considerably faster. For example, both India and China have followed this approach recently in increasing agricultural productivity and growth. In China, there have been recent reductions in direct and indirect taxation of agriculture, removal of controls on land use and production, and public investments, resulting in increased productivity. In India, over the last 20 years, policies have been followed to bring domestic prices closer to international prices while substantial investments in irrigation and high yielding grain varieties have turned the food grain sector from a deficit to a surplus.

MACROECONOMIC POLICIES AGAINST AGRICULTURE IN LDCs

In addition to distortion caused by trade and sector policies, developing countries have pursued monetary and fiscal policies coupled with an exchange rate rigidity, further increasing the bias against agriculture.

LDCs have pursued inappropriate fiscal policies, with recurring deficits. Since access to international capital markets by these countries is limited, and because of scarce domestic savings, these deficits have to be financed by creating money. This leads to inflation. However, the exchange rate is not allowed to adjust because of the differences between the domestic and international inflation rates, resulting in the overvaluation of the nominal exchange rate due to the introduction of exchange and trade controls to manage the balance of payments position.

This overvaluation of the exchange rate lowers the returns to traded goods, especially agricultural exports, and makes agricultural imports cheaper relative to domestic substitutes. Also, the expansionary monetary and fiscal policies increase the level of effective protection to domestic industry relative to agriculture because, first, the balance of payments worsens with the overvalued exchange rate, resulting in the application of *ad hoc* trade controls primarily on industrial goods; and second, the domestic prices of goods subject to quotas or other non-tariff restraints will increase relative to world prices. The creation of excess credit means that the increase in demand for goods whose importation is restricted will be reflected primarily in increased prices. Thus the relative prices of the unprotected agricultural sector will be lower.

AGRICULTURAL WORLD TRADE

The history of agricultural production and trade from 1960 to the 1980s has been one of overreaction, overproduction and domestic policies that prevent adjustment to changing world market conditions. The combination of excess capacity, increased productivity, the declining long-term trend in real agricultural commodity prices, and predatory trade policies, has destabilized world commodity markets. The increased use of export subsidies and falling commodity prices has brought rising international tension. Several countries brought their concerns to GATT for negotiations, and have pressed for widespread reforms for trade in agriculture.

Europe and Japan increased their nominal protection of agriculture to high levels in the 1960s. Protection has persisted for Europe in the 1980s while increasing for Japan. For the US, protection levels increased in the 1970s and 1980s, but were lower than those for Europe. In order of importance, the nations responsible for depressing international market prices for agriculture were the EU, the US and Japan (Roningen and Dixit 1989). The effect of EU policies on international market prices was greater than the combined impact of the US and Japan. In 1986–87, the farm programmes of the EU transferred \$33.3 billion to farmers. Farmers and governments elsewhere in the world lost \$26.7 billion as a result.

Most developing countries have maintained internal agricultural prices, both for consumers and producers, at below world market levels. These have subsidized the urban consumers and increased demand and import dependence. They have also reduced incentives for domestic production. Urban consumers are subsidized for political reasons. In some countries, to overcome the new effects of low prices, governments have heavily subsidized fertilizers, agricultural credit, and other imports. These subsidies often accrue to wealthier farmers, and further distort the incentives and the structure of agriculture and the economy. Many studies such as Trela et al. (1987), Anderson (1992), Loo and Tower (1988) and Tyers and Anderson (1992) have provided quantitative estimates of the costs of protection and their impact on agricultural trade and welfare of both the developed and the developing countries.

EVALUATION AND CONCLUSIONS

Having highlighted agricultural policies in the EU and developing countries over the past 35 years, we wish now to identify some key lessons learned from these policies.

First, unlike many developing countries that have neglected their agricultural development, the CAP of the EU offers strong evidence that agriculture has received great support. It is not clear, nor does it matter, whether such support took place because of the enormous lobbying and political pressures of farmers or because of the EU's explicit prioritization of agriculture. What is currently a fact is that the EU has developed a dynamic comparative advantage in numerous agricultural products which it might not have achieved otherwise. However, the costs of these policies have become very high and may not be sustainable in the future.

Second, although the EU's foremost economic goal was the establishment of a customs union to promote growth through trade, it is obvious that such a goal was not pursued exclusively. Our brief historical overview documents that the CAP was a significant complementary goal.

Third, the numerous efforts by the EU to coordinate national agricultural policies and its willingness to assess, review and revise them, as documented in Swinbank (1989, 1993), clearly demonstrates that simple rules do not exist. This experience should help developing countries realize that as they engage in agricultural programmes, such programmes should be frequently revised.

Fourth, it is instructive to note how flexible exchange rates contributed to the numerous complexities of the CAP. Such complexities offer living proof that customs unions are more successful with stable exchange rates than with volatile ones, and offer a powerful argument for the necessity of monetary coordination and eventual monetary integration.

Fifth, since the CAP has largely achieved its purpose of promoting agricultural development within the EU, one may wonder what will be its future. Much in the spirit of the infant industry argument, one would hope that the EU would gradually prepare its agricultural industry to compete worldwide under global market conditions. This is very much the spirit of the Uruguay Round of the GATT which started in September 1986 in Puenta del Este, Uruguay and concluded in 1993.

Sixth, in contrast to the CAP, most LDCs have neglected their agricultures by following policies that favour industrial development. Thus, the world agricultural markets are dominated by the industrial countries' farm policies which are contributing substantially to declining and fluctuating prices for farm products. A solution to this problem is for all countries to agree to act jointly to reduce protection and thus avoid the classic free-rider problem. However, different countries vary in their willingness to participate, due to dissimilar domestic and political costs. For example, EU farmers would lose substantially from unilateral (about $66 billion per year) as well as multilateral liberalization ($53 billion per year) as reported in Tyers and Anderson (1992). By contrast, for the US, unilateral liberalization would reduce US producers' welfare by $19 billion per year, and multiliberalization would result in a gain of $3 billion per year (in 1985 US dollars).

Finally, a gradual liberalization of tariffs would entail substantial global economic benefits. Risks associated with trade in food would be reduced and LDCs would be encouraged to reform their policies also. Developing countries would benefit economically if agricultural protection and insulation policies were reformed. International food prices would fluctuate less, and opportunities would arise to expand net foreign-exchange earnings. If the developing countries also agreed to reduce their degree of insulation and lowered the effective taxation of their farm sectors, the economic benefits to them and the world would be even larger.

REFERENCES

Anderson, K. (1992), 'Agricultural Trade Liberalization and the Environment: A Global Perspective', *World Economy*, January, 153–71.

Bautista, R.M. and A. Valdes (eds) (1993), *The Bias Against Agriculture: Trade and Macroeconomic Policies in Developing Countries*, San Francisco: International Food Policy Research Institute, ICS Press.

Buckwell, A.E., D.R. Harvey, K.J. Thompson and K.A. Parton (1982), *The Costs of the Common Agricultural Policy*, London: Croom Helm.

Chhibber, A. and J. Wilton (1986), 'Macroeconomic Policies and Agricultural Performance in Developing Countries', *Finance and Development*, September, 6–9.

Gupta, S., L. Lipschitz and T. Mayer (1989), 'The Common Agricultural Policy of the EU', *Finance & Development*, June, 37–9.

Hathaway, D. (1987), *Agriculture and the GATT: Rewriting the Rules*, Washington, DC: Institute for International Economics.

Hill, B. (1984), *The Common Agricultural Policy: Past, Present and Future*, London: Methuen.

Kondonassis A.J. and A.G. Malliaris (1991), 'New and Old Themes in Economic Development: From Antithesis to Synthesis', *Major Issues of Global Development*, University of Oklahoma, pp. 281–98.

Krueger, A.O. (1992), 'Global Trade Prospects for the Developing Countries', *World Economy*, July, 457–74.

Loo, T. and E. Tower (1988), 'Agricultural Protection and the Less-Developed Countries', Conference Paper, *Agricultural Policies and the Non Farming Economy*, Washington, DC: AEI for Public Policy Review.

Moyer, H.W. and T.E. Josling (1990), *Agricultural Policy Reform*, Ames, Iowa: Iowa State University Press.

Pearce, J. (1981), *The Common Agricultural Policy: Prospects for Change*, London: Routledge & Kegan Paul.

Pelkmans, J. (1987), 'The EU's Trade Policy Towards Developing Countries', in Christopher Stevens and Joan Verloren van Theman (eds), *EU and Third World: A Survey*, London: Hodder and Stoughton.

Ray, A. (1986), 'Trade and Pricing Policies in World Agriculture', *Finance and Development*, September, 2–5.

Roningen, V.O. and P.M. Dixit (1989), 'How Level is the Playing Field? An Economic Analysis of Agricultural Policy Reforms in Industrial Market Economies', Economic Research Service, USDA, no. 239.

Schiff, M. and A. Valdes (1992), *The Plundering of Agriculture in Developing Countries*, Washington, DC: World Bank.

Swinbank, A. (1989), 'The Common Agricultural Policy and the Politics of European Decision Making', *Journal of Common Market Studies*, **27**, 303–22.

Swinbank, A. (1993), 'European Agenda: CAP Reform, 1992', *Journal of Common Market Studies*, **31**, 359–72.

Trela, I., J. Whalley and R. Wigle (1987), International Trade in Grains: Domestic Policies and Trade Impacts', *Scandinavian Journal of Economics*, no. 3, 271–85.

Tyers, R. and K. Anderson (1992), *Disarray in World Food Markets: A Quantitative Assessment*, Cambridge, UK: Cambridge University Press.

17. Foreign direct investment in the EU: integrating or disintegrating effects?

Mike Pournarakis and Nikos C. Varsakelis*

INTRODUCTION

Multinational enterprises (MNEs) have emerged as a major factor in the development process for both developing and developed countries. Furthermore, because of the dramatic changes in international production during the last decade, the role of foreign direct investment (FDI) is becoming increasingly important. FDIs experienced a spectacular growth in the second half of the 1980s. The three members of the 'Triad' (the US, the EU and Japan) are the protagonists in the flow of international investment. The Triad accounts for about 75 per cent of the world's outflows of FDIs while intra-Triad FDIs represent a large share of the world total.

The interaction between national states and MNEs could be represented by a two-player game. The formation of the EU is expected to alter the rules of this game. The global strategies of the MNEs will be affected by this formation while individual states will react to EU policies on inward investment activity. Such policies are expected to pursue the dual objective of the attraction of FDIs and the best possible allocation of this investment activity in the regions of the EU.

This chapter examines the effects of FDI activity on European integration. It concentrates on inward FDIs in the EU. The discussion draws on the evidence of transnational activity in the EU by the members of the Triad. Given the current FDI policy of the EU, which does not accommodate adequately the regional disparities, the chapter concludes that transnational activity in Western Europe could become a source of economic rivalry with a mix of integrating and disintegrating effects on the EU process.

*We express our gratitude to Panos Hadjipanayotou for his helpful comments. The usual disclaimer applies.

FDI INFLOWS TO THE EU FROM THE TRIAD MEMBERS

FDI inflow to the EU from the Triad members was particularly impressive during the 1980s and early 1990s. US and Japanese transnational corporations sought to position themselves strategically in the EU in response to the EC 1992 programme, although with a considerable time lag. Furthermore, intra-EU foreign investment is characterized by massive restructuring with intense cross-border activity. In this section, we examine the basic trend in the behaviour of intra- and extra-EU FDI.

The US

The US-based transnationals have had a strong presence in Europe for a long time and compared to other non-EU transnationals, possess high local content levels. Unlike other industrial economies the US relies on investment-based exports to the EU. Almost 80 per cent of total US goods purchased by European citizens are produced by the US MNEs' affiliates in the EU (UN 1992).

The already strong foreign investment position of the US in the EU may explain the relatively low rates of FDI inflows in the late 1980s and early 1990s. Thus, capital outflows from the US to the EU fell from US$9669m in 1988 to US$9101m in 1990. This overall slow-down of the growth rate in US FDI also characterizes US FDI in the EU for the year 1991. This trend may also be attributed to an unexpected levelling off of the rush to gain presence in the EU before 1992 and to the shifting priorities by US investors due to the NAFTA agreement (USITC 1992). This explanation may be reinforced by the fact that the category of investment referred to as 'equity capital outflows' or 'new' investment in the EU was very low in 1991, the lowest compared to US FDIs in other parts of the world.

It should be added that large-scale restructuring of US investment in the EU was already underway in 1988 and 1989 (UN 1990; Table 17.1). American transnationals placed their bulk of interest on the adjustment of their investment to the new regional environment. As a result of the market unification and the elimination of trade barriers, the region-based affiliates are expected to continue to engage in realignment of their investment activity. Cross-border investment, with mergers and acquisitions, is expected to characterize corporate restructuring and investment in new ventures. In terms of geography, the persistent centripetal tendencies are obvious since, with the exception of Spain, the periphery of the EU does not fall within the main poles of attraction for US affiliates (Table 17.1).

Finally, EU-based affiliates of US transnationals enjoy a definite competitive advantage compared to their rivals from Japan and other non-European

Table 17.1 US direct investment position abroad on a historical-cost basis, EC (US$m)

Host country	1988	1989	1990	1991
UK	44459	59827	68224	68261
Germany	21832	24550	27259	32942
Netherlands	16145	18133	22658	24711
France	13041	14069	18874	20495
Italy	9496	10294	13117	13825
Belgium	7501	7941	9050	8838
Spain	4966	6096	7704	7712
Ireland	5886	5522	6880	7450
Denmark	1161	1234	1597	1835
Luxembourg	841	1127	1390	1455
Portugal	546	488	598	893
Greece	195	264	288	291
Total EEC	131069	149545	177642	188710

Source: *Survey of Current Business*, August 1991; US Department of Commerce, BEA Statistics, 1992.

countries. The US transnationals' affiliates are now in a position to capitalize on their experience and exploit the advantage of market unification to shift their scope of competition from the national environment of the individual member country to the European level. This competitive advantage constitutes a major factor in the formation of their globalization strategies during the 1990s (Divinney and Hightower 1991). In addition, we should mention that this US FDI inflow targets some specific sectors which are expected to improve their competitiveness after the completion of the internal market. Among these sectors are pharmaceuticals, motor vehicles, finance and business. In general, we could say that US-based firms have turned their interest towards the high- and medium-technology industrial sectors.

Japan

Japan's importance as a source of FDI outflow has increased dramatically since the early 1980s with an impressive acceleration towards the end of the decade. Japan became the single most important overseas investor during these years.

After peaking in 1990, Japanese investment outflows followed the general trend of decline in world FDI but retained the first position in the next two years. The pace of Japan's FDI outflow to the EU was even faster. When combined with the considerable slow-down of Japanese investment to the US, it becomes evident that there is a shift of interest for certain fields of FDIs in favour of the EU.

In the case of Japanese FDI inflow in the EU, the challenge is big, considering that the penetration of Japanese products to the EU is primarily export-based. Japanese affiliates in the EU supplied only 20 per cent of their country's sales, and the remaining part came from exports (UN 1990). Furthermore, greenfield investment of Japanese-owned plants was directed mainly to finance, banking and insurance services rather than manufacturing until the mid-1980s (UN 1992). In recent years, however, Japanese firms have exhibited a tendency to converge to the US prototype with more investment-based exports to the EU in order to exploit the benefits of the EC 1992 programme (Encarnation 1993).

Geography-wise, Japanese investment exhibits a tendency for a balanced distribution among the more advanced countries. With the exception of Spain, no centrifugal tendencies are exhibited. The UK is the main host country of Japanese FDI in Europe. Almost 35 per cent of the total Japanese FDI targeted the UK for the period 1984–88 (Jovanovic 1992). This trend reached 51 per cent by 1990 and then it slowed down during 1991 and 1992, when it

Table 17.2 Japanese direct investment abroad, 1990–92, European Communities (US$m)

Host country	1990	1991	1992
UK	6806	2948	2553
Netherlands	2744	1960	1144
Luxembourg	1242	1115	1371
Germany	224	266	68
Denmark	1257	817	456
France	854	223	295
Spain	320	378	332
Belgium	367	222	281
Ireland	49	102	113
Italy	217	322	216
Portugal	68	10	12
Greece	4	1	–
Total	13369	9004	6766

Source: Ministry of Finance, Japan.

was 32 per cent and 38 per cent respectively. The six core country members, France, Germany, the Netherlands, Italy, Belgium and the UK hosted 95 per cent of the total Japanese FDI in the EU for the period 1984–88, but during 1990–92 there was a slow-down for these countries, with a relative increase in the share of Denmark and Spain (Table 17.2).

Despite the slow-down of Japanese FDI activity in 1991 and 1992, Japanese firms engaged in a variety of strategic alliances, acquisitions and joint ventures, breaking away from their insistence in the past on greenfield foreign investment. This type of investment activity was directed primarily by the single market implementation, that is a policy of 'Europeanization' of Japanese firms. Dunning (1993) estimates that, in the 1988–90 period, 40 per cent of the value of new Japanese investment in the EU took place in the form of acquisitions and mergers.

Intra-EU Investment

FDI investment inside the EU borders exceeds inward investment. Intra-union direct investment underwent a spectacular increase in the period 1984–89. In terms of geographical allocation, investment in the EU exhibits preferences for closeness to the centre (Tables 17.3 and 17.4). Thus, 95 per

Table 17.3 Intra-Community inward direct investment (ECUm)

Host country	1984	1985	1986	1987	1988	1989
Belgium and Luxembourg	1051	504	959	1182	3816	5330
Denmark	8	6	72	177	136	523
Germany	632	612	595	425	1367	4815
Greece	15	107	136	102	86	254
Spain	570	592	1164	1519	1889	3406
France	1216	1233	1435	1349	4424	3864
Ireland	140	281	62	160	301	1051
Italy	971	489	1106	770	1278	2355
Netherlands	2802	700	2800	1283	3791	4532
Portugal	82	188	114	192	313	681
UK	1899	1614	2819	5237	2566	7555
not allocated	271	81	65	321	303	977
Total EUR 12	4053	6233	11336	12634	20269	35344

Source: Eurostat, European Community Direct Investment, 1992.

Table 17.4 Mergers and acquisitions in the EC, involving the top 1000 European firms by industry, 1987–91

Sector	1986–87	1987–88	1988–89	1989–90	1990–91
Food	52	51	76	102	71
Chemicals	71	85	107	148	100
Electrical and electronics	41	36	49	46	48
Machinery	31	38	55	52	25
Computers	2	3	4	2	7
Metal manufacturing	19	40	35	64	47
Vehicles	21	15	14	32	21
Wood paper, furniture	25	34	61	79	49
Mining	9	12	19	19	13
Textiles	6	14	20	13	12
Construction	19	33	39	39	47
Other manuf.	7	22	13	26	15
Distribution	49	57	58	52	38
Banking	35	78	83	113	75
Insurance	28	40	33	46	28
Total	415	558	666	596	596

Source: CEC XXIst Report on Competition Policy, 1992.

cent of the total FDI activity in the EU targets the core countries as defined above.

The EC 1992 programme affected positively inward foreign investment in the EU during the 1980s. The shift of the EU from trade policy-led to production based integration *via* the EC 1992 programme in the 1985 is attributable primarily to the fact that Europe lags behind in the technology race between the members of the Triad. In the years that followed it became evident that regional rather than national economic policies on trade and investment would dominate intra-EU economic activity. An unprecedented level of intra-regional FDI in the second half of the 1980s led to the 'regionalization' of EU-owned industry. Many EU transnational firms regionalized their activities in their effort to prepare themselves to move up from 'national champions' to 'EU champions'. Corporate strategies aimed at rationalizing operations on a regional scale with massive merger and acquisition activity. EU corporations have undergone a period of restructuring with intense cross-border activity following the EC 1992 programme. It seems that realignment and rationalization of FDIs rather than new greenfield investment will be the priority in the 1990s.

The boom of mergers and acquisitions since 1986 at the national, intra-EU and international level characterizes investment activity (Table 17.4). The increasing trend of 'big' mergers and acquisitions levelled off in 1990–91. The big member states, France, Germany and the UK, are the protagonists in the EU merger activity while among the foreign buyers the US and Japan are the most active countries. For example, mergers and acquisitions of European firms by US companies between 1986 and 1988 were increasing at three times the rate of previous years.

EFFECTS OF INWARD FDI ON EU INTEGRATION

Before 1992, MNEs with their foreign direct investment activity in the EU tried to exploit the location-specific advantages as defined by Dunning (1993) in the eclectic paradigm of international business. Thus, there is a spatial distribution of the economic activity of business firms, both European and foreign, across the regions of the EU for the exploitation of regional differences in the resource endowments (comparative advantage of the region), transport and communication cost, and the price, quality and productivity of inputs. In addition, MNEs tried to overcome the artificial barriers in the trade of goods and services such as subsidies, public procurements, technical standards etc. to further increase their profits.

The EC 1992 programme intends to eliminate all non-tariff barriers, leading the way towards the intensification of competition in national and European markets. Thus, European economic integration is expected to harmonize the conditions of production and lower the cost of intra-EU trade. This process will encourage European-based firms to exploit intra-regional product and process specialization, economies of scale and fresh economies of scope (Dunning 1990).

To the extent that the establishment of the internal market will bring about the virtual elimination of the non-tariff barriers, some location-specific advantages that were due to the existence of these artificial barriers will cease to exist. Thus, MNEs may not continue to produce in some regions and may concentrate their economic activity in the core areas of the EU. Some of the location-specific advantages such as investment incentives, communication and transportation costs, societal and infrastructure provisions etc. will start to converge to the EU average. Finally, some of the location-specific advantages, such as the special endowments of different regions, e.g. quality of labour and capital, resources etc. will still remain even after the completion of the internal market which, in turn, may affect the competitive advantage and the location of production of both foreign investors and EU-owned firms.

Therefore, several FDIs will not be as eager to remain or to go multinational since the factors that lead to multinational advantage, such as the exploitation of cross-border arbitrage, will tend to diminish. As a result, there will be some shrinkage in the extent to which firms produce in two or more countries, having important implications for the periphery of the EU (Itaki and Waterson 1990).

The development of this trend will depend among other things on the extent to which creation of the so-called 'Euro-organizations' will materialize (Vandermerwe 1993). According to this thesis, Europe-wide decentralized networks may be the new structure, leading firms to strongly favour regions that are exhibiting comparative advantage. Thus the Europe-based firms, instead of centralizing their economic activity, might prefer to reallocate their activity throughout Europe in order to exploit the comparative advantages of every possible region.

European economic integration brings into conflict two trends. The first is in favour of the centralization of the MNEs' economic activity and the second is in favour of the integration of a decentralized system for European organizational structure. In the first case, the FDI activity will have disintegrating effects, since there will be a slow-down of investment in the peripheral regions and an increase in investment in the core countries. In the second case, FDI activity in the EU will have integrating effects. Intensification of foreign investment activity in the peripheral regions will help convergence in the core countries through the distribution effect of FDI activity. This intensification will be in accordance with the comparative advantage of each region.

THE NEED FOR A COMPREHENSIVE FDI POLICY IN THE EU

The above discussion suggests the need for a comprehensive FDI policy in the EU. Of course, the complexity of the issue of inward investment in the Union must be appreciated. Figure 17.1 shows the potential conflict of interests that may arise in an integration scheme like the EU. This conflict could stem from three sources: the union, the state and the MNE investor, both external and European.

The problems at the state–MNE investor level of interaction arise from the complete lack of a comprehensive regulatory framework on FDI activity in the global economy. Unlike the fields of international trade and finance,

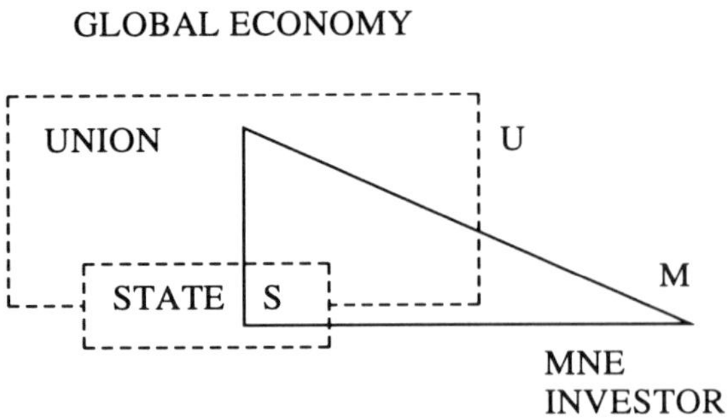

Figure 17.1 Possible conflict of interests in the EU integration scheme

international investment activity does not have to conform to any general principle of a comprehensive agreement. The lack of an institutional framework to facilitate the needs of the global economy explains the usual tactics adopted by foreign investors to circumvent economic policies of national governments. These problems reached an unprecedented level during the 1970s, when many national governments, especially those of developing countries introduced an aggressive policy towards the domestic affiliates of the MNEs (Kennedy 1992). During the 1980s, however, because of the burden of debt and deficits, developing countries as well as the developed ones changed their attitude towards the attraction of FDI.

So far, individual states and MNEs play a bargaining game in which both try to maximize their corresponding objective function given existing constraints. The bargaining outcome depends on the relative bargaining power that each player has in the process of achieving its objective (Grosse and Behrman 1992). The policies of other states on the attraction of the FDI are included as constraints in the model. When the individual state enters into an economic union the formulation of the model is modified. The extra constraint that emerges is the supranational FDI policy that the economic union adopts, and which the member state must take into account (the model could take the form of three players: union, state and MNE investor).

At the union–FDI level of interaction a union-wide FDI policy could act as a shock absorber in this triangular conflict. Active and consistent policies could address the important issues of market imperfections at the union level and provide the prototype for a global approach to the issue of FDI activity. The EU, currently, lacks a consistent and well coordinated policy on FDI. At best, present policies could be viewed as an extention of the more general EU target to secure competitiveness and equal treatment of insiders and newcomers under the proviso that reciprocity is observed by the outside world. In practice, however, due to the lack of an explicitly stated common policy on

FDI inflow, individual states often resort to beggar-thy-neighbour practices with frequent use of increased national subsidies in order to recruit the type of multinationals that suit their development needs.

During the last period the existing EU policy aimed to implement articles 85 and 86 of the Rome Treaty, which promote competition and guard against 'excessive' concentration, and this affected FDI restructuring. The EC 1992 programme created the need to widen the scope of these policy measures so that the issue of mergers and acquisitions could be accommodated in such a way that market efficiency and rationalization of cross-border investment activity could materialize. The EC regulation no. 4064 of 1989 and the major control regulation of 1990, reflect the spirit of the globalization process and emphasize market efficiency in the framework of strengthening competition policy.

The FDI policies of the EU are so far characterized by a relative atrophy compared to other policy areas. Due to insufficient focus and lack of consistency, regional FDI policy does not guard against unbalanced developments that can accentuate regional disparities. The reduced competitive bidding for FDI attraction by the periphery of the EU is not offset by an accommodating regional policy of incentives. Furthermore, large-scale cross-border restructuring entails dislocation costs due to centripetal preferences of investors. As a result, widely divergent policies of the member states frequently lead to beggar–thy-neighbour practices. To the extent that these persistent asymmetries imply a lack of consensus in the central authorities on the primacy of regional over national FDI policies, foreign investment activity in EU could be the source of serious economic rivalry with disintegrating rather than integrating effects that hinder the objectives of the Maastricht Agreement.

CONCLUSION

MNEs will play an increasingly important role in the global economy of the 1990s. The formation of large economic blocs raises the interesting question of the interaction between corporate integration and regionalization. Integration schemes with market unification of the member states are expected to lead to regionally integrated FDI activity. Then, the active and consistent policies of regional authorities may provide an appropriate framework for transnationals to facilitate the process of market unification.

A major question that arises in the economics of European integration is whether inward FDI activity has overall integrating or disintegrating effects in the framework of the EU scheme. In this chapter we have tried to identify the effects of economic integration on FDI strategies. Also, we looked at the effects of these FDI decisions on the convergence process, especially for the peripheral regions. We expect that MNEs, both European and external, will pursue a strategy which will lead to a mix of integrating and disintegrating effects. The realities of the post-EC 1992 FDI activity suggest definite preferences for centripetal policies of investment, both internal and external. The need emerges, therefore, for a comprehensive FDI policy consistent with the objective of competition intensification, which at the same time will accommodate the EU convergence targets.

REFERENCES

Burgenmeier, B. and J. Muchielli (eds) (1991), *Multinational Firms and European Integration*, London: Routledge.

Divinney, T. and W. Hightower (1991), *European Markets after 1992*, London: Lexington Books.

Dunning, J. (1990), *European Integration and Transatlantic FDI: The Record Assessed*, University of Reading, Working Paper Series B, no. 144, September.

Dunning, J. (1993), *Multinational Enterprises and the Global Economy*, Wokingham, UK: Addison Wesley.

Dunning, J. and J. Cantwell (1991), 'Japanese Direct Investment in Europe', in Burgenmeier and Muchielli (1991).

Encarnation, D. (1993), 'A Common Evolution? A Comparison of United States and Japanese Transnational Corporations', *Transnational Corporations*, **2**, (February), 7–32.

Grosse, R. and J.N. Behrman (1992), 'Theory in International Business', *Transnational Corporations*, **1** (February), 93–126.

Itaki, M. and M. Waterson (1990), *European Multinationals and 1992*, University of Reading, Working Paper Series B, no. 141, August.

Jovanovic, M.N. (1992), *International Economic Integration*, London: Routledge.

Kennedy, C.R. (1992), 'Relations Between Transnational Corporations and Governments of Host Countries: A Look to the Future', *Transnational Corporations*, **1** (1) (February), 67–91.

Kline, J. (1992), 'International Regulation of Transnational Business: Providing the Missing Leg of Global Investment Standards', *Transnational Corporations*, **1**, 153–64.

Panic, M. (1992), *National Management of the International Economy*, London: Macmillan.

UK Department of Trade and Industry (1991), *A Study into the Knock-On Effects of Inward Investment in English Regions*, London: DTI.

United Nations (1992), *World Investment Report for 1991*, New York: UN.

United Nations (1990), *Regional Economic Integration and Transnational Corporations in the 1990s: Europe 1992, North American and Developing Countries*, Series A, no. 15, July, New York: UN.

United Nations (1992), *From the Common Market to EC 92,* ST/CTC/144, New York: UN.

United Nations (1993), *World Investment Report, 1993*, New York: UN.

US Department of Commerce, International Trade Administration (1993), *Europe Now, A Report*, January, Washington, DC.

US International Trade Commission (1992), *The Effects of Economic Integration within the European Community and the United States*, April, Washington, DC.
Vandermerwe, S. (1993), 'A Framework for Constructing Euro-Networks', *European Management Journal*, **11** (1), 55–61.
Young, S. and N. Hood (1993), 'Inward Investment Policy in the European Community', *Transnational Corporations*, **2** (August), 35–60.

18. The Community's technology policy: its role and effects on European economic integration

George M. Korres and Yannis G. Paraskevopoulos

INTRODUCTION

Economists measure economic integration for three main purposes: to compare the degree of economic integration found in one regional group with that of another, and to measure the progress of integration in a particular grouping over time; to quantify the aggregate effects of integration on variables that influence the welfare of the group; and to quantify the effects of integration on the distribution of its benefits among the participating countries. Technological change has been widely considered for many years as an 'engine of growth' as well as an important factor in development and economic growth. Today, there is intensive technological competition among the EU, the US and Japan. European technology policy aims to reinforce existing technological capabilities, to take greater advantage of the international scene, to increase convergence between member states, to reduce the disparities of the less favoured regions, and to contribute to European economic integration.

In this chapter, we examine the Community's research policy and the effects on European economic integration, and evaluate the development of European technology policy. We shall also analyse the way that European technology policy works and how it is implemented through various 'channels' to the member states. We shall look at the implications of the transfer of technological to economic growth and estimate the effect on the member states. For this reason, we shall apply a demand model to measure the results from the flow of financial resources.

THE COMMUNITY'S TECHNOLOGY POLICY AND EUROPEAN ECONOMIC INTEGRATION

During the past quarter-century or so, many arrangements for international economic integration have emerged. The most important of these blocs is the European Economic Community (EEC) which has enabled European integration to proceed rapidly by completing a customs union, providing for the free movement of persons and capital, and finally, applying the integration plan in a number of areas such as agricultural policy, transport and technology policy.

In the first phase of the history of the Community's research policy only eight articles from the Euratom Treaty were devoted to the promotion of research activities. During the 1960s, several attempts were made to develop cross-national research groupings. Until the end of the 1980s, the Community's research policy was oriented towards coordinating the national technology policies of member states rather than pursuing a coherent technology policy. During the period 1982–90 there was a more coherent and clearer technology policy. The Single European Act (SEA) and the Treaty of Maastricht have worked in this direction. The SEA makes substantial amendments to the Treaty of Rome. It contains provisions that intend to accelerate the process of European integration by completing a large single market, strengthening economic and social cohesion and cooperating in financial matters. The principles introduced by the SEA are repeated, confirmed and extended in the Maastricht Treaty, which offers a double perspective on technology policy.

THE IMPLEMENTATION OF EUROPEAN TECHNOLOGY POLICY: THE FRAMEWORK PROGRAMMES

Today, the Community's research policy is implemented through specific programmes. In the 1980s, the first step in the direction of the Community's research policy was the formulation of the first framework programme (1984–87). This has introduced medium-term planning of research activities at EC level.

The second framework programme started in September 1987, when approximately 60 per cent of the funds from the second framework programme were allocated to industrial research. The decisive breakthrough to a comprehensive political strategy for the technological sectors came with the second and third framework programmes. The second (1987–91) and the third (1990–94) programmes are based on the Single European Act.

In April 1990, the Council of Ministers adopted the third framework programme (1990–94), overlapping the second programme by two years. The fourth programme complies with the provisions made by the Maastricht

*Table 18.1 The Community's framework research programmes**

Focal areas	Total mECUs	Percentage of total budget
First framework programme (1984–87)		
Agricultural competitiveness	130	3.50
Industrial competitiveness	1060	28.20
Improving raw materials	80	2.10
Improving energy resources	1770	47.20
Stepping up development aid	150	4.00
Improving working conditions	385	10.30
Improving the science & technology potential	85	2.30
Horizontal action	90	2.40
Total budget	3750	100
Second framework programme (1987–91)		
Quality of life	375	6.90
Towards an information society	2275	42.30
Modernization of industry	845	15.60
Biological resources	1173	5.20
Energy	280	21.70
S/T for development	80	1.50
Exploiting marine resources	80	1.50
Improvement of science & technology cooperation	288	5.30
Total budget	5396	100
R&D programmes already adopted or in hand	1084	
Total budget	6840	

Third framework programme (1990–94)		
Enabling technologies	3000	38.90
Information technologies & communications	1200	15.60
Industrial & material technologies		
Management of natural resources	700	9.10
Environment	1000	13.00
Life sciences & technologies	1100	14.30
Energy		
Management of intellectual resources	700	9.10
Human capital & mobility	7700	100
Total budget		
Fourth framework programme (1994–98)		
Area I Technological & demonstration of research & technology	11600	78.91
Area II Cooperation of non-EC countries & international organizations	1400	9.52
Area III Circulating and exploiting research funding	700	4.76
Area IV Improving training and mobility for researchers	1000	6.80
Horizontal support measures	(1600)	
Total	14700	100

Note: * Community's financial contribution only.

Source: CEC 'EC Research Funding', Brussels, Belgium, 2nd & 3rd editions, 1990, 1991.

Treaty and therefore covers the Community's R&D activities. Table 18.1 shows the Community's framework research programmes.

The most significant objectives of the Community's framework programmes are the following:

- to strengthen European industry and the industrial competitiveness;
- to set up a vast solid market by promoting standardization and open procurement;
- to improve the effectiveness of the Community's scientific and technical cooperation;
- to promote agricultural competitiveness;
- to speed up the marketing of new technologies by carrying out programmes for the application of information technologies;
- to help the least favoured regions of the Community gain access to new technologies; and
- to apply accelerator factors, such as encouraging small and medium enterprises (SMEs) and continuing training.

However, the lack of economic infrastructure in the smaller member states and the advanced level of research projects has restricted the participation of smaller member states under the 'normal quotation'.

THE TRANSFER OF FINANCIAL AND TECHNOLOGICAL FLOWS THROUGH CSFs

The transfer of financial and technological flows to the member states has a large impact on the establishment of research and technological infrastructure. These resources are intended to establish the appropriate industrial infrastructure, to enhance the research units and the traditional agricultural activities.

The CSFs (Community's structural funds) consist of the following two main categories:[1] 'national section', which aims to develop and improve research activities in the whole country; these activities are concerned with the training, the transfer of know-how and advanced technologies; and 'regional section', composed of some special projects corresponding to each of the regions. These are aimed at improving the infrastructure and exploiting the local resources of each region. Figure 18.1 shows the expenditures from structural funds among the member states for the period 1987–92. The CSFs focus mainly on the fields of transport, telecommunications, and the research and energy sectors. Apart from the funds that were allocated directly to technological infrastructure through research framework programmes, a large amount is devoted to research activities through CSFs. The IMPs (integrated

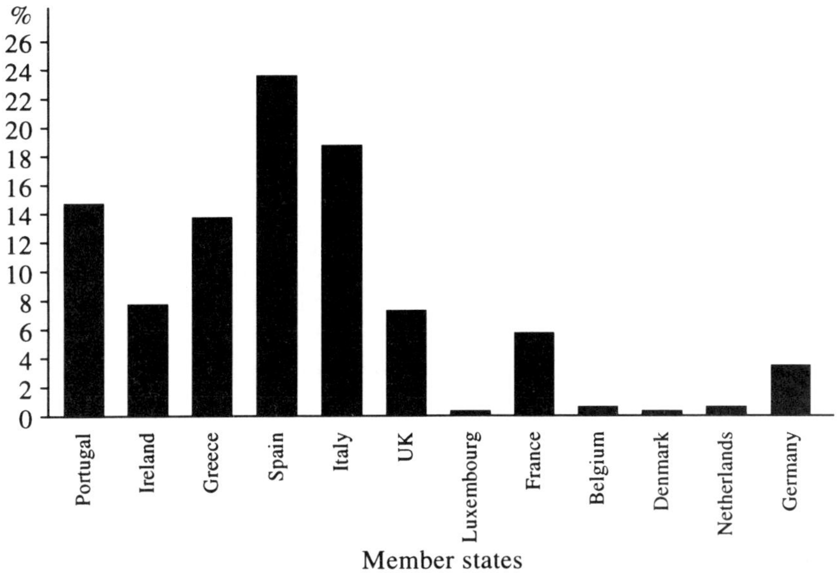

Figure 18.1 Structural funds' expenses, % of total Community funding, 1987–92

Mediterranean programmes) worked in this direction; they were approved by the European Council in July 1985, in order to help the Mediterranean regions (France, Greece and Italy). Since 1990, all these IMPs have been included within the framework of CSFs.

ESTIMATION ON THE EFFECTS OF THE TRANSFER OF THE COMMUNITY'S FINANCIAL AND TECHNOLOGICAL FLOWS

The Theoretical Model: the Demand Side

Consumption

Equation (1) indicates the consumption, where the variable of consumption (*CON*) indicates the logarithm of per capita consumption which is equal to the logarithm of national disposal income deflated by the index of consumer prices. The variables *DCON* and *DLYD* are in a dynamic form which indicates the change between two periods.

$$DCON = a_0 + a_1\,DLYD + a_2\,(CON_{t-1} - LYD_{t-1}) \qquad (1)$$

We added two lagged variables, one for the consumption $(CON)_{(t-1)}$ so that the influence from the past on the present consumer behaviour gives a distributed lag of the Koyck-type transformation, and one for the national disposable income $(LYD)_{(t-1)}$.

Investment

Equation (2) is a dynamic form and the variable (*DTINV*) indicates the change between two periods of total investment that is equal to the (*DGDP*) argument which is the difference of GDP between two periods, *t* and (*t*–1). The variable (*DFLBFE*) is the total bank lending in agricultural and manufacturing deflated by the GDP deflator, which is a proxy for the CSFs' flows. Finally, the dummy variable D_1 indicates the firm's profitability.

$$DTINV = a_0 + a_1\, DGDP + a_2\, DFLBFE + a_3\, D_1 \tag{2}$$

Imports

The equation of total imports (of goods and services) is expressed in per capita units and in real terms. In the import equation the dependent variable is the log of per capita imports (those aged between 15 and 64 years). As an explanatory argument, we used the log difference of per capita GDP (in constant prices), the log difference of terms of trade and the price of exports over the price of imports and finally a lag-dependent term. It is worth noting that we have incorporated the price effect too.

$$LMQ = a_0 + a_1\, DLGDP + a_2\, DTRD + a_3\, LMQ_{t-1} \tag{3}$$

Employment

The employment equation is expressed in logarithms and the variable (*LEM*) is a logarithm of total employment in manufacturing which is equal to the variable (*GDP*) that is the logarithm of total final demand (corresponding to the GDP in constant prices), plus the log of deflated wage rate (the wage rate deflated by the private consumer price index) plus the logarithm of the lag variable of total employment $(LEM_{(t-1)})$. This formulation applies the partial adjustment technique. *LEM* and *GDP* are cointegrated by Okum's law.

$$LEM = a_0 + a_1\, GDP + a_2\, LEM_{(t-1)} \tag{4}$$

Determination of wages

We have expressed the wage price level in a logarithm-dynamic form. The dependent variable (*DLDFL*) is the change between two periods in the GDP deflator which shows the inflation rate. This is equal to a constant term plus the argument of (*DWGDFL*) which is a difference of logarithms of the deflated shares of wages and salaries in GDP, plus the lag of the previous period variable ($DWGDFL_{(t-1)}$), as well as the variable of differences of logarithm of import prices (*DPLM*).

$$DLDFL = a_0 + a_1\ DWGDFL + a_2\ DWGDFL_{(t-1)} + a_3\ DLPM \qquad (5)$$

The Empirical Results

We estimated the previous five-equation system simultaneous equation model by using the iterative non-linear least square method (INLSQ), which provides parameter estimates asymptotically with those taken out of the maximum likelihood method. The advantage of this method is that we get the cross-effect along the error term. Table 18.2 shows these estimations. The R^2 for the whole model is 0.61 and the D–W statistic 1.832.

The Community's financial flows have a macroeconomic impact on the economies of member states. Tables 18.3 and 18.4 show the effects of CSFs on the major macroeconomic aggregates for the economies of member states. The estimates have been made according to two scenarios: the first includes the CSFs; the second does not. The transfer of financial and technological flows has a direct impact on the economic and technological infrastructure of the sectors. For instance, these flows affect the establishment of new tech-

Table 18.2 Empirical results of simultaneous equation model: Greece (1989–93)

Empirical results

$$DCON = 2.05 + 0.97DLYD + 0.66(CON_{(t-1)} - LYD_{(t-1)}) \quad (1)$$
(3.10) (2.242) (6.184) $R^2 = 0.61$, D–W = 1.778

$$DTINV = -134916 + 465363DGDP + 81.33DFLBFE + 198084D_1 \quad (2)$$
(–5.08) (2.09) (11.05) (3.97) $R^2 = 0.13$, D – W = 0.537

$$LMQ = 0.167 + 0.820DLGDP + 0.535DTRD + 0.972LMQ_{(t-1)} \quad (3)$$
(1.23) (2.78) (2.39) (38.3) $R^2 = 0.98$, D – W = 2.58

$$LEM = 0.70 - 0.236GDP - 0.0540LEM_{(t-1)} \quad (4)$$
(12.48) (–4.33) (–1.54) $R^2 = 0.98$, D – W = 0.805

$$DLDFL = -1.312 + 0.134DWGDFL - 0.056DWGDFL_{(t-1)} + 0.811DLPM \quad (5)$$
(–4.38) (4.05) (–3.69) (13.92) $R^2 = 0.86$, D – W = 1.763

Note: The numbers in parentheses are the *t*-statistics. The numbers are the growth rates except the number of investment which are in absolute values.

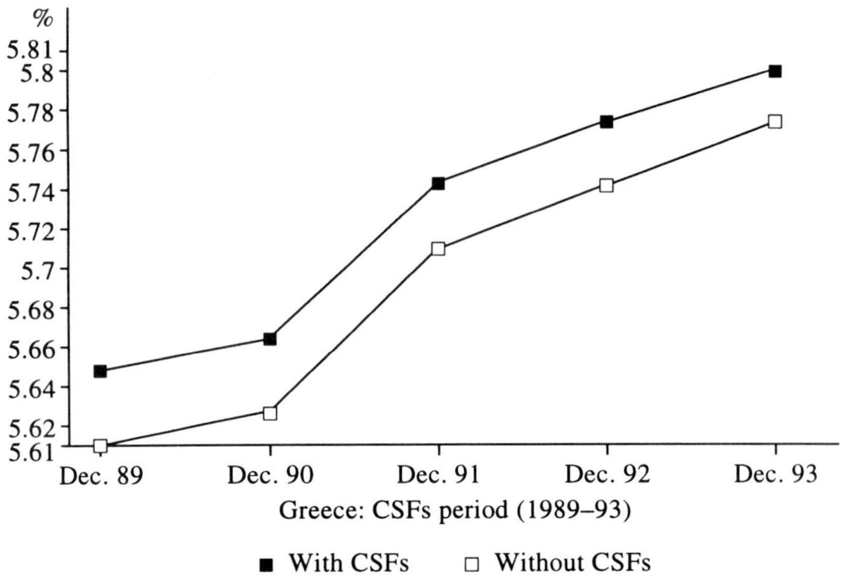

Figure 18.2 *Rate change, per capita imports (1989–93) with and without CSFs*

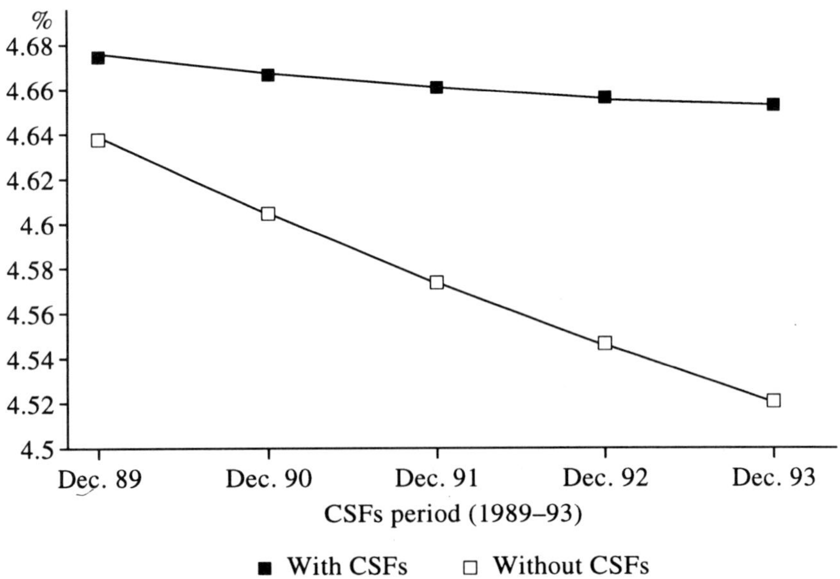

Figure 18.3 *Greece: rate change, employment (1989–93) with and without CSFs*

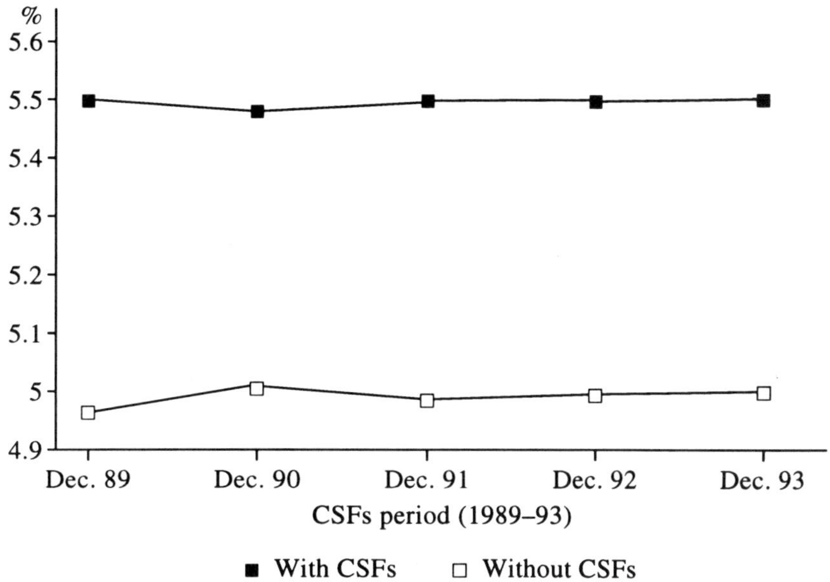

Figure 18.4 *Greece: rate change, investment (1989–93) with and without CSFs*

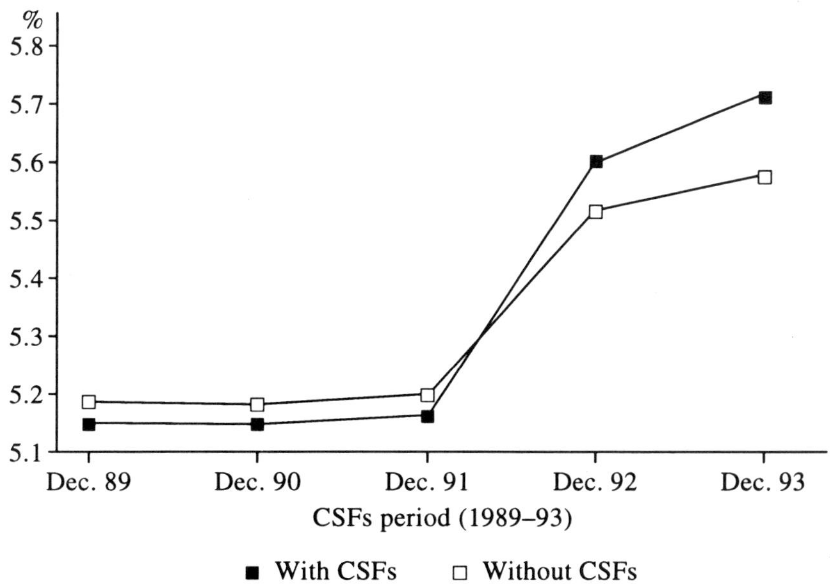

Figure 18.5 *Greece: rate change, consumption (1989–93) with and without CSFs*

nologies in small and medium enterprises, the development of human resources, and so forth. CSFs figure largely in the Greek economy. For example, according to our estimates for the period of CSFs (1989–93), the growth rate in consumption was 2.4 per cent higher, there was a 51.6 per cent increase in the investment rate, an 8.5 per cent increase in the employment rate and an increase of about 3.4 per cent in imports compared with the estimates for the alternative scenario – that without CSFs. The growth rates of consumption, employment, investment and imports are shown in Figures 18.2–18.5, where we have developed the two scenarios (with and without CSFs). Finally, Tables 18.3 and 18.4 show the Commission's results for other member states.

In addition to a substantial increase in the financial transferred flows, the CSFs also entail an improvement in human capital and an increase in the rate of investment.

The main economic results can be divided into demand- and supply-side effects. The short-term impacts on the demand side result either directly or indirectly from the transfer of the CSFs and induce an increase in the total

Table 18.3 CSFs and gross fixed capital formation

	Average growth rate, 1989–93	% of GFCF on CSF, 1993	% of GFCF on Community grant, 1993
Portugal	7.9	23.2	8.3
Ireland	8.4	17.7	7.5
Spain(obj.1)	8.4	6.9	3.5
Italy(obj.1)	4.1	6.3	2.8
UK(obj.1)	3.2	12.5	4.8

Note: The above results are based on econometric models that the Commission used for the estimation of CSFs' impact on these countries.

Table 18.4 Estimated workforce dependent on Community grants (1993)

	Absolute thousands	% of total occupied population
Portugal	116.7	3.1
Ireland	17.0	1.5
Spain(obj.1)	54.2	0.7
Italy(obj.1)	47.1	0.9
UK(obj.1)	4.1	0.7

Note: The above results are based on econometric models that the Commission used for the estimation of CSFs' impact on these countries.

demand. The impacts on the supply side are coming from the creation of new productive processes, improved skills in the workforce, dissemination of technological progress, and an alteration in the capacity of production technology.

However, the technological gap among member states still exists and is broadening. Most of the Community's research projects are appropriate and allocated to the advanced technological Northern European member states. This mainly happened because in these countries the necessary infrastructure had already been established from the early stages of development and consequently it was easier for them to participate in advanced research projects.

In summary, we can say that positive micro and macro effects on the small member states are mainly derived from the transfer of financial flows. In the Community's technology policy what really needs greater attention are the specific needs of the less favoured regions, which have particular problems.

CONCLUSIONS

Economic integration presupposes the unification of monetary, fiscal and other policies and the setting up of a supranational authority whose decisions are binding for member states (these involve progressive loss of national autonomy). This process of integration is not smooth and continuous. In the last years of European economic integration, the mobility of the factors of production has substantially increased. Also, there has been a tendency towards cooperation and towards the replacement the national policies of member states with a common European policy in the sectors of agriculture, transport, research and technology, etc.

The essence of convergence is a product of dynamic factors; thus it cannot be demonstrated by an absolute indicator. However, what it implies is a reduction in the existing gaps between different member states and not simply the improvement of a firm or a country against its previous situation. Community action for smaller member states in the field of research and technology has to be fostered and to be reconsidered carefully, in order to achieve a higher level of efficiency. Technology policy was heavily preoccupied with the external gap of the EEC *vis-à-vis* Japan and the US. However, a similar sized gap also exists among EU countries.

According to the Community's plans, the following criteria are essential for the selection and implementation of technological policy:

- research must contribute to strengthening the economic and social cohesion and competitiveness of the Community's areas, and furthermore must secure scientific and technical quality;

- there should be recognition that the individual member states cannot provide the necessary finance and personnel for research;
- research must contribute to the achievement of the common market and to the unification of European scientific and technical areas, in order to establish uniform norms and standards.

Decision-making on technology policy has been largely transferred to the Community level, although national policies tend to be harmonized.

Up until now, most of the Community's framework research programmes have been allocated to the technologically advanced countries. For instance, about 25 per cent of the Community's research budget corresponding to joint research centres is allocated to only four countries. The international demand for research activities can reinforce the weak internal market demand for the small member states. This creates the opportunity to expand activities that otherwise would probably remain at much lower levels.

In the light of the above remarks, the Community's technology policy has to be reinforced and reoriented on a range of fronts:

- it must begin to establish a coherent technology policy;
- coordination with the broader parts of Community instruments and resources (CSFs) could create a much more favourable effect on the productive capabilities of these countries;
- the Community's research programmes should be launched with the aim of meeting the specific needs of small member states;
- traditional industries that are quite important for the small member countries should be supported by different research and technological programmes;
- the Community could outline specific programmes for technological diffusion to the small member states;
- the Community should promote linkages between 'theoretical and applied' scientific and technological activities in the small member states.

NOTE

1. The Community's Structural Funds consist of the European Social Fund (ESF), the guidance section of the European Agricultural Guidance and Guarantee Fund (EAGGF) and the European Regional Development Fund (ERDF).

REFERENCES

Aked N.H. and P.J. Gummett (1976), 'Science and technology in the European Communities: the history of the cost projects', *Research Policy*, **5**, 270–94.

CEC (1985a), *The European Community research policy.*

CEC (1985b), *Community R&D policy up to 1984.*

CEC (1986), *New technologies in Europe.*

CEC (1986 and 1987), *Research and Technological development in Less Favoured Regions of the Community*, (STRIDE), final reports (two vols).

CEC (1987a), *The Single European Act.*

CEC (1987b), *Research and technological development for Europe.*

CEC (1988a), *Research and technological development policy.*

CEC (1988b), *Technology in Europe, 1988–1991*, Brussels: Eurotech.

CEC (1990a), *Trends in scientific R&TD in the EEC*, (by A. Quinn).

CEC (1990b), *Community Support Framework 1989–1993, Greece (objective 1).*

CEC (1992a), *Research after Maastricht: an assessment – a strategy.*

CEC (1992b), *Second annual report on the implementation of the reform of the Structural Funds*, Brussels: CEC.

CEC (1992c), *IMP – Progress report for 1990*, SEC(92)690, final.

CEC (1992d), *European economy*, no. 2, chap. 4.

CEC (1992e), *Science, Technology and Community cohesion: research results and R&TD policy recommendations*, MONITOR/FAST programme.

CEC (1992f), *Science and technological policy, scientific potential policies in EEC member states.*

Eastwood, B. (1988), European Community Structural Funds in Greece', (with research assistance of Helen Katsouli), British Embassy in Athens.

EIB (1982–91), *Annual reports*, Luxembourg.

Godferoy, Dang N'Guyen and R. Owen (1992), 'High-tech competition and industrial restructuring in light of the single market', *American Economic Review*, **82** (2), May.

Grahl, J. and P. Teague (eds) (1990), *1992–The big market: the future of European Community*, Lawrence and Wishart.

Jorgenson W.D., M.F. Gollop and M.B.Fraumeni (eds.) (1987), *Productivity and U.S. economic growth,* Cambridge, Mass.: Harvard University Press.

Lolos, S.E.G. and G.N. Zonzilos (1992), 'The impact of European Structural Funds on Growth: the case of Greece', Economic Research Department of Greece.

OECD (1989), 'Science and technology indicators: R & D production and diffusion of technology', report no. 3.

OECD (1992), *Science and technology policy – review & outlook in 1991*, Paris: OECD.

Sharp M. (1990), 'Technology and the dynamics of integration', chap. 3 in W. Wallace (ed.), *The dynamics of European integration*, London: Royal Institute of International Affairs.

Sharp, M. and C. Shearman (1987) 'European technological collaboration', Chatham House Paper no. 36, London: Royal Institute for International Affairs.

Tsipouri L. (1989), 'The Greek technological policy and the entrance of European Communities 1981–1986', Athens: Foundation of Mediterranean Studies.

Woolcock, S. (1984), 'Information technology: the challenge to Europe', *Journal of Common Market Studies*, **22** (4).

19. Economic integration and the EU: the Spanish experience

Miren Etxezarreta

BACKGROUND

Democracy has recently been restored in Spain. After 50 years of dictatorship a transitional period was experienced with democratic elections in 1977 and a new democratic constitution in 1978, in the midst of a grave economic crisis. In 1977, with a right–centre government, an adjustment plan – Pactos de la Moncloa – was approved by the democratic powers. Through this plan, the working classes accepted the burden of the consequences of the crisis in exchange for the consolidation of democracy and some promised structural reforms. A period of tough economic policy followed and the situation improved rapidly, albeit at the expense of the working population.

Towards the end of 1981, stagnation, unemployment, new external disequilibria, high inflation levels and public deficits were prominent again. Social unrest increased. In October 1982 the Spanish socialist party (PSOE), of the moderate left, won the elections with a large majority.

THE ECONOMIC POLICY OF THE NEW GOVERNMENT

To face a difficult economic situation the policy adopted was a quasi-neoliberal economic policy: measures of a short-term character involving a hard adjustment programme, combined with structural measures leading to liberalization of external relations, internal deregulation, directed especially at the labour market, and restructuring of productive activities.

The only difference between this model and a strict neoliberal programme was the unavoidable need for public intervention, both for the restructuring of the productive and financial apparatus and for the improvement of the very weak system of social welfare.[1] However, both approaches followed a clear neoliberal pattern.

This economic policy was possible because Spaniards accepted that sacrifices were unavoidable in order to begin a new period of prosperity, and the majority were prepared to afford the socialist government a long period of goodwill.

Two main axes can be recognized in the pattern of action of successive socialist governments: first, the choice of private capital and the market as the main agents to alleviate the crisis and to promote economic recovery; and second, the internationalization of the Spanish economy. Internationalization was seen in a wider context than simply becoming a member of the then European Economic Community (EEC), even though this integration constituted one of the cornerstones of the economic policy of the government, and was now a feasible goal, due to the advent of Spanish democracy.[2]

INTERNATIONALIZATION OF THE ECONOMY AND ENTRY TO THE EEC

The internationalization of the Spanish economy and its integration into the EEC were basic objectives, assumed without reservation, for the socialist government since coming to power. This unqualified will implied the passive acceptance of all the consequences of the internationalization process, and the renunciation of all means through which to guide it. The world economic powers and the market guided the path towards integration. The government not only accepted this situation but distinguished itself through its disciplined adherence to all international recommendations.

A good example of this was the government's attitude towards entry to the EEC. Three main reasons seem to form the basis of the acute interest of the government in Spain becoming a member country:

1. During the dictatorship, integration into Europe was seen as one of the main guarantees of democracy and international recognition. Membership of the EEC was not only an economic issue, but an important political achievement.
2. Economic benefits were expected to accrue from membership. It was considered that modernization of the economy would be strongly enhanced because, owing to Spain's cheap reserves of labour, foreign enterprises would be enticed to settle in the country, bringing improved technology. Furthermore, a larger European market would be opened to Spanish products.
3. Political factors played an important role in the establishment of the timetable for joining. Against what was proposed in their own electoral programme, the government decided that Spain should join NATO. Pub-

> lic opposition to joining NATO then forced a referendum on the subject. In order to bolster the NATO proposal and win the referendum, the government linked it to membership of the EEC in what was basically a propaganda ploy.[3]

All these elements led to increased pressure to join and to the acceptance of almost any conditions that would be imposed on the country by the EEC (the countries with similar economic structures were rather reticent about Spain's entry). As a result, the Spanish entry took place on 1 January 1986, with very tough, if not outright unfair conditions imposed on Spain's economy.

The situation of Spanish society at the time led to a passive acceptance of these unfavourable conditions: the working class was afraid of high unemployment, and had been led to believe that membership in the EEC would create jobs; moreover, it had very little capacity for response because of the crisis and the unions' close cooperation with the government. Medium and small entrepreneurs were also suffering under the impact of the crisis with very little group organization. Meanwhile, big enterprises favoured entry and financial capital was in the process of abandoning previously important industrial interests. Even the policy-makers seemed misled in their enthusiasm about the possibilities that the EEC seemed to offer. A lack of reliable information and a heavy propaganda campaign combined to promote 'Europe', almost without opposition, as the one solution to the many evils afflicting Spain.

THE OPERATION OF THE MODEL: RESTRUCTURING WITHOUT CHANGE

Legitimized by the triumph in the successive elections of 1986, 1989 and 1993, the socialist government has maintained the same lines of economic policy without significant change. Obviously, different circumstances have led to different specific measures, but the philosophy, and the patterns of action, have remained constant.

Spain suffered from an acute economic crisis from late 1974 to 1985. The years 1982–85 were particularly hard, with GDP growing at only around 1.8 per cent, real wages falling and unemployment above the 22 per cent level.

From 1986 onwards a more satisfactory rate of growth was achieved (4.7 per cent yearly average for 1986–89). Due to international recovery and the economic and political stimulus provided by entry into the EEC, investment rates increased (gross capital formation 1986–89 24.5 per cent as against 23.3 per cent for 1974–85), and by the end of the decade, economic activity flourished. Flows of external capital entered Spain in abundance, entrepreneurial surplus improved, important new public works were started (especially in relation to two important events – the Barcelona Olympic Games and the Universal Exhibition of Seville), real state operations and prices increased enormously, and the peseta reached the highest rate of exchange in its history. In 1989, the Spanish government even decided to join the European monetary system (EMS) before the due date for adjustment and with a high rate of exchange. It was a 'golden' period.

The labour market also started a recovery. Real wages improved, new employment was generated, if mainly of a short-term nature. At the end of 1989, temporary workers accounted for 28.1 per cent of waged work. Consumption increased, welfare services were improved, and an appreciable advance in the living conditions of the working class and the general population could be observed. Expectations were high. Recovery followed at a satisfactory rate and produced extraordinary enthusiasm within the state and business sectors, culminating in the summer of 1992, with the very successful organization of the Barcelona Olympic Games. The whole country was optimistic (in spite of an employment rate of more than 15 per cent).

It was argued that this situation fully vindicated the economic policy of adjustment imposed on the country since 1982. According to this interpretation, the model had achieved its objectives.

In the overall strategy, the influence accorded to EEC membership was paramount. Spanish presence and success in Europe was highlighted and celebrated. The country felt it was, at long last, an important partner among the industrialized countries of the world. It seemed to have achieved not only a successful economic incorporation but an increased political stature within Europe for the nation and its leadership.

The importance of European membership was further stressed in relation to the enormous flows of foreign capital entering the country (from 1986 to 1990 total inflows increased yearly from 11.7 per cent to 16.8 per cent of gross domestic capital formation; from 1985 to 1989 such inflows increased sixfold). Foreign direct investment flooded the country, taking key positions in all sectors of the economy, except finances. Meanwhile portfolio capital, lured by very high rates of interest resulting from the tight monetary policy and public deficits, bought a huge number of Spanish financial assets and have been a prominent part of the financial network ever since. This important flow of foreign capital was also extremely useful in balancing the very high trade deficit caused by external liberalization. These results seemingly proved the wisdom of the government and the folly of those critics who had worried about the effects of integration.

Nevertheless, the period did not pass without problems. In spite of the increase in real wages that took place, high levels of unemployment, new forms of labour contracts, restructuring and austerity resulting from the Pactos de la Moncloa, had negatively affected important parts of the working class and other sectors of the population. Employed people were increasingly divided between people with good, permanent jobs with rising wages, and a majority of workers constituting the 'flexible' labour force, i.e. those without qualifications, in temporary, low-wage jobs, and suffering from higher rates of unemployment.[4]

At the other end of the spectrum of wealth and income, the picture was exactly the reverse. The characteristic features were increasing business profits – the banks had the highest profits in their history – and incomes for the richest part of the population, a noticeable adoption of a philosophy of rapid enrichment and individual benefit, and particularly the acceptance that this deeply divided society was the *normal* state of social life. A minority of the richest people very rapidly improved their position, in contrast with substantial groups of poorer people experiencing great financial difficulties which were structural in origin.[5]

The population was dissatisfied. Although political parties and unions had cooperated with the strategy of the socialist government, they were in some way forced by their rank and file to express their discontent. In December 1988 a general strike took place, with the participation of most of the population, against what was considered to be a government of the left.

DISAPPOINTMENT AND THE PROBLEMS SINCE 1992

Optimism and enthusiasm did not last long. By the end of 1991 some negative indicators could be perceived. Very serious problems remained in the depths of the Spanish economy. These resurfaced very rapidly when a new world recession revealed the grave consequences of the economic policy followed since 1982. The position taken in the face of requirements implied by the Maastricht Treaty worsened the already difficult position.

Important macroeconomic disequilibria remained even during the golden period; indeed, some were generated by it. Among these, the deficit and the overvaluation of the rate of exchange (because of the demand for currency by foreign capital flows), deserve special consideration. External liberalization with an overvalued currency, buoyant investment and consumption, and the influx of new branches of multinational firms settling into Spanish markets, led to a tremendous rise of imports not matched by exports. The Spanish trade deficit became the third highest in the world by total volume and the first in per capita terms. The rate of exports to imports fell from 79.5 per cent in 1985 to 64.7 per cent in 1992. Also, integration implied a substantial diversion of trade, since it had concentrated on the EU countries (at the time of writing more than 60 per cent of imports and 68 per cent of exports) at the expense of trade with the rest of the world.

Demand was too high, credit was well above desirable levels, and the inflation rate improved but was still high (7 per cent), especially in relation to Spain's European partners. And despite all the economic expansion, the rate of unemployment reached 16 per cent in 1991.

By the last quarter of 1992, deterioration was clearly in evidence. The economic crisis reappeared, aggravated by the international recession which reduced substantially the activity of modern transnational firms, and by the external liberalization of trade that destroyed thousands of traditional enterprises (net rate of change in the number of firms was negative (–2.6 per cent) between 1979 and 1987 and the 1990s have not been better). Economic activity slowed down substantially, investment fell, the real estate boom ended abruptly, and many firms went bankrupt and closed down. Unemployment began again to climb very rapidly (between 1993 and 1994 330 000 industrial jobs have been lost).

The government blamed the difficulties on the international recession. However, even accepting that it had negatively affected the Spanish economy, the real situation was that Spain was paying heavily for the economic policies implemented during the1980s.[6]

Unfortunately the government did not recognize the problem and maintained, and even reinforced, the same economic policy that created many of the problems. The economic policy of restraint, which was never fully abandoned, has been revived and strengthened. It is argued that the low competitiveness of the economy is mainly due to high labour costs, which, of course, leads again to diminished wages and to the increased flexibility of the labour market, whereas, in spite of some critical voices, the rate of interest and the rate of exchange of the peseta were maintained (for the sake of keeping up the high capital flows).

It was under these conditions that the Maastricht Treaty entered the picture, with its well known requirements for economic and monetary union. The Spanish government promptly declared that every effort would be made to accomplish the tight conditions required by the Treaty. It meant reinforcing the restrictive economic policy, which could only lead to further deterioration of the already noticeable recession.[7] The seriousness of the crisis and the instability of foreign capital flows, together with the European monetary crisis, led to three successive devaluations in eight months between 1992 and 1993.

The years 1993 and 1994 have been extremely difficult for the Spanish economy and society. The crisis has reached absolutely unexpected levels: GDP deteriorated by 1 per cent in 1993; even with rapidly diminishing rates of interest (allowed by the general lowering of rates in the industrial world) investment decreased, economic activity stagnated, the outlook was bleak; unemployment reached the unbelievable rate of 25 per cent – more than double that of the European Union (reaching more than 45 per cent among the young). There are no new jobs. Wages are diminishing even in absolute terms and internal demand has fallen by more than two points. And, after an improvement due to the crisis and devaluation, the trade balance is deteriorating rapidly again: the Spanish economy is suffering a deep crisis and expectations are bleak.

ATTEMPTING AN ASSESSMENT

What went wrong? The most important single element seems to be the deterioration of the industrial structure of the country. This has taken place since Spain's entry into the EEC, and has been caused by a complete liberalization of the external sector without any careful steering of the process or considerations of the competitive capacity of the country's productive system to face it. The enthusiasm for the market sponsored by the socialist leaders prevented them from establishing any industrial policy to help the firms cope with the increased competition created by the entry of European firms (they firmly argued that the best industrial policy was no policy at all).

Spain expected from the market and external investment the necessary technology and management for the modernization of its industry and the expansion of its activities. Therefore, the flow of external capital was encouraged in a variety of ways without any discrimination as to its character or conditions. But the attractiveness of Spain for foreign industrial corporations was its booming market of almost 40 million people and the possibility of being able to restructure multinational firms according to the European space. Most direct investment bought existing firms which then did not expand but were restructured according to the European or world economic space,[8] often eliminating existing jobs or substituting the product with imports from other European plants.

There has not been any policy in regard to linking foreign investment with the productive apparatus of the country, nor a strategy to achieve a dynamic comparative advantage or find adequate space in international markets. Comparative advantage has been sought on the basis of low prices and wages (elements in which Spain can hardly compete with South East Asia), ignoring the fact that in European markets other elements may be more relevant. Spain's technology lags behind the competition, R&D activities are very few (in 1994 total expenses in R&D were below 0.87 per cent as compared with 2 per cent in the EU), institutional support for small enterprises is very low and falling because of the pressure to cut public expenditure. The industrial fabric has been destroyed and is now highly vulnerable to any alteration – internal or external – of a socioeconomic character.[9] Internationalization has become an end in itself. It is assumed that it will promote by itself efficiency and competitiveness. At the same time, small industries working for the internal market have hardly been affected at all by the inhibited competition from imports.

Today, a dual productive structure has been consolidated. The Spanish economy is characterized by a few, modern firms of a transnational character, operating with foreign technology, connected with financial capital, responding increasingly to transnational objectives and programmes, and generating very little employment. At the other extreme are many traditional small enterprises – those that sustain employment – that can hardly survive the effects of external competition. It is generally recognized now that the productive system has suffered a profound weakening, with a great distortion of the industrial fabric. The shortcomings of this strategy are demonstrated when it is noted that increases in productivity have been extremely weak throughout the recovery period (1986–90) and, particularly, that they have been much lower than for the period in which the crisis was at its peak.[10] Forecasts for the immediate future are for a continuation of this trend.

To sum up, the main result of the difficult period (for the working population) of the last 15 years has not been the building of a dense, solid and efficient productive system. The policies chosen tended to compound indiscriminate growth instead of consolidating a productive apparatus with relative autonomy. After 20 years of great effort, external restrictions are tighter (rates of interest have increased again and the central bank is supporting the currency after three successive devaluations), the country's most dynamic industries respond to alien accumulation patterns, the industrial system lacks any internal logic and productivity is stagnant. The government does not seem to have any project whatsoever and its policy is reduced literally 'to preparing the country to take advantage of the expected international'. It seems as if all responsibility for steering the economy and the country has been abandoned by the government.

The situation regarding portfolio and real estate foreign investment also requires comment. The volume here has exploded since 1986. These high foreign capital flows facilitated the financing of public deficits and, especially, prevented the trade deficit from operating as an external bottleneck, even permitting an increase in reserves. But both portfolio flows and foreign capital directed to the real estate market have also experienced negative consequences.

Foreign flows require a healthy rate of exchange as well as high profits and rates of interest to compensate for the risk to the country. Above all, they are extremely sensitive to all types of instability. The slightest alteration can lead to important outflows of great destabilizing power, as has been clearly shown in the monetary crises of 1992, 1993 and the events of late 1994 and early 1995.

These elements increase Spain's economic dependence and diminish its freedom to design its own policy. On the one hand, control of inflation becomes crucial. On the other, high rates of interest and a stable rate of exchange gradually become basic elements of economic life that are not any longer part of the equilibrium variables but convert themselves, with inflation, into *the* basic economic variables. External restrictions will come to govern the country's level of investment, exports, growth and employment. It might be asked whether the facilities for financing the trade balance disequilibrium with foreign portfolio flows will eventually become, in fact, a disadvantage (e.g. the Dutch disease). Also, the increasing demands of servicing the external debt have to be taken into account, especially with such high rates of interest.

Further, membership of the European monetary system from 1989 forced Spain to maintain a high rate of exchange (which had been fixed at a high level upon its entry). Implicitly, the hypothesis of a rigidity of external relations is accepted, and external constraints are interpreted rather as a lack of adjustment of the productive apparatus to external conditions, compelling it to modify industrial and labour positions. The operation of the economy around external equilibrium eventually becomes reinforced.

Membership of the EU means a much weaker capacity for an autonomous economic policy at all levels, and the Maastricht Treaty reinforces that voluntary dependence. In spite of this, it is almost impossible to find among Spanish policy-makers any type of qualification or caution against the requirements established by integration. They seem to believe that the mere fact of European membership is enough to provide with advantages those nations which accept the rules of the game. The integration of Spain in the EMS and the position regarding the Treaty of Maastricht are the best examples of this attitude. In both cases, doubts have been expressed as to whether the policy-makers' readiness to accept the conditions of these institutions was not a back door through which to introduce a policy of austerity and discipline for labour, desired also by the domestic policy-makers wary of imposing such conditions in their own right.

The extremely favourable attitude of the Spanish government regarding internationalization is sometimes difficult to reconcile with the groups that support it. Some interpretations of the role of the state in a global economy provide some food for thought concerning this theme. According to some groups, the state is no longer an institution primarily concerned to promote the national interest; its role is rather to facilitate global accumulation in a complex articulation of dominant international forces, significant sectors of national capital, and provide the necessary legitimation of power at the national level in the context of some sort of 'transnationalized or proto-international state'.[11] We offer no analysis of these hypotheses *vis-à-vis* the Spanish economy, but they present an interesting argument, since it is otherwise difficult to understand the behaviour of the Spanish state.

Great capital flows led to a boom in transactions of all types: buying of enterprises, real estate speculation, and financial flows that converted the country into a sort of paradise for speculators. Worse yet, it turned the whole of the business community into speculators and financial traders. Entrepreneurs became lured by the riches that selling their enterprises could provide,[12] builders and real estate businesses could not believe their good fortune. There was easy money that expanded all sorts of transactions, making ordinary businessmen feel stupid for not profiting from the limitless possibilities. The urge to become rich rapidly took hold at almost all levels of the leadership of the country, economic and political as well (even the Minister of Finance asserted that Spain was the best country in which to become rich quickly).

Alas, the reawakening has been rude. In 1993 and 1994 it was discovered that corruption had been widespread; that honesty has been in scarce supply, as high-level civil servants and famous businessmen have been imprisoned for robbery and deceit.

To this we have to add the very serious suggestions of great irregularities in the practices of the government. Not only has corruption at high levels of the political body been hinted at, but still more serious accusations are underway at the time of writing regarding the possible implication of the government in the setting up and operation of an illegal underground group devoted to attacking Basque terrorists. This has led to significant political instability with important economic consequences, among them the outflow of large amounts of portfolio capital, and a consequent fall in the exchange rate, which has reached its lowest level ever *vis-à-vis* the German Deutschmark.

Within a couple of years the whole structure of success, brilliance and high expectations of becoming first-class Europeans has collapsed. Moreover, none of the Maastricht requirements have been fulfilled, and any hopes of being among the first group of countries in the economic and monetary union have disappeared. The country seems utterly immersed in an atmosphere of crisis, bewilderment and confusion.

At the time of writing – mid February 1995 – the government maintains that on the basis of international expansion, economic recovery is taking place and that it is only being hindered by 'artificially created political instability'. They contend that the GDP has grown 2 per cent in 1994, that the yearly inflation rate has diminished to 4.4 per cent, that the public deficit will be greatly contained in 1995, and that foreign capital and business confidence will be recovered; in short, that the outlook is for 1995–96 is optimistic.

Let us hope they are right. However, the situation is far from clear: the trade balance is again deteriorating rapidly, currency is barely maintaining the very low levels reached recently, foreign capital is not yet returning to the country, internal demand has not recovered and there are no signs of a different policy for the productive system. Above all, there is very little hope for an improvement in the rate of unemployment, and it is officially accepted that it will not diminish in the next two years. In any case, the fact that the Spanish economy in the best case might improve on the basis of an international recovery says very little about its own robustness and soundness. It would seem that the model of economic policy that has been followed during the last 15 years should be thoroughly reassessed.

WHICH WAY TOWARDS INTEGRATION?

To analyse the negative consequences of an economic policy that favours the integration of Spain into the EU does not necessarily imply a position favouring a closed economy, still less advocating autarky. In the present world economy, such positions would be not only wrong but impossible. The internationalization of capital at present is a constituent element of all economic activity. *But different positions in regard to the process of integration are possible*. One specific form and model of economic integration has, up to now, been presented as the only possible one. In fact, it is only one option among several. All countries are being integrated within a global economy, but not all of them adopt the same position or take a passive stand. Cases such as those of Denmark, the UK, or the unyielding negotiations which have taken place between Sweden and Austria for entrance into the EU, show that other positions are possible. The strategy we have analysed here implies an unqualified acceptance of total and rapid economic liberalization that means the subordination of the country to the most powerful economic forces of the world without safeguards. In that model, external transactions are not based on internal objectives, with external flows and global decisions articulated around them but, on the contrary, it is maintained that by means of inhibited competition, a happy result will be achieved. The 'painful extroversion' (an expression of R. Boyer) should produce fruit through market dynamics. In opposition to that model, it is our contention that economic integration should be debated realistically (we cannot forget, for instance, that Spain is a small country). The objectives, magnitude, form and conditions under which Spanish society must integrate itself into the EU and into the world economy, must be discussed in order to ensure that the basic interests of its population are taken into account; and to assert that the central objective of the economic life of any community must be to improve the quality and standard of living of its population.

NOTES

1. Due to political circumstances and the heavy negative impact of the economic crisis of the 1970s, it was necessary to develop some sort of a limited welfare state which previously was extremely reduced under the 50 years of dictatorship. However, most of the basic measures leading to the new system had already been established by the previous government.
2. Membership of the EEC had been constantly denied by the Community due to the dictatorial character of the political regime. On the other hand, for the opposition to the dictatorship, the EEC was always seen as a guarantee of democracy.
3. The referendum was won by the government by a very small margin after an extremely pressing campaign at all levels.
4. The share of national income going to labour remained constant and personal income distribution was in 1987 the same as in 1980. The percentage of disposable family income in the 30 per cent of the families with the lowest income in 1987 was 2.12 per cent *lower* than in 1982 while 10 per cent of the families with higher incomes received 2.34 per cent *more*. Marginality and poverty of important groups of the population increased so that for the first time a basic income for destitute families had to be established. In the income of the families, social security benefits represented 12.1 per cent in 1975 and 20.2 per cent in 1989. Nevertheless, public expenses in social security absorbed the same percentage of GDP from 1982 to 1990 (14 per cent) (it only increased to 17 per cent in 1993 due to the high level of unemployment that increased expenses in unemployment benefits (Alcaide Inchausti 1990).
5. This situation, together with the division of the working class in two segments, and the fiscal effort necessary to support the welfare state, so that it takes the majority of funds from waged workers and not from the profits of capital, may lead to an electoral alliance between the privileged groups and the 'aristocracy of workers' as it seems has happened in the UK during Thatcherism. It would be of great interest to analyse whether a similar alliance is also taking place in Spanish society.
6. One of its consequences being precisely that it renders the Spanish economy highly vulnerable to the slightest international difficulty.
7. It can even be thought that the eager acceptance of all the Maastricht conditions was due to the fact that they legitimated an austerity policy propounded independently by the Spanish government at the time.
8. A very good example of this is the Volkswagen car factory. After a few years of operation, due to new plants of the consortia for Eastern Europe, they are in the process of closing down the factory, dismissing 9000 workers and transforming the site into an industrial park for small enterprises. The original enterprise (SEAT) had been a public undertaking, and the first car producer in the country, until it was bought by FIAT and then by the German consortium. And after this, a substantial amount of public funds were pumped in so as to equilibrate its balance sheet.
9. The great instability of the currency in January 1995, caused by the great outflow of portfolio capital due to the political instability caused by corruption and other political problems of the government, show very clearly the extreme vulnerability of this model.
10. With some differences according to the source, all data express a slow-down in productivity. For example:

1976	'77	'78	'79	'80	'81	'82	'83	'84	'85	'86	'87	'88	'89
8.4	7.1	6.3	3.1	7.7	4.5	10.0	6.2	7.5	5.7	0.4	1.9	1.5	–1.1

11. See Gill and Law (1988), especially chap. 17.
12. 'A selling fever situated Spain as the fourth country in the world selling enterprises, arriving to the point where the good entrepreneur became identified as the one who sells his enterprise' (Velasco 1989/90, p. 19).

REFERENCES

Alcaide, J. (1989/90), 'Política de rentas', *Información comercial española*, Madrid, nos 676–7.
Etxezarreta, M. (ed.) (1991), *La restructuración del capitalismo en España*, Barcelona: Fuhem/Icaria.
Garcia Delgado, J.L. (ed.) (1990), *Economía española de la transición y la democracia*, CIS.
Gill, S. and D. Law (1988), *The global political economy*, Brighton, UK: Harvester Wheatsheaf.
Montes, P. (1993), *La integración en Europa*, Madrid: Trotta.
Velasco, L. (1989/90), 'La insoportble gravedad del deficit exterior', *Información comercial española*, Madrid, nos 676–7.
Viñals, J. (ed.) (1992), *La economía española ante el Mercado Unico europeo*, Madrid: Alianza.

PART VI

Greece and the European Union

20. European integration and industrial structure in Greece: prospects and possibilities for convergence

George C. Petrakos and Spyros E. Zikos

INTRODUCTION

European economic space has been going through a complex, often conflicting, but also rapid process of integration, the major elements of which are: the operation of the single European market (SEM); movement towards economic and monetary union (EMU); the unification of Germany, the enlargement of the European Union (EU); and the westward orientation of Eastern and Central European (ECE) countries. This process involves states and regions with different levels of development, different endowments of resources, infrastructure and technology, and different rates of success in organizing efficiently their productive bases.

The great diversity with respect to economic, cultural and institutional characteristics that exists in Europe has often been viewed with scepticism, but also, at times, with enthusiasm. Nevertheless, it is commonly agreed that a crucial question for the common future of Europe is whether, under what conditions and to what extent the process of integration among basically unequal partners promotes convergence or divergence. Considering that the Union has passed from a period of convergence and high growth that ended in the mid-1970s to a period of divergence and low growth at both the national and the regional level thereafter (CEC 1991; Dunford and Perrons 1993), this question warrants increasing attention.

Several studies have already indicated that the dynamics of this complex process of integration may have an overall unfavourable impact on the performance of the less developed states and regions of the EU. In the first place, the operation of the SEM through the simplification of border formalities, the harmonization of technical standards, the liberalization of financial services and the opening up of public procurement, will intensify competition among firms and regions and will strengthen the competitive advantages of the core regions that house the most efficient European enterprises (Amin et al. 1992; CEC 1991). Also the elimination of trade barriers seems to alter the spatial behaviour of large enterprises, reinforcing on a larger scale the importance of geographical factors such as distance, centrality or market accessibility and a more ordered spatial organization of activities at the European level. As a result, central regions and metropolitan areas will strengthen their position, benefiting from market size, agglomeration economies and changes in the strategic behaviour of large European firms, while intermediate regions will also enjoy significant gains by offering similar advantages in a less congested and lower-cost environment (CEC 1992). On the contrary, laggard regions will suffer directly from the impact of the SEM, since they contain the highest share of sensitive sectors (CEC 1990; Camagni 1992), the weakest and most vulnerable productive bases, insufficient infrastructure, and an overall unfavourable geographical index for strategic location.

Second, policies towards economic and monetary union (EMU) have a disproportionately adverse effect on the weaker member states and regions of the Community by largely depriving them of the means of fiscal policy that are necessary for the creation of modern infrastructure, and of the means of monetary and exchange rate policy that allow them to compete on a comparative advantage basis with the more efficient members of the EU (Camagni 1992). As a result, less developed states are obliged to implement 'convergence criteria' that seem to have a disproportionate effect and to be at variance with the Commission's goal of social and economic cohesion. To the extent that the Maastricht Treaty is not revised or extended, the peripheral states and regions of the Community may find themselves sliding towards a position of absolute disadvantage with respect to the set of multiple constraints within which they have to operate in their effort to actively intervene in and reform their productive bases.

Third, the unification of Germany and the economic and political transformation of the ECE countries pose a potential threat to the less developed regions of the EU, through the diversion of public funds and mobile investment to the east, and through direct competition from the labour-intensive, low-cost industries of these countries (CEC 1991, 1993a).

Given that the process of integration itself is expected to have an overall unfavourable impact on the less developed areas of the EU, the important issue that has to be addressed is whether any parallel developments or policies capable of offsetting this impact exist at the European or national level. Clearly, in the andipode of these polarizing trends and dynamics, and largely because of them, we find the recently reformed and drastically upgraded and strengthened regional policy of the Commission (CEC 1991, 1993d) emphasizing the provision of basic and economic infrastructure and the stimulation of indigenous potential in the laggard regions.

An equally important element that could work in favour of the less developed regions and become a promising factor for the success of regional policy could be the existence of a visible trend of structural adjustments towards a modern and more competitive industrial base in these regions. Despite the increasing weight of the service sector in the output and the employment of most economies, its contribution to wealth and economic prosperity should not be overestimated, since its existence and growth are strongly bound to industry (Peschel 1992). As a result, industrial activity remains the basic determinant of the spatial distribution of economic development, which means that any signs of industrial restructuring in peripheral states and regions should be understood as an important first element in a (perhaps long) process of economic convergence.

The purpose of this chapter is to examine the changes that have taken place in the industrial structure of Greece, a state classified by the European Commission as an Objective 1 area, to assess the impact of existing policies to evaluate the prospects for the economy within the integrated European space, and to determine the policies necessary for the period of adjustment. As the discussion about the new Europe and the nature of the changes expected in the spatial organization of activities is gaining momentum, gathering knowledge of the prospects, opportunities and constraints faced by the structurally weak countries will be in our view a useful contribution.

THE STRUCTURE OF GREEK INDUSTRY

The performance of the Greek economy in the postwar period is already known from the reports of international organizations such as the OECD, the IMF, and the EU as well as from many scholarly papers and publications. Although in the 1960s Greece was placed second among the fastest growing OECD economies with an average GDP growth rate of about 7 per cent, in the 1980s it was ranked last among the EU economies with an average GDP growth rate of about 1.5 per cent and a GDP per capita constantly falling below the EU average. As a result of the collapse of the growth rate of output, the economy was unable in the 1980s to create sufficient numbers of new jobs, despite the huge expansion of the public sector. The unemployment rate increased from about 2 per cent in 1979 to 8 per cent in 1992, exceeding that of the OECD countries and approaching the higher average rate of the EU.

Although available statistics and reports provide sufficient information about the internal and external macroeconomic imbalances of the economy, little attention has been paid to its structure, and especially to the structure of industry. Therefore, we examine in this section the structural changes that have taken place in Greek industry during the last 15–20 years, emphasizing the performance of the two-digit, ISIC branches, and the performance of industrial firms by size.

The Structure of Industrial Sectors in Greece

The post-1973 period has been a time of crisis for Greek manufacturing. Although in the 1960s industrial activity was the vehicle of development, in the 1970s and the 1980s this dynamism has been exhausted. This is shown in the declining average annual growth rate of industrial output which, from 9.5 per cent in the 1961–70 period, fell to 5.0 per cent between 1971 and 1980, to 1.0 per cent in 1981–90 and to 1.6 per cent in 1991–92. In the same direction the average annual growth rate of investment declined from 10.7 per cent in the 1961–70 period to 2.9 per cent in the 1971–80 period, to become negative (–2.9 per cent) in the period 1981–90 and only slightly positive (0.6 per cent) in the period 1991–92. As a result of these developments the share of manufacturing in GNP has declined from 21.3 per cent in 1980 to 19.3 per cent in 1988 and to 17.6 per cent in 1992 which, compared with an average share of about 30 per cent for the other European countries, indicates the declining competitiveness of Greek industry. This is clearly expressed both domestically, with the rapid increase of imports, and internationally, with the sluggish performance of exports (Giannitsis 1985). Especially after Greece's entry into the EU, import penetration from the Union has doubled, while the share of manufacturing output that is exported to the EU has hardly grown at all (CEC 1993c).

The crisis of Greek manufacturing in the post-1973 period is also expressed through a shift of investment and employment towards traditional activities and a contraction of the already weak and undeveloped intermediate and capital goods sector. As can be estimated from Table 20.1, in the period 1963–73 the intermediate and capital goods sectors (30–38) increased their employment at a faster rate than did the consumption sectors (20–29), creating in this period 85 335 new jobs compared to 43 217 new positions in the consumption goods sectors.

In contrast, during the period 1973–88, Greek industry experienced a retreat of the intermediate and capital goods sectors and a return to traditional activities and the consumption goods sectors. In this period the consumption sectors increased their employment by 70 189 new positions while the capital and intermediate goods sectors created only 30 284 new positions. It is ironic that the return of Greek industry to traditional activities and sectors that characterize early stages of development took place during a period when domestic demand, because of improvements in the standard of living, was moving away from the old consumption patterns. At the same time in the international markets traditional industries shifted towards developing coun-

Table 20.1 Employment in Greek industry by sector (1963–88)

ISIC no.	Number of employees 1963	1973	1988	Composition of employment per branch 1963	1973	1988
20	76443	89285	104307	16.21	14.78	14.77
21	8556	12307	13530	1.81	2.04	1.92
22	16959	9049	12895	3.60	1.50	1.83
23	55916	68419	66403	11.86	11.33	9.40
24	71358	72030	116924	15.13	11.92	16.55
25	28495	34406	30949	6.04	5.70	4.38
26	21685	29445	30467	4.60	4.87	4.31
27	6135	7971	12011	1.30	1.32	1.70
28	13227	15963	22621	2.80	2.64	3.20
29	9945	13061	12018	2.11	2.16	1.70
30	7938	15832	19296	1.68	2.62	2.73
31	12584	20255	27768	2.67	3.35	3.93
32	1378	3765	7483	0.29	0.62	1.06
33	28089	37465	37848	5.96	6.20	5.36
34	2287	7859	10418	0.48	1.30	1.47
35	38658	47850	47081	8.20	7.92	6.67
36	15556	23697	22320	3.30	3.92	3.16
37	13589	30473	28424	2.88	5.04	4.02
38	34581	52808	69650	7.33	8.74	9.86
39	8185	12102	13893	1.74	2.00	1.97
20–39	471564	604042	706306	100.00	100.00	100.00

Source: NSSG (various years).

tries that appeared to have significant comparative advantages in order to compete for a larger share of the market (Giannitsis 1985). This orientation of Greek industry towards traditional sectors has been, as Table 20.1 shows, a structural weakness in the past, which, however, began to intensify after the 1973 crisis. In that respect Greece, compared to the other countries of the European South, has the closest proximity to industrial structures characterizing the old international division of labour (Lipietz 1987; Getimis and Economou 1992).

Industrial Structure and Firm Size in Greece

In Table 20.2 we provide data about the number of firms, by size, in the Greek industrial sector for the 1973–88 period. It becomes obvious from the beginning that the industrial sector in Greece is characterized by very small production units (by international standards). We observe that in 1988, 93.5 per cent of industrial firms being classified as light manufacturing or handicraft units employed one to nine persons.[1] We also see that this share remains unchanged for the entire period 1973–88. The total number of industrial firms in this period increased by 19.25 per cent, but this change is attributable to the creation of new small-scale enterprises, and especially those between one and nine employees. As a result the average size of firms has remained unchanged for the entire period at the very small figure of 4.8 employees per firm which is the lowest in Europe (Portugal's average for example is 15

Table 20.2 Number of firms in Greek industry by size (1973–88)

	Number of firms				Composition by size			
Size	1973	1978	1984	1988	1973	1978	1984	1988
1–9 pers.	113479	120321	135666	135327	93.51	93.28	93.91	93.51
10–49	6667	7139	7378	7935	5.49	5.53	5.11	5.48
1–49	120146	127460	143044	143262	99.00	98.82	99.02	98.99
50+	1211	1528	1419	1455	1.00	1.18	0.98	1.01
Total	121357	128988	144463	144717	100.00	100.00	100.00	100.00

Source: NSSG (various years).

Table 20.3 Number of employees in Greek industry by size (1973–88)

	Number of employees				Composition of employment by size			
Size	1973	1978	1984	1988	1973	1978	1984	1988
1–9 pers.	254905	264140	293868	301468	42.20	39.34	42.95	42.68
10–49	127454	139174	141058	151955	21.10	20.73	20.62	21.51
1–49	382359	403314	434926	453423	63.30	60.06	63.57	64.20
50+	221683	268183	249220	252884	36.70	39.94	36.43	35.80
Total	604042	671497	684146	706307	100.00	100.00	100.00	100.00

Source: NSSG (various years).

employees per establishment – CEC 1990). Thus the problem of fragmentation of production in Greek manufacturing remains, since the increase in demand seems to be met by the creation of new small family firms while the expansion or the merging of existing firms is slow or stalled. Given this structure of industry, Greece maintains the most fragmented production base of all European countries.

Looking at Table 20.3 we see that in the same period (1973–88) employment in manufacturing increased by 16.93 per cent. This change is again attributable to the increase of employment by small-scale firms and especially those employing one to nine persons. On the contrary, large firms employing more than 50 persons, after an increase in employment in the period 1973–78, are faced with significant reductions in jobs. In fact, this reduction would have been much greater if one, were to count the number of industrial rescues undertaken by the state in order to avoid the social cost of unemployment. Comparing the figures in Tables 20.2 and 20.3 with data from other European countries we see that in Greece the share of small industry (1–49 employees) is much greater.[2] Note here that in Greece the category of firms employing 1–49 persons has a very unbalanced distribution, dominated by small firms with an average size of a little more than three employees (Table 20.4). This is explained by the disproportionate weight of family firms that either employ one to two persons (usually owner plus spouse) and account for 45 per cent of the total number of industrial firms, or employ one to four persons (in most cases the entire family) and account for 85 per cent of the total number of firms.

Examining the developments that took place in industrial employment in the post-1973 period, we see that small industry shows a significant ability to adjust and survive recessions and demand variations that is not found in its large counterpart. This finding is consistent with the increasing international recognition of the importance of the flexibility and adaptability of small firms

Table 20.4 Average firm size in Greek industry (1973–88)

Size	1973	1978	1984	1988
1–9 pers.	2.25	2.20	2.17	2.23
10–49	19.12	19.49	19.12	19.15
1–49	3.18	3.16	3.04	3.16
50+	183.06	175.51	175.63	173.80
Total	4.98	5.21	4.74	4.88

Source: NSSG (various years).

in a changing economic environment. Recent empirical studies (Hadjimichalis and Vaiou 1987; Andrikopoulou 1987; Lyberaki 1988) have found that small firms are more flexible and more adaptive, having a better record with respect to employment, investment, loan burden and effectiveness compared to large firms.

These findings, however, should be used with care since they do not justify any kind of optimistic scenario about the future of Greek industry. They should rather be taken as a warning to those who might consider small firms as a relic of the past, and a confirmation that they are active participants in the economy, and that their potential should not be underestimated (Lyberaki 1988). It is, however, doubtful whether small industry will be able to carry out by itself the kind of restructuring and the technological upgrading that is necessary for industrial development in Greece

Flexibility and adaptability do not seem to be oriented towards dynamic markets, product differentiation or quality improvements, but rather towards activities of secondary importance. According to the statistics of the 1984 survey of industry, from the 15 504 new small firms with one to nine employees, 6076 were in car repair, 1362 in wood processing, 1167 in metal products and 1099 in electrical appliances service and repair. With these facts, it is questionable whether small firms are able to seriously assist in the restructuring of the productive base of the economy, especially when flexibility during the business cycles seems to be associated with the contraction or expansion of family employment in order to meet the variations in demand (Hadjimichalis and Vaiou 1990; Petrakos et al. 1991).

PROSPECTS AND POSSIBILITIES FOR CONVERGENCE

Given the main characteristics of industry presented in the previous section and the fact that the performance of industry is decisive for the future of Greece in the European economy, we cannot be optimistic. We do not observe any significant signs indicating that structural deficiencies have been in the process of being removed, or that a new paradigm of development is emerging. Even worse, recent studies show the impact of EU membership on industrial output to be negative for most industrial sectors (Petrakos and Zikos 1991) and that the elimination of trade barriers will seriously affect most labour-intensive sectors which are protected to a greater degree than the, in terms of output, relatively significant capital-intensive sectors (CEC 1990; Hassid and Katsos 1992).

Based on the analysis of the structure of Greek industry, some commonly held views about the performance of peripheral states and the process of integration may be found to be unjustified. First, there is a perception that

Greece is a special case of failure in the EU, usually associated with the policies of the 1980s. Although Greece as a country is considered an extreme case of structural weakness within the EU, the fact is that, at the EU regional level, there are many larger or smaller areas (some the size of Greece) having similar characteristics to those of Greece. Almost all the Objective 1 Regions (O1Rs) of the Union have the same or greater difficulties in restructuring their industrial bases and are equally threatened by the forces of SEM and EMU. However, what makes Greece a really special case within these regions is its overall unfavourable geographical position with respect to the other members of the Union.

In a single European market, factors such as distance, lack of adjacency, and limited accessibility to the European developmental centre, although rarely mentioned, play a very important role in the prospects of the country for growth and development. Under a more protected and fragmented economic environment, national markets maintained a significant degree of independence and the locational choices of firms had a greater spread in order to overcome trade barriers. The elimination of barriers and the unification of markets, however, altered previous locational needs and patterns, highlighting the significance of the geographical characteristics of regions, making centrality and accessibility at the European level a decisive factor. Rosenblat and Pumain (1993) have found that multinational enterprises in Europe and also their subsidiaries, follow such a locational pattern that favours by far the core areas of the EU. A simple European level gravity index is found to explain 65 per cent of this locational pattern. A similar gravity index is also found by Petrakos (1993) to have a correlation coefficient of over 90 per cent with the level of GDP, industrial product and total exports of the European countries. That implies that less strategic and perimetric locations with respect to the European centre of gravity are bound to a certain extent to lead to peripheral and inferior economic structures independently of the success or failure of domestic policies. Distance may also explain why Greece and Ireland are the only European countries that, despite market unification and the experience of the other countries, continue to maintain a very low share of intra-industry trade[3] and tend to undertake at the European level an inter-industry specialization. A Heckscher–Olin type of specialization and economic relation, however, implies a geographically divided pattern of integration, with the more advanced economies specializing in technology-, capital- or knowledge-intensive goods and the less advanced in labour-intensive and assembly activities.

A second commonly met but, in our opinion, unjustified view is that if all countries abide by the Maastricht criteria of strict macroeconomic management, then economic convergence will take place. Although macroeconomic stabilization policies are necessary, there is no known mechanism based on monetary policies that will convert structurally weak and less developed economies into healthy ones. On the contrary, there are fears that the deprivation of fiscal, monetary and exchange rate tools will put these economies in a more disadvantageous situation with respect to their economic and social infrastructure, as well as their competitive position *vis-à-vis* more efficient countries in international markets. Thus, even if nominal convergence is achieved this does not imply that real convergence will follow. The structural problems of Greek industry with respect to its orientation, composition, size and regional bias will not be removed by a more balanced macroeconomic environment. The latter may stimulate the expansion of output, as it is expected to do, but this will be an expansion of the same type – a replication of existing patterns of production that reproduce structural deficiencies on a larger scale. As a result, it is easier to conceive how real convergence will lead to a nominal Maastricht-type convergence than the opposite. Real convergence, which remains the goal, depends more on structural adjustment policies, technological diffusion, access to information and a favourable institutional environment, which are not central to the logic of Maastricht.

Third, there is in our opinion a fallacy related to the belief that the regional and structural policies of the EU have a temporary character and will be terminated with the completion of the second stage of EMU. Regional policies in the form of assistance to less developed regions and regions in crisis, should be seen as a permanent ingredient of the new Europe for a number of reasons. Despite strong neoclassical expectations of the opposite, regional disparities will increase as a result of integration and will further increase with the next enlargement of the EU to include the Central and Eastern European countries, at least for the foreseeable future (Petrakos 1993). As a result, regional policies will be necessary to offset largely destabilizing and undesired population flows that will be impossible to deter administratively in a single market. In addition, regional policies will be the necessary counterbalancing force to sectoral, R&D and 'excellence' policies supporting large and efficient enterprises in the advanced regions of the Union, in an effort to create 'European champions' that will effectively compete with US and Japanese firms in world markets. In the absence of regional policies it will be really difficult to maintain huge sectoral programmes in information technology, aerospace, etc. that favour exclusively the largest and most efficient European firms, located in the more dynamic and prosperous regions. Also, to the extent that social stability is a precondition for the realization of the benefits of economic integration, support to the less developed areas of the EU should not be seen as a luxury. The possible marginalization of these regions will generate tensions and conflicts that will undermine in the long-run the vision of the common European future. Finally, the deficiency of less developed countries in domestic fiscal and monetary means of intervention should be remedied at a higher level as it becomes clear that weak states and regions cannot compete with advanced ones, given their deficiencies in social and economic infrastructure. This requires a federal-type EU budget to fill the gap created by the Maastricht Treaty if a further increase in disparities is to be avoided. All this leads to a totally different attitude towards the necessity of EU regional policy, implying that it has to be seen as a permanent ingredient of the integration process.

Therefore, EU regional and structural policies have to be maintained along with other national initiatives and institutional arrangements to facilitate the efforts of emerging social partnerships at the local and national level to pursue development and restructuring strategies based on their special characteristics, comparative advantages, creativity and resource potentials. Given the small size of industrial units in Greece, the paradigm of 'Third Italy' appears to be a much more suitable development strategy than the large-scale massive production modes of Western Europe. In that respect, the support of local small industry institutions and community service centres, facilitating information flows, technology transfers, product design assistance, R&D cost sharing, cooperation with universities and training, is essential. These institutions, participating in regional, national or even international networks, can maintain and transmit to local productive bases the high level of knowledge required to survive in a world of unstable markets and rapid technological change. They can also be used as a vehicle for the Balkan strategy of Greek firms, especially the small and peripherally sited ones. This Balkan strategy is a necessary development dictated by the intolerably long distance of Greece from the Western European centre of gravity. In fact, under certain conditions it could be a successful positive response to unification, one that attempts to convert peripherality at the European level to centrality at a sub-European level by promoting a regional Balkan market in which Greece, by definition, has a increasing role.

Attempting the creation of a peripheral growth pole in the Balkan peninsula, while at the same time integrating with the other countries of the EU, and perhaps serving as a link between Western Europe and the emerging markets in the Balkans and the East Mediterranean basin, may be the best strategic response to the challenges and the problems lying ahead.

NOTES

1. In Greece the division of industrial enterprises into small, medium and large is based on the number of employees. More specifically, small are those with one to nine employees, medium those with 10–49 and large those with over 50 employees.
2. For the EU countries, the contribution to employment of firms with a size smaller than 50 persons was 22.0 per cent in Germany (1970), 37.6 per cent in Italy (1970), 11.3 per cent in

the UK (1972), 22.5 per cent in Denmark (1973), 24.9 per cent in the Netherlands (1973), 20.1 per cent in Ireland (1968) and 17.4 per cent in France (1976) (CPER 1989, p. 59), while in Greece it is 64.0 per cent (1988). That implies that the role of small industry in maintaining and expanding industrial employment levels in Greece is decisive.

3. For Ireland see Grimwade (1989). For Greece we estimated the intra-industry trade ratios for the nine ISTC sectors for the period 1985–90 and found that they range from 35 per cent to 56 per cent with no increasing trend.

REFERENCES

Amin A., R. Charles and J. Howells (1992), 'Corporate Restructuring in the New Europe', *Regional Studies*, **26** (4), 319–31.

Andrikopoulou, E. (1987), 'Regional policy and local development in a Greek peripheral region: the case of Thraki', *Antipode*, **19** (1), 7–24.

Camagni, R. (1992), 'Development Scenarios and Policy Guidelines for the Lagging Regions in the 1990s', *Regional Studies*, **26** (4), 361–74.

CEC (1990), Social Europe, *European Economy*, Brussels: CEC.

CEC (1991), *The Regions in the 1990s*, Fourth Periodic Report, Brussels: CEC.

CEC (1992), *Urbanisation and the Future of Cities in Europe, Regional Development Studies no. 4*, Brussels: CEC.

CEC (1993a), *New Location Factors for Mobile Investment in Europe, Final Report, Regional Development Studies, no. 6*, DG XVI Brussels: CEC.

CEC (1993b), *Regional Development Studies, no. 7*, Trade and Foreign Investment in the Community's Regions: the Impact of Economic Reform in Central and Eastern Europe, Brussels: CEC.

CEC (1993c), *Towards a Competitive Economy, A New Approach to Policy for Greek Industry*, Athens: CEC.

CEC (1993d), *The Structural Funds of the European Communities, 1994–1999*, Brussels: CEC.

CEPR (1989), *Small scale enterprises*, Athens: Center for Economic Planning and Research (Greek).

Dunford, M. and D. Perrons (1993), 'Regional Inequality as a Cause and Consequence of Slower Growth', *TOPOS*, special edition, Athens: URDP.

Getimis P. and D. Economou (1992), 'New geographical disparities and spatial policies in Greece', *TOPOS, The review of urban and regional studies*, **4**, 3–44 (Greek).

Giannitsis T. (1985), *The Greek industry, development and crisis*, Athens: Gutenberg (Greek).

Grimwade, N. (1989), *International Trade, New Patterns of Trade, Production and Investment*, London: Routledge.

Hadjimichalis, C. and D. Vaiou (1987), 'Changing patterns of uneven regional development and forms of social reproduction in Greece', *Society and Space*, **5**, 319–33.

Hadjimichalis, C. and D. Vaiou (1990), 'Whose flexibility? The politics of informalization in Southern Europe', *Capital and Class*, **42**, 76–106.

Hassid, J. and G. Katsos (1992), 'The Impact of European Integration on Greek Industry', *Institute for Economic and Industrial Research*, Athens (Greek).

Lipietz, A. (1987), *Miracles and Mirages: The Crisis of Global Fordism*, London: Verso.

Lyberaki, A. (1988), 'Flexible specialization and small firms in Greece', PhD thesis, Sussex University.

NSSG (1965, 1975, 1985, 1992), *Surveys of Industry, Handicraft and Commerce*, Athens: National statistical service of Greece.

Peschel, K. (1992), 'European integration and regional development in northern Europe', *Regional Studies*, **26** (4), 387–97.

Petrakos, G. (1993), 'The Regional Dimension of Transition in Eastern and Central European Countries: An Assessment', presented at a conference for the Redevelopment of Regions Expected to Experience Severe Impacts from Technological and Environmental Reconstruction, ACE/PHARE Program, Katowice, Poland, 24–27 September 1993.

Petrakos, G. and S. Zikos (1991), 'The Decline of Greek Industrial Growth, 1963–1983', *Vierteljahreshefte zur Wirtschaftsforschung*, **3/4**, 156–65.

Petrakos, G., S. Zikos and T. Zacharopoulos (1991), 'SSEs and strategies of local development. A case study of the prefecture of Karditsa', *TOPOS, The review of urban and regional studies*, **3**, 69–91 (Greek).

Rosenblat C. and D. Pumain (1993), 'The Location of Multinational Firms in the European Urban System', *Urban Studies*, **30** (10), 1691–709.

21. Interactions between agricultural credit and private investment: empirical evidence and policy implications

Nicholas C. Baltas*

INTRODUCTION

The aim of this chapter is to quantify, on the one hand, Greek farmers' investment behaviour both at the aggregate level and by broad type of investment and, on the other hand, their demand for loans to finance this investment. Such a quantitative approach to these two closely interrelated issues should provide valuable guidelines in any attempt to formulate efficient credit policies for institutional lenders to the farming sector.

A simultaneous equations econometric model was used to describe the demand for credit and investment by Greek farmers. In particular, credit needs for agricultural investment were estimated using a combination of a partial adjustment model and the adaptive expectations model. Farmers' investment behaviour was investigated by employing a synthesized traditional model for both the aggregate and three individual types of investment.

Since the classical econometric model of adaptive expectations and partial adjustment have been criticized mainly for their inadequate theoretical basis, the rational expectations model is also used. Then, the empirical results derived from the rational expectations model are compared with those obtained from the application of the classical model.

The chapter is divided as follows. In the next section, the developments with regard to both credit and capital formation policy are outlined for the period 1952–92. Then, the interrelationship between credit and investment is depicted in the form of a simultaneous equations model followed by the presentation of the rational expectations model. The sources of the data used as well as a few general characteristics of the method of estimation are given next. Then the estimates of the model's parameters are presented and the empirical results

*I am indebted to A. Andrikopoulos and P. Grevenites for their comments. Many thanks are also due to E. Vasilatos for computational assistance.

derived from the rational expectations model's parameters are compared with those obtained from the application of the classical model. Finally, the main findings are summarized and some policy implications are drawn.

CREDIT AND CAPITAL FORMATION POLICY IN GREEK AGRICULTURE

Between 1950 and 1992, total gross fixed asset formation in Greek agriculture increased in real terms at an average annual rate of 2.6 per cent. The year-on-year rates of increase were considerably higher during the period up to 1973. After that year, there was a marked slow-down in investment activity, which accelarated in the 1980s, with the exception of 1985. This phenomenon has also characterized the entire Greek economy (Baltas and Sakellis 1988). Again, we observe more or less the same trend in private investment, despite the financial support provided to the agricultural sector by FEOGA since 1981.

In the same period, the shares of agricultural gross value-added in GDP and agricultural investment in total investment gradually declined, with minor yearly fluctuations, from 33 per cent and 10 per cent in 1950 to 15 per cent and 6 per cent in 1990 respectively, reflecting the farming sector's decreasing weight in the overall economy as the industrialization process got underway. When we break total agricultural investment into its private and public components, we observe a fairly steady relationship of 1:2 in favour of private investment, the share of which fluctuated from just under half, for a few years in the early 1960s and in the late 1980s.

Private fixed asset formation in agriculture is broken down in official statistical sources into the following types of investment: non-residential buildings; machinery and equipment; and other constructions and works. About 50 per cent or more of private investment went to machinery and equipment, followed by other constructions and works (around 30 per cent or more) while the rest was taken up by non-residential buildings. Private investment in machinery and equipment showed a continuous increase up to 1979, reflecting the need for mechanization in the Greek agricultural sector. After that year investment in machinery and equipment began to decline, except in 1984 and 1985 when it reached its 1979 level, stabilizing at a lower level in recent years. The other two types of agricultural private investment increased up to 1973 and then, showing a declining trend, more or less stabilized at considerably lower levels. As for public agricultural investment, by far the largest share, around 90 per cent or more, was channelled to fixed assets other than machinery and equipment and, predominantly, to land improvements, which alone typically took up to 60 per cent or more of the total.

Turning now to the financing of private investment activity in the farming sector, the first thing to note is that until very recently the exclusive institutional lender to agriculture had been the Agricultural Bank of Greece (ABG). As a result, bank financing of the primary sector's investment is no other than the amount of medium- and long-term credit extended by the ABG. Throughout the postwar period up to the early 1980s, an easy credit policy was adopted towards the farming sector: the main tools were a low interest rate regime (many of which were subsidized), longer pay-off periods, etc. The rationale for this treatment was twofold: first, the recognition, given the overwhelming small family farm character of Greek agriculture, of the owner-occupier's limited scope for self-finance; second, the provision of a strong incentive for the sector's modernization and structural improvement.

Since 1984 credit has been increasingly tight, because of the liberalization of the banking system following Greece's entry to the EC. Controls imposed on the size of agricultural credit and its distribution among various crops started to relax and were eventually removed. The final stage in this development was the conversion of the ABG from a state-owned bank to a *société anonyme*.

Throughout the period under discussion, ABG loans covered about 50 per cent of private farm investment. In fact ABG finance has followed the same trend as that of private farm investment. ABG loans increased from 39 per cent in 1958 to 1 per cent in 1973 following with some fluctuations a declining trend, which was rapid during the later years of the period, resulting in its lower level (18 per cent) in 1989 and rising to 31 per cent in 1991. The rapid increase of real interest rates has played a crucial role in recent developments.

Throughout the period nominal interest rates granted to the agricultural sector by the ABG lagged behind those granted by commercial banks to the other sectors of the economy. Moreover, nominal interest rates to agriculture showed a relative stability in relation to the rapid and frequent fluctuations of inflation rates. The adjustment of interest rates to changes of inflation occurred at considerably lower levels and with a time lag, except in the 1957–63 and 1987–92 periods. The recent developments in interest rates and their adjustment to levels equal to or even higher than inflation rates explain the drop in the demand for loanable funds by farmers.

Regarding the share of ABG loans by type of investment we can notice that in the case of 'non-residential buildings'[1] these ranged from 70 to 90 per cent, while for 'machinery and other equipment' its share fluctuated between 14 and 86 per cent. Lastly, bank lending for 'other constructions and works' covered 40 per cent of realized investment of this type, the major part of which was granted at subsidized interest rates until the late 1970s (Baltas 1980).

THE CLASSICAL MODEL

In order to describe the interrelationship between financing and capital formation at the aggregate level, and by type of investment, a simultaneous equations econometric model was employed comprising two behavioural equations: investment finance and private investment expenditure.

To express the need for financing agricultural investment, a partial adjustment model combined with adaptive expectations is used (e.g. Baltas 1983; Alogoskoufis and Baltas 1991).[2]

The traditional approach to modelling investment behaviour requires assumptions about both the adjustment process and the desired level of capital. Various theories about the adjustment process have been proposed (Weersink and Tauer 1989). The traditional investment models have been criticized because they have been based on *ad hoc* specifications for the adjustment process and desired capital. More recent models have cast the firm in a dynamic optimization framework in order to derive the investment behaviour equation.

Although dynamic models of investment behaviour have a more consistent theoretical framework than the traditional ones, it is not evident that the former are unambiguously better than the latter. For instance, the results obtained by Weersink and Tauer (1989) indicate that the investment behaviour of New York dairy farms is explained more appropriately by using the traditional approach.

For this purpose, we employ a synthesized traditional model to examine investment behaviour with respect to the aggregate and the three types of investment. The independent theories were integrated into a single unified approach.

THE RATIONAL EXPECTATIONS MODEL

The adaptive expectations and partial adjustment models have been criticized mainly for their inadequate theoretical basis and the statistical estimation problems arising when the ordinary least squares method is used (Baltas 1987; Baltas and Apostolou 1988).

In order to study farmers' behaviour in allocating their limited productive resources (predominantly land and fixed capital, but also intermediate inputs and labour) to growing various crops and their risk-taking entrepreneurship in an uncertain environment of future prices and yields, we can make use of a simplified model of rational expectations which consists of two behavioural equations. We assume that farmers are rational in the sense that they respond to the various signals given out by the economic environment and formulate their own expectations about their agricultural income taking into consideration the developments in the CAP, credit policy, etc.

THE DATA AND THE METHOD OF ESTIMATION

The behavioural equations of the model have been estimated using annual data obtained from the National Accounts of Greece and the Agricultural Bank of Greece. The data employed for capital stock have been supplied by Papaelia's study (1992) covering the period 1972–90. For the estimation of the model at the aggregate level the data used cover the period 1951–91, while the 'by type of investment' available data cover the period 1958–91. A list of the variables employed in the model is provided in the Appendix.

As is known, the OLS method is inappropriate[3] for estimating the parameters of the model as a whole. Thus, a simultaneous equations technique was chosen, which was provided by the 2SLS method. Since lagged endogenous variables were included among the explanatory variables and autocorrelation may be present in the error term, we tried to remove autocorrelation using the Cochrane–Orcutt iterative technique first and second order.

EMPIRICAL RESULTS

The use of the rational expectations model in our attempt to explain the interrelationship between financing and capital formation in Greek agriculture does not always provide clearly superior results to those obtained under the classical model of adaptive expectations and partial adjustment (see Tables 21.1–21.4). This will be made evident below when we consider investment financing and capital formation at the aggregate level and by type of investment. It must be said at the outset, however, that this limited explanatory capacity is a feature of all rational expectations models employed in our analysis and may have been caused by the elimination of the trend in the endogenous variables.

Specifically, in the case of the credit function for aggregate private investments some differences between the two models are readily noticeable (Table 21.1). First, the number of explanatory variables increases in the rational expectations model. Thus we can see that, in addition to capital formation, which is the main explanatory variable, credit extended in the previous year and the rate of interest affect the level of credit in the current period. As to the influence exerted on the level of borrowing by the amount of credit supplied only in the previous year, this should be attributed to the fact that agricultural investment, and especially on-farm investment, tends to be of a smaller scale

Table 21.1 Aggregate private investment expenditure

Classical model

(*a*) $\log RM_t = -5.833 + 1.633\log RI_t - 0.059\log r_t$
$\quad\quad (5.250)\ (12.527)\quad\quad (0.697)$

$N = 37,\quad \bar{R}^2 = 0.903,\quad DW = 1.897,\quad \hat{R}_1 = 0.248\ (1.479)$

$a_0 = -5.833,\quad a_1 = 1.633,\quad a_2 = -0.059,\quad \lambda = \mu = 1$

(*b*) $\log RI_t = -2.569 + 0.682\log RY_{t-2} - 0.183\log r_t + 0.270\log G_t + 0.232\log RM_t$
$\quad\quad (1.356)\ (3.034)\quad\quad (2.117)\quad\quad (2.714)\quad\quad (2.262)$

$N = 37,\quad \bar{R}^2 = 0.930,\quad DW = 2.064,\quad \hat{R}_1 = 0.479\ (2.825),\quad \hat{R}_2 = -0.400\ (2.333)$

Rational expectations model

(*i*) $\Delta^2\log R\hat{M}_t = 0.030 - 0.633\Delta^2\log RM_{t-1}$
$\quad\quad (0.419)\ (4.431)$

$\bar{R}^2 = 0.335\quad F_{1,36} = 19.634$

$DW = 2.175$

(*ii*) $\Delta^3\log R\hat{I}_t = 0.006 - 0.540\Delta^3\log RI_{t-1}$
$\quad\quad (0.101)\ (3.769)$

$\bar{R}^2 = 0.263\quad F_{1,36} = 14.205$

$DW = 2.237$

(*a*) $\log R\hat{M}_t = -1.030 + 0.674\log R\hat{I}_t + 0.446\log R\hat{M}_{t-1} - 0.179\log r_t$
$\quad\quad (0.569)\ (2.489)\quad\quad (3.857)\quad\quad (1.931)$

$N = 34,\quad \bar{R}^2 = 0.791,\quad DW = 1.961,\quad \hat{R}_1 = 0.049\ (0.209)$

$a_0 = -1.859,\quad a_1 = 1.217,\quad a_2 = -0.323,\quad \mu = 1,\quad \lambda = 0.554$

(*b*) $\log R\hat{I}_t = -3.711 + 1.038\log RY_{t-2} - 0.323\log r_t + 0.190\log R\hat{M}_t$
$\quad\quad (1.175)\ (2.584)\quad\quad (2.026)\quad\quad (1.261)$

$N = 34,\quad \bar{R}^2 = 0.505,\quad DW = 2.264,\quad \hat{R}_1 = 0.055\ (0.344),\quad \hat{R}_2 = -0.526\ (2.899)$

Note: Figures in parentheses denote *t*-statistics. The values $\hat{R}_1$ and $\hat{R}_2$ express the first- and second-order autoregressive coefficients. The values a_0, a_1, a_2, μ and λ show the estimates of the parameters of equations (1), (2) and (3).

and to have a shorter gestation period than that undertaken in the other economic sectors. Similar results were obtained in our previous study (Baltas 1983). Second, it should be noted that the interest rate elasticity value is low

(–0.18). This can be attributed to the easy credit conditions that prevailed over most of the period, which greatly reduced the cost of credit.

Turning now to the aggregate investment function, while the decisive variable was medium- and long-term (Baltas 1983), this holds to some extent valid exclusively on the classical model. Farmers' decisions on new investment are also influenced by the rate of interest, which of course expresses the cost of credit, although not much is shown by its low elasticity, ranging from –0.18 to –0.32. The coefficient of the agricultural income, lagged two years, depicts the dynamic process of farmers' expectations building in a satisfactory manner. Finally, the classical model shows that farmers' investment decisions are quite sensitive to public policy due to the complementarity between private and public investment.

Considering the empirical results obtained for credit and investment in 'non-residential buildings', we can see that the two models are almost identical (Table 21.2). Thus, the speed of adjustment is the same for both credit and investment ($\mu = \lambda = 0.8$), which means that this type of investment is completed within a two-year period. With regard to the investment equation, the empirical results reveal that credit is the decisive factor in this case as well, while farmers' decisions to invest are influenced by the interest rate.

Next, we have the two functions relating to investments in 'machinery and other equipment' (Table 21.3). The results under the rational expectations model were not substantially different from those under the classical econometric model. From the first equation it is clear that the demand for loans is related to the level of investment and to the interest rate. The partial adjustment coefficient is $\lambda = 0.99$ and that for adaptive expectations is $\mu = 1$. In other words, credit adjustment takes place within a little over one year while the rate of investment adjustment is even faster. This is explained by the ready availability of credit that has provided a strong incentive for the mechanization of Greek agriculture for many years. Now, the ABG only finances cases where there is a proven 'real need' for doing so.

Coming now to investment in 'machinery and other equipment', we see that this is heavily influenced by the level of agricultural income in the previous year, which indicates a high elasticity (3). As for the capital stock, it does have the anticipated sign and seems to play a negative role on farmers' decision to mechanize their production given the high degree of mechanization of the farming sector in recent years and the sector's structural weakness (small and multi-fragmented farms). In contrast to our previous study, the amount of credit fails the statistical significance test in both models.

Finally, in the case of investment in 'other constructions and works' a comparison of the estimates arrived at under the two approaches reveals that the rational expectations model of the credit equation has a slightly higher explanatory power than that of the classical model (Table 21.4). The invest-

Table 21.2 Non-residential buildings

Classical model

(*a*) $RMK_t = 28.009 + 0.435\,RIK_t + 0.417\,RMK_{t-1} - 0.065\,RMK_{t-2}$
(0.890) (4.953) (1.799) (0.440)
$N = 30$, $\bar{R}^2 = 0.850$, $DW = 1.996$, $\hat{R}_1 = 0.627$, $\hat{R}_1 = -0.115$
(1.857) (0.440)
$a_0 = 43.224$, $a_1 = 0.671$, $\mu = \lambda = 0.792$, $\bar{e}_{RIK} = 0.592$

(*b*) $RIK_t = 400.944 - 22.881\,rK_t + 1.019\,RMK_t$
(1.387) (1.635) (3.295)
$N = 30$, $\bar{R}^2 = 0.891$, $DW = 2.162$, $\hat{R}_1 = 0.388$, $\hat{R}_2 = 0.052$
(1.847) (0.261)
$\bar{e}_{rK} = -0.291$, $\bar{e}_{RMK} = 0.749$

Rational expectations model

(*i*) $\Delta^2 R\hat{M}K_t = -1.181 - 0.623\Delta^2 RMK_{t-1}$ $\bar{R}^2 = 0.360$ $F_{1,36} = 21.776$
(0.024) (4.667) $DW = 2.363$

(*ii*) $\Delta^2 R\hat{I}K_t = 11.265 - 0.347\Delta^2 RIK_{t-1}$ $\bar{R}^2 = 0.091$ $F_{1,29} = 4.009$
(0.166) (2.002) $DW = 2.266$

(*a*) $R\hat{M}K_t = -32.106 + 0.404 R\hat{I}K_t + 0.586 R\hat{M}K_{t-1} - 0.187 R\hat{M}K_{t-2}$
(0.782) (5.681) (3.448) (1.477)
$N = 27$, $\bar{R}^2 = 0.828$, $DW = 2.020$, $\hat{R}_1 = 0.517$, $\hat{R}_2 = -0.419$
(1.823) (1.712)
$a_0 = 49.540$, $a_1 = 0.623$, $\mu = \lambda = 0.707$, $\bar{e}_{RIK} = 0.543$

(*b*) $R\hat{I}K_t = 366.780 - 21.473 rK_t + 1.058 R\hat{M}K_t$
(1.303) (1.419) (4.008)
$N = 27$, $\bar{R}^2 = 0.795$, $DW = 1.312$, $\bar{e}_{rK} = -0.274$, $\bar{e}_{RMK} = 0.786$

Notes: As for Table 21.1.

ment equation, however, yields less satisfactory results. The explanatory power shown in Table 21.2 has diminished and, more importantly, so has the statistical significance of the various variables (agricultural income lagged by two years, public investment and credit). Of particular importance is the statistical indication that these three variables do not influence farmers' investment decisions, these being disproved not only by our previous study but also by what happens in the real world. Indeed, in the classical model the level of investment in 'other constructions and works' is satisfactorily explained by the relevant amount of credit provided, by the level of farm income in the two previous years, the interest rate and, finally, by the level of

Table 21.3 *Machinery and other equipment*

Classical model

(*a*) $RMM_t = 659.892 + 0.302\,RIM_t + 0.035\,RMM_{t-1} - 41.133rM_t$
$\quad(1.053)\ (1.489)\quad(0.095)\quad(1.926)$
$N = 17,\quad \bar{R}^2 = 0.623,\quad DW = 1.883,\quad \hat{R}_1 = 0.240\ (0.639)$
$a_0 = 683.826,\quad a_1 = 0.313,\quad a_2 = -42.625,\quad \mu = 1,\quad \lambda = 0.965$
$\bar{e}_{RIM} = 0.808,\quad \bar{e}_{rM} = -0.610$

(*b*) $RIM_t = -2985.915 + 60.798\,RPY_{t-1} - 0.118\,MK_{t-1} + 0.498\,RMM_t$
$\quad(1.078)\ (2.270)\quad(1.467)\quad(0.860)$
$N = 17,\quad \bar{R}^2 = 0.424,\quad DW = 2.165,\quad \hat{R}_1 = 0.004\ (0.019)$
$\bar{e}_{RPY-1} = -3.267,\quad \bar{e}_{MK-1} = -1.158,\quad \bar{e}_{RMM} = 0.186$

Rational expectations model

(*i*) $\Delta^2 R\hat{M}M_t = 3.091 - 0.281\Delta^2 RMM_{t-1}$ $\quad(0.070)\ (1.762)$ $\quad \bar{R}^2 = 0.054,\ DW = 2.265$ $\quad F_{1,36} = 3.104$

(*ii*) $\Delta^2 RIM_t = 4.375 - 0.480\Delta^2 RIM_{t-1}$ $\quad(0.037)\ (2.908)$ $\quad \bar{R}^2 = 0.199,\ DW = 2.253$ $\quad F_{1,29} = 8.455$

(*a*) $R\hat{M}M_t = -615.652 + 0.349R\hat{I}M_t + 0.010R\hat{M}M_{t-1} - 138.329rM_t$
$\quad(1.087)\ (1.794)\quad(0.037)\quad(2.581)$
$N = 17,\quad \bar{R}^2 = 0.630,\quad DW = 2.278,\quad \hat{R}_1 = 0.077\ (0.335),\quad \hat{R}_2 = -0.464\ (2.138)$
$a_0 = 621.871,\quad a_1 = 0.353,\quad a_2 = -139.726,\quad \mu = 1,\quad \lambda = 0.990,$
$\bar{e}_{RIM} = 0.955,\quad \bar{e}_{IM} = -2.070$

(*b*) $R\hat{I}M_t = -1367.835 + 53.491RPY_{t-1} - 0.136Mk_{t-1} + 0.138R\hat{M}M_t$
$\quad(0.234)\ (0.775)\quad(0.936)\quad(0.183)$
$N = 17,\quad \bar{R}^2 = 0.320,\quad DW = 2.493,\quad \hat{R}_1 = 0.213\ (0.890),\quad \hat{R}_2 = -0.416\ (1.686)$
$\bar{e}_{RPY-1} = 2.834,\quad \bar{e}_{MK-1} = -1.335,\quad \bar{e}_{RMM} = 0.050$

Notes: As for Table 21.1.

public investment. The statistical significance of the last variable is explained by the fact that, public investment being overwhelmingly devoted to major land improvement and irrigation schemes, its infrastructural character is a precondition for undertaking on-farm investment.

In the credit equation, it is worth noting the strong influence exerted by the medium- and long-term loan variable lagged by two years, in contrast to what we found in the previous two types of investment. The obvious reason for this

Table 21.4 Other constructions and works

Classical model

(*a*) $\log RML_t = -5.140 + 1.230\log RIL_t + 0.428\log RML_{t-2}$
$\quad(5.441)\ (5.939)\quad(2.752)$
$N = 30,\ \bar{R}^2 = 0.686,\ DW = 1.749,\ \hat{R}_1 = 0.176,\ \hat{R}_2 = -0.632$
$\quad(0.825)\quad(2.208)$

(*b*) $\log RIL_t = -0.786 + 0.516\log RY_{t-2} - 0.047\, rL_t + 0.225\log G_t$
$\quad(0.444)\ (2.905)\quad(4.624)\quad(1.964)$
$+0.153\log RML_t$
(2.208)
$N = 30,\ \bar{R}^2 = 0.863,\ DW = 2.473,\ \hat{R}_1 = 0.021,\ \hat{R}_2 = -0.688$
$\quad(0.136)\quad(4.401)$

Rational expectations model

(*i*) $\Delta^2\log R\hat{M}L_t = 0.035 - 0.874\Delta^2\log RML_{t-1}$ $\quad\bar{R}^2 = 0.597\quad F_{1,29} = 45.517$
$\quad(0.328)\ (6.747)$ $\quad DW = 2.430$

(*ii*) $\Delta^2\log RIL_t = 0.020 - 0.435\Delta^2\log RIL_{t-1}$
$\quad(0.329)\ (2.549)$
$\bar{R}^2 = 0.155\quad F_{1,29} = 6.495$
$DW = 2.319$

(*a*) $\log R\hat{M}L_t = -8.628 + 1.522\log R\hat{I}L_t + 0.635\log R\hat{M}L_{t-2}$
$\quad(4.232)\ (5.058)\quad(3.234)$
$N = 27,\ \bar{R}^2 = 0.743,\ DW = 1.954,\ \hat{R}_1 = 0.277,\ \hat{R}_2 = -0.300$
$\quad(1.235)\quad(1.113)$

(*b*) $\log R\hat{I}L_t = -1.723 + 0.715\log RY_{t-2} - 0.059rL_t + 0.116\log G_t + 0.110\log R\hat{M}L_t$
$\quad(0.326)\ (1.404)\quad(2.740)\quad(0.424)\quad(0.865)$
$N = 27,\ \bar{R}^2 = 0.651,\ DW = 2.491,\ \hat{R}_1 = 0.119,\ \hat{R}_2 = -0.691$
$\quad(0.701)\quad(3.537)$

Notes: As for Table 21.1.

divergence is that because this category of investment mainly refers to on-farm land improvement and irrigation projects and to tree and vineyard planting, a longer gestation period is necessary.

CONCLUDING REMARKS AND POLICY IMPLICATIONS

Having compared the empirical results obtained by the classical model with those obtained by the rational expectations model, it is evident, on the basis of economic criteria, that one cannot be in favour of the latter approach. On the contrary, in most of the cases results were less satisfactory (aggregate private investment, machinery and other equipment, other constructions and works). Only in one case (non-residential buildings) was a slight improvement observed.

Overall, the empirical analysis shows that capital formation is the major explanatory variable of the demand for credit followed in some cases by the credit extended in the previous year and by the nominal interest rate. On the side of capital formation, we may conclude that the ready availability of credit on easy terms has proved to be instrumental in stimulating agricultural investments in the past decades, followed by farmers' expectations on agricultural income, and in some cases by the government's public investment policy. Thus, the unfavourable developments that were observed with regard to the above-mentioned policy variables explain the marked slow-down in investment activity that occurred in Greek agriculture in the 1980s.

NOTES

1. For a few years the share of ABG loans in investment on 'non-residential buildings' exceeded 100 per cent. This can be attributed to the fact that some investment projects might have been realized first and financed by the ABG later when the required credits had become available.
2. Specifically, this derives from the following three relationships:

$$M_t^* = a_0 + a_1 I_t^* + a_2 \tau_t + u_t \qquad (1)$$

$$M_t - M_{t-1} = \lambda \, (M_t^* - M_{t-1}) + v_t \quad 0 \prec \lambda \leq 1 \qquad (2)$$

$$I_t^* - I_{t-1} = \mu \, (I_t - I_{t-1}^*) + w_t \quad 0 \prec \mu \leq 1, \qquad (3)$$

   where M^* and I^* are the desired level of financing and investment respectively and τ is the nominal interest rate.
3. The inappropriateness of OLS can be attributed to three main reasons: first, the estimates of the parameters would be biased; second, since both lagged and non-lagged endogenous variables are included in the system, the estimates would be inconsistent; and third, OLS cannot trace out the interdependence of economic phenomena. Only a simultaneous consideration of the interaction between the model's variables can achieve this.

REFERENCES

Alogoskoufis, G. and N. Baltas (1991), 'Price and Quantity Adjustment in a Dual Character Market: The Case of the Greek Poultry Sector', *Agricultural Economics*, **6**, 79–89.
Baltas, N. (1980), 'An Empirical Investigation of the Production and Trade of Greek Peaches', *Oxford Agrarian Studies*, **9**, 89–114.
Baltas, N. (1983), 'Modelling Credit and Private Investment in Greek Agriculture', *European Review of Agricultural Economics*, **10**, 389–402.
Baltas, N. (1987), 'Supply Response for Greek Cereals', *European Review of Agricultural Economics*, **14**, 195–220.
Baltas, N. and N. Apostolou (1988), 'A Rational Expectations Model for the Poultry Sector in Greece', *Applied Economics*, **20**, 917–27.
Baltas, N. and M. Sakellis (1988), 'Greek Agriculture in the National Economic Context', *Oxford Agrarian Studies*, **17**, 112–41.
Papaelia, T. (1992), *Investment, Capital and Productivity in the Agricultural Sector*, Agricultural Bank of Greece, Research and Planning Division, no. 44, Athens.
Weersink, A.J. and L.W. Tauer (1989), 'Comparative Analysis of Investment Models for New York Dairy Farms', *American Journal of Agricultural Economics*, **71**, 136–45.

APPENDIX: ENDOGENOUS AND EXOGENOUS VARIABLES

Variables are generally defined in their order of appearance, beginning with the endogenous variables and followed by the predetermined variables.

Endogenous Variables

RM Medium- and long-term loans for agricultural private investment deflated by the implicit price index of agricultural private investment, *P* (1970=100).

RI Agricultural private investment at constant 1970 prices.

RMK Medium- and long-term loans for agricultural private investment in non-residential buildings deflated by the implicit price index of agricultural private investment in non-residential buildings, *PK* (1970=100).

RIK Agricultural private investment in non-residential buildings at constant 1970 prices.

RMM Medium- and long-term loans for agricultural private investment in machinery and other equipment deflated by the implicit price index of agricultural private investment in machinery and other equipment, *PM* (1970=100).

RIM Agricultural private investment in machinery and other equipment at constant 1970 prices.

RML Medium- and long-term loans for agricultural private investment in other constructions and work deflated by the implicit price index of agricultural private investment in other constructions and works, PC (1970=100).

RIL Agricultural private investment in other constructions and works at constant 1970 prices.

Predetermined Variables

RM_{-i} Real medium- and long-term loans for agricultural private investment lagged *i* years (*i*=1,2).

RMK_{-i} Real medium- and long-term loans for agricultural private investment in non-residential buildings lagged *i* years (*i*=1,2).

RMM_{-i} Real medium- and long-term loans for agricultural private investment in machinery and other equipment lagged *i* years (*i*=1,2).

RML_{-i} Real medium- and long-term loans for agricultural private investment in other constructions and works lagged *i* years (*i*=1,2).

ΔY Changes in gross agricultural income at constant 1970 prices.

RY_{-n} Gross agricultural income lagged *n* years at constant 1970 prices.

RPY_{-n} Implicit price index of agricultural income deflated by the implicit price index of gross domestic product (1970=100), lagged *n* years.

r Nominal interest rate paid for medium- and long-term loans for agricultural private investment.

rK Nominal interest rate paid for medium- and long-term loans for agricultural private investment in non-residential buildings.

rM Nominal interest rate paid for medium- and long-term loans for agricultural private investment in machinery and other equipment.

rL Nominal interest rate paid for medium- and long-term loans for agricultural private investment in other constructions and works.

G Agricultural public investment at constant 1970 prices.

K_{-1} Agricultural private capital stock lagged one year at constant 1970 prices.

KK_{-1} Agricultural private capital stock in non-residential buildings lagged one year at constant 1970 prices.

MK_{-1} Agricultural private capital stock in machinery and other equipment lagged one year at constant 1970 prices.

LK_{-1} Agricultural private capital stock in other constructions and works lagged one year at constant 1970 prices.

22. An empirical study of the effects of economic integration of Greece with the EU

George Zestos*

INTRODUCTION

Greece became an associate member of the European Union (EU) in 1962, and a full member in 1981. During this period Greece and the EU countries liberalized trade among each other and adopted common policies. The most important of these policies is the Common Agricultural Policy (CAP). The purpose of this chapter is to examine how the entry of Greece into the EU affected the Greek economy. The case is interesting since Greece is a developing country with substantially lower standards of living and a relatively large agricultural sector in comparison with the other EU countries. In contrast the other EU countries are developed industrialized economies with small agricultural sectors.[1] The effect on the Greek economy of entry into the EU can partly be gauged by a comparison of the per capita income in Greece before and after entry in 1981. The Greek economy practically ceased growing after this time, but the different sectors of the economy were affected differently. This will be demonstrated in this chapter by estimates and comparisons of the elasticity of substitution of the Greek sectors with the corresponding sectors of the French and German economies.

The elasticity of substitution in production between capital and labour, σ, is a crucial parameter for the firm. Relatively high values of σ must be associated with relatively high efficiency levels for the firm, and low values of σ with relatively low efficiency levels. The reason for this is that when σ is relatively high, a small change in the factor–price ratio, i.e. the ratio of the wage rate to interest rate, causes large changes in the demands of the two inputs, and consequently a large change in the capital to labour ratio.[2] This indicates flexibility of the firm regarding its ability to make substitution between the two inputs employed. The above analysis suggests that it will be

* The author wishes to express his gratitude to his assistant, Grigorios Zimonopoulos.

useful to both business managers and government policy-makers to know the value(s) of σ for all business firms. This may be difficult, considering the proliferation of such firms. An alternative approach is to estimate σ for the main sectors of the economy. This approach is followed here, with the capital to labour corresponding elasticities of substitution of the agricultural, service and industrial sectors of Greece, France and Germany estimated and compared for convergence or divergence.[3] A tendency for convergence of the Greek sectoral elasticities towards the corresponding French and German elasticities of substitution should be interpreted as the Greek sector(s) becoming similar to the corresponding French and German sectors. Non-convergence of the Greek elasticities of substitution to the corresponding French and German elasticities means that the Greek sectors remain different from the corresponding French and German sectors.

The elasticity of substitution can be estimated empirically provided there are data available on inputs and outputs of production. This occurs when production functions are estimated either at the firm or industry level. The most popular production functions which practically dominate all economic literature on this topic are: the Cobb–Douglas function (CD), the constant elasticity of substitution (CES), and the transcendental production function.

Despite the fact that the CD production function is a very popular model and has economically meaningful parameters, it suffers from one major drawback: the elasticity of substitution between capital and labour for a CD production function is equal to one. This is indeed a very strong and unrealistic assumption to be imposed on a parameter of such great economic importance. It should be noted that there was never disagreement among economists that σ is a parameter whose value(s) can only be estimated empirically. The elasticity of substitution based on a transcendental constant returns to scale production function has an additional economically meaningful and desirable feature – it varies with time.[4]

ESTIMATION OF THE CES PRODUCTION FUNCTION USING THE KMENTA APPROXIMATION

A production function that partially overcomes the drawback of the CD production function is the constant elasticity of substitution (CES). This production function yields elasticity of substitution estimates that are constant but not necessarily equal to one. The CES production function for the case of constant returns to scale (CRS) is given below:

$$Y = \gamma e^{\lambda t}[\delta K^{-\rho} + (1-\delta)L^{-\rho}]^{-\frac{1}{\rho}} \tag{1}$$

All parameters of the CES production function are economically meaningful; this is one reason for its popularity.[5] The estimation of the CES production function in this study is carried out using the Kmenta approximation method. The latter is based on Taylor's expansion formula up to the second order, disregarding the rest of the terms and around $\rho = 0$; this formula is given below.

$$\ln\frac{Y}{L} = \ln\gamma + \lambda t + \delta \ln\frac{K}{L} - \frac{1}{2}\rho\delta(1-\delta)[\ln\frac{K}{L}]^2 + u \qquad (2)$$

This equation was estimated for the full sample (1961–87), for all the sectors of the Greek, German and French economies. It is however impossible to estimate equation (2) in the exact form as stated above, since each term does not contain a single coefficient. An indirect method is used to estimate (2) by rewriting the equation as follows:

$$\ln\frac{Y}{L} = \beta_0 + \beta_1 t + \beta_2 \ln\frac{K}{L} + \beta_4[\ln\frac{K}{L}]^2 + u \qquad (3)$$

The above is the restrained form of the Kmenta approximation formula of the CES production function. This equation can be estimated using ordinary least squares (OLS), or any other regression estimation method. Once estimates for β_0, β_1, β_2, and β_4 are obtained, the values of the original CES parameters γ, λ, δ, and ρ are obtained.[6] Once an estimate for ρ is obtained, an estimate for the elasticity of substitution can be found, since $\sigma = 1/(1 + \rho)$.

Before the sectoral elasticities of the three countries are reported it must be mentioned that the estimated production functions were tested for structural stability. The Chow test was performed for the year 1973–74, the oil crisis, and for 1980–81, the year of Greece's entry into the EU. Two more structural stability tests were performed, the Cusum and the Cusum of squares. Based on the results of the Chow test, the elasticity of substitution was calculated. Whenever the Chow test indicated no structural break, σ was calculated from the estimated parameters of the entire sample regression, resulting in only one value for σ for the entire sample. If, on the other hand, the Chow test indicated structural break(s), then σ was constructed by taking into consideration the structural break(s). In the case of only one break, two values for σ were constructed. If two structural breaks were revealed according to the Chow test, then three different values for σ were constructed. In order to understand what affected σ we report and compare the estimated production functions of the Greek agricultural and industrial sectors.

GREEK AGRICULTURE

The estimated CES production function of the Greek agricultural sector is stable along the entire sample period. This is demonstrated with the Chow test, the Cusum test, and the Cusum of squares test. The last two are presented in Figure 22.1. Since the graphs of the test statistics of both tests stay within the 95 per cent critical bound lines, this is evidence for structural stability of the agricultural sector.

The estimated production function of Greek agriculture is:

$$\ln\frac{Y}{L} = -.53 - .01t + 1.18\ln\frac{K}{L} + .08[\ln\frac{K}{L}]^2 \quad (4)$$

$$(.78)\,(.01)\quad(.37)\qquad(.04)$$

$$R^2 = .98 \qquad F = 583 \qquad DW = 2.2$$

in which the numbers in parentheses are standard errors.

The stability of the Greek agricultural sector is also supported by the graphs of the recursive coefficients (Figure 22.2), which are converging very drastically and without fluctuations to their values.

The stability of the Greek agricultural sector must be attributed to the protection the sector enjoys from the EU. First the Greek government subsidized the agricultural sector and after entry into the EU, the EU continued to subsidize agriculture. Protection allowed farmers not to be very responsive to global market conditions. The end result was overproduction and inefficiency.

GREEK INDUSTRY

Three different sub-samples were estimated for the industrial sector of Greece, as shown in Table 22.1. Consequently three different values for σ were constructed based on the estimated parameters from each of the three sub-samples. The elasticity of substitution of the Greek industrial sector increased during the period 1974–80, but declined in 1981–87. The fluctuation in σ of the Greek industrial sector is attributed to the instability of the sector. The instability of the industrial sector is indicated by the Chow test, the Cusum test, the Cusum of squares test, and the graphs of the recursive coefficients. The graphs of the Cusum, the Cusum of squares tests and the recursive coefficients are presented below in Figures 22.3 and 22.4.

It is clear from these graphs that the industrial sector has experienced structural changes during the 1961–87 period. The main cause of the instability of this sector is the openness of the sector to the EU and the international competition. This is attributed to the entry of Greece into the EU, starting

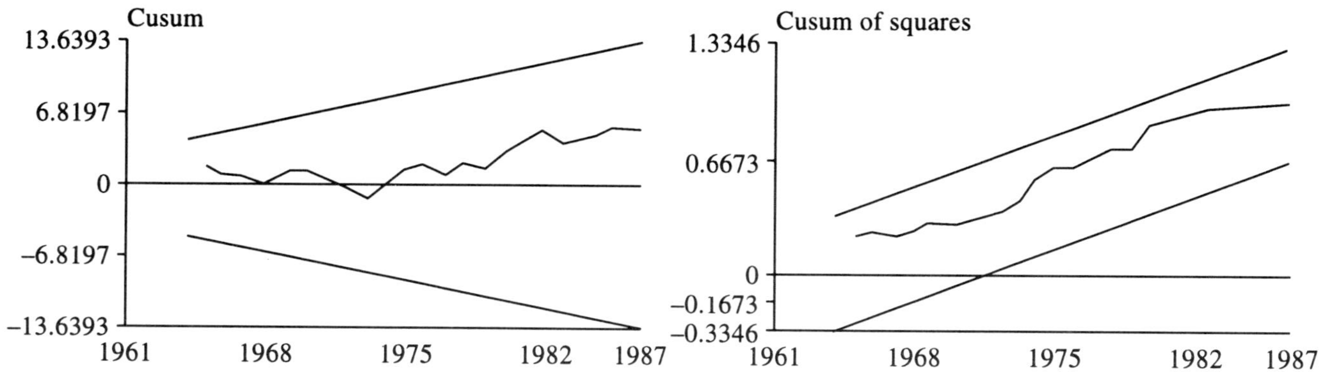

Figure 22.1 *Stability of the Greek agricultural CES production function*

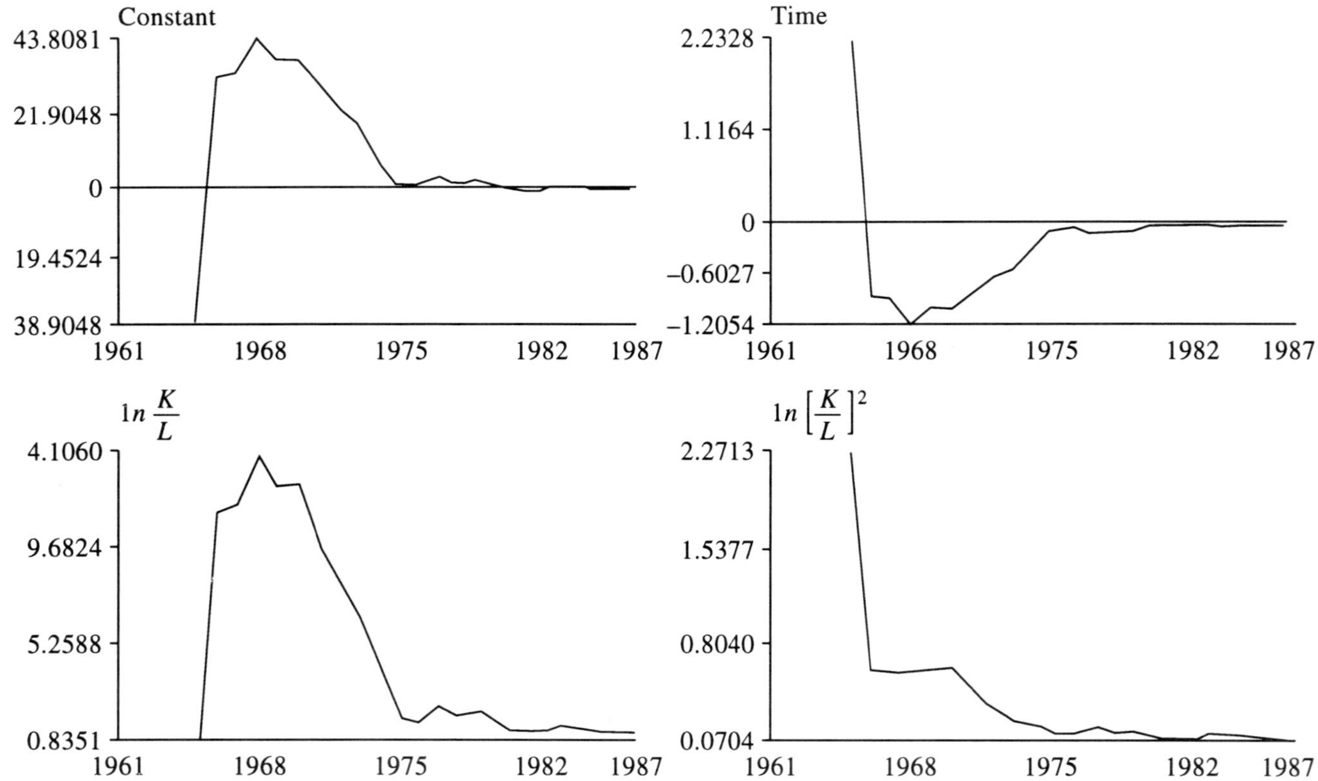

Figure 22.2 Recursive coefficients of the Greek agricultural CES production function

Table 22.1 Estimated CES production function of Greek industry

Period	β_0	β_1	β_2	β_4	γ	λ	δ	ρ
1961–73	–0.81	0.04	1.62	0.31	0.44	0.04	1.62	0.61
	(1.40)	(0.04)	(0.61)	(0.14)				
1974–80	–17.1	0.02	–21	–7.5	0.0	0.02	–21	–0.03
	(5.4)	(0.01)	(7.2)	(2.4)				
1981–87	4.78	–0.04	9.17	3.48	119	–0.03	9.1	0.09
	(2.77)	(0.01)	(3.17)	(1.30)				

Note: The numbers in parentheses are standard errors.

with the Athens Agreement in 1962 when Greece became an associated member. Greece gradually reduced trade barriers against the EU member countries and accepted the common EU tariffs against non-EU member countries. Greek tariffs against third countries were usually higher than the corresponding common tariffs.

Table 22.2 portrays the sectoral elasticities of the three countries. A careful examination of this table reveals several interesting findings. The Greek agricultural sector displayed low elasticity of substitution (0.57), denoting very low responsiveness of the agricultural firms to changes in the factor–price ratio. This behaviour indicates inefficiency in the agricultural sector since firms do not act as rational cost minimizers that respond rapidly to changes in the factor market conditions.

A similar story is told by the Greek service sector where σ is relatively low, below unity at 0.25 and 0.88 for the 1960–80 and 1981–87 sub-periods respectively. These relatively low values of σ denote a slow response of the Greek service firms to changes in the factor–price ratio. Low values of σ suggest inefficiency in this sector. Comparison of the Greek agricultural and service elasticities with the corresponding German and French elasticities indicates that neither the agricultural nor the service elasticities converged. The Greek agricultural and service elasticities are low and below unity; the corresponding German and French elasticities of substitution are close to unity. The inefficiency of the Greek agricultural sector is attributed to protection which the sector received from the Greek government and after joining the EU. The non-convergence of the Greek service elasticity of substitution to the corresponding German and French elasticities is attributed to the lack of external competition in this sector since many services are not traded internationally and are therefore indirectly protected.

Table 22.2 also reports the elasticity of substitution of the Greek industrial and manufacturing sectors. The Greek industrial elasticity of substitution

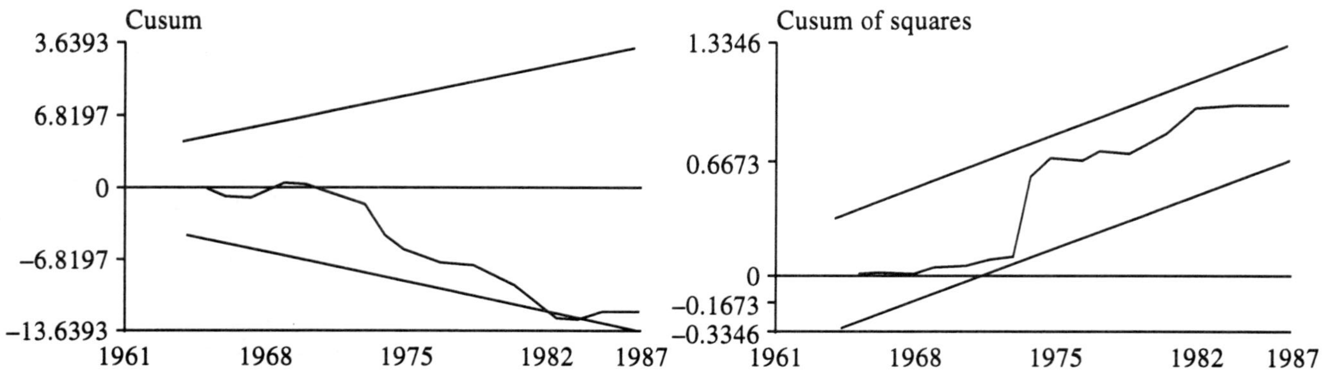

Figure 22.3 Instability of the Greek industrial sector

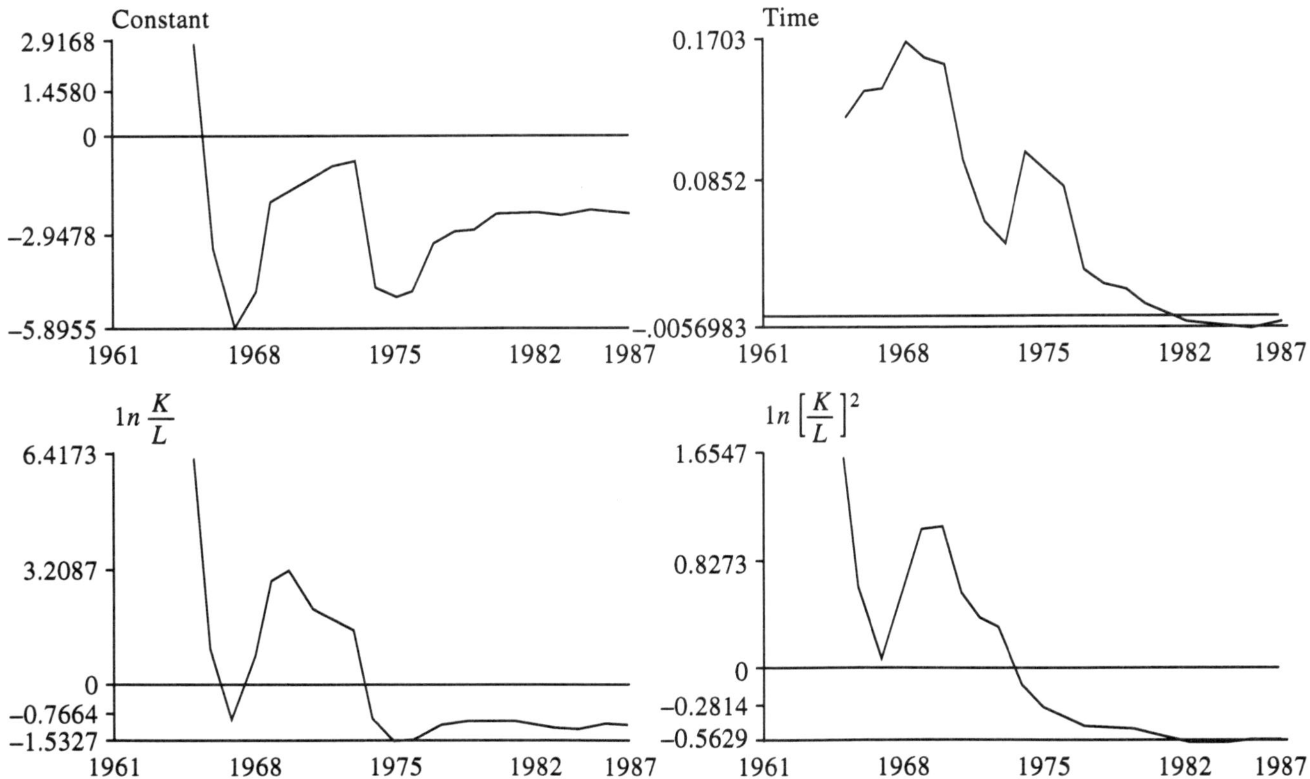

Figure 22.4 Recursive coefficients of the Greek industrial CES production function

Table 22.2 Elasticity of substitution based on CES Kmenta approximation production function

		Elasticity of substitution		
Sector	Period	Greece	Germany	France
Agriculture	1960–87	0.57		
	1960–73		1.13	0.96
	1974–80			0.99
	1981–87			1.00
	1974–87		1.01	
Industry	1960–87			
	1960–73	0.62	0.87	1.03
	1974–80	1.03		0.99
	1981–87	0.91		1.09
	1974–87		1.00	
Manufacturing	1960–87			
	1960–73	1.04	0.86	0.22
	1974–80			1.00
	1981–87			1.06
	1974–87	1.02	1.01	
Services	1960–87			
	1960–73		0.68	0.95
	1974–80			
	1981–87	0.88		
	1961–80	0.25		
	1974–87		1.23	0.97

increased from 0.62 during 1973–74 to 1.03 during 1974–80 and declined to 0.91 in the last sub-period 1981–87. While there is indeed some fluctuation in the Greek industrial σ, the fluctuation is small and σ remains close to unity. The elasticity of substitution of the industrial sectors of France and Germany tend to take values close to unity as well.

Similarly the elasticities of substitution of the manufacturing sectors of the three countries converged towards unity. Convergence of the elasticities of substitution of the industrial and manufacturing sectors of the three countries is explained by competition. Cross-border firms compete in the same market.

Competition requires that firms minimize cost and thus become equally sensitive to factor price changes. This type of firm behaviour in the three countries brought about convergence.

While the above findings are economically meaningful, one only wonders why the elasticities of substitution of the industrial and manufacturing sectors tended to converge to unity. Another study, by Zestos (1996), which utilized the same data but a transcendental production function, arrived at similar conclusions regarding the tendency for convergence or divergence of the sectoral elasticities of the three countries. The transcendental production function permitted the construction of σ as a vector of different values for each year. Estimates of σ based on the transcendental production function of the three countries did not converge in the agricultural or the service sectors. On the contrary, estimates of the traded, industrial and manufacturing sectors converged towards zero. One can now question which production function allows the correct estimation of σ. One way to pursue this question is to calculate σ using the two models with other sets of data. This will be only a starting point in shedding light on this problem, and investigating which of the two production functions yields unbiased estimates of the elasticity of substitution.

NOTES

1. Exceptions are Portugal and Spain; these countries joined the EU in 1986 towards the end of the period of this study.
2. The elasticity of substitution is defined as the ratio of the change in the capital to labour ratio divided by the change in the marginal product of labour to the marginal product of capital ratio; the latter is equal to the change in the factor price ratio when the firm is in equilibrium.
3. The elasticity of substitution of the manufacturing sector, a large sub-sector of industry, is also estimated and compared.
4. Elasticities of substitution of the sectoral Greek, French and German economies based on the transcendental production function were estimated in Zestos (1996). This chapter compares the estimated elasticities based on the transcendental production function with the elasticities based on the CES production functions.
5. The economic meaning of the CES parameters is given as: γ = efficiency parameter; δ = distribution parameter; ρ = substitution parameter; λ = a parameter measuring technical change.
6. This can be done by solving the system of equations below:

$$\gamma = e^{\beta_0}, \lambda = \beta_1, v = 1, \delta = \beta_2, \rho = \frac{-2\beta_4}{\beta_2(1-\beta_2)}$$

Such a system was solved and the estimates of γ, λ, δ, ρ were obtained.

REFERENCES

Kmenta, J. (1967), 'On Estimation of the CES Production Function', *International Economic Review*, **8** (2), June.

Zestos, G. (1996), 'The Elasticity of Substitution as a Proxy Measure of Economic Integration', *Atlantic Economic Journal*, **24** (1), March.

23. Purchasing loyalty: Greece and the EU

Dimitris Bourantonis and Constantine Tsoutsoplides

THE EMERGENCE OF A PRO-COMMUNITY CONSENSUS

On 1 January 1981, Greece formally joined the EC. This was the result of energetic campaigning in the European capitals by the Greek Prime Minister Constantine Karamanlis, who managed to overrun the Commission's scepticism, on the strength of political argumentation. His claim was that Greece's entry into the EC would secure its fragile democratic regime that in 1974 replaced seven years of dictatorship. His aim was to integrate Greece irreversibly into the West.

Greece applied for membership in July 1975, following an association agreement from the early 1960s that had been frozen during the seven years of dictatorship. Joining the EC became the central foreign policy objective during the 1974–81 New Democracy administration.

Only ten months after the Treaty of Accession came into effect, the Panhellenic Socialist Movement (PASOK) was swept to power by a 48.7 per cent share of the national vote. Pasok was elected on a platform that, among others, rejected the fundamental wisdom of Greece's entry into the EC. Parties opposing participation in the Community gained another 12 per cent of the national vote in the October 1981 elections. In total, the political parties that explicitly opposed Greece's entry into the EC gained 60.7 per cent of the national vote.

PASOK, which became the major opposition party after the 1977 elections, unequivocally opposed Greece's planned entry into the Community on both economic and political grounds.[1] PASOK argued that entry would impede Greece's economic development and create insurmountable adjustment problems both to the agricultural and industrial sector. Moreover, PASOK argued that full membership 'would consolidate the peripheral role of the country as a satellite of the capitalist system' (Clogg 1979) though it would not oppose a loose association based on the Norwegian model.

On 31 July 1992, the Greek Parliament ratified the Maastricht Treaty by an overwhelming majority. Out of the 300 members of Parliament, 286 voted in favour, 8 voted against and 5 abstained. From the 1970s' anti-Community camp, only the Communist Party of Greece (KKE) remained firmly in place. PASOK and the non-Stalinist left had become enthusiastic converts. The almost total political acceptance of the country's membership of the Community was underlined in the most emphatic way.

What happened in a decade that altered Greek political attitudes towards the EC option so radically? In 1981 PASOK was given for the first time the chance to test its political platform against the harsh realities of government. Its pre-election militancy was immediately softened. Outright opposition to full membership was dropped. Instead, the new institutional reality was taken for granted and the government focused its efforts on improving the terms of participation. At the same time, an attempt was made to gradually broaden the popular support for such a significant change of policy.

Indeed, increasing political acceptance of EC membership was accompanied by widening popular acceptance. It is interesting to note that, although the anti-Community platform gained considerable support in the 1981 elections, there was considerably greater underlying popular support for the European orientation option. This support broadened and deepened in the course of the decade. These developments are lucidly illustrated by evidence from the opinion polls organized by the Eurobarometer.

At the time of Greece's entry into the Community, as much as 60 per cent of the public favoured the unification of Western Europe, with a mere 23 per cent against it.[2] At the time, European unification had the support of almost three-quarters of the public in the ten member states and the opposition of some 13 per cent. By the mid-1980s, public support for European unification in Greece was around the EC-10 average. At the beginning of the 1990s the Greek public had become more enthusiastic than the European (EC-10) average, most notably at the level of the core share that supported integration unequivocally.

Accession took place with a solid support of some 40 per cent of the public.[3] Although the anti-Community platform gained some 60 per cent of the popular vote in the 1981 elections, outright opposition to membership of the Community was only limited to around 20 per cent of the public. At the beginning of the 1980s, over 50 per cent of the EC-10 public supported their countries' membership of the Community and opposition was less than 20 per cent. By 1986, support for membership exceeded 50 per cent in Greece. By the end of the decade support for membership was clearly greater than the EC-10 average. Three in four Greeks favoured their country's membership of the Community, with those opposing now reduced to less than 10 per cent.

The sharp increase in acceptability of membership of the Community over the course of the 1980s certainly relates to the Greek public's perception of benefit from it.[4] In the early 1980s, one in two Greeks already appeared to believe that membership of the Community would be beneficial to the country. Between a third and a quarter believed that membership did not serve the country's interests. This division of opinion was similar to the EC-10 average. While the average Community picture did not change, Greek perceptions had altered considerably by the late 1980s. By the end of the decade, no less than three in four Greeks believed that their country had benefited from membership. Dissenters were limited in the region of 10–15 per cent. It should however be noted that a slight reversal of the trend has been discernible in the early 1990s.

Public acceptance of membership of the Community is not only coloured by perceptions of the country's cost–benefit calculus, but by perceptions of the opportunity cost as well. It appears that the Greek public sees its future welfare inextricably linked to membership of the EC. Reactions to a potential scrapping of the Community illustrate the point.[5] At the time of Greece's entry into the EC, one in two Greeks did not care if the Community were scrapped. Only between a quarter and a third of the public had negative feelings about such a possibility. Overall, attachment to the Community was greater for the EC-10 average. From the late 1980s onwards, however, more than one in two Greeks said they would feel 'very sorry' if the Community ceased to exist. Obviously, the emerging attachment to the Community, in combination with the perception of the clear majority that the country benefits overall from participation in the Community, underlines the public perception that the country would find it hard to sustain its welfare outside the Community's framework.

The sharp increase in acceptability of membership and attachment to the European orientation, both by politicians and the public in Greece during the decade that followed the country's entry, requires a systematic explanation. What was it that made anti-Community Greek political parties accept membership, to the point that the Community option has arguably the widest support across the political spectrum observed among EC member states? What changed public attitudes and built an unusually deep public consensus in favour of the country's European orientation? What sustains these attitudes and what might possibly erode them?

This chapter aims to offer an insight into the reasons for the emergence of the wide pro-Community consensus in Greece during the first decade of its membership. The thesis we shall examine is whether there is a positive relationship between the net income transfer from the EC to Greece and the level of acceptance of the EC. The analytical tool for this discussion will be the model of a market where political influence is exchanged for real resources.

GREECE IN THE EC SPHERE OF INFLUENCE: A CONCEPTUAL MODEL

According to Knorr, influence can be non-coercive as well as coercive. It is coercive when B's conduct is affected by his fear of sanctions of one kind or another. B's choice of behavior is consequently restricted by A's influence. Influence is noncoercive, if B's choices are enriched rather than limited by A's influence, for example if A persuades B that a proposed cooperative venture is mutually beneficial' (Knorr 1973).

In view of the fact that membership of the EC became increasingly acceptable and instrumental in Greek politics, it could be said that the EC's non-coercive influence on Greece has increased considerably since 1981. Greece is a net recipient from the EC (Georgakopoulos 1994). It could be argued that EC political influence on Greece was greatly enhanced through the increasing dependence of Greek economic welfare on income transferred from the EC.

There is a long history of efforts to establish the causality of the relationship between economic and political power throughout the evolution of the political economy.[6] Postwar literature concentrated mostly on examining two phenomena: the use of aid as a lever, and preferential trade as a means for the acquisition of political influence.

If everything has a price, so too does political influence. In effect, the price of political influence could be determined in a conceptual market where political influence has a demand and a supply curve.

The supply of influence curve is determined by a country's vulnerability to external influence. This vulnerability depends on a number of factors that may be grouped under three generic headings:

1. Urgency for extra income.
2. Substitutability of sources of income by alternative ones.
3. Resistance towards foreign influence.

A nation's urgency for extra income may be approximated by:

- its real income per capita; and
- its marginal utility for income.

In other words, the poorer a country, the greater its urgency and consequently its vulnerability.

A nation's ability to switch sources of income depends on:

- the demand for influence curve of alternative sources; and
- the extra costs a switch would entail.

Overall, the more difficult it is for a nation to secure income from alternative sources, the greater its vulnerability to the influence of the current income providing source.

A nation's resistance to external political influence is the expression of its preference to forgo additional income in order to secure wider political choice. This preference may be defined along three generic categories:

1. The depth of the nationalist feeling prevailing in the nation. The deeper the nationalist feeling runs in a nation, the greater its resistance.
2. The similarity of its political objectives to the source of influence. The greater the similarity, the smaller the resistance, as its political choices compromise less by yielding to influence.
3. The size and structure of local vested interests that derive their income from the source of influence. The greater and more influential locally these vested interests are, the less the resistance.

Of the three determinants of vulnerability, the urgency for extra income is exogenously given for a nation's supply curve. The other two, ability to switch and resistance, are very much dependent on who the influential party is and the medium of transaction employed.

The impact on Greece's economic welfare from its participation in the Community depends on the effects of bilateral trade and real resources transferred. It could thus be said that to the extent that Greece's net welfare increases as a result of its participation in the Community, so does the latter's scope for influence on the former.

In the case of capital transfers from the EC, the relationship is clear. To the degree that Greece is a net recipient from the EC, the country secures extra income on which she has gradually and increasingly come to depend. In the case of income effects from the trade relationship, the analysis is more complex. Generally speaking, the more monopolistic or monopsonistic the position of the EC is *vis-à-vis* Greece, the more difficult it is for Greece to switch to other trading partners. A number of observations can be made regarding Greece's facility to switch away from trade with the EC to an equally profitable trading relationship with a third party:

1. Joining the EC increased the share of Greek trade with the Community, thus making it more difficult to switch away to alternative sources.
2. Trade between Greece and the rest of the Community is vastly asymmetrical in terms of the share it represents in the total trade of each side.
3. The greater the incidence of monopolies and/or monopsonies in particular products, the more difficult it is to find alternative trading partners.
4. The greater the complementarity, particularly of an exclusive nature –

when for example Greek exports have little demand outside the Community market – the harder it is to interrupt the trade link.

5. The more differentiated the trade products are, the more difficult it is to switch suppliers.
6. Because that it is more difficult to conquer an export market than find a supplier, the party with the negative trade balance is the one favoured in terms of influence. Bilateralism, however, makes it difficult to switch imports if it is difficult to switch exports.
7. Handling transit trade is a source of influence.
8. The more economically integrated two regions are, the more difficult it is to find alternative trade partners outside the relationship.

Turning to considerations of resistance to influence, the following observations help define the degree of vulnerability: new countries tend to be more nationalistic (Johnson 1965). Nationalism is a preference, and the utility derived from its consumption is in terms of psychic income rather than that of goods or services with a normal down-sloping demand curve. Appearances then probably matter as much as the content of the relationship. Other things being equal, a 'covert' way of 'purchasing' influence is cheaper than an 'apparent' one (Marrese and Vanous 1983) as it is less likely to mobilize adverse nationalist feeling. Similarity of political orientation between the two partners linked by an influence relationship lessens resistance.

The owners of factors of production engaged in the production of goods and services traded with the dominant country have a vested interest in the continuation of this trade relationship. A country's resistance to external political influence is inversely related to the political influence these vested interests have locally. An assessment of this relationship may be attempted through the interest group model of public choice (Caves 1976). Other things being equal, this influence will be greater:

- the more open the economy is;
- the smaller the mobility of resources within the economy; and
- the more concentrated these interests are regionally and sectorally.

It is important to underline the dynamic nature of vested interests favouring the continuation of a foreign trade relationship. Indeed, a given trade relationship will tend to develop vested interests that favour conditions for the expansion of trade which, in turn, will strengthen the interest group and reinforce its claims for expansion.

Turning to the demand for influence curve, a fundamental distinction has to be made between the demand for influence of politicians and that of the general public. The EC Commission, which is motivated by its vision of building a united Europe, will devote resources to gain support for its vision much more readily than will taxpayers and consumers of the net contributing member states of the Community. In that respect, a 'covert' means of 'purchasing' influence will also be favoured by politicians, as this will permit them to operate closer to their own demand for influence curve rather than that of the general public.

What is clear from this discussion is that between any pair of countries, or group of countries, operates a market for political influence, where demand and supply depend on the particular sides involved and the medium of transaction employed.

INCOME AND LOYALTY: THE EVIDENCE

In order to assess whether Greece's entry into the EC increased its vulnerability to the EC, it is sufficient to establish the dynamics of the determinants of its vulnerability, as this was defined in the conceptual model presented above on the one hand, and the net welfare effects of the relationship on the other.

We have identified two channels through which income can be transferred between Greece and the EC: capital transfers and trade. Greece is a net recipient at the fiscal level (Georgakopoulos 1994). Inflows from the EC became increasingly important for Greece. By the end of the 1980s, they represented 5 per cent of the GDP, 10 per cent of the budget and covered around a quarter of the country's external trade deficit. The estimation of net resource transfer, however, should take into consideration two factors: first, that the bulk of resources from the EC come from the FEOGA (Georgakopoulos 1992). During the first half of the 1980s, around 75 per cent of the total capital inflows from the EC went to price guarantees of agricultural produce. These resources mostly went to final consumption which, given the country's negative trade balance, partly financed imports from other EC member states. After 1985, however, the share of structural funds increased, exceeding 40 per cent by the end of the decade. Moreover, it is fair to assume that a comparable sum of money would have been paid to agricultural guarantees from national resources, as the agricultural income traditionally enjoyed heavy protection anyway. Second, direct income transfers through trade have to be deducted from fiscal transfers in order to find net resource transfers between Greece and the EC. Community protection through the common external tariff and countervailing duties on imported agricultural products mean that the resulting increases in final prices represent an income transfer from consumers to producers.

According to studies cited by Georgakopoulos (1994) during the first half of the 1980s no less than a third of Greece's fiscal benefits from the EC were matched by negative direct income transfers from trade. Subsequently, their relative importance must have dropped, first, to the extent that fiscal inflows increased quicker than Greece's trade deficit with the EC; and second, in the near future, Greece's net position will further improve, as Community protectionism gradually recedes following the conclusion of the GATT agreement and the reform of the Common Agricultural Policy (CAP).

Greece's entry into the EC translated into a considerably more extrovert posture for the country. Openess, however, mostly boosted imports, while exports largely stagnated. This led to a considerable deterioration of the country's trade balance deficit, which doubled from around 10 per cent to 20 per cent of the GDP. This loss represents almost 75 per cent of Greece's net fiscal revenues from the Community. Yet, it is impossible to determine what part of this is due to joining the Community. The country had a long association agreement which makes it difficult to employ existing tests; there is no comparable *antimonde* situation when Greece had no preferential relationship to the Community.

Indeed, any trade expansion effects in the aftermath of Greece's entry into the Community were less the result of changes in the prevailing bilateral or external tariff structure, and more of institutional changes (such as quantitative, administrative and taxation barriers to EC imports to Greece), the abolition of Greek export subsidies and the impact of participation in the CAP (that changed the Greek agricultural trade import cover ratio from 1.3 in 1980 to 0.65 in 1981).

With regard to the welfare effects of Greece's entry into the Community from trade, some clarification is needed. The worsening trade balance was partly the result of trade diversion of Greek imports from cheaper sources, which worsened Greece's terms of trade, and partly the result of trade creation that increased imports from the EC at the expense of more expensive Greek products, which benefited Greek consumers (Georgakopoulos 1992).

Overall, fiscal transfers from the EC to Greece were identifiable and favoured particular constituencies, such as the farmers. Direct returns of income from trade and the effects of trade diversion were less perceptible as they spread thinly across consumers, who were already immune to price rises after almost a decade of sustained double-digit inflation. On the contrary, income lost to local producers through trade creation was counterbalanced by income gained by consumers, who found price reductions an altogether unexpected, if extraordinary, blessing.

NO WAY OUT: LOCKING IN THE EFFECTS OF INCOME ON LOYALTY

The dynamic implications of income transfers on Greece's vulnerability are even more far-reaching for locking Greece politically into the EC. Greece's urgency for income has increased since joining the Community. Indeed, the differential in per capita income compared to the EC average fell from almost 44 per cent at the beginning of the 1980s to almost 41 per cent by the end of the decade, despite net capital transfers from the EC (OECD 1991).

Even more important for the determination of Greece's real urgency is the evolution of the role of EC financing in the running of the economy. Net fiscal revenues from the EC represent an increasingly important share of the GDP, the trade deficit and the budget. By the end of the 1980s, the climax of Greece's conversion into a Euro-enthusiast, net fiscal transfers from the EC represented as much as 4.5 per cent of the GDP, 23.9 per cent of the trade deficit and 8.4 per cent of the budget (Georgakopoulos 1994).

EC financial participation increases any Greek government's future economic reliance upon it. This means that not only has the public an urgent need for its income, but the government has as well. Indeed, EC participation permitted the government to realize its natural tendency for growth. Total government expenditure grew from 35 per cent of the GDP in 1980 to as much as 55 per cent in 1990.

On the other hand, Greece's ability to switch to other sources of income was seriously limited as time went by. The US, which had been Greece's major assistance provider in the postwar period, gradually reduced its contributions to military aid within the NATO framework. Certainly, resistance to the US, in terms of perceived harmony of political aims, was greater than that to the EC. In that light, other things being equal, the Greek public would rather be within the EC's sphere of political influence.

The inflow of foreign direct investment from non-EC countries declined, as Greece's location-specific advantages became less attractive. It suffices perhaps to say that while Greece received an annual average of 2 per cent of EC inward foreign direct investment in 1984–86, its share fell to 0 per cent for 1987–89 (Eurostat 1992). Most importantly, however, the advancing process of integration of the Greek economy with the EC increases the costs of switching to non-EC trade partners. The participation of the single market should be seen as a decisive leap forward in terms of integration.

Resistance to the EC also decreased during the 1980s. The gradual shift in world politics and the eventual disintegration of the socialist bloc eroded ideologically motivated opposition to the EC. As the Greek economy adjusts to the realities of the participation in the EC, vested interests that derive their income from a protected national economy weaken in relative terms to vested interests that derive their income from the new economic environment.

According to public opinion measurement in the Eurobarometer, the beginning of the 1990s saw the climax of Euro-enthusiasm in Greece. Subsequently, a slow but clearly discernible reversal of the trend took place. Since net resource transfers are on the increase, what accounts for these early hints that public support for the Community will not always be obvious.

Indeed, the forthcoming second Community support framework translates into a gigantic injection of Community resources into the Greek economy. In view of the considerable needs for investment in the country's infrastructure and the poor fiscal condition of the government, the urgency of these inflows from the EC becomes apparent. Moreover, the expected reflation from this increase in public spending is anticipated by the economy as the missing ingredient for the relaunch of growth. Given the obviously urgent need for the income Greece derives from the Community, one can only speculate about the factors that work in the opposite direction.

The impact of the perception of alternative sources of income, as a determinant of Greece's vulnerability *vis-à-vis* the EC, is neutralized to the degree that the public gets used to the idea of sustained income transfers from the EC. On the other hand, a number of developments may have increased public resistance. Income benefits from membership are not readily identified by the public. Instead, the general level of disposable income is seen as a proxy for the net benefits derived from the partnership. The early 1990s were a period of austerity, which contrasted unfavourably with the increase in income despite falling productivity in the 1980s.

Market deregulation and privatization had a negative impact on segments of the population. It could be said that the adjustment of the Greek economy, with its inevitable negative effects on specific vested interests, did not really take place until almost a decade after entry. It could be argued that it was not until the early 1990s that Greeks realized that there is a price tag to European integration. This price is equal to the income sacrifices needed to attain the objectives of convergence. Special constituencies also felt other adjustment costs, such as farmers following the reform of the CAP and the new GATT agreement.

Political as well as economic considerations lead to an increase in resistance. For the first time, fundamental Greek political objectives diverged clearly from what was perceived as the Community consensus in the case of the break-up of Yugoslavia. With hindsight, Greece was proved right in sensing the danger in the hasty disintegration of Yugoslavia. It is widely held that war was brought to Greece's doorstep by the actions of some of its partners pursuing their own political objectives.[7]

What fuelled nationalist feelings and underlined diverging political objectives, however, was a by-product of the Yugoslav crisis: Greece's problems with its new neighbour, namely, the Former Yugoslav Republic of Macedonia (FYROM). FYROM is genuinely perceived as a potential threat in the future, if acting as an instrument of other regional powers.[8] Most importantly, however, sustained efforts coming from FYROM to build a distinct 'Macedonian' national identity, using historical references to ancient Macedonia, is perceived by the public as a direct challenge to Greece. This issue motivated widespread nationalist feelings of a magnitude that has not been observed in Greece since the time of the Cyprus independence effort in the late 1950s.

In this context, Community consensus is perceived to be unsympathetic to the Greek case. There have been arguments that Greece's partners have not acted in the spirit of Community solidarity. In the context of this debate, even cultural differences with the rest of the Community are brought to the forefront. Certainly such considerations increase the country's resistance and eventually shift the country's supply of influence curve.

In the future, Greece should be expected to remain in the Community's sphere of influence. Urgency for income will not decrease in the medium term. The enlargement of the Community to gradually include the rest of Europe in terms of full membership or association agreements certainly limits Greece's alternatives. The new rapprochement with the US should be seen as a policy for building up alternative economic and political support. Resistance, however, both politically motivated and from vested economic interests, will continue to rise, thus moderating public support for the Community.

By the end of the 1990s Greece's relationship with the European Union (EU) will be very different from that of the late 1980s. Verbal qualification of Greek political participation in the EU, as registered in the 1980s, will implicitly be replaced by concrete measures. As economies converge and politics diverge, Greece will maintain its fundamental commitment to the Union, but will acquire a more eclectically critical posture. Perhaps this will augur well for a more mature relationship.

NOTES

1. See PASOK (1975, 1979).
2. The questions submitted to the sample were: In general, are you for or against efforts being made to unify Western Europe? If FOR, are you very much for this, or only to some extent? If AGAINST, are you only to some extent against or very much against?
3. The question submitted to the sample was: Generally speaking, do you think that (your country's) membership of the European Community is a good think, a bad thing, or neither good nor bad?

4. The question submitted to the public was: Would you say that (your country) has on balance benefited or not from being a member of the European Community?
5. The question submitted to the public was: If you were to be told tomorrow that the European Community had been scrapped, would you be very sorry, indifferent, or relieved?
6. For a discussion of the pursuit of political objectives through economic policy see Kindleberger (1970); for an across-the-spectrum discussion of issues involved from an economist's point of view, Knorr (1973, 1975); for a pioneering contribution on strategic foreign trade policy that aims to establish political spheres of influence, McCulloch and Pinera (1977) and Marrese and Vanous (1983); for a more contemporary approach of the same issue, Mosley (1987); on the discussion of the use of aid for the achievement of political goals, Gilpin (1987) and Frey (1984).
7. See interview of Prime Minister A. Papandreou (*Newsweek*, 9 May 1994, p. 60).
8. A. Papandreou at joint press conference with President Bill Clinton (1994).

REFERENCES

Caves, R.C. (1976), 'Economic Models of Political Choice', *Canadian Journal of Economics*, May, 278–300.

Clogg, R. (1979), 'The Greek Political Context' in L. Tsoukalis (ed.), *Greece and the European Community*, Aldershot, UK: Gower.

Eurobarometer (1993), *Trends 1974–1992*, Brussels: EC Commission.

Eurostat (1992), *European Community Direct Investment 1984–1989*, Theme 6, Series D, Luxembourg.

Frey, B. (1984), 'Public Choice View of International Political Economy', *International Organization*, **38** (1), Winter, 199–223.

Georgakopoulos, T. (1992), 'Greece in the European Community: Transfer of resources and trade balance during the first decade', *Epiloghi*, Yearly Special Edition Review 1991–92, February, 77–81.

Georgakopoulos, T. (1994), 'Economic Integration and Unequal Development', in T. Georgakopoulos, C. Paraskevopoulos and J. Smithin (eds), *Economic Integration Between Unequal Partners*, Aldershot, UK: Edward Elgar, pp. 98–109.

Gilpin, R. (1987), *The Political Economy of International Relations*, Princeton, NJ: Princeton University Press.

Hirschman, A. (1945), *National Power and the Structure of Foreign Trade*, Berkeley and Los Angeles: University of California Press.

Johnson, H.G (1965), 'A Theoretical Model of Economic Nationalism in New and Developing Nations', *Political Science Quarterly*, **80** (2), 169–85.

Kindleberger, C.P. (1970), *Power and Money*, London: Macmillan.

Knorr, K. (1973), *Power and Wealth*, London: Macmillan.

Knorr, K. (1975), *The Power of Nations*, New York: Basic Books.

Marrese, M. and J. Vanous (1983), 'Unconventional Gains From Trade', *Journal of Comparative Economics*, **7**, 382–99.

McCulloch, B. and D. Pinera (1977), 'Trade as Aid: The Political Economy of Tariff Preferences for Developing Countries', *The American Economic Review*, December, 959–67.

Mosley, P. (1987), *Overseas Aid: Its Defence and Reform*, Brighton, UK: Wheatsheaf Books.

OECD (1991), *Economic Outlook*, Paris: OECD.

PASOK (1975), *3rd of September Proclamation of Basic Principles and Goals of the*

Panhellenic Socialist Movement, International Relations Committee, Series A, Publication no. 1.

PASOK (1979), *Statement of Andreas Papandreou on the Occasion of Greece's Accession to the EEC*, Press Office, Athens, 26 May.

Secretariat General of Press and Information (1994), Joint Press Conference of Prime Minister Andreas Papandreou and President Bill Clinton, Athens, 22 April.

Index